Loneliness Updated

> "To be alone is to be different. To be different is to be alone, and to be in the interior of this fatal circle is to be lonely. To be lonely is to have failed" (Susan Schultz, 1976)

Loneliness carries a significant social stigma, as lack of friendship and social ties is socially undesirable, and social perceptions of lonely people are generally unfavourable. Lonely people often have very negative self-perceptions, believing that the inability to establish social ties is due to personal inadequacies or socially undesirable attributes.

This book is divided into three parts. The first part reviews loneliness in general, describing what it is and how it affects us. The second part examines loneliness throughout the life cycle, analysing how it affects us in childhood, adulthood and as we age. The final part explores the connection between loneliness and other conditions such as arthritis, eating disorders and depression.

Loneliness Updated offers the latest research on how loneliness can affect us in our daily lives, and how it is expressed as we travel through life from childhood to old age. It will be a highly interesting read for scholars, students and researchers of clinical psychology, particularly those interested in further exploring the effects and consequences of loneliness.

This book was originally published as a special issue of *The Journal of Psychology*.

Ami Rokach is a clinical psychologist who has been exploring loneliness and its effects for the past 30 years. Aside from helping people deal with their loneliness and pain, he also teaches in the psychology departments at York University in Toronto, Canada, and The Centre for Academic Studies, in Israel.

Dedicated with love and the greatest appreciation to Natalie and Benny.

Loneliness Updated

Recent research on loneliness and how it affects our lives

Edited by
Ami Rokach

Routledge
Taylor & Francis Group
LONDON AND NEW YORK

First published 2013
by Routledge
2 Park Square, Milton Park, Abingdon, Oxfordshire OX14 4RN

Simultaneously published in the USA and Canada
by Routledge
711 Third Avenue, New York, NY 10017

First issued in paperback 2015

Routledge is an imprint of the Taylor & Francis Group, an informa business

This book is a reproduction of *The Journal of Psychology*, volume 146, issues 1-2. The Publisher requests to those authors who may be citing this book to state, also, the bibliographical details of the special issue on which the book was based.

British Library Cataloguing in Publication Data
A catalogue record for this book is available from the British Library

ISBN 13: 978-1-138-94538-8 (pbk)
ISBN 13: 978-0-415-62325-4 (hbk)

Typeset in Times New Roman
by Taylor & Francis Books

Publisher's Note
The publisher would like to make readers aware that the chapters in this book may be referred to as articles as they are identical to the articles published in the special issue. The publisher accepts responsibility for any inconsistencies that may have arisen in the course of preparing this volume for print.

Contents

Citation Information

The following chapters were originally published in *The Journal of Psychology*, volume 146, issues 1-2 (2012). When citing this material, please use the original page numbering for each article, as follows:

Chapter 1
Loneliness Updated: An Introduction
Ami Rokach
The Journal of Psychology, volume 146, issues 1-2 (2012)
pp. 1-6

Chapter 2
Is Loneliness the Same as Being Alone?
Daniel W. Russell, Carolyn E. Cutrona, Cynthia McRae and Mary Gomez
The Journal of Psychology, volume 146, issues 1-2 (2012)
pp. 7-22

Chapter 3
Loneliness, Optimism, and Well-Being Among Married, Divorced, and Widowed Individuals
Hasida Ben-Zur
The Journal of Psychology, volume 146, issues 1-2 (2012)
pp. 23-36

Chapter 4
Loneliness and Emotional Intelligence
Leehu Zysberg
The Journal of Psychology, volume 146, issues 1-2 (2012)
pp. 37-46

Chapter 5
Is It Lonely at the Top? An Empirical Study of Managers' and Nonmanagers' Loneliness in Organizations
Sarah Wright

The Journal of Psychology, volume 146, issues 1-2 (2012)
pp. 47-60

Chapter 6
Children's Loneliness, Sense of Coherence, Family Climate, and Hope: Developmental Risk and Protective Factors
Adi Sharabi, Uzi Levi and Malka Margalit
The Journal of Psychology, volume 146, issues 1-2 (2012)
pp. 61-83

Chapter 7
The Prevalence of Loneliness Among Adults: A Case Study of the United Kingdom
Christina R. Victor and Keming Yang
The Journal of Psychology, volume 146, issues 1-2 (2012)
pp. 85-104

Chapter 8
Association Between Loneliness and Suicidality During Middle Childhood and Adolescence: Longitudinal Effects and the Role of Demographic Characteristics
Katherine C. Schinka, Manfred H. M. Van Dulmen, Robert Bossarte and Monica Swahn
The Journal of Psychology, volume 146, issues 1-2 (2012)
pp. 105-118

Chapter 9
Family of Origin Environment and Adolescent Bullying Predict Young Adult Loneliness
Chris Segrin, Natalie Nevarez, Analisa Arroyo and Jake Harwood
The Journal of Psychology, volume 146, issues 1-2 (2012)
pp. 119-134

Chapter 10
"When It's Just Me at Home, It Hits Me That I'm Completely Alone": An Online Survey of Adolescents in Self-Care
Mónica Ruiz-Casares
The Journal of Psychology, volume 146, issues 1-2 (2012)
pp. 135-153

Chapter 11
Loneliness, Depression, Social Support, and Quality of Life in Older Chronically Ill Appalachians
Laurie A. Theeke, R. Turner Goins, Julia Moore and Heather Campbell
The Journal of Psychology, volume 146, issues 1-2 (2012)

pp. 155-171

Chapter 12
Life Events and Personality Predicting Loneliness Among Centenarians: Findings From the Georgia Centenarian Study
Bob Hensley, Peter Martin, Jennifer A. Margrett, Maurice MacDonald, Ilene C. Siegler and Leonard W. Poon
The Journal of Psychology, volume 146, issues 1-2 (2012)
pp. 173-188

Chapter 13
No Place Like Home? Potential Pathways to Loneliness in Older Adults Under the Care of a Live-In Foreign Home Care Worker
Liat Ayalon, Sharon Shiovitz-Ezra and Yuval Palgi
The Journal of Psychology, volume 146, issues 1-2 (2012)
pp. 189-200

Chapter 14
Cross-National Differences in Older Adult Loneliness
Tineke Fokkema, Jenny De Jong Gierveld and Pearl A. Dykstra
The Journal of Psychology, volume 146, issues 1-2 (2012)
pp. 201-228

Chapter 15
Loneliness in Patients with Rheumatic Diseases: The Significance of Invalidation and Lack of Social Support
Marianne B. Kool and Rinie Geenen
The Journal of Psychology, volume 146, issues 1-2 (2012)
pp. 229-241

Chapter 16
Loneliness and Eating Disorders
Martha Peaslee Levine
The Journal of Psychology, volume 146, issues 1-2 (2012)
pp. 243-257

Chapter 17
Loneliness and Depressive Symptoms: The Mediating and Moderating Role of Uncontrollable Ruminative Thoughts
Janne Vanhalst, Koen Luyckx, Filip Raes and Luc Goossens
The Journal of Psychology, volume 146, issues 1-2 (2012)
pp. 259-27

Notes on Contributors

Analisa Arroyo is a graduate student at the University of Arizona, USA. Her current research interests are shyness, social skills, and identity.

Prof. **Liat Ayalon** is a clinical geropsychologist and a researcher in the School of Social Work at Bar Ilan University, Israel. Her interests include the integration of mental health in primary care, ageism, and formal and informal care alternative for older adults.

Hasida Ben-Zur has a Ph.D. in psychology and is an associate professor in the School of Social Work, Faculty of Welfare & Health Studies, at the University of Haifa, Israel. Her current research areas are stress and coping and decision making.

Robert Bossarte is an assistant professor in the Department of Psychiatry at the University of Rochester, USA, and chief for Epidemiology and Populations Research at the VISN 2 Center of Excellence for Suicide Prevention (Department of Veterans Affairs). His current research interests are connectedness and suicide prevention.

Heather Campbell is an undergraduate student in the Division of Social Work at West Virginia University, USA.

Carolyn E. Cutrona is a Professor in the Department of Psychology, Iowa State University, USA.

Jenny De Jong Gierveld is Emeritus Professor, VU University, Amsterdam and Honorary Fellow of the Netherlands Interdisciplinary Demographic Institute (NIDI) in The Hague. Her research interests are living arrangements, social networks, social integration and loneliness of older adults.

Manfred H. M. van Dulmen is an associate professor in the Department of Psychology at Kent State University, USA. His current research interests include adolescence, aggression, suicide, romantic relationships, and quantitative methodology.

Pearl A. Dykstra is Full Professor of Empirical Sociology at the Erasmus University, Rotterdam, the Netherlands. Her publications focus on ageing and the life course, intergenerational family relationships, and the division of responsibilities between families and the state.

Tineke Fokkema is a senior researcher at the Netherlands Interdisciplinary Demographic Institute (NIDI) in The Hague. Her main research interests are cross-national studies in intergenerational solidarity and older adult loneliness, including the evaluation of interventions.

Rinie Geenen is professor and head of the research group Psychorheumatology at Utrecht University, department of Clinical and Health Psychology, and at the University Medical Center Utrecht, department of Rheumatology and Clinical Immunology, in the Netherlands. His current research interest is in the mutual interaction between biological, psychological, and social factors in chronic diseases, especially with respect to rheumatic diseases.

Mary Gomez is a Teacher in the Cherry Creek School District, Englewood, Colorado, USA.

Luc Goossens is a full professor in Developmental Psychology at the Catholic University of Leuven, Belgium. His major research interests are adolescent identity, autonomy, and loneliness.

Jake Harwood is a professor at the University of Arizona, USA. His current research interests are identity, intergroup communication, and stereotyping.

Robert B. Hensley is an assistant professor at The College of Saint Scholastica, USA. His current research interests are adult development and aging, adaptation in late adulthood, and relationship termination adjustment in college students.

Marianne B. Kool is a PhD student and psychologist at the Utrecht University, department of Clinical and Health Psychology, and at the University Medical Center Utrecht, department of Rheumatology and Clinical Immunology, in the Netherlands. Her current research interests are psychosocial aspects of rheumatic diseases and, in particular, invalidation for chronic (invisible) diseases.

Uzi Levi, PhD, is a social psychologist and a lecturer at Peres Academic Center, Israel. His current research interests are social comparisons, methodological approaches, and the dynamic of stereotype threat.

Koen Luyckx is a postdoctoral researcher at the Fund of Scientific Research (FWO) at the Catholic University of Leuven, Belgium. His current research interests are identity, personality, parenting, and chronic illness.

Maurice MacDonald is the Director of the School of Family Studies and Human Services and a professor at Kansas State University, USA. His current research interests include socioeconomic resources and economic burden of support for the oldest old, family economic and public policy, and financial literacy among college students.

Malka Margalit, PhD, is a professor and head of the school of Social Sciences at Peres Academic Center and a professor emeritus at Tel-Aviv University, Israel. Her current research interests are children's loneliness and hope theory as well as and social–emotional aspects of individuals with learning disabilities.

Jennifer A. Margrett is an assistant professor at Iowa State University, USA. Her current research interests are adult development and aging, everyday problem solving, and health and functioning.

Peter Martin is Director of the Gerontology Program and a professor at Iowa State University, USA. His current research interests include work with the Exceptional Longevity Initiative, survival and longevity of the oldest old in the Georgia Centenarian Study, and rural aging.

Cynthia McRae is a Professor in the College of Education, University of Denver, USA.

Julia Moore is a registered nurse and a graduate research assistant at the West Virginia University School of Nursing, USA.

Natalie Nevarez is an undergraduate student at the University of Arizona, USA, majoring in communication.

Yuval Palgi is lecturer and a senior clinical psychologist at the Department of Gerontology, Faculty of Social Welfare and Health Sciences, University of Haifa, Israel. He received his Ph.D. from Tel Aviv University. His main research interests include gerontology, psychological aspects of PTSD, and well-being.

Martha Peaslee Levine, MD, is an assistant professor of pediatrics, psychiatry and humanities at Penn State College of Medicine, USA. Her current research interests include the emotional effects of eating disorders, journaling and health, communication in healthcare, media literacy, and empowerment of women.

Leonard W. Poon is Director Emeritus, Institute of Gerontology, at the University of Georgia, USA. His current research interests include survival and longevity of the oldest old in the Georgia Centenarian Study, cognitive aging, and public health and older adults.

Filip Raes is an assistant professor at the Catholic University of Leuven, Belgium. He is a clinical psychologist and a trained behavior therapist. His current research interests include depression, autobiographical memory, rumination, behavior therapy, psychosis, and neuropsychology.

Ami Rokach is a clinical psychologist who has been exploring loneliness and its effects for the past 30 years. Aside from helping people deal with their loneliness and pain, he also teaches in the psychology departments at York University in Toronto, Canada, The Centre for Academic Studies, in Or Yehuda, Israel and Walden University, USA.

Ben Rokach completed his MD degree in 2009 from McMaster University, and is now a medical resident in radiology at Memorial University in Newfoundland Canada. Having completed a BSc in Psychology, he became aware, during his medical training, not only of patients' physical problems that needed attending to, but of their emotional turmoil, mental anguish, and loneliness during illnesses and/or hospitalization. He hopes to highlight this phenomenon and encourage more research and intervention programs to ease patients' suffering.

Mónica Ruiz-Casares is an Assistant Professor in the Division of Social and Cultural Psychiatry, at the Center for Research on Children and Families at McGill University, USA, and in the Transcultural Research and Intervention Team at the CSSS de la Montagne, Montreal, Canada. Her research focuses on the determinants and consequences of leaving children home alone cross-culturally.

Daniel W. Russell is a Professor in the Department of Human Development and Family Studies, Iowa State University, USA.

Katherine C. Schinka is a graduate student in the Department of Psychology at Kent State University, USA. Her current research interests include loneliness and suicide during adolescence.

Chris Segrin is a professor at the University of Arizona, USA. His research interests are family communication and mental health.

Adi Sharabi, PhD, is a lecturer at the Kibbutzim College of Education Technology and the Arts, and at Tel Aviv University, Israel. Her current research interests are socioemotional and familial aspects of children and adolescents with and without learning disabilities.

Sharon Shiovitz-Ezra is a lecturer at the Paul Baerwald School of Social Work and Social Welfare at the Hebrew University of Jerusalem, Israel. Her research focuses on loneliness in the second half of life. She examines predictors and outcomes of loneliness such as morbidity and mortality in later life. She also explores the chronicity aspect of loneliness.

Ilene C. Siegler is a Senior Fellow at the UNC Institute on Aging and a professor at Duke University, USA. Her current research interests are in developmental psychology and behavioral epidemiology, racial differences in emotional responses to caregiving, and the role of personality in health and disease at midlife.

Monica Swahn is an associate professor at the Georgia State University, USA. Her current research interests pertain to involvement in health risk behaviors among adolescents and young adults and specifically to early alcohol misuse and its adverse health consequences.

Laurie A. Theeke is an assistant professor at West Virginia University, USA. Her research interests include loneliness, use of story as intervention for loneliness, and physical health outcomes related to loneliness.

R. Turner Goins is an Associate Professor in the Department of Community Medicine and Associate Director for Research at the Center on Aging, School of Medicine, West Virginia University, USA.

Janne Vanhalst is a PhD student at the Catholic University of Leuven, Belgium. Her major research interests include the development of loneliness during adolescence and associations with depressive symptoms, self-esteem, and interpersonal factors.

Christina Victor, BA, MPhil, PhD, is Professor of Gerontology at Brunel University, UK, and the Programme Director for Health Ageing at the Brunel Institute for Ageing Studies (BIAS). Her research interests focus upon loneliness and social isolation in later life, healthy ageing, and ageing among ethnic minority and new ageing populations.

Sarah Wright is a senior lecturer at the University of Canterbury, New Zealand. Her current research interests are loneliness in the workplace, social relationships at work, and meaningful work.

Dr. **Keming Yang**, Ma, PhD, is Lecturer in Sociology at Durham University, UK. His research interests focus on three key areas: economic sociology broadly and more specifically entrepreneurship with an empirical focus on China's economic and political development; research methods, especially quantitative methods; social gerontology, with a focus on the social relations.

Leehu Zysberg is a senior lecturer in the Department of Psychology, Tel Hai College, Israel. His current research interests include measurement and assessment, coping with stress in various life conditions, and the study of emotional intelligence as a psychological resource.

Additional authors for The Georgia Centenarian Study (Chapter 12):

Jonathan Arnold is a professor in the Department of Genetics at the University of Georgia. USA. As part of the Georgia Centenarian Study he has examined the impact of genetics, nutrition, and life style on human longevity.

Adam Davey is Associate Professor of Public Health at Temple University, USA, and Director of the Doctoral Program in Health Ecology. His research addresses the epidemiology exceptional survivors and novel applications of missing data in longitudinal research.

Marla Gearing is an assistant professor at Emory University, USA. Her research focuses on the pathogenesis of and neuropathologic overlap among neurodegenerative diseases.

Robert C. Green is Associate Professor of Medicine in the Division of Genetics, Department of Medicine at Brigham and Women's Hospital and Harvard Medical School, USA. His research interests have evolved from a focus on clinical trials and genetic epidemiology to a focus on translational genomics and health outcomes.

Dorothy B. Hausman is an associate research scientist at the University of Georgia, USA. Her research interests are biochemical assessment of nutritional status, older adults, and obesity.

Mary Ann Johnson is the Bill and June Flatt Professor in Foods and Nutrition at the University of Georgia, USA. Her research interests are in nutrition, health, and aging.

S. Michal Jazwinski is a professor at Tulane University, USA. His current research is in the biology of aging, with emphasis on genetics and molecular biology and the interdisciplinary interface with the psychosocial sciences.

Willard Rodgers is a research professor emeritus at the University of Michigan, USA. His current research interests are cognitive aging and methodological issues related to longitudinal studies of the elderly.

Christoph Rott is senior research scientist at Heidelberg University, Germany. His current research interests are centenarians, functional health in old age, valuation of life, and psychological strengths in very old age.

Joyce Lisa Tenover is a geriatrician, Professor of Medicine (Affiliate) at Stanford University, USA, and GRECC Associate Director for Clinical Programs at the Palo Alto VA. Her research interests include androgen replacement therapy in older men, and improving ambulatory care for the frail elderly.

John L. Woodard is an associate professor of Psychology at Wayne State University, USA. His research interests include neurobehavioral and neuroimaging studies of memory in aging and Alzheimer's disease and cognitive and affective processes in exceptional longevity.

Loneliness Updated: An Introduction

The whole conviction of my life now rests upon the belief that loneliness, far from being a rare and curious phenomenon, peculiar to myself and to a few other solitary men, is the central and inevitable fact of human existence.

—Thomas Wolfe

CHANCES ARE that you would disclose a sorry family history, medical problems, and even depression, but few would openly admit to being lonely. Susan Schultz (1976) poignantly wrote that "To be alone is to be different. To be different is to be alone, and to be in the interior of this fatal circle is to be lonely. To be lonely is to have failed" (p. 15). There is a stigma to being lonely. The public and therefore us researchers seem to not look favorably on anyone who admits to suffer its pain. When I present, or teach, and ask my audience whether there is anyone in the group who has never experienced loneliness, no one raises a hand. When I further inquire whether anyone is lonely now—dead silence. No one, in my 30 years of researching this topic, has ever had the courage to admit, in public, that he or she is lonely. Loneliness carries a significant social stigma, as lack of friendship and social ties are socially undesirable, and the social perceptions of lonely people are generally unfavorable. Lonely people often have very negative self-perceptions, and the inability to establish social ties suggest that the person may have personal inadequacies or socially undesirable attributes (Lau & Gruen, 1992).

Loneliness has become an almost permanent and all-too-familiar way of life to millions of North Americans: the single people, divorced individuals, adolescents, housewives, and the scores of people who call suicide prevention centers and hot lines. It is so widespread and aversive, that a billion-dollar loneliness industry has been developed to meet the desire of those who do not know what to do about their loneliness (Rokach, 1988). The loneliness business includes videotaping clubs, health spas, self-help books and mate-finding agencies and is an extremely fast-growing business. It tempts us with an array of relational possibilities, social-skills upgrading, and semiforced joined activities. Many lonely people join the ride in an attempt to become unlonely and frequently end up more hopeless than they were when they started. Dating online and the explosive growth of Facebook are but two attempts at creating virtual communities that for many may replace flesh-and-blood friends.

Ours is the age of relationships. We tend to believe in the uniqueness, importance, and availability of relating to others, thinking that we know how to conquer the barriers against closeness that we erect. Whereas in the past, work was seen as the valued solution to self-fulfillment, today it is relationships that appear to be the main—if not the only—means by which self-esteem can be affirmed. A paradox is thus created where on the one hand we yearn for close intimate relationships, and on the other hand our social conditions are not conducive to the development of human relations. Our life style in the dawn of the 21st century both creates isolation and makes it more difficult to cope with it (Rokach, 2000). Everyone is seeking companionship, and everyone seems to be having trouble finding it. Good, close, intimate relationships have become scarce, and when scarcity occurs, there is usually somebody around to exploit it (Gordon, 1976).

Observed Friedman (2007),

> Indeed the social fabric of American life is rapidly changing, in reaction to the collision of contemporary social forces, touching most of us in one way or another. Increased mobility and social isolation, the stress of a fast paced and high pressure lifestyle changes in the family unit, the impact of technology and the rise in consumerism are forces that disrupt our ability to create strong and lasting social connections (p. 3).

In today's fast-paced ever-changing world, when virtual reality sometimes replaces the real one, people have no time or energy for establishing a connection with anything beyond the narrow frame of their own hurried lives in a culture that gives little priority to human relationships and that rewards nothing but the individual acquisition of power and money (Carter, 1995).

Loneliness is a prevalent, common, and disconcerting social phenomenon (Cacioppo and Patrick, 2008). Recent estimates suggest that up to 32% of adults experience loneliness and that up to 7% report feeling intense loneliness (see Hawkley et al., 2010). It is clear that all of us wish to avoid experiencing it. But what is that experience we dread so much? While some writers describe loneliness as a specific and unique pain, an undifferentiated stressor, others view loneliness as a response to various needs, circumstances, and situations and accordingly finely differentiate it into several *types* of loneliness. Although such differentiation may be useful as an intellectual tool, these types are artificial. They conceive of loneliness as a unified experience and, in so doing, fail to capture the complexity of this experience.

Cacioppo et al. (2006) suggested that—just like physical pain, which, while it is unpleasant, has a protective function and serves as an alarm bell to guard against damage to the organism—loneliness is a social pain that is triggered by disconnection from others, from the group to which the human individual belongs and that can assure us of food, defense, social connection, and support in the struggle to survive (as it did especially for our ancestors). Based on the various theoretical sources and my own research, I proposed three distinguishing characteristics of all loneliness experiences:

1. Loneliness is a universal phenomenon that is fundamental to being human (see also Peplau & Perlman, 1982; Wood, 1986).
2. Although shared by all of us periodically, loneliness is in essence a subjective experience that is influenced by personal and situational variables (see also Rook, 1984).
3. Loneliness, which is a complex and multifaceted experience, is always very painful, severely distressing, and individualistic (see also Moustakas, 1961; Rokach & Brock, 1997).

Since Moustakas wrote, in 1961, his seminal book on loneliness, there has been growing research and academic interest in this common experience. All of us experience it, but only in the past 2 decades has there been an open quest to understand it and learn how to cope with it.

The present, special issue, includes a wide variety of interesting, creative, enlightening, and even groundbreaking research on loneliness and its relationships to other human conditions.

This special issue is divided into three parts. The first includes articles that review loneliness in general; the second examines loneliness and its effects and expression throughout the life cycle; and the third examines the connection between loneliness and other conditions.

Russell, Cutrona, McRae, and Gomez present the cognitive discrepancy model, which predicts that loneliness will be experienced when a person perceives that his or her social involvement is less than what that person would want it to be. Ben-Zur looked at the interaction of loneliness and optimism and how they affect the well-being of people with various marital status, that is, married, divorced, and widowed people. Zysberg suggested that emotional intelligence may contribute to our understanding of, and possibly coping with, loneliness. Wright examined the question whether people "at the top" of their organization are lonelier than the rest of us. She discovered that they are not. Managers were no more or less lonely than their non-manager counterparts.

In the second part were included studies that examined loneliness throughout the life cycle. Sharabi, Levi, and Margalit examined the contributions of individual and familial variables for the prediction of loneliness as a developmental risk and the sense of coherence as a protective factor. Looking at children in Grades 5–6, those researchers found that family cohesion was, indeed, a protective factor as far as loneliness is concerned. Victor and Yang examined loneliness as experienced by those 15 years of age and older. It was found that those either younger than 25 years or older than 65 are the loneliest. Depression, physical health, and social involvement were associated with loneliness at different stages in life. Schinka, Van Dulmen, Bossarte, and Swahn explored the association between loneliness and suicidability of youth aged 10–14 years. Suicide among them is a growing problem and concern, and it appears that loneliness, while not the only factor, is a poignant one in contributing to the decision of youngsters to take their own lives. Segrin, Nevarez, Arroyo, and Harwood found that the loneliness of youths' parents and the youths' having suffered bullying were significant predictors of youth loneliness. Ruiz-Casares examined adolescents' loneliness and solitude and found that those who were lonely enjoyed being home alone much less than those who were not lonely. Possibly, being alone increased their perception and amplified their experience of loneliness.

Loneliness of elderly individuals and its affects on their health and quality of life form a growing social concern. We have, thus, included four articles on that topic. Theeke, Goins, Moore, and Campbell examined the relationship between loneliness, depression, social support, and quality of life in chronically ill older Appalachians. Those researchers found that loneliness, as could be expected, was a significant problem for that population. Hensley, Martin, Margrett, MacDonald, Siegler, Poon, and additional researchers from the Georgia Centenarian Study examined the loneliness of Georgian centenarians, who are functionally limited and commonly experience social isolation. They found that lifetime negative events, neuroticism, and perceived competence were all significant predictors of loneliness. Ayalon, Shiovitz-Ezra, and Palgi examined the loneliness of frail elderly individuals, who commonly have a foreign aid worker looking after them. Those researchers argued that the elderly individuals, living in such conditions of physical limitations, being cared for by someone whom they do not know well, and with limited social involvement, are particularly prone to loneliness. And last, Fokkema, Gierveld, and Dykstra investigated elderly loneliness in a cross-comparative perspective. They examined the loneliness of European elderly individuals. Their study showed significant difference between levels of loneliness of elderly individuals in Northern Europe (i.e., Denmark and Switzerland) and higher loneliness levels in those in the Southern part of Europe (i.e., Greece and Spain). To understand and explain these cross-national differences, those authors examined the demographic data, socioeconomic data, health, and social network of the elderly individuals.

Our third section includes articles that examine loneliness in relation to other conditions. For instance, Kool and Geenen explored the loneliness that people afflicted with Rheumatic disease, fibromyalgia, and ankylosing spondylitis experience. Those researchers suggested that social support is highly important for the sick. Levine examined the link between loneliness and eating disorders (anorexia and bulimia). She found that negative interpersonal relationships and experiences of loneliness exacerbate eating disorders. Loneliness, negative emotions, and reduced social connection are highly significant in maintaining eating disorders. Examining loneliness and depression, Vanhalst, Luyckx, Raes, and Goossens explored whether rumination functioned as a mediator or moderator in the relationship between two types of loneliness (the relationship with parents and those with peers) and depressive symptoms. They found that rumination partially mediated between peer-related loneliness and depression, and moderated between parent-related loneliness and depressive symptoms.

I cannot close my introductory remarks without wholeheartedly thanking all those reviewers who gave so kindly of their time, expertise, knowledge, and—mostly—their wish to help in creating the best and most highly relevant and interesting special issue.

My heartfelt thanks to the following professors:

Chris Segrin
Ron Downey
Amiram Raviv
Malka Margalit
Tricia Orzeck
Liora Findler
Sid Strauss
Mary Wells
Liat Ayalon
Sharon Shiovitz-Ezra
Laurie Theeke
David Teplin

We all hope that you will find this issue enlightening, helpful, engaging, and enriching.

Ami Rokach
Guest Editor

REFERENCES

Cacioppo, J. T., Hughes, M. E., Waite, L. J., Hawkley, L. C., & Thisted, R. A. (2006). Loneliness as a specific risk factor for depressive symptoms: Cross-sectional and longitudinal analyses. *Psychology and Aging, 21*, 140–151.

Cacioppo, J. T., & Patrick, W. (2008). *Loneliness: Human nature and the need for social connection*. New York: W. W. Norton.

Carter, B. (1995). Focusing your wide-angle lens. *The Family Therapy Networker, 19*(6), 31–35.

Friedman, R. L. (2007). *Widening the therapeutic lens: Sense of belonging as an integral dimension of the human experience*. A dissertation submitted to the Wright Institute Graduate School.

Gordon, S. (1976). *Lonely in America*. New York: Simon & Schuster.

Hawkley, L. C., Thisted, R. A., Masi, C. M., & Cacioppo, J. T. (2010). Loneliness predicts increased blood pressure: 5-year cross-lagged analyses in middle-aged and older adults. *Psychology and Aging, 25*(1), 132–141.

Lau, S., & Gruen, G. E. (1992). The social stigma of loneliness: Effect of target person's and perceiver's sex. *Personality and Social Psychology Bulletin, 18*(2), 182–189.

Moustakas, C. E. (1961). *Loneliness*. Englewood Cliffs, NJ: Prentice-Hall.

Peplau, L. A., & Perlman, D. (1982). Perspectives on loneliness. In L. A. Peplau & D. Perlman (Eds.), *Loneliness: A sourcebook of current theory, research and therapy* (pp. 1–20). New York: Wiley & Sons.

Rokach, A. (1988). Theoretical approaches to loneliness: From a univariate to a multidimensional experience. *Review of Existential Psychology and Psychiatry, 19*(2–3), 225–254.

Rokach, A. (2000). Correlates of loneliness as perceived by the terminally ill. *Current Psychology, 19*(3), 237–248.

Rokach, A., & Brock, H. (1997). Loneliness and the effects of life changes. *Journal of Psychology, 131*(3), 284–298.

Rook, K. S. (1984). Research on social support, loneliness, and social isolation: Toward an integration. In P. Shaver (Ed.), *Review of personality and social psychology: Emotions, relationships, and health* (Vol. 5, pp. 239–264). Beverly Hills, CA: Sage.

Schultz, S. (1976). *Bittersweet: Surviving and growing from loneliness.* New York: T. Crowell.

Wood, L. A. (1986). Loneliness. In R. Harré (Ed.), *The social construction of emotions* (pp. 184–208). Oxford: Blackwell.

PART I: A REVIEW OF LONELINESS

Is Loneliness the Same as Being Alone?

DANIEL W. RUSSELL
CAROLYN E. CUTRONA
Iowa State University

CYNTHIA MCRAE
University of Denver

MARY GOMEZ
Cherry Creek School District

ABSTRACT. The cognitive discrepancy model predicts that loneliness occurs when individuals perceive a difference between their desired and actual levels of social involvement. Using data from a sample of high school sophomore students, the present investigation was designed to go beyond previous research that has tested this model by examining the predicted nonlinear relationships between desired and actual social contact and feelings of loneliness. Analyses indicated that support for the cognitive discrepancy model of loneliness was found only for measures of close friendships. Specifically, the discrepancy between the students' ideal number and actual number of close friends was found to be related in a nonlinear fashion to feelings of satisfaction with close friendships and loneliness after control for the number of close friends. Implications of these findings for theoretical models of loneliness are discussed.

LONELINESS RESEARCHERS commonly distinguish between the experience of loneliness and being alone (Cutrona, 1982; Paloutzian & Janigan, 1987; Perlman & Peplau, 1982; Russell, 1982). This reflects the recognition that some individuals may be alone or socially isolated and be quite happy with that situation. In contrast, other individuals may be involved in a large number of interpersonal relationships yet be dissatisfied with important aspects of their relationships (e.g., the quality of the relationships; lack of a particular type of relationship, such as a romantic relationship) and experience feelings of loneliness.

To understand the distinction between social isolation and loneliness, the *cognitive discrepancy* model of loneliness was developed (Peplau & Perlman, 1982). According to this model, individuals develop an internal standard or expectation against which they judge their interpersonal relationships. If their relationships with others exceed this standard, then individuals are satisfied with their relationships and do not experience feelings of loneliness. If their current relationships with others are below this standard, then individuals are dissatisfied with their relationships and experience feelings of loneliness.

The cognitive discrepancy model of loneliness represents an extension of earlier theoretical ideas developed by Thibaut and Kelley (1959). They present an analysis of satisfaction and attraction in dyadic relationships based on the individual's Comparison Level (CL). If the outcomes experienced by the individual from a given relationship are above the CL, then the individual is satisfied and attracted to the relationship. If the outcomes experienced by the individual for that relationship are below the CL, then the individual is dissatisfied and not attracted to the relationship. The cognitive discrepancy model of loneliness proposes that the individual develops a CL for his or her entire network of social relationships. This CL can be thought of as representing the quantity or quality of social contact the person desires and is used by the individual to evaluate the adequacy of his or her current social network. Thus, the cognitive discrepancy model hypothesizes that satisfaction with social relationships and feelings of loneliness are jointly determined by the person's current social relationships and his or her CL for social relationships.

One factor hypothesized by Thibaut and Kelley (1959) to determine the person's CL is social comparison. That is, the individual formulates expectations concerning the number and type of social relationships he or she should have in part based on the social relationships of similar others. So, for example, students should develop expectations regarding their interpersonal relationships based in part on the relationships of other students who are perceived as being similar to themselves.

An interesting issue concerns how discrepancies between the person's actual interpersonal relationships and desired or expected relationships are related to satisfaction with relationships and loneliness. Kelley and Thibaut (1978) suggest that this relationship may not be linear. That is, near the person's CL a unit increase or decrease in the quantity or quality of relationships may be especially important to the person in determining satisfaction and loneliness. Thus, there may not be a simple linear relationship between changes in the discrepancy between current relationships and the CL and feelings of satisfaction and loneliness.

To understand this prediction, imagine that a student desires four close friends. If this student has four close friends and loses one, that loss may affect greatly his or her satisfaction with friendships and loneliness. What if the same student has eight close friends and loses one, or has two close friends and loses one? Clearly, in these latter cases the person is so far above or below the CL that a loss of one friend has very little meaning in terms of changes in relationship satisfaction or loneliness. Thus, the units of satisfaction or loneliness may be "stretched" in the area surrounding the CL.

The cognitive discrepancy model of loneliness was tested by Russell, Steffen, and Salih (1981). Using data from a randomly selected sample of over 500 college students (including nearly equal numbers of the four undergraduate classes and graduate students), measures were taken of students' current social relationships, CL for social relationships, typical social relationships of college students, and satisfaction with social relationships in three relationship domains: friendships, romantic/dating relationships, and family relationships. In addition, participant's level of loneliness was measured using the UCLA Loneliness Scale (Russell, Peplau, & Cutrona, 1980). Analyses were conducted examining the relationship between a discrepancy score, formed by subtracting the person's current relationships from his or her CL, and satisfaction with each type of relationship.

As predicted by Kelley and Thibaut (1978), nonlinear associations were found between this discrepancy score and relationship satisfaction and loneliness for all three types of relationships. For example, Russell, Steffen, and Salih (1981) found that the relationship between increases in the number of close friendships and satisfaction with friendships and decreases in loneliness was linear until the point where the person's current friendships and his or her CL for friendships were equal. Above that point, there was no further increase in satisfaction or decrease in loneliness with further increases in the number of close friendships above the CL. These results were also found for measures of the quality of relationships. For example, the association between increases in the intimacy of romantic relationships and satisfaction with romantic relationships and decreases in loneliness was linear until the point where the person's current relationship intimacy and his or her CL for intimacy were equal; there were no further increase in satisfaction or decrease in loneliness with further increases in intimacy. These results indicate that, as suggested by Kelley and Thibaut (1978), individuals are differentially sensitive to increases or decreases in the quantity or quality of their interpersonal relationships, depending upon how their current relationships compare to the CL. Below the CL, satisfaction and loneliness are determined by the number of close friends and the level of romantic relationship intimacy. Above the CL, further increases in the number of close friendships or the intimacy of the romantic relationship had no effect on relationship satisfaction or loneliness.

Archibald, Bartholomew, and Marx (1995) attempted to test the cognitive discrepancy model of loneliness in a sample of high school sophomores. They assessed the current social relationships of these students, their ideal social relationships (i.e., the CL), and their perceptions of the relationships of the typical high school student. Feelings of satisfaction with social relationships and loneliness were also assessed. After controlling for the current social relationships of these students, Archibald et al. (1995) found that the discrepancy between their ideal and actual social relationships was strongly related to relationship satisfaction ($\Delta R^2 = .14$) but was unrelated to feelings of loneliness. By contrast, the discrepancy between the typical student's social relations and their own social relationships was only weakly predictive of either relationship satisfaction or loneliness ($\Delta R^2 = .02$).

Ward and Rana-Deuba (2000) also examined the effects of actual social contact versus desired social contact on satisfaction with social relationships and loneliness for a sample of foreigners living in Nepal (*M* Age = 39.6 years). They assessed the amount of actual social contact and desired social contact in 12 areas (e.g., going to social functions, discussing social and political issues, celebrating holidays) for relationships with Nepalese and individuals from their own country. Their results indicated that the discrepancy between their actual and desired social contacts across these 12 areas was related to satisfaction with the quality and quantity of relationships with Nepalese and conationals ($r = .35$–$.48$). The measures of relationship satisfaction were also significantly related to feelings of loneliness. However, as Archibald et al. (1995) found, the discrepancy measures were unrelated to loneliness.

Unfortunately, these investigations did not test for the nonlinear relationships between their discrepancy measures and feelings of satisfaction and loneliness predicted by Kelley and Thibaut (1978) and found by Russell et al. (1981). As a consequence, it is unclear whether or not their results are consistent with the predictions of the cognitive discrepancy model of loneliness. The present study collected data from a sample of high school sophomores using the measures of social relationships employed by Archibald et al. (1995). In addition, data were collected using the measures of close friendships employed by Russell et al. (1981). Using these data, analyses were conducted to test for both linear and nonlinear relationships between the cognitive discrepancy measures and feelings of satisfaction with relationships and loneliness.

Method

Participants

A sample of 188 sophomore students from a suburban high school participated in the study. In recruiting participants, teachers were first contacted to determine if they would permit students in their class to participate during class time. A total of 195 students, representing approximately 45% of the 435 sophomores in the school, were allowed to participate in the study. The final sample represented 43% of the sophomore class, or 96% of those who were permitted by their teachers to participate.

Participants were 85 males and 95 females. The remaining eight students did not indicate their sex. The students were 15–16 years of age. A majority of the sample (57%) was white, 14% were African American, 7% were Hispanic, and 6% were Asian. Remaining participants were either of mixed racial background (9%) or in another racial group (7%).

List-wise deletion of cases with missing data on the measures was used to ensure that the results were consistent for the different sets of analyses that were conducted. As a consequence, the number of cases used in the analyses was 169. Individuals with missing data on one or more of the variables (n = 19) were compared to cases with complete data (n = 169) in terms of demographic characteristics and the measures of interpersonal relationships and loneliness. Perhaps not surprisingly, male students (12.9%) were more likely to have missing data on these measures than female students (2.1%), $\chi(1, N = 180) = 6.33$, $p < .05$. None of the differences between these two groups on the remaining measures were statistically significant ($p < .05$).

Measures

Social Life Questionnaire. This measure was developed by Archibald et al. (1995) to assess various aspects of the social lives of high school students. It consists of 78 items that ask students about their actual and ideal levels of social activity as well as their perceptions of the social activities engaged in by the typical high school student. The measure covers activities with social friends, close friends, romantic relationships, and specific social events. For example, one item asks participants, "How often before classes start: (a) do you get together with friends? (b) would you like to get together with friends? and (c) does the typical student get together with friends?" Students responded to these items using a 9-point Likert scale that ranged from "every school day" to "almost never."

Scores were computed following the procedures used by Archibald et al. (1995). A measure of *actual* social activity was derived by standardizing and summing together the 26 questions that dealt with student involvement in social activities. This measure was found to be highly reliable ($\alpha = .95$). *Ideal-actual* discrepancy was derived by subtracting students' ratings of their actual social activities from their ideal social activities, standardizing these scores, and then summing them. This measure was also found to be reliable ($\alpha = .94$). An identical procedure was used to derive scores for the *typical-actual* discrepancy measure, which was also found to be reliable ($\alpha = .95$).

A final set of seven questions asked the students to rate how satisfied they were with various aspects of their interpersonal relationships on a 7-point Likert scale that ranged from "completely satisfied" to "completely dissatisfied." So, for example, students were asked, "How satisfied are you with the amount of weekday social activity you engage in?" Responses to these items were standardized and summed together to form a measure of social satisfaction ($\alpha = .90$).

Close friendships. A series of questions identical to those used by Russell et al. (1981) was asked concerning close friendships. First, students were asked to indicate their current number of close friends on a 7-point scale that ranged from "none" to "11 or more." They were also asked to indicate their ideal number of close friends and how many close friends they thought the typical sophomore at their high school has, using the same 7-point scale. Finally, they were asked to indicate how satisfied they were with their current number of close friends on a 9-point scale that ranged from "not at all" to "very satisfied."

To be consistent with the measures computed from the Social Life Questionnaire, measures of ideal-actual discrepancy and typical-actual discrepancy were also calculated from the measures of close friendships.

Loneliness. Loneliness was assessed using Version 3 of the UCLA Loneliness Scale (Russell, 1996). This latest version of the Loneliness Scale was designed to improve on earlier versions of the scale (e.g., Russell et al., 1980) by simplifying both the wording of the questions and the response format. Data presented by Russell (1996) provide support for the reliability and validity of the loneliness scale for a variety of populations. The measure was found to be reliable in this sample ($\alpha = .90$).

Results

Descriptive Statistics

The average loneliness score for this sample was 40.57 ($SD = 9.16$). This is comparable to the average scores on Version 3 of the UCLA Loneliness Scale for college student samples (Russell, 1996). Male students ($M = 41.86$) reported higher levels of loneliness than female students ($M = 39.91$), although the difference was not statistically significant, $t(168) = 1.38$. It should be noted that most studies have not found sex differences in loneliness using the UCLA Loneliness Scale (see review by Borys & Perlman, 1985).

Students in the present study reported a higher level of ideal social activity than their actual level of social activity, $t(168) = 8.90, p < .001$. Similarly, students also reported a higher number of ideal close friendships than their actual number of close friends, $t(168) = 5.44, p < .001$. They rated the typical student's level of social activity as higher than their own, $t(168) = 6.63, p < .001$. However, their rating of the typical student's number of close friends did not differ from their own actual number of close friends, $t(168) < 1$. There was also no difference in their rating of the ideal and typical level of social activity, $t(168) < 1$. Finally, students rated their ideal number of close friends as higher than the number of close friends of the typical high school sophomore, $t(168) = 3.86, p < .001$.

Correlations among the measures of loneliness, satisfaction, and social activity are presented in Table 1, along with the parallel measures for close friendships. The measures derived from the Social Life Questionnaire (Archibald et al., 1995) were all very highly correlated. By contrast, the measures of close friendships were less strongly related to one another. The two sets of measures were nearly equally related to scores on the loneliness measure. Finally, the measures of social activity and the two discrepancy scales were all correlated above .40 in magnitude with the satisfaction measure derived from the Social Life Questionnaire.

TABLE 1. Correlations Among the Measures of Loneliness, Satisfaction, Social Activity, and Close Friendships

Variable	Social Activity	Ideal-Actual Discrepancy	Typ.-Actual Discrepancy	Satisfaction	# of Friends	Ideal-Actual Friends	Typ.-Actual Friends	Satisfaction w/ Friends
Social Activity	1.00							
Ideal-Actual Discrepancy	−.71***	1.00						
Typ.-Actual Discrepancy	−.85***	.81***	1.00					
Satisfaction	.46***	−.44***	−.44***	1.00				
# of Friends	.31***	−.26**	−.31***	.22**	1.00			
Ideal-Actual Friends	−.23**	.36***	.25**	−.22**	−.26**	1.00		
Typ.-Actual Friends	−.33***	.29***	.41***	−.19*	−.61***	.28***	1.00	
Satisfaction w/ Friends	.34***	−.17*	−.28***	.40***	.25**	−.13	−.29***	1.00
Loneliness	−.35***	.23**	.35***	−.44***	−.31***	.23**	.43***	−.49***

Note. $N = 169$. Typ. = Typical.
*$p < .05$. **$p < .01$. ***$p < .001$.

Prediction of Satisfaction

Analyses were conducted to evaluate the ability of the cognitive discrepancy measures to predict the two measures of satisfaction (i.e., satisfaction with social activities and satisfaction with close friendships) over and above the influence of actual social relationships. A series of hierarchical regression analyses was conducted. In these analyses, sex of student was included as a predictor in Step 1 of the regression analyses. The measure of actual relationships was entered in Step 2, followed by the linear discrepancy measure (e.g., ideal-actual relationships) in Step 3 and the square of the discrepancy measure in Step 4. Inclusion of this latter term permitted us to test for the nonlinear relationships of the discrepancy measures predicted by Kelley and Thibaut (1979) and found by Russell et al. (1981).

Table 2 presents the results of the regression analysis predicting satisfaction with social activities. Sex of the student was not related to satisfaction, whereas the level of actual social activity was a highly significant predictor ($R^2 = .24$). The ideal-actual discrepancy score was also a statistically significant predictor, accounting for an additional 3% of the variance in the satisfaction measure. The typical-actual discrepancy score accounted for only 1% of the variance in satisfaction. Finally, in contrast to our predictions, there was no evidence of a nonlinear relationship between the discrepancy measures and satisfaction, with neither of the squared discrepancy measures found to be statistically significant.

Hierarchical regression results for the measure of satisfaction with close friendships are presented in Table 3. Sex of student was not significantly related to satisfaction with close friendships, whereas the number of close friends was found to be a statistically significant predictor ($R^2 = .06$). After control for these two predictor variables, the ideal-actual discrepancy measure was not related to satisfaction. However, as predicted, the squared discrepancy measure was found

TABLE 2. Hierarchical Regression Analyses Predicting Satisfaction with Social Activities

Step	ΔR^2	F
1. Sex	.01	2.13
2. Social Activity	.24	53.51***
3. Ideal-Actual Discrepancy	.03	5.57*
4. Ideal-Actual Discrepancy Squared	.01	1.50
3. Typical-Actual Discrepancy	.01	2.42
4. Typical-Actual Discrepancy Squared	.00	<1

Note. $N = 169$.
***$p < .001$. **$p < .01$. *$p < .05$.

TABLE 3. Hierarchical Regression Analyses Predicting Satisfaction with Close Friendships

Step	ΔR^2	F
1. Sex	.00	<1
2. # of Close Friends	.06	10.89**
3. Ideal-Actual Discrepancy	.01	1.06
4. Ideal-Actual Discrepancy Squared	.03	6.20*
3. Typical-Actual Discrepancy	.03	6.22*
4. Typical-Actual Discrepancy Squared	.00	<1

Note. $N = 169$.
$^{***}p < .001$. $^{**}p < .01$. $^{*}p < .05$.

to be a statistically significant predictor, accounting for an additional 3% of the variance in satisfaction with close friendships. For the typical-actual discrepancy measure, only the linear term was found to be a statistically significant predictor after control for sex and the number of close friends, accounting for an additional 3% of the variance in satisfaction.

These latter results therefore appear to be consistent with the findings of Russell et al. (1981) concerning the nonlinear relationship between the ideal-actual discrepancy measure and satisfaction with close friendships. Figure 1 presents a plot of the relationship between the ideal-actual discrepancy score and a standardized residual satisfaction score, wherein the effects of sex and the number of close friends have been removed statistically. Satisfaction with close friends increased as the actual number of close friends became closer to the student's ideal number of close friends. However, in contrast to predictions, the level of satisfaction was found to *decrease* as the actual number of close friends became greater than the ideal number of close friends. Satisfaction with close friends was found to be the greatest when there was a match between the ideal and actual numbers of close friends.

Prediction of Loneliness

An identical set of regression analyses was conducted to predict loneliness from the measures of social activity and close friendships. Table 4 presents the results of the analyses predicting levels of loneliness from the measures of social activity. After control for sex of the student, actual level of social activity accounted for 11% of the variance in loneliness scores. The ideal-actual discrepancy measure was not a statistically significant predictor, whereas the typical-actual discrepancy measure was marginally significant, accounting for 2% of the variance in loneliness. In contrast to predictions, neither of the squared discrepancy terms was a statistically significant predictor of loneliness.

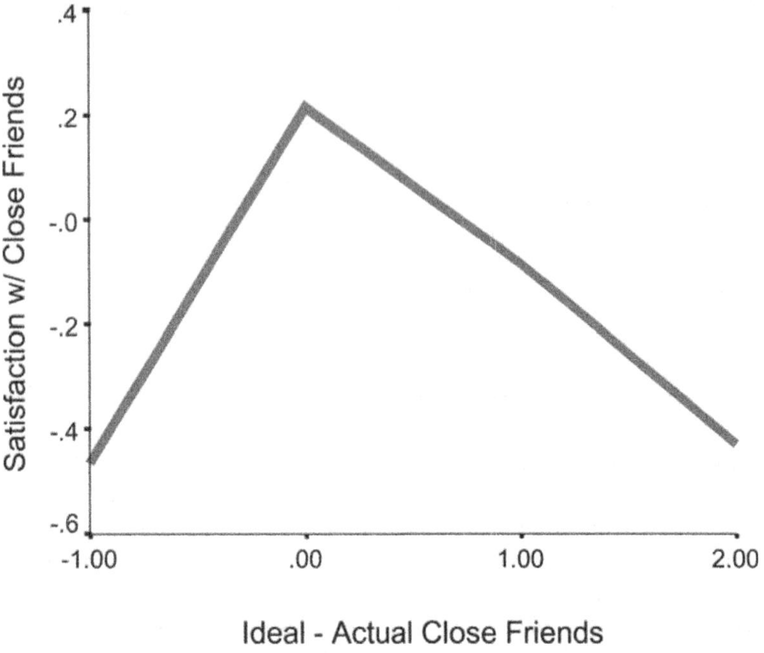

FIGURE 1. Ideal–actual close friends and standardized level of residual satisfaction with close friends.

TABLE 4. Hierarchical Regression Analyses Predicting Loneliness from Measures of Social Activity

Step	ΔR^2	F
1. Sex	.01	1.91
2. Social Activity	.11	19.47***
3. Ideal-Actual Discrepancy	.00	<1
4. Ideal-Actual Discrepancy Squared	.01	1.21
3. Typical-Actual Discrepancy	.02	3.52
4. Typical-Actual Discrepancy Squared	.00	<1

Note. $N = 169$.
$^{***}p < .001$. $^{**}p < .01$. $^{*}p < .05$.

TABLE 5. Hierarchical Regression Analyses Predicting Loneliness from Measures of Close Friendships

Step	ΔR^2	F
1. Sex	.01	1.91
2. # of Close Friends	.09	16.99***
3. Ideal-Actual Discrepancy	.03	5.75*
4. Ideal-Actual Discrepancy Squared	.07	13.69***
3. Typical-Actual Discrepancy	.08	15.83***
4. Typical-Actual Discrepancy Squared	.01	1.16

Note. $N = 169$.
$^{***}p < .001$. $^{**}p < .01$. $^{*}p < .05$.

Table 5 presents parallel results using the measures of close friendships to predict loneliness scores. The actual number of close friends was found to predict 9% of the variance in loneliness scores. After control for the number of close friends, the ideal-actual discrepancy measure for close friends was found to be statistically significant, accounting for 3% of the variance. Consistent with predictions, the squared discrepancy term was also statistically significant, accounting for an additional 7% of the variance in loneliness scores. Finally, as was found for the measure of satisfaction with friendships, only the linear term for the typical-actual discrepancy measure was statistically significant, accounting for 8% of the variance in loneliness scores.

The relation between the ideal actual discrepancy score and the standardized residual measure of loneliness (with control for the effects of sex and number of close friends) is presented in Figure 2. As expected, the results are essentially a mirror image of the findings for satisfaction with close friendships. Loneliness decreased as the actual number of close friends approached the ideal number of close friends reported by the students. However, loneliness *increased* as the actual number of close friends exceeded the ideal number of close friends. Once again, the lowest levels of loneliness were reported by students for whom there was a match between their ideal and actual numbers of close friends.

Discussion

The current study tested the nonlinear association between the ideal-actual discrepancy and relationship outcomes such as loneliness. According to Kelley and Thibaut (1978), discrepancies around the ideal level or CL are most important to the individual, having the greatest effect on relationship satisfaction and loneliness. Discrepancies that are farther away from the ideal level or CL are hypothesized to

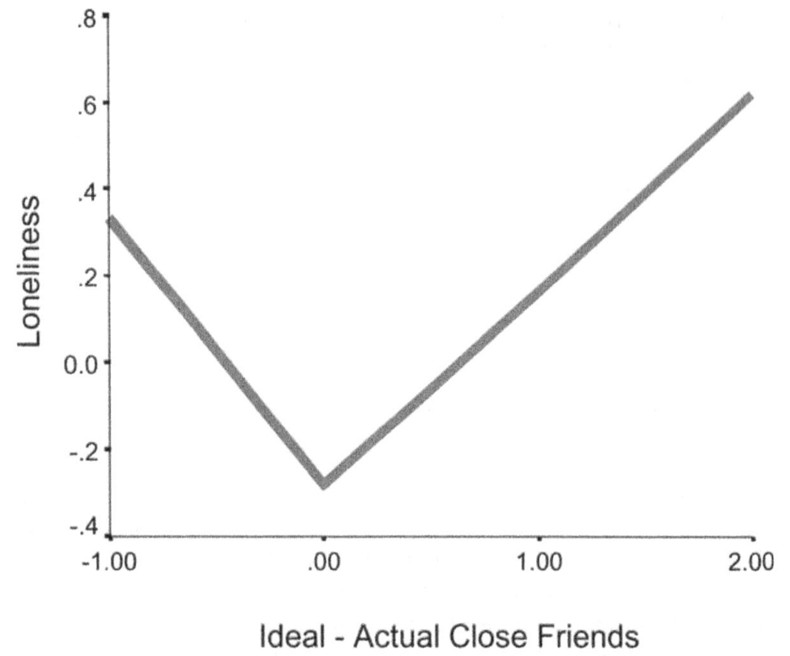

FIGURE 2. Ideal–actual close friends and standardized level of residual loneliness.

have less effect on satisfaction and loneliness, leading to the hypothesized nonlinear relationship. Recent studies testing for the relationship between the difference between ideal and actual relationships and satisfaction and loneliness have not evaluated this nonlinear relationship. The present study therefore builds on the analyses presented by Archibald et al. (1995) and Ward and Rana-Deuba (2000) by adding a test for nonlinear association between the ideal-actual relationship difference and relationship satisfaction and loneliness.

The results of this investigation provide mixed support for this cognitive discrepancy model of loneliness. There was no evidence of the predicted nonlinear relationship between the ideal-actual discrepancy measure for social activities and either satisfaction with social activities or loneliness. By contrast, a statistically significant nonlinear relationship was found between the ideal-actual discrepancy measure for close friendships and both satisfaction with close friendships and loneliness. This latter relationship was found after control for the number of close friendships reported by the students.

What might account for these differences in results for social activities versus close friendships? One possible explanation concerns the nature of the measures themselves. An assumption of the cognitive discrepancy model is that individuals have developed a clear expectation concerning the quantity and/or quality of their interpersonal relationships, which is in turn employed by individuals in evaluating those relationships. Given the importance and salience of close friendships, it is easy to believe that high school sophomores have a clear idea concerning the number of close friendships they would ideally like to have. By contrast, these students may not have a clear conception of how often they would like to participate in various social activities (e.g., getting together with friends before classes start). That is, these students may have a CL for close friendships but not for social activities.

A second possible explanation involves colinearity between the measure of actual social activity and the discrepancy measures derived from the Social Life Questionnaire. As can be seen in Table 1, the two discrepancy measures were strongly related to the measure of actual social activity; these correlations are very similar to those reported by Archibald et al. (1995). Furthermore, scores on the discrepancy measures were only weakly related to the measures of ideal or typical social activities. So, for example, the correlation between the ideal-actual discrepancy score and the measure of actual social activities was highly significant ($r = -.71$); the fewer was the number of social activities reported, the greater was the discrepancy. By contrast, the correlation of the ideal-actual discrepancy score with the measure of ideal social activities was nonsignificant ($r = .06$). This indicates that scores on the discrepancy measures were primarily a function of the actual level of social activity reported by the students and in turn may explain why the ideal actual discrepancy measure was not predictive of either satisfaction with social activity or loneliness after control for the level of actual social activity.

The parallel measures concerning close friends were less strongly related to the number of close friends. For example, the correlation between the number of close friends and the ideal-actual discrepancy score was –.26 (see Table 1). In addition, the ideal number of close friends was much more strongly related to this discrepancy score ($r = .48$), suggesting that the scores on the discrepancy measure were not solely determined by the actual number of close friends reported by the students.

Although we did find evidence supporting a nonlinear relationship between the ideal-actual discrepancy measure for close friendships and both satisfaction with close friendships and loneliness, the *form* of that relationship was clearly different from that found by Russell et al. (1981) for college students. Among high school sophomores, having both more and fewer close friends than desired was associated with decreased satisfaction with close friendships and increased loneliness. By contrast, Russell et al. (1981) found that decreased satisfaction and increased loneliness occurred only if college students reported having fewer close friends than they desired.

An important issue for future research concerns why these high school students would find having more friends (relative to their CL) to be negative or aversive. It is possible that having too many close friends is burdensome to these students and overloads them with social obligations. Indeed, we may have caught some of these students in the midst of a process wherein they are discovering how many friends they desire or formulating their CL for close friendships. So, for example, some students may have formed a large number of close friendships early in their high school career, only to discover the negative aspects of being involved in a large number of relationships. Indeed, these high school students reported a greater number of close friends ($M = 5.26$) than did the college students surveyed by Russell et al. (1981; $M = 3.86$). Over time, students may adjust their CL downward and reduce the size of their social network. If true, we should expect to see declines in the number of close friends over time among those students who indicated that their actual number exceeded their ideal number of close friends.

In contrast to the nonlinear relationship found for the ideal-actual discrepancy measure, the typical-actual discrepancy measure was related to satisfaction and loneliness in a linear fashion. High school students reported greater satisfaction with friendships and less loneliness to the extent that their close friendships exceeded those of the typical high school student. According to Kelley and Thibaut (1978), such social comparison information should serve as one determinant of the person's CL. Support for this prediction was found for the present sample. The ideal number of close friends was correlated with the typical number of close friends ($r = .34$). However, these two measures clearly operate differently in relation to the actual number of close friends reported by students, given the different pattern of relationships with satisfaction and loneliness. The discrepancy between typical and actual close friendships remained a significant predictor of both satisfaction and loneliness after control for the discrepancy between ideal and actual close friendships. That is, in a regression model that included the ideal-actual score as a predictor (and that controlled for both sex and actual number of friendships), the typical-actual score was predictive of both satisfaction with close friendships ($\beta = -.23$, $p < .05$) and loneliness ($\beta = .33$, $p < .001$). This suggests that students may compare their current friendships to both their CL and their perceptions of the relationships of other similar students in evaluating the adequacy of those relationships.

An important limitation of the measure of social activities that was employed in this study should be noted.[1] The Social Life Questionnaire does not involve contact with others using different forms of technology, such as the Internet or cell phones, that are commonly employed by high school students. These new methods of social contact may be particularly important for lonely students. Although studies indicate that loneliness is not related to the formation of friendships over the Internet (Russell, Flom, Gardner, Cutrona, & Hessling, 2003; Subrahmanyam & Lin, 2007), loneliness among high school students has been found to be related to compulsive use of the Internet (Van der Aa, Overbeek, Engels, Schotte, Meerkerk, & Fejnden, 2009). Incorporating an assessment of social contact via the Internet and other forms of technology may have altered the relationship between loneliness and the measure of social activity.

In summary, our results indicate that loneliness is not synonymous with being alone, at least in the context of certain aspects of interpersonal relationships. High school students who are lonely do not necessarily report having fewer close friendships. Instead, it appears from our findings that in predicting loneliness, we must take into consideration the number of close friendships desired by these students. Individuals who report a match between their desired and actual numbers of close friends are both the individuals who are most satisfied with their close friendships and the individuals who are least lonely. In contrast, students who report having more or fewer close friendships than they desire are the most likely to be dissatisfied with their friendships and to be lonely. Future studies should examine why these high school students found it aversive to have more friends than they desired and should evaluate changes over time in both their CL for friendships and their actual number of friendships. Measures of social contact via the Internet and other technologies should also be incorporated into future examinations of the relationship between loneliness and social contact.

NOTE

1. The authors thank an anonymous reviewer for noting this limitation of the measure.

REFERENCES

Archibald, F. S., Bartholomew, K., & Marx, R. (1995). Loneliness in early adolescence: A test of the cognitive discrepancy model of loneliness. *Personality and Social Psychology Bulletin*, *21*, 296–301.

Borys, S., & Perlman, D. (1985). Gender differences in loneliness. *Personality and Social Psychology Bulletin*, *11*, 61–74.

Cutrona, C. E. (1982). Transition to college: Loneliness and the process of social adjustment. In L. A. Peplau & D. Perlman (Eds.), *Loneliness: A sourcebook of current theory, research, and therapy* (pp. 291–301). New York: Wiley Interscience.

Kelley, H. H., & Thibaut, J. W. (1978). *Interpersonal relations: A theory of interdependence*. New York: Wiley Interscience.

Paloutzian, R. F., & Janigan, A. S. (1987). Models and methods in loneliness research: Their status and direction. *Journal of Social Behavior and Personality*, *2*, 31–36.

Perlman, D., & Peplau, L. A. (1982). Theoretical approaches to loneliness. In L. A. Peplau & D. Perlman (Eds.), *Loneliness: A sourcebook of current theory, research, and therapy* (pp. 123–134). New York: Wiley Interscience.

Russell, D. (1982). The measurement of loneliness. In L. A. Peplau & D. Perlman (Eds.), *Loneliness: A sourcebook of current theory, research, and therapy* (pp. 81–104). New York: Wiley Interscience.

Russell, D. (1996). The UCLA Loneliness Scale (Version 3): Reliability, validity, and factor structure. *Journal of Personality Assessment, 66*, 20–40.

Russell, D. W., Flom, E. K., Gardner, K. A., Cutrona, C. E., & Hessling, R. S. (2003). Who makes friends over the Internet? Loneliness and the "virtual" community. *International Scope Review, 5*(10), 1–19.

Russell, D., Peplau, L.A., & Cutrona, C. E. (1980). The revised UCLA Loneliness Scale: Concurrent and discriminant validity evidence. *Journal of Personality and Social Psychology, 39*, 472–480.

Russell, D., Steffen, M., & Salih, F. A. (1981, August). *Testing a cognitive model of loneliness*. Paper presented at the symposium New Directions in Loneliness Research at the annual convention of the American Psychological Association in Los Angeles, California.

Subrahmanyam, K., & Lin, G. Adolescents on the net: Internet use and well-being. *Adolescence, 42*, 659–677.

Thibaut, J. W., & Kelley, H. H. (1959). *The social psychology of groups*. New York: Wiley.

Van der Aa, N., Overbeek, G., Engles, R. C. M. E., Scholte, R. H. J., Meerkerk, G., & Van den Eijnden, R. J. J. M. (2009). Daily and compulsive Internet use and well-being in adolescence: A diathesis-stress model based on Big Five personality traits. *Journal of Youth and Adolescence, 38*, 765–776.

Ward, C., & Rana-Duba, A. (2000). Home and host culture influences on sojourner adjustment. *International Journal of Intercultural Relations, 24*, 291–306.

Loneliness, Optimism, and Well-Being Among Married, Divorced, and Widowed Individuals

HASIDA BEN-ZUR
University of Haifa

ABSTRACT. The study explored feelings of loneliness and dispositional optimism and their unique contribution to well-being. The sample included 196 women and men (*M* age = 45.94 years; 54% were women; 34% were married, 34% were divorced, and 32% were widowed) who completed inventories assessing feelings of loneliness, dispositional optimism, and well being measured by life satisfaction and negative affect. Widows and widowers scored higher than married respondents on loneliness and negative affect and lower on life satisfaction and optimism. Divorced persons scored lower on life satisfaction than married respondents but higher than widows and widowers on optimism. Loneliness was negatively correlated with optimism. Multiple regression analyses using demographics, family status, loneliness, and optimism as independent variables showed that loneliness contributed negatively to well-being, while optimism contributed positively to well-being. A Structural Equation Modeling analysis and mediation tests showed that both loneliness and optimism mediated the effects of widowhood on well-being. The findings are in support of Conservation of Resources (COR) theory (S. E. Hobfoll, 1989, 2001).

THE AIM of the present research was to investigate the contribution of loneliness and optimism to the well-being of married, divorced, and widowed individuals. It has been claimed that being married contributes to positive effects on the subjective well-being of both spouses (Waite, 1995), and the association between marital status and subjective well-being is strong, universal, and stable (Diener, Gohm, Suh, & Oishi, 2000; Mastekaasa, 1993). Changes in marital status are considered the most significant transitions in the social life of adults. Indeed, the work of Holmes and Rahe (1967) on life events suggests widowhood and divorce as the two most stressful events experienced in adulthood. The loss of a spouse can lead to reduced mental health (e.g., Stroebe & Stroebe, 1987; Zisook, Paulus,

Shuchter, & Judd, 1997), as well as greater financial and economic problems (Aber, 1992; Stroebe & Stroebe, 1993). Separation or divorce may lead to similar outcomes, such as impairment of psychological health (Aseltine & Kessler, 1993; Hope, Power, & Rodgers, 1999), loss of social and emotional ties, and economic hardship (Amato, 2000).

Based on the above research, it can be assumed that marital events such as becoming a widow or widower and divorcing lead to a great loss of resources. The present study focused on two such resources: personal and social resources. Such traits as self-esteem, optimism, mastery, and self-efficacy are considered to be important personal resources, while spousal and social support is seen as an important social resource that contributes to adjustment following stressful life events. Theoretical conceptualizations of stress incorporate these characteristics as major components of the coping process (e.g., Hobfoll, 1989, 2001; Lazarus & Folkman, 1984; Moos & Schaefer, 1993; Pearlin, 1999). For example, Lazarus (1999), Lazarus and Folkman (1984), and Moos and Schaefer (1993) assigned personal characteristics and social support the role of antecedents that affect people's appraisals of their capacity to cope with stressful encounters as well as their subsequent coping efforts, thus leading to lower short-term distress and better long-term life satisfaction and health. Sometimes such traits are seen as moderators or mediators (e.g., Pearlin, 1999) of the relationship of the stressful encounter and outcomes. They are also called *protective mechanisms* that contribute to personal resilience (e.g., Garmezy, 1991; Major, Richards, Cooper, Cozzarelli, & Zubek, 1998; Richardson, 2002) and help people adjust to devastating life experiences.

In the context of the Conservation of Resources (COR) theory (Hobfoll, 2001), a sense of optimism (a personal characteristic) and being with a partner or having companionship (a condition) are viewed as resources that people value. These resources can be depleted or lost as a result of major life events. Several studies have shown that changes in resources mediated the effects of stress on distress. Hobfoll, Johnson, Ennis, and Jackson (2003), for example, show material loss to be related to changes in women's sense of mastery and social support, which in turn led to depression and anger. It may be expected, therefore, that following major life changes such as loss of spouse or separation, people experience loss of social ties and spousal support, which can be reflected in greater loneliness and higher levels of depression and helplessness, which may be expressed by reduced optimism, in contrast to married individuals.

Loneliness is conceived as involving psychological as well as social aspects (Holmen, Ericsson, & Winblad, 2000) and consists of emotional loneliness, a loss or absence of confiding in and forming an attachment to a special and beloved person; and social loneliness, the absence of meaningful friendships. As tested in the present study, loneliness is reflected in a perception that one lacks social ties and social relationships. It signals difficulties in social relationships and is related to the quality of these relationships rather than to the frequency of contact (Heinrich & Gullone, 2006; Pinquart & Sorensen, 2001), as shown by the relative independence of measures of loneliness and nonintegrated social network (Golden et al., 2009). Research has shown that marital disruption due to death, divorce, or separation increases the loss of support in older age especially (Glaser, Tomassini, Racioppi, & Stuchbury, 2006), in as much as spouses are the primary source for providing emotional and instrumental support and fulfill most needs for intimacy and attachment (Wang & Amato, 2000; Pinquart, 2003). Thus, widowhood has been found to be a powerful predictor of loneliness (Beal, 2006; Golden et al., 2009; Savikko, Routasalo, Tilvis, Strandberg, & Pitkala, 2005) and more so among men than among women (Pinquart, 2003).

Dispositional optimism is defined as the generalized expectancy that good outcomes will occur when confronting major problems (Scheier & Carver, 1985). In the context of behavioral self-regulation theory, optimism can be considered a strong determinant of continued efforts to deal with problems, in contrast to turning away and giving up (Carver & Scheier, 2000). In general, dispositional optimism is found to be related to better adjustment following diverse stressors (see Nes & Segerstrom, 2006): It has been found to enhance adaptation following stressful medical encounters (e.g., Ben-Zur, Rapaport, Amar, & Uretzki, 2000; Bjorck, Hopp, & Jones, 1999; Epping-Jordan et al., 1999) and to contribute to successfully coping with blindness (Ben-Zur & Debbi, 2005) and with marital loss (O'Rourke, 2004).

The present study's aims were threefold: First, to replicate previous findings regarding the effects of widowhood and divorce on feelings of loneliness and optimism; second, to assess the contribution of loneliness and optimism to well-being; and third, to assess loneliness and optimism as mediators of the effects of marital status influences on well-being. Well-being is assessed in the present study using two indicators: life satisfaction and negative affect. *Life satisfaction* is conceived as a sense of satisfaction with various life areas and as a cognitive component of subjective well-being (Diener & Fujita, 1995). *Negative affect* describes subjective distress and dissatisfaction and consists of negative emotional states (Tellegen, 1985; Watson & Clark, 1992; Watson, Clark, & Tellegen, 1988).

To summarize, the main novel feature of the present study is the assessment of the effects of widowhood and divorce on well-being as mediated by feelings of loneliness and dispositional optimism. The conceptual model depicting mediation effects is given in Figure 1. As can be seen in the figure, marital status is assumed to contribute to well-being through loneliness and optimism.

The following hypotheses were posited:

> *H1:* Loneliness and negative affect will be higher among the widowed individuals than among the divorced individuals and higher among the divorced individuals than among the married individuals.

> *H2:* Optimism and life satisfaction will be lower among the widowed individuals than among the divorced individuals and lower among the divorced individuals than among the married individuals.

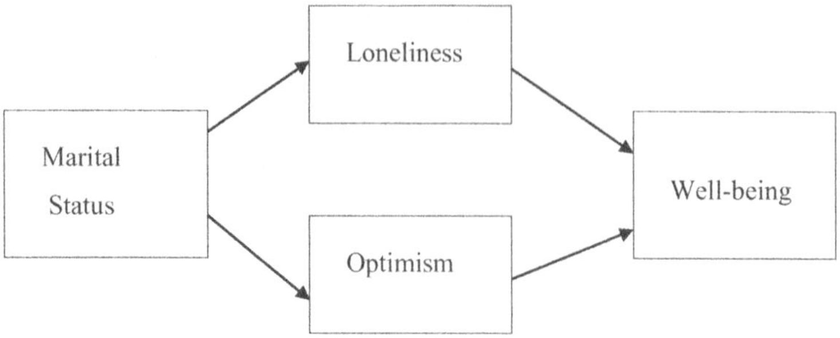

FIGURE 1. The conceptual model.

H3: Loneliness will be related to higher negative affect and lower life satisfaction, whereas optimism will show opposite associations with these well-being measures.

H4: Loneliness and optimism will mediate the effects of marital status on well-being measures.

Method

Sample and Procedure

A sample of 196 respondents completed the inventories. A quota sampling was used with stratifications according to family status and gender. Thus, of the respondents, 34% were married, 34% were divorced, and 32% were widowed. The three groups were comparable in gender percentages (48%, 42%, and 49%, respectively), $\chi^2(2, N = 190) = 0.86, p = 0.65$; number of children ($M = 2.45$, 2.26, and 2.76; $F = 2.97$, *ns*), and reported economic status ($M = 2.75$, 3.08, and 2.82; $F = 2.08$, *ns*). The widowed and divorced group were comparable on number of years following loss or separation ($M = 5.72$ and 5.78, respectively; $t < 1$). The widowed group, however, were older than the divorced and married participants (years), $M = 55.92$, 43.38, and 38.89; $F(2, 190) = 45.22, p < .0001$; less educated (years), $M = 13.48$, 14.92, and 15.49; respectively, $F(2, 185) = 7.35, p < .001$; and lower on reported health status (1 = *very good*, 5 = *not good at all*), $M = 2.60$, 2.12, and 1.84, respectively, $F(2, 167) = 8.21, p < .0001$.

The inventories were distributed by graduate students among persons in their community, or at work, with instructions to collect data from divorced, widowed, and married men and women in equal proportions. The research was approved by the internal review board of the university.

Inventories

Demographic data. A demographic questionnaire requested information on age, gender, education, health and family status, number of children, place of origin, work status, and length of marriage as well as number of years since divorce or widowhood.

Life satisfaction. This three-item scale (Ben-Zur, 2003) contains items depicting general satisfaction (e.g., "Generally speaking, I am satisfied with my life"), with high internal reliability values ($\alpha = .90$–$.92$). In the present study, the psychometric properties were satisfactory ($M = 3.60$, $SD = 0.81$, $\alpha = .89$).

Negative affect. This 10-item subscale was taken from the Positive and Negative Affect Schedule (PANAS; Watson et al., 1988). The total scale contains 20 adjectives depicting various mood and affective states (e.g., *enthusiastic*, *hostile*): 10 positive and 10 negative. The two subscales, namely positive affect (PA) and negative affect (NA), showed high internal reliabilities ($\alpha = .84$–$.90$) and were validated through their correlations with anxiety and depression (Watson et al., 1988). In the present study, the items were rated on a 5-point scale, ranging from 1 = *not at all* to 5 = *a lot*, in relation to current everyday life. The present study used only the negative affect scale ($M = 2.20$, $SD = 0.67$, $\alpha = .86$).

Loneliness. The Hebrew version of the revised UCLA loneliness scale (Russell, Peplau, & Cutrona, 1980) was used. The scale includes 20 items that refer to satisfaction with social relationships. The total score is computed by summing up the item ratings after reversing the direction of 10 items toward a high level of loneliness ($M = 35.34$, $SD = 10.05$, $\alpha = .91$).

Dispositional optimism. The Hebrew version of the Life Orientation Test (LOT), constructed by Scheier and Carver (1985), was used. It contains eight items rated on a 5-point scale (1 = *strongly agree*, 5 = *strongly disagree*), with a high score indicating an optimistic tendency. The internal reliability and test–retest of the original version were satisfactory ($\alpha = .76$, test–retest = .79; Scheier & Carver, 1985), and satisfactory values were obtained in the present study ($M = 3.79$, $SD = 0.81$, $\alpha = .84$).

Social desirability scale (SDS). This eight-item measure is based on Crowne and Marlowe's social desirability questionnaire (1964). The SDS represents the mean of the eight items (marked true/untrue) after reversing the direction of four items toward social desirability. In the present study, $M = 1.53$, $SD = 0.27$, and $\alpha = .71$.

Results

Table 1 shows the results of the one-way analyses of variance (ANOVA) of the research variables. All the variables showed significant differences between the three groups, with the exception of social desirability, along with an overall significant effect in multivariate ANOVA, Wilks's $\lambda = 0.817$, and $F(10, 370) = 3.94$, $p < .0001$. Loneliness and negative affect were higher in the widowed group

TABLE 1. Ms (SDs) of the Study Variables of Widowed, Divorced and Married Respondents

	M (*SD*)			
Group variable	Widowed	Divorced	Married	Statistical test *F*
Loneliness	39.38 (1.24)[a]	35.29 (1.17)[a b]	31.73 (1.18)[b]	9.97***
Optimism	3.49 (0.81)[a]	3.85 (0.83)[b]	4.00 (0.70)[b]	7.06**
Life satisfaction	3.24 (0.81)[a]	3.54 (0.84)[a]	3.97 (0.61)[b]	15.19***
Negative affect	2.38 (0.67)[a]	2.21 (0.68)[a b]	2.03 (0.61)[b]	4.44*
Social desirability	1.54 (0.28)	1.50 (0.28)	1.56 (0.27)	0.86

n = 193–196. *M*s with the same superscript letter do not differ significantly ($p = .05$) in a Scheffe test.
*$p < .01$; **$p < .001$; ***$p < .0001$.
M = mean; *SD* = standard deviation.

than the married group, while life satisfaction and optimism were lower among the widowed group than the married group. Thus, H1 and H2 were confirmed in regard to widowed persons.

The divorced group scored higher than the widowed group on optimism and lower than the married group on life satisfaction. No differences were found between the divorced group and the widowed or married participants on loneliness or negative affect. Thus, H1 and H2 were partially confirmed in regard to divorced persons.

Medium-level correlations were found between loneliness and optimism ($r = -.55$, $p < .001$), and between these variables and life satisfaction and negative affect (range = $-.61$ to $.55$, $p < .001$, for all correlations). A set of hierarchical regressions was applied to the well-being indices, using demographic variables, marital status dummy variables (widowhood and divorce; Table 2), loneliness, optimism, and social desirability as the independent variables. As can be seen in Table 2, both widowhood and divorce contributed negatively to life satisfaction, whereas only widowhood contributed positively to negative affect. Furthermore, loneliness contributed negatively to life satisfaction, while optimism contributed positively to this outcome. Loneliness also contributed positively to negative affect, while optimism contributed negatively to this outcome. Thus, H3 was fully supported.

Table 2 also shows the multiple regressions applied to loneliness and optimism, using all demographics including marital status as predictors, suggesting that widowed persons were again found to be higher on loneliness and lower on optimism. On the basis of these data, which suggest that widowhood is the marital

TABLE 2. Standardized Coefficients and Multiple R^2 of Hierarchical and Multiple Regressions

Independent Variable	Dependent Variable					
	Life satisfaction Step 1	Life satisfaction Step 2	Negative affect Step 1	Negative affect Step 2	Loneliness	Optimism
Gender	−.02	−.01	.17*	.15	−.11	−.12
Age	−.08	−.09	−.21*	−.20*	−.00	.01
Years of education	.03	.00	−.10	−.07	−.12	.01
Health status (reported)	−.18*	−.08	.29***	.17	.16*	−.27**
Economic status (reported)	−.33***	−.26***	.18**	.09	.21**	−.13
Social desirability	.21**	.12	−.32***	−.21**	−.08	.27***
Widowhood	−.36***	−.25*	.20*	.07	.30**	−.22*
Divorce	−.20**	−.18*	.05	.03	.12	.04
Loneliness	—	−.19*	—	.21*	—	—
Optimism	—	.26**	—	−.33***	—	—
R^2	.44	.54	.37	.53	.26	.29
F	13.94***	16.85***	10.50***	15.84***	6.47***	7.30***
df	8,145	10,143	8,145	10,143	8,145	8,145

Health status, reported (1 = *very good*; 5 = *not good at all*); economic status, reported (1 = *very good*; 5 = *not good at all*). Widowhood: 1 = widowed, 0 = divorced and married. Divorce: 1 = divorced, 0 = widowed and married.

$^{*}p < .01$. $^{**}p < .001$. $^{***}p < .0001$.

df = Degrees of freedom.

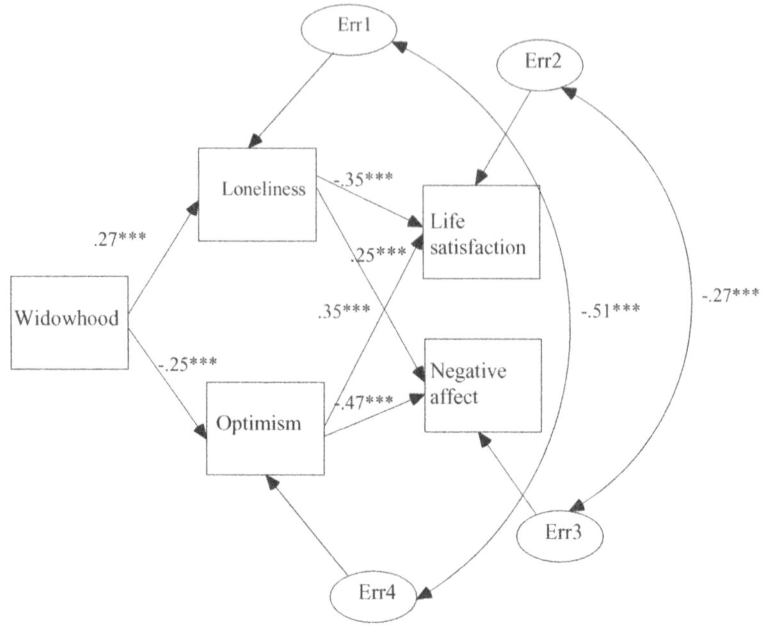

FIGURE 2. Testing the research model.

status mostly contributing to loneliness and optimism, the research model was tested, with widowhood (widowed vs. divorced and married persons) expected to affect loneliness and optimism, which, in turn, would affect life satisfaction and negative affect. The model was tested using Structural Equation Modeling (SEM) with AMOS 7.0 (Arbuckle, 2006). We evaluated the model by using five fit indices: Chi-square goodness-of-fit test, NFI, CFI, TLI, and RMSE. For NFI, CFI, and TLI, values greater than .90 are acceptable, while the RMSE should be smaller than .08. The resulting model is depicted in Figure 2. As can be seen in the figure, all paths are significant, in line with the hypotheses. The fit indices follow: $\chi^2(2) = 4.90$, $p = .09$; NFI = .98; CFI = .99; and TLI = .92. Only the RMSE was a bit high, with a marginal result of .086. An alternative model was also assessed, testing widowhood as contributing to life satisfaction and negative affect, which, in turn, affect loneliness and optimism. This analysis showed values that were almost identical to those of the first model: $\chi^2(2) = 4.96$, $p = .08$; NFI = .98; CFI = .99; TLI = .92; and RMSE = .087.

The hierarchical regressions presented in Table 2 show that the effect of widowhood (Marital status 1) on well-being (Step 1) is reduced when loneliness and optimism are entered (Step 2). These results suggest that loneliness and optimism may mediate the effects of widowhood on life satisfaction and negative affect. Mediation tests were conducted using the Baron and Kenny (1986) guidelines and the Sobel test (Sobel, 1982) by means of an Internet-based interactive software program (Preacher & Leonardelli, 2006). The first column (path c) in Table 3 shows regression results of each dependent variable (DV) on the independent variable (IV); the second (path a) shows regression results of each mediator on IV; the third (path b) and forth (path c') columns show the regression results of each DV on each mediator and IV, respectively; and the fifth column presents the Sobel test results. As can be seen in the table, in each analysis the inclusion of the mediator (i.e., loneliness or optimism) lowered the association of marital status 1 (widowhood) with life satisfaction and rendered it insignificant with negative affect. Thus, H4 was partially supported, suggesting that some of the effects of widowhood on life satisfaction and negative affect may have been mediated by loneliness and optimism.

Discussion

The study shows that even after an average of 5.7 years following separation or loss, the widows and widowers scored higher than married people on a variety of well-being and adjustment measures, including negative aspects of life, such as loneliness and negative affect; and lower on positive aspects, such as current life satisfaction and optimism. Divorced persons differed from widows and widowers in scoring higher on optimism but showed a similarity to them in scoring lower than the married sample on current life satisfaction. Evidently, people vary in their reactions to loss. Some recover from the loss of a spouse relatively quickly and thus are considered to be high in resilience, while others remain chronically depressed over long periods (e.g., Bonnano et al., 2002).

The data are in support of the Conservation of Resources (COR) theory (Hobfoll, 1989, 2001), which holds that the loss of resources is the most important element in a stressful encounter and that such a loss can increase vulnerability to other losses, sometimes leading to a loss cycle that is difficult to counteract. In the present study, almost 6 years following their loss, the widowed scored lower than the married participants on well-being indicators as well as in optimism and scored higher on loneliness. Thus, based on the COR theory, a major life event such as the death of a spouse can bring about the loss of vital resources as the loss of a meaningful relationship and support of a spouse, presumably leading to loneliness, which cannot be corrected easily.

In the present study, marital status was related to life satisfaction independently of optimism and loneliness, and these two resources were also found to be related independently to the well-being measures, that is, life satisfaction and negative affect. Optimism has been researched intensively in the context of a variety of life events (e.g., Bjorck et al., 1999; Epping-Jordan et al., 1999; O'Rourke, 2004) and is an important resource that can help people cope with blindness (Ben-Zur

TABLE 3. Explaining Effects of Widowhood on Life Satisfaction and Negative Affect: Mediation Analyses Results—Beta Coefficients (and t-tests)

Mediator	Path c	Path a	Path b	Path c'	Sobel Z
Dependent variable: Life satisfaction					
Loneliness	−.29 (−4.28***)	.27 (3.88***)	−.50 (−8.08***)	−.17 (−2.73**)	3.50***
Optimism	−.29 (−4.28***)	−.25 (−3.61***)	.50 (8.15***)	−.17 (−2.75**)	3.30***
Dependent variable: Negative affect					
Loneliness	.18 (2.54**)	.27 (3.88***)	.50 (7.71***)	.05 (*ns*)	3.47***
Optimism	.18 (2.54**)	−.25 (−3.61***)	−.60 (−10.19***)	.03 (*ns*)	3.40***

** $p < .01$.; ***$p < .001$; Note: Path c: dependent variable regressed on marital status 1 (independent variable); Path a: mediator regressed on marital status 1 (independent variable); Path b: dependent variable regressed on mediator, together with marital status 1; Path c': dependent variable regressed on marital status 1 (independent variable), together with mediator; t-tests for beta coefficients are given in parentheses.

& Debbi, 2005) or open-heart surgery (Ben-Zur et al., 2000). Loneliness is emphasized in studies of marital loss (e.g., Glaser et al., 2006; Pinquart, 2003), and its counterpart, social support, has also been explored in a variety of contexts (see Hobfoll & Vaux, 1993) and is considered to be an important resource in times of stress and crisis (e.g., Hobfoll, 2001; Lazarus & Folkman, 1984; Moos & Schaefer, 1993). As can be seen in the present results, loneliness contributes to well-being as much as optimism, and both were found to be mediators of the effects of widowhood on well-being. Upon losing a spouse, one often loses spousal support and company, in some cases after many years of marital life. Additionally, social relations that were initiated by the deceased spouse may be lost with the social environment becoming poorer and more restricted. These processes may result in intense feelings of loneliness that can harm well-being in the long run. In sum, both loneliness and optimism may be important reference points in any intervention aimed at alleviating distress and improving well-being among the widowed.

One limitation of the study is that it is correlational and cross-sectional. Thus, the conceptual model depicted marital status as a precursor of loneliness and optimism, which in turn affect negative affect and life satisfaction; but it could be the opposite case, namely, that lower levels of life satisfaction and higher negative affect result in intensive feelings of loneliness and a pessimistic tendency towards one's future. The present study tested both models using SEM, but the model fit indices were almost identical and could not differentiate between the two models, and even with the use of SEM it is not possible to determine the direction of causality in a cross-sectional study. Another limitation is that the three groups tested—married, divorced, and widowed individuals—were not matched in demographic aspects such as age, number of years of marriage, and health and economic status. However, when comparing the present sample in terms of age, education levels, and work status with a representative sample collected in Israel (Gilbar & Ben-Zur, 2002), we observed the same demographic patterns. Moreover, the effects of marital status, loneliness, and optimism were observed after demographic variables and social desirability were controlled. Finally, marital quality, which might contribute to feelings of loneliness, was not investigated in the present study. Future studies might well continue the investigation of lack of personal and social resources in the context of divorce and widowhood using longitudinal research, objective (physiological, performance) measures of well-being, and finer assessments of marital quality.

REFERENCES

Aber, C. S. (1992). Spousal death, a threat to women's health: Paid work as a "resistance resource image." *Journal of Nursing Scholarship, 24*(2), 95–99.

Amato, P. R. (2000). The consequences of divorce for adults and children. *Journal of Marriage and the Family, 62*(4), 1269–1287.

Arbuckle, J. L. (2006). *Amos 7.0 user's guide* [computer manual]. Chicago: SPSS.

Aseltine, R. H., & Kessler, R. C. (1993). Marital disruption and depression in a community sample. *Journal of Health and Social Behavior, 34*, 237–251.

Baron, R. M., & Kenny, D.A. (1986). The moderator-mediator variable distinction in social psychological research: Conceptual, strategic, and statistical considerations. *Journal of Personality and Social Psychology, 5*, 1173–1182.

Beal, C. (2006). Loneliness in older women: A review of the literature. *Issues in Mental Health Nursing, 27*, 795–813.

Ben-Zur, H. (2003). Happy adolescents: The link between subjective well-being, internal resources, and parental factors. *Journal of Youth and Adolescence, 32*, 67–79.

Ben-Zur, H., & Debi, Z. (2005). Optimism, social comparisons and coping with vision loss in Israel. *Journal of Visual Impairment and Blindness, 99*, 151–164.

Ben-Zur, H., & Michael, K. (2009). Social comparisons and well-being following widowhood and divorce. *Death Studies, 33*, 220–238.

Ben-Zur, H., Rapaport, B., Amar, R., & Uretzki, G. (2000). Coping strategies, life style changes and pessimism after open-heart surgery. *Health and Social Work, 25*, 201–209.

Bjorck, J.P., Hopp, D. P., & Jones, L. W. (1999). Prostate cancer and emotional functioning: Effects of mental adjustment, optimism, and appraisal. *Journal of Psychosocial Oncology, 17*, 71–85.

Bonnano, G. A., Wortman, C. B., Lehman, D. R., Tweed, R.G., Haring, M., Sonnega, J., et al. (2002). Resilience to loss and chronic grief: A prospective study from preloss to 18-months postloss. *Journal of Personality and Social Psychology, 83*, 1150–1164.

Carver, C. S., & Scheier, M. F. (2000). On the structure of behavioral self-regulation. In M. Boekaerts, P. R. Pintrich, & M. Zeidner (Eds.), *Handbook of self-regulation* (pp. 41–84). San Diego, CA: Academic Press.

Crowne, D. P., & Marlowe, D. (1964). The approval motive: Studies in evaluative dependence. New York: Wiley.

Diener, E., & Fujita, F. (1995). Resources, personal strivings, and subjective well-being: A nomothetic and idiographic approach. *Journal of Personality and Social Psychology, 68*, 926–935.

Diener, E., Gohm, C. L., Suh, E., & Oishi, S. (2000) Similarity of the relations between marital status and subjective well-being across cultures. *Journal of Cross Cultural Psychology, 31*(4), 419–436.

Epping-Jordan, J. E., Compas, B. E., Osowiecki, D. M., Oppedisano, G., Gerhardt, C., Primo, K., & Krag, D. N. (1999). Psychological adjustment in breast cancer: Processes of emotional distress. *Health Psychology, 18*, 315–326.

Garmezy, N. (1991). Resilience in children's adaptation to negative life events and stressed environments. *Pediatric Annals, 20*, 459–466.

Gilbar, O., & Ben-Zur, H. (2002). *Cancer and the family caregiver: Distress and coping*. Springfield, IL: Charles C. Thomas.

Glaser, K., Tomassini, C., Racioppi, F., & Stuchbury, R. (2006). Marital disruptions and loss of support in later life: A longitudinal study of the United Kingdom. *European Journal of Ageing, 3*, 207–216.

Golden, J., Conroy, R. M., Bruce, I., Denihan, A., Green, E., Kirby, M., & Lawlor, B.A. (2009). Loneliness, social support networks, mood and well-being in community-dwelling elderly. *International Journal of Geriatric Psychiatry, 24*, 694–700.

Heinrich, L. M., & Gullone, E. (2006). The clinical significance of loneliness: A literature review. *Clinical Psychology Review*, *26*, 695–718.
Hobfoll, S. (1989). Conservation of resources: A new attempt at conceptualizing stress. *American Psychologist*, *44*, 513–524.
Hobfoll, S.E. (2001). The influence of culture, community, and the nested-self in the stress process: Advancing conservation of resources theory. *Applied Psychology: An International Review*, *50*, 337–421.
Hobfoll, S.E., Johnson, R.J., Ennis, N., & Jackson, A. P. (2003). Resource loss, resource gain, and emotional outcomes among inner city women. *Journal of Personality and Social Psychology*, *84*, 632–43.
Hobfoll, S.E., & Vaux, A. (1993). Social support: Resources and context. In L. Goldberger & S. Breznitz (Eds.), *Handbook of stress: Theoretical and clinical aspects* (2nd ed.) (pp. 685–705). New York: Free Press.
Holmen, K., Ericsson, K., & Winblad, B. (2000). Social and emotional loneliness among non-demented and demented elderly people. *Archives of Gerontology and Geriatrics*, *31*, 177–192.
Holmes, T. H., & Rahe, R. H. (1967). The social readjustment rating scale. *Journal of Psychosomatic Research*, *11*(2), 213–218.
Hope, S., Power, C., & Rodgers, B. (1999). Does financial hardship account for elevated psychological distress in lone mothers? *Social Science and Medicine*, *29*, 381–389.
Lazarus, R. S. (1999). *Stress and emotion: A new synthesis*. London: Free Association Books.
Lazarus, R. S. & Folkman, S. (1984). *Stress, appraisal and coping*. New York: Springer.
Major, B., Richards, C., Cooper, M. L., Cozzarelli, C., & Zubek, J. (1998). Personal resilience, cognitive appraisals, and coping: An integrative model of adjustment to abortion. *Journal of Personality and Social Psychology*, *74*, 735–752.
Mastekaasa, A. (1993). Marital status and subjective well-being: A changing relationship? *Social Indicators Research*, *29*(3), 249–276.
Moos, R. H., & Schaefer, J. A. (1993). Coping resources and processes: Current concepts and measures. In L. Goldberger & S. Breznitz (Eds.), *Handbook of stress: Theoretical and clinical aspects* (2nd ed.) (pp. 234–257). New York: Free Press.
Nes, L. S., & Segerstrom, S.C. (2006). Dispositional optimism and coping: A meta-analytic review. *Personality and Social Psychology Review*, *10*, 235–251.
O'Rourke, N. (2004). Cognitive adaptation and women's adjustment to conjugal bereavement. *Journal of Women & Aging*, *16*, 87–104.
Pearlin, L. I. (1999). Stress and mental health: A conceptual overview. In A. V. Horwitz & T. L. Scheid (Eds.), *A handbook for the study of mental health: Social contexts, theories and systems* (pp. 161–175). Cambridge, UK: Cambridge University Press.
Pinquart, M. (2003). Loneliness in married, widowed, divorced, and never-married older adults. *Journal of Social and Personal Relationships*, *20*, 31–53.
Pinquart, M., & Sorensen, S. (2001). Influences on loneliness in older adults: A meta-analysis. *Basic and Applied Social Psychology*, *23*, 245–266.
Preacher, K. J., & Leonardelli, G. J. (2006). Calculation for the Sobel test. http://www.people.ku.edu/~preacher/sobel/sobel.htm
Richardson, G. E. (2002). The metatheory of resilience and resiliency. *Journal of Clinical Psychology*, *58*, 307–321.
Russell, D., Peplau, L. A., & Cutrona, C. E. (1980). The revised UCLA loneliness scale: Concurrent and discriminant validity evidence. *Journal of Personality and Social Psychology*, *39*, 472–480.
Savikko, N., Routasalo, P., Tilvis, R. S., Strandberg, T. E., & Pitkala, K. H. (2005). Predictors and subjective causes of loneliness in an aged population. *Archives of Gerontology and Geriatrics*, *41*, 223–233.

Scheier, M. F., & Carver, C. S. (1985). Optimism, coping, and health: Assessment and implications of generalized outcome expectancies. *Health Psychology*, *4*, 219–247.

Sobel, M. E. (1982). Asymptotic intervals for indirect effects in structural equations models. In S. Leinhart (Ed.), *Sociological methodology* (pp. 290–312). San Francisco: Jossey-Bass.

Stroebe, W., & Stroebe, M. S. (1987). *Bereavement and health: The psychological and physical consequences of partner loss*. New York: Cambridge University Press.

Stroebe, W., & Stroebe, M. S. (1993). Determinants of adjustment to bereavement in younger widows and widowers. In M. S. Stroebe, W. Stroebe, & R. O. Hansson (Eds.), *Handbook of bereavement: Theory, research, and intervention* (pp. 208–226). New York: Cambridge University Press.

Tellegen, A. (1985). Structures of mood and personality and their relevance to assessing anxiety with an emphasis on self-report. In A. H. Tuma & J. D. Maser (Eds.), *Anxiety and the anxiety disorders* (pp. 681–706). Hillsdale, NJ: Lawrence Erlbaum.

Waite, L. J. (1995). Does marriage matter? *Demography*, *32*, 483–507.

Wang, H., & Amato, P. P. R. (2000). Predictors of divorce adjustment: Stressors, resources, and definitions. *Journal of Marriage and the Family*, *62*, 655–668.

Watson, D., & Clark, L. A. (1992). On traits and temperament: General and specific factors of emotional experience and their relation to the five-factor model. *Journal of Personality*, *60*, 442–476.

Watson, D., Clark, L. A., & Tellegen, A. (1988). Development and validation of brief measures of positive and negative affect: The PANAS scale. *Journal of Personality and Social Psychology*, *54*, 1063–1070.

Zeidner, M., & Ben-Zur, H. (1994). Individual differences in anxiety, coping, and post-traumatic stress in the aftermath of the Persian Gulf War. *Personality and Individual Differences*, *16*, 459–476.

Zisook, S., Paulus, M., Shuchter, S. R., & Judd, L. L. (1997). The many faces of depression following spousal bereavement. *Journal of Affective Disorders*, *45*(1–2), 85–94.

Loneliness and Emotional Intelligence

LEEHU ZYSBERG
Tel Hai College

ABSTRACT. The possible associations of loneliness with Emotional Intelligence (EI), 2 of its correlates (life satisfaction and a sense of meaning), and several background variables were tested on a sample of 134 young adults attending college in northern Israel. Structural Equation Modeling (SEM) analysis provided support for the model, suggesting that the presence of meaning, EI, and size and availability of an individual's social network are the strongest correlates of loneliness. EI therefore emerges as a potentially important factor in our understanding of loneliness, and the model provides a framework for future studies. The results are discussed vis-à-vis existing findings in the literature and possible directions for approaching loneliness as a theoretical concept and a social phenomenon.

THE CONCEPT OF LONELINESS has been the focus of scientific attention since the 1980s, though it remains in need of further investigation. While often addressed as part of a broader condition involving personal and interpersonal distress and even pathology (McWhirter, 1990; Heinrich & Gullone, 2006), loneliness is also a prevalent condition among normative, functioning populations, inflicting distress and psychological irritation (Arslan, Hamarta, Ure, & Osyesil, 2010). Actually, some influential authors see loneliness as a social plague of modern times, a common source of unrest and distress for an ever-growing portion of the general population, with some subpopulations, such as the elderly and marginalized youth, being at an even higher risk (Perlman & Peplau, 1984; McPherson, Smith-Lovin, & Brashears, 2006; Dykstra, 2009; Arslan, Hamarta, Ure, & Osyesil, 2010).

Loneliness is often defined as the subjective discrepancy between one's desired and one's (perceived) existing interpersonal relations. It has been traditionally associated with a broad range of adverse psychological outcomes, such as anxiety, depression, increased likelihood of substance abuse, and social deviance, as well as

The author thanks Ms. Neta Arazy for her invaluable help in the preparation of the study and data collection.

milder outcomes, such as lower social skills, a more critical view of self, and perfectionism (Perlman & Peplau, 1984; McWhirter, 1990; Hughes, Waite, Hawkley, & Caccioppo, 2004; Arslan, Hamarta, Ure, & Osyesil, 2010). The literature also proposes tactics for interventions with persons suffering from loneliness, ranging from cognitive-behavioral techniques to socially focused interventions, such as training in social skills and providing a framework for social support (Young, 1982; McWhirter, 1990).

The effectiveness of identification of at-risk populations, prevention, and necessary treatment to reduce the experience of loneliness depend on our understanding of the correlates, indicators, and antecedents of loneliness. A meta-analysis by Pinquart and Sorenson (2003) identified loneliness as a concept related to conditions and concepts of self-esteem, mood, anxiety, anger, and optimism, fear of negative evaluation, shyness, social skills, social support, dysphoria, and sociability (see also Shaver & Brennan, 1991). Most of these concepts are also associated with a relatively new concept: that of Emotional Intelligence (EI; Mayer, Salovey, & Caruso 1999). EI is a concept describing a group of personal characteristics allowing the identification and management of emotions in oneself and others (Mayer, Salovey, & Caruso 1999; Mayer, Roberts, & Barsade, 2008). The concept is still in its infancy, and there remains disagreement on its definitions and measures (Bradberry & Su, 2006).

In current literature, EI is conceptualized in two competing manners: The first sees EI as a group of personality traits and general behavioral predispositions (e.g., High motivation, self-consciousness, Optimism), while the other envisions EI as an ability that is equivalent in almost every aspect to traditional intelligence: Rather than processing cognitive information to correctly solve problems, EI refers to our ability to effectively and correctly process emotional information to solve personal and interpersonal problems (Mayer, Salovey, & Caruso 1999; Bradberry & Su, 2006). The most widely accepted ability model for EI described it as a compound concept pertaining to (a) emotion recognition in self and others, (b) the integration of emotion in thought and problem solving, (c) effectively processing complex emotions, and (d) emotion modification and management (Brackett & Mayer, 2003). Despite the disagreements, some encouraging results show support of the ability approach to EI. A recent review of the existing literature proposes that ability EI is correlated with the quality and perceived satisfaction with interpersonal relationships in childhood and adolescence, social well-being, satisfaction with family relationships (with only sporadic evidence regarding satisfaction with romantic attachments), and effective communication style and skills. The effects appear to be maintained even when the researcher controls for personality traits or cognitive abilities (Mayer, Roberts, & Barsade, 2008).

Though (to the best our knowledge) never before directly tested, the association between EI and Loneliness emerges from the literature: EI has been linked to satisfaction with social relations in a variety of contexts and the quality of social ties and relations in a few studies utilizing ability-based EI measures (Lopes,

Salovey & Straus, 2003; Mavroveli, Petrides, Rieffe & Bakker, 2007). Additional evidence suggests EI plays a significant role in determining social well-being and perceived social competence (Lopes, Brackett, Nezlek, Schultz, Sellin & Salovey, 2004). Satisfaction and distress based on social factors also associated with EI (Gannon & Ranzijn, 2005). Such findings not only lend support to the construct validity of EI but also position EI as a factor associated with a wide range of social, inter-, and intra-personal behaviors and symptoms. Findings linking EI with a sense of well-being, satisfaction, and emotional resilience may suggest a link with a somewhat overlapping conceptual frame, that of "positive psychology" (Antonovsky, 1987): EI and concepts from the content world of positive psychology, central among them the finding of meaning in life, have shown both theoretical and empirical association. These commonalities, in turn, are also conceptually akin to many of the factors and outcomes associated with loneliness (as shown in the literature review above).

Given the evidence, it may be of interest to study and explore the potential associations of EI and some of its prominent theory-based correlates with loneliness. To date, no such study linking the conceptual frames of EI and positive psychology with the concept of loneliness has been published. Such an investigation may shed new light on the nature and antecedents of loneliness in people's lives as well as offer ways of identifying "at risk" populations and thereby point to future interventions, or so-called "emotional immunization," for loneliness. Using a sample of young adults attending college in northern Israel, we therefore tested the potential associations of a generally accepted measure of loneliness with a measure of ability EI and two of its correlates from the existing literature: general satisfaction with one's life (Ganon & Ranzijn, 2005) and a sense of meaning in one's life (Steger, Frazier, Oishi, and Kaler, 2006). Such associations never take place in a "social vacuum", and the literature does point out to the importance of background variables such as age and the characteristics and availability of social support systems (Jones, Hobbs & Hockenberry, 1982). We therefore hypothesized a model comprising background and demographic factors, personal attributes (including EI level), and loneliness, as depicted in Figure 1.

The model reflects a hypothesized negative association between EI level and level of reported loneliness, since EI is widely purported to be instrumental in effective management of self and relationships with others (Mayer, Salovey, & Caruso, 1999). Based on the existing literature, the model also reflects positive associations between EI, age, satisfaction with life, and meaning in life. On the basis of these associations, we also hypothesized associations between the correlates of EI and loneliness. The model also represents some background variables that are mentioned in the existing literature as restrictions or factors associated with loneliness, such as the size of the social network, the availability of members of the social network, and the type of community (e.g., a large city vs. a village) in which an individual resides. At this point, with what was more an exploratory

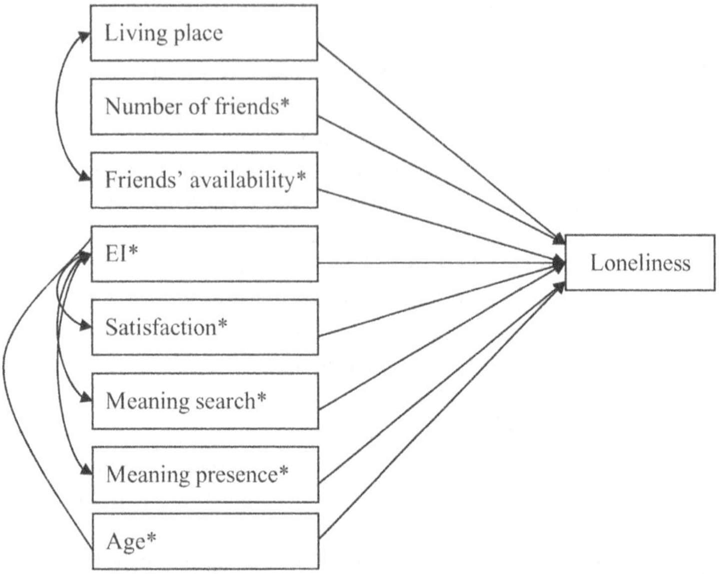

FIGURE 1. The proposed model for the study, linking Emotional Intelligence, its correlates, and its background variables to loneliness. * = a hypothesized negative association.

model, we did not attempt to examine more complex associations (e.g., mediation or moderation) between the study variables.

Method

Sample

We used a correlational study design, easily allowing exploratory examination of associations among variables. Participants were 134 students enrolled in undergraduate psychology programs at several colleges in northern Israel whom we had asked to participate in a study on "young people's life." About half of them received credit for participation, while the rest volunteered to participate. They were all 1st-year students, mainly since this was a convenience sample, and since course requirements in the psychology program encourage 1st-year students to participate in studies on campus. Of all participants, 106 were women, and 28 were men. As reported by the participants in a demographic questionnaire administered, the mean age was 23.98 years ($SD = 2.95$ years). Most of the students were single (54%), only 3% were married, and 43% reported being in a romantic relationship. The vast majority (86.5%) was Jewish, 4.5% were Muslim, about 3%

were Christian, and about 6% reported belonging to "another religion." Regarding religious observance, most of the sample (72%) reported being secular, 24% reported being "traditional," and the rest (4%) reported being "religious."

Measures

Loneliness was assessed using the Hebrew version of the Revised UCLA scale (Russel, Peplau, & Cutrona, 1980). This self-report measure of loneliness is widely used in the literature and demonstrates good reliability and acceptable validity (McWhirter, 1990).

EI was assessed with the AVEI (Audio-Visual Test of Emotional Intelligence; Zysberg, Zisberg & Levy, 2010), a computer-based test using the ability-EI approach (Mayer, Roberts, & Barsade, 2008). This instrument includes 27 items comprising still images or short video clips depicting people in various situations. Respondents are requested to identify the emotions that a target person is experiencing in each item. The test has shown evidence of acceptable reliability and good predictive validity, with diverse criteria associated with the concept of EI (Zysberg, in press).

Correlates of EI. The existing literature associates EI with a wide range of behavioral and psychological outcomes, of which two were deemed most relevant to the context of this study: life satisfaction and a sense of meaning.

Life satisfaction was assessed by the Hebrew version of the Life Satisfaction Scale by Diener et al. (1985). This simple self-report scale shows adequate reliability and validity in a broad range of studies (Pavrot & Diener, 1993).

Meaning in life was assessed by the Meaning in Life questionnaire (Steer, Frasier, Oishi, & Kaler, 2006). This self-report questionnaire assesses two aspects: the presence of meaning in one's life and the extent to which one seeks meaning in life. Evidence of reliability and consistency beyond culture and gender have been established by the authors, and while evidence of the scale's validity is sporadic, it is sufficient to justify use in this study.

Demographic and background variables. In addition to the above data, demographic information was collected on gender, age, socioeconomic status, and religious orientation. Background data related to the participants' social network were also collected, including place of residence (city, town, village, kibbutz, other small community), number of friends, and their physical availability. Some information on family members, such as number of siblings and family cohesiveness, was also collected.

Procedure

After obtaining the college's committee approval, students were approached in class and were requested to participate in a study on "various aspects in young adults' life." With the exception of one student, all the students whom we tried to recruit agreed to participate. They filled out the questionnaires and took the computer-based AVEI in a large computer lab in groups of 5–10. The full procedure took about 35–40 min to complete. Students were promised an update of the study results once completed, if interested. The data were entered in the SPSS 16.0 program and processed using the same program, as well as the AMOS 16 module.

Results

First, the distributions of the main study variables were examined. As shown in Table 1, the main distribution indices suggest close to normal distribution. The samples were also tested for possible differences between participants from different colleges, and no significant differences were found on any of the main variables. Thus, the database was treated thereafter as one for the rest of the analyses.

In order to test the model proposed in this study, the AMOS 16 software package was used to run Structural Equation Modeling analysis. This model allows for a single-run analysis, testing for both unique associations between each of the variables and the target variable (loneliness), while testing the interactions and intercorrelations between the variables according to the hypothesized model (Kaplan, 2000). The results of the analysis are summarized graphically in Figure 2.

The results provide evidence to support the hypothesized model. In descending order, the most prominent associates of loneliness were finding meaning in one's life, EI, number of friends, and their availability. As expected, EI was also associated with age and life satisfaction. However, it was not found to be associated with meaning. The goodness-of-fit indices for the overall model were generally within the acceptable range, with the exception of Chi-square, which is usually found to be significant in larger samples.

In order to test for the possibility of demographic variables intervening with the effects or the model, a series of multiple hierarchical regressions were used to test for the possible effects of gender, parents' level of religiosity, self-religiosity,

TABLE 1. Distribution Indices of the Main Study Variables ($n = 134$)

Variable	M (SD)	Minimum–maximum range	Skewness kurtosis
Loneliness	2.24 (0.45)	1.30–3.40	.18–.09
Meaning (presence)	5.15 (0.94)	2.50–7.00	–.69.56
Meaning (search)	4.68 (1.37)	1–7	–.29–.36
Satisfaction	4.76 (0.99)	2.20–6.80	–.36.07
EI	17.64 (3.36)	7–24	.53.70

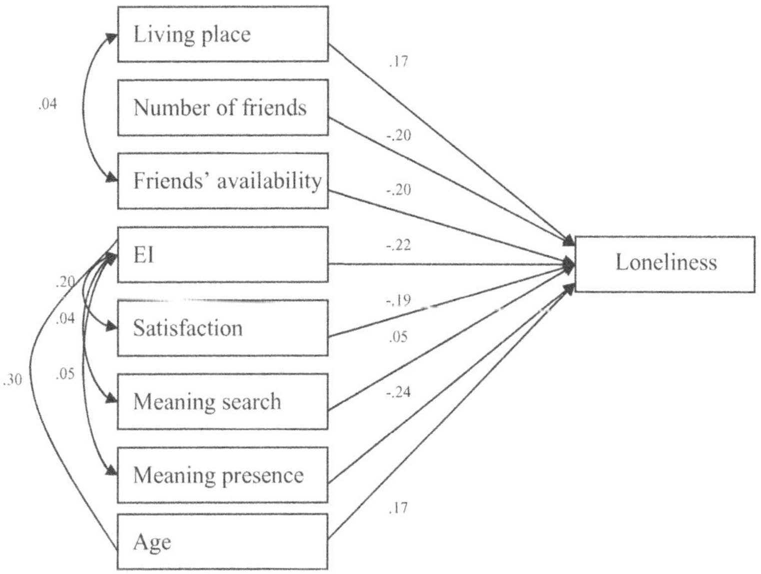

FIGURE 2. Results of the SEM analysis. Model coefficients over .13 are considered statistically significant at the .05 level or better. Model goodness-of-fit indices: Chi-square = 73.8; *df* = 21, *p* < .001; GFI = .93; NFI = .94; RMSEA = .05.

ethnicity, and number of siblings. No statistically significant effect was found for any of the above.

Discussion

This study looked at the possible role played by EI and two of its correlates in our understanding of loneliness as a psychological construct and phenomenon. Given that EI is proposed in the literature to be associated with skills and abilities related to individuals' processing of emotions and relations with others, the present study hypothesized that EI would be negatively associated with loneliness. In order to attain a broader picture of factors associated with both EI and loneliness, we examined additional background variables, including age, life satisfaction, and a sense of meaning in life, which are theoretically or empirically associated with EI (Diener et al., 1984; Gannon & Ranzijn, 2005; Steger et al., 2006), as well as social network size, availability of friends, and type of living environment, which are associated with loneliness (McWhirter, 1990; McPherson, Smith-Lovin, & Brashears, 2006).

The results generally provide support for the hypothesized model. The presence of meaning in life, EI, number of friends, and their availability were found to be the strongest associates of loneliness, with the only exception being a lack of association found between loneliness and the searching-for-meaning score. The model also included the hypothetical associations between EI, age, satisfaction, and the two aspects of meaning in life (presence of meaning in life and searching for meaning in life), based on the existing literature. The analysis indeed confirmed most associations, with the exception of the meaning indices, thus at least partially supporting the construct validity of the EI measure (as did the negative correlation with loneliness). Additional associations between some of the background variables were mostly supported by the data.

Two unexpected results are worth discussing here: First is the low, yet positive, association between age and loneliness, contrary to the hypotheses. This association is especially intriguing given that the study did not include elderly participants, who are often identified as an at-risk group for loneliness. Since the sample consisted exclusively of young adults, and in any case persons over 40 years were excluded from participation, this result may be an artifact stemming from the social detachment of older young adults from the company of young adults aged mainly 20–29 years. The second surprise was the lack of association between EI and the meaning indices, while meaning (only the presence-of-meaning score) did play a significant role in accounting for the variance in loneliness. This result raises the question of whether EI and sense of meaning play different roles in the experience of loneliness: It may be that searching for meaning in itself is not an "emotional" or "social" strength, as opposed to finding and attaining meaning, which seem to provide a sense of social and personal strength in the face of social adversity (as in loneliness). So why is it not correlated with EI? One may suggest that meaning may be attained through many paths: religious, social, contemplative, and so on. These do not necessarily overlap with the content world of EI per se.

Although the study design did not allow for a direct causal test of the relationships between the main variables, it does shed some new light on our understanding of loneliness. EI is seen by proponents of the ability-EI model as a mental resource that is pivotal in processing emotional information (e.g., identifying emotions and incorporating emotions in thought) and in coping with emotional interpersonal situations (e.g., managing or regulating emotions in self and in others). Can better managing such resources serve as a buffer to protect individuals against the detrimental effects of feeling lonely? Can we use measures of EI to identify people who might be more prone than others to suffer loneliness, especially in transitional stages (e.g., moving from home to college or moving from one country to another for work)? This possibility is further supported by the association found between loneliness and the size and availability of the social network.

The design of this study, though adequate for the purpose of exploring potential associations among the main study variables, dictated some limitations that need to be addressed when interpreting the results. The sample size, while adequate for analysis purposes, is not very large. The use of an Israeli sample is another factor to consider in generalizing the results. The correlational design, dictated by ethical considerations, also limits the ability to discuss the results in causal terms. However, for purposes of a preliminary discussion of the role of EI in loneliness, the results provide good-enough support and justification for a guiding model to be used in future studies testing the relevance of EI to our understanding of loneliness.

REFERENCES

Antonovsky, A. (1987). *Unraveling the mystery of health: How people manage stress and stay well.* San Francisco, CA: Jossey-Bass.

Arslan, C., Hamarta, E., Ure, O., & Ozyesil, Z. (2010). An investigation of loneliness and perfectionism in university students. *Procedia Social and Behavioral Sciences, 2*, 814–818.

Brackett, M. A., & Mayer, J. D. (2003). Convergent, discriminant and incremental validity of competing measures of Emotional Intelligence. *Personality and Social Psychology Bulletin, 29*, 1–12.

Bradberry, T., & Su, L. D. (2006). Ability versus skill-based assessment of emotional Intelligence. *Psicotema, 18*(suppl.), 59–66.

Diener, E., Emmons, R. A., Larsen, R. J., & Griffin, S. (1985). The Satisfaction with Life Scale. *Journal of Personality Assessment, 49*, 1–5.

Dykstra, P. A. (2009). Older adult loneliness: Myths and reality. *European Journal of Aging, 6*, 91–100.

Gannon, N., & Ranzijn, R. (2005). Does Emotional Intelligence predict unique variance in life satisfaction beyond IQ and personality? *Personality and Individual Differences, 38*, 1353–1364.

Heinrich, L. N., & Gullone, E. (2006). The Clinical significance of loneliness: A literature review. *Clinical Psychology Review, 26*, 695–718.

Jones, W. H., Hobbs, S. A., and Hockenberry, D. (1982). Loneliness and social skills deficits. *Journal of Personality and Social Psychology, 42*(4), 682–689.

Kaplan, D. (2000). *Structural equation modeling: Foundations and extensions.* (Advanced Quantitative Techniques in the Social Sciences series, Vol. 10). Thousand Oaks, CA: Sage.

Lopes, P. N., Brackett, M. A., Nezlek, J. B., Schultz, A., Sellin, I., & Salovey, P. (2004). Emotional intelligence and social interaction. *Personality and Social Psychology Bulletin, 30*(8), 1018–1034.

Lopes, P. N., Salovey, P., & Straus, R. (2003). Emotional intelligence, personality and the perceived quality of social relationships. *Personality and Individual Differences, 35*, 641–658.

Mavroveli, S., Petrides, K. V., Rieffe, C., & Bakker, F. (2007). Trait emotional intelligence, psychological well-being and peer rated competence in adolescence. *British Journal of Developmental Psychology, 25*, 263–275.

McPherson, M., Smith-Lovin, L., & Brashears, M. E. (2006). Social isolation in America. *American Sociological Review, 71*(3), 353–375.

McWhirter, B. T. (1990). Loneliness: A review of the literature with implications for counseling and research. *Journal of Counseling and Development, 68*(4), 417–422.

Pavrot, W., & Diener, E. (1993). Review of the Satisfaction with Life Scale. *Psychological Assessment, 5*, 164–172.

Perlman, D., & Peplau, L. A. (1984). Loneliness research: A survey of the empirical findings. In L. A. Peplau and S. Goldston, (Eds.), *Preventing the harmful consequences of severe and persistent loneliness*. Washington, DC: U.S. Government Printing Office.

Russel, D., Peplau, L. A., & Cutrona, C. E. (1980). The revised UCLA loneliness scale: Concurrent and discriminant validity evidence. *Journal of Personality and Social Psychology, 39*(3), 472–480.

Steger, M. F., Frazier, P., Oishi, S., & Kaler, M. (2006). The Meaning in Life Questionnaire: Assessing the presence of and search for meaning in life. *Journal of Counseling Psychology, 53*, 80–93.

Young, J. E. (1982). Loneliness, depression and cognitive therapy. In L. A. Peplau & D. Perlman (Eds.), *Loneliness: A sourcebook for current theory, research and therapy*. New York: Wiley.

Is It Lonely at the Top? An Empirical Study of Managers' and Nonmanagers' Loneliness in Organizations

SARAH WRIGHT
University of Canterbury

ABSTRACT. Loneliness is often assumed to be an occupational hazard for senior-ranked members of an organization. However, most of what researchers hear about being "lonely at the top" is anecdote. This article provides empirical evidence from three separate studies assessing loneliness in managers and nonmanagers. Across all three studies, loneliness did not differ by managerial status. Managers were no more or less lonely than their nonmanager counterparts. This suggests that factors beyond seniority may be contributing to loneliness in organizational settings. Ideas for future research are discussed.

IN THE POPULAR PRESS, people at the top of an organization are often characterized as lonely. Undoubtedly, social isolation is built into certain professional occupations, with the enforced hierarchy being an occupational hazard for some individuals. Thus, the need for certain roles to maintain professional and social distance from their subordinates is often assumed to cause loneliness. Loneliness is not a new phenomenon to study empirically, and loneliness at work is not a new concept for journalists to report on. For instance, the words "loneliness" and "isolation" are often mentioned in the media in relation to being at "the top," as in, "British business leaders battle against office politics and loneliness" (Beckman, 2004); "It's not just lonely at the top; it can be disengaging' too"(Jones, 2005); "You're the new boss, but it's lonely at the top" (Wallington, 2005); and "Lonely at the top of Yahoo (Weinstein, 2007)." Popular business articles also reinforce the notion that it is lonely for employees who rise the ranks within an organization, with comments such as, "It's lonely at the top is as cliché as you can get—but like most popular clichés, there is often a lot of truth in the statement" (Kearns, 2005). Many pop-psychology websites and online articles also offer remedies for being lonely in senior positions, with articles on "Lessening loneliness of life at top" (McIntyre, 2009; Donadio, 2004).

Research suggests that the least lonely people have strong friendships, are emotionally connected to others in their social network, and experience a sense of intimacy and membership in a wider social group (McWhirter, 1990). Managerial and leadership positions within organizations do not often foster work environments where friendship, emotional connection and social intimacy within that environment are possible, thereby creating a context in which loneliness may develop. This is evidenced by research indicating that the role of school principal is often a lonely managerial position (e.g., Cubitt & Burt, 2002). Managers are expected to influence (and sometime coerce) people to achieve objectives, and work to maintain cooperative relationships and manage competitive relationships (Goleman, 2004). Managers often have to simultaneously enlist support from subordinates and superiors, often in ways that can alienate others around them (Stokes-Berry, 2010). The pyramid shape of most organizations suggests that the "top" is not typically a crowded place. Senior organizational members may therefore have very little lateral support and opportunity to develop meaningful interpersonal relationships, creating an environment that may foster isolation and loneliness. However, most of what researchers hear about loneliness at the top is anecdote and conjecture. This article empirically tests whether it is indeed "lonely at the top" in various organizational settings.

Literature Review

In the 1970s, an American sociological theorist, Philip Slater, recognized that cultural values and social institutions could exacerbate loneliness. Slater (1976) argued that social institutions such as private corporations emphasize individualism and personal success through competition and independence, which he argued go against the basic human needs for belonging, community and engagement with others. Similarly, Seidenberg (1980, p. 186) argued that "corporate men are lonely both in their travels and in their offices . . . they secretly yearn for more trust and genuine friendship, which are absent both from competitors on the outside and inside from the organization."

Literature on occupational stress also touches on isolation and loneliness as both a cause and a consequence of stress at work. For instance, Cooper (1981; Cooper & Quick, 2003) described the problem of isolation as being a factor that adds to the strain of the manager. Not surprisingly, being higher in the organization results in fewer opportunities for feedback and social dialogue from others, simply because the top is not a very crowded place. As such, there are fewer people around at that level to provide support and feedback. There is also some evidence in the literature to suggest that personal communication is not reciprocal in situations where the parties have unequal status. As such, there is more willingness to self-disclose up the status hierarchy (i.e., from subordinate to manager) than down it (Earle, Giuliano, & Archer, 1983). Commercial research from Adamson and Axmith (2003) suggests that for two thirds of chief executive officers (CEOs), the most difficult issue they face is feeling disconnected from others at work.

Contrary to the conceptual links between seniority and loneliness, empirical research by Bell, Roloff, Van Camp, and Karol (1990) found a small but negative (–.12) correlation between organizational level and loneliness, indicating that loneliness is associated with those at the bottom of the hierarchy. This correlation was surprising given that those higher up in the organization worked longer hours and shared fewer hours with family. The correlation remained even after commitment, hours worked per week, job satisfaction, age, education, and family income were controlled for. In explanation, the researchers argued that people at higher levels of their organizations may differ on individual or interpersonal dimensions, such as social skills, marital satisfaction and interpersonal orientation. It may be that the social skills that lead these individuals to move up the organization's ladder may also be responsible for their lower levels of loneliness. Gender and marital status did not affect the respondents' reports of loneliness. In subsequent analysis, lack of work-group cohesion was the best predictor of loneliness. Interestingly, there was a strong positive relationship between hours worked and loneliness but only for those who thought their work-group was not close. The authors argue that if the work environment is oppressive, working long hours will more likely contribute to loneliness. Not surprisingly, the number of hours worked is irrelevant to loneliness if the work environment is cohesive and the employee has high job satisfaction. However, Bell, Roloff, Van Camp, and Karol's (1990) study was conducted with participants from a cross section of organizations. It is unlikely that the self-reported "top" and "bottom" of the organization mean the same thing for different employees from different organizations. That is, being at the top of the hierarchy in a small retail shop is not comparable to being at the top of a large corporation.

Page and Cole (1991) suggest that managers and those with professional occupations tend to experience less loneliness than other occupational groups, such as technicians, sales staff, and clerical staff. Page and Cole's research suggests that economic status influences loneliness, in that reduced income and poorer education status are influential factors in reported loneliness. Those in professional or managerial occupations who typically have a higher income and more advanced education are, according to Page and Cole, less likely to be lonely due to their economic and social wellbeing. This conclusion runs counter to previous claims that the role of manager tends to be isolating and lonely.

Reinking and Bell (1991) conducted a field study in a civil service organization to examine how one's career situation interacts with his or her communication competence to influence a person's level of loneliness. The researchers hypothesized that individuals who occupy low positions in organizational hierarchies would be more prone to loneliness. Similar to previous findings (Bell et al., 1990; Page & Cole, 1991), Reinking and Bell (1991) found that loneliness was associated with those respondents in lower level positions, even when communication competence was controlled for. In explanation for this finding, the authors argue that success in the workplace may be more important for many people than closeness to others. Moreover, an individual may not see a deficit in personal relationships when achievement at work fulfils primary goals. However, given the nature of civil service, the authors suggest that the results may not generalize beyond the specific parameters of the organization. The authors also concede that their measurement of "the top" (based purely on self-reported job title) may have been insufficient to capture the essence of what it means to be at the "top."

In a study of Australian managers, Lindorff (2001) addressed the issue of social support and workplace stressors, hypothesizing that the majority of workplace stressors identified by managers would include concerns about relationships. Lindorff supported this tenet, indicating that 75% of the stressors nominated by managers included a relationship appraisal component. For example, the majority of issues related to lack of support, assistance or understanding from superiors, performance confrontations with subordinates, failure to communicate, and poor leadership within the organization. The author implies that managers who receive limited support when experiencing work-related stress may feel "lonely at the top" (p. 281). However, this study did not directly assess loneliness in organizations.

Purpose of the Current Study

From the above review, there is some evidence to suggest that it is *not* lonely at the top. However, previous studies have had methodological weaknesses in terms of measuring "the top" and measuring loneliness. The current study seeks to rectify these methodological limitations by using a validated measure of loneliness in the workplace and a consistent measure of organizational status. Empirical data is gathered across three separate studies in several different public and private organizations to determine whether managers are lonelier than nonmanagers. For a subsection of this analysis, the current study also seeks to investigate whether very young managers are lonelier than older managers and whether women are lonelier than men in managerial roles. There is some anecdotal evidence to suggest that younger managers have a difficult time adjusting to the managerial role and can often experience the "isolation of command." This is thought to be because of the social impact of making difficult decisions (Longnecker, Moore, Petty, & Palich, 2006). The current study therefore analyses whether very young managers are lonelier than their older counterparts. There is also anecdotal discussion to suggest that women experience greater isolation in the managerial role than men (Deng, Hassan, & Jivan, 1905). This study is the first to empirically test these anecdotal relationships. The literature on loneliness and organizational hierarchy is now somewhat dated. Many studies with titles related to being "lonely at the top" do not report on loneliness (e.g., Sala, 2001) and often relate to topics not directly studying loneliness (e.g., the need for executive coaching; Turner, 2006).

Although previous research has questioned whether it is lonely at the top, no study has used valid and comprehensive measures of workplace loneliness or managerial status across both public and private organizations to answer this question. This study contributes to the loneliness literature by more comprehensively determining whether occupational hierarchy influences loneliness in a workplace environment.

Method

Study 1

Procedure. Participants were recruited from six privately owned companies. Key contacts from within those organizations sent out an e-mail to invite employees to participate in the research. Employees completed the questionnaire online.

Instruments. The instruments that were used are as follows.

Loneliness at Work Scale. Loneliness was measured using Wright, Burt, and Strongman's (2006) 16-item scale. The items described emotional deprivation and lack of social companionship at work. The alpha coefficient for the scale was .94.

Demographics. Participants were asked to provide their age and gender. They were also asked to identify whether they were in a management position within the organization and how many employees they supervised. This, coupled with looking at their job title (self-report), determined whether they were coded as a manager or a nonmanager.

Participants. I received 360 usable responses. The average age of participants was 37.74 years (SD = 11.11 years), with ages ranging between 18 and 62 years. Of the sample, 67% were female. Of the participants, 39% were in a management position.

Study 2

Procedure. Participants were recruited from a government regulatory organization as part of a wider study on organization retention. The human resources manager sent out an email inviting employees to participate in the research. Responses were collected online.

Instruments. The instruments that were used are as follows.

Loneliness at Work Scale. Loneliness was measured using Wright, Burt, and Strongman's (2006) scale as described in Study 1.

Demographics. Participants were asked to provide their age and gender. Management status was identified in the same method as Study 1 but the respondent's job title and number of employees they supervised was gathered from organizational personnel records.

Participants. I received 225 useable responses. The average age of participants was 44.38 years (SD = 14.6 years), with ages ranging between 19 and 69 years. Of participants, 56% were female. Of the participants, 33% were in a management position.

Study 3

Procedure. Participants were recruited from a government service organization as part of a study on competency development. Employees were invited to participate in the research during a training event within the organization. The participants completed the questionnaire on paper and posted it back to the researcher.

Instruments. The instruments that were used are as follows.

Loneliness at Work Scale. An alternative measure of loneliness was used for this study. From the three facets in Hawkley, Browne, and Cacioppo's (2005) measure of loneliness, 12 items was used, worded as in the original text for general loneliness, and worded to be specific to the workplace. This scale was originally based on the revised UCLA Loneliness Scale (Russell, Peplau, & Cutrona, 1980). Items related to isolation, relational connectedness, and collective connectedness. The alpha coefficient for the general version was .862, and that for the work-specific version was .919. The correlation between the two different scales was .695.

Demographics. Participants were asked to provide their age and gender. Management status was identified in the same method as Study 2.

Participants. Participants were 188 employees. The average age of participants was 44.18 years (SD = 11.8 years), with ages ranging between 20 and 65 years. Of participants, 52% were female. Of the participants, 29% were in a management position.

Normality

Prior to analysis, the distributional properties of the dependent variables were evaluated. The work loneliness variables in Study 1 and Study 2 were found to have a skewness z score over 3, indicating that the distribution was not normally distributed (6.87, 4.19, respectively). A logarithmic transformation was conducted on these variables to normalize distribution. The descriptive statistics for the dependent variables are shown in Table 1.

Results

Table 1 shows the descriptive data for the loneliness variables. For Study 1 and Study 2, there was a possible range of 16–112, and for Study 3, there was a possible range from 12 to 60). For all loneliness measures, higher scores indicated higher levels of loneliness at work. The alpha coefficient for the loneliness scales were .93 in Study 1, .92 in Study 2, and .89 in Study 3.

Age was dichotomized into two categories: $\geq$34 years and $<$34 years to determine very young managers in the sample. Very young managers were defined as aged 34 years or younger, while "not-very-young" managers were defined as aged 35 years or older. Chi-square was used to compare managerial position (manager or nonmanager) with age (very young manager $<$35 years old) and

TABLE 1. Descriptive Statistics for the Dependent Variables

Variable	*M*	*SD*	Median	Minimum	Maximum	Skewness *Z* score	Kurtosis *Z* score
Study 1 ($n = 360$)							
Loneliness (work)[a]	42.60	18.54	39.00	16	104	6.87	1.78
Loneliness (work) (transformed)	1.59	0.19	1.59	1.20	2.02	–0.54	–2.16
Study 2 ($n = 255$)							
Loneliness (work)[a]	35.96	8.93	35.97	21	73	4.19	2.75
Loneliness (work) (transformed)	1.54	0.11	1.55	1.32	1.86	0.28	–0.67
Study 3 ($n = 188$)							
Loneliness (work)[b]	22.61	6.49	22.61	12	35	2.61	–0.53
Loneliness (general)[b]	20.44	5.28	20.44	12	42	1.44	–1.34

[a]16-item scale from Wright, Burt, and Strongman (2006).
[b]12-item scale from Hawkley, Browne, and Cacioppo (2005).

gender. For Study 1, age was found to be significant ($\chi^2 = 16.64$, $p < .001$) indicating that there was a higher frequency of managers that were 35 years of age or older (69.0%) as compared to nonmanagers (47.2%). For Study 2, a significant difference was found between age and managerial position ($\chi^2 = 6.02$, $p < .05$) indicating that there was a higher frequency of managers who were 35 years of age or older (84.0%) as compared to nonmanagers (68.7%). For Study 3, a significant difference was found between age and managerial position ($\chi^2 = 11.80$, $p < .001$), indicating that there was a higher frequency of managers who were 35 years of age or older (92.1%) as compared to nonmanagers (67.2%). No gender differences were found.

Table 2 provides the results from the ANOVAs used to investigate differences in work loneliness scores by managerial position. ANCOVAs were used to assess differences in work loneliness scores by managerial position after adjusting for available covariates. For studies 1, 2, and 3, no significant differences were found on loneliness scores between managers and nonmanagers in the unadjusted (ANOVA) and adjusted analysis (ANCOVA). Table 3 presents further analysis which suggests that among managers, age and gender was not found to be significantly associated with work loneliness across all three studies. That is, female managers do not have statistically different work-related loneliness scores than male managers. Very young managers (less than 35 years old) do not have statistically different work-related loneliness scores than older managers.

Table 4 provides the results from the ANOVAs used to investigate differences in general loneliness scores (Study 3) by managerial position. ANCOVAs are used to assess differences in general loneliness scores by managerial position after adjusting for available covariates. No significant differences were found on general loneliness scores between managers and nonmanagers in the unadjusted and adjusted model. Post hoc power analyses were conducted to explain these nonstatistically significant results and to help determine if low power threatened the internal validity of the findings. Post hoc power values for the three studies were .92, .82, and .75, respectively. Power of .80 and above is typically (but arbitrarily) judged to be adequate (Murphy & Myors, 2004). Statistically nonsignificant results in studies with adequate power contribute to the body of knowledge because power can be ruled out as a threat to internal validity. Therefore, explanations other than low power are necessary to explain the nonsignificant findings.

Discussion

This study set out to examine whether it is lonelier at the top of the organization than at the bottom. Those in management positions were compared to those in nonmanagement positions across three studies in separate organizations. The studies were systematically developed to include samples from several organizations across public and private sectors and included multiple measures of

TABLE 2. ANOVA and ANCOVA Results for Work-Related Loneliness

Variable	Study 1[d]				Study 2[d]				Study 3			
	n	*M*	*SD*	*F* (*p*)	*n*	*M*	*SD*	*F* (*p*)	*n*	*M*	*SD*	*F* (*p*)
Managerial position[b]				3.15 (.08)				3.47 (.06)				1.28 (.26)
Manager	145	40.43	17.62		75	34.41	8.72		54	21.77	6.80	
Nonmanager	215	44.04	19.03		150	36.74	8.97		134	22.94	6.35	
Managerial position[c]				3.40 (.07)				2.62 (.11)				.69 (.41)
Manager	145	40.43	17.62		75	34.41	8.72		51	22.07	6.79	
Nonmanager	215	43.80	18.78		147	36.85	8.99		119	23.03	6.49	

[b]ANOVA model does not include any covariates.
[c]ANCOVA model includes age and gender as covariates
[d]Statistics run on transformed values but raw means and standard deviations are provided in the table.

TABLE 3. ANOVA Results for Work-Related Loneliness Among Managers

	Study 1[b]				Study 2[b]				Study 3			
Variable	*n*	*M*	*SD*	*F* (*p*)	*n*	*M*	*SD*	*F* (*p*)	*N*	*M*	*SD*	*F* (*p*)
Manager's Age				0.22 (.64)				0.01 (.92)				0.50 (.48)
Young	45	41.91	19.33		12	34.62	10.15		4	19.75	5.68	
Old	100	39.77	16.86		63	34.38	8.51		47	22.26	6.89	
Manager's Gender				0.10 (.92)				0.11 (.74)				1.52 (.22)
Male	54	40.46	18.88		37	34.96	10.12		28	22.86	7.93	
Female	91	40.42	16.94		38	33.88	7.20		26	20.59	5.22	

[b]Statistics run on transformed values but raw means and standard deviations are provided in the table.

TABLE 4. ANOVA Results for General Loneliness (Study 3)

Variable	*n*	*M*	*SD*	*F* (*p*)
Managerial position[b]				0.32 (.58)
Manager	54	20.10	5.86	
Nonmanager	134	20.58	5.04	
Managerial position[c]				0.17 (.68)
Manager	51	20.26	5.76	
Nonmanager	119	20.53	5.05	

[b]ANOVA does not include any covariates.
[c]ANCOVA includes age and gender as covariates.

loneliness. The results consistently indicate that across all the organizations studied and across all measures, managers were no more or less lonely than their nonmanager counterparts, either in work or more generally. The results from this study do not suggest that managers are not lonely per se, merely that there are no significant differences between managers' and nonmanagers' loneliness scores.

The notion that it is lonely at the top does seem to be paradoxical when studying the literature. On the one hand, effective leaders are portrayed as socially and personally well-adjusted individuals (who should, therefore, not be lonely), while lonely people are socially and personally lacking and find their isolation exceedingly painful (see several studies and articles by Rokach, 2007, 2001, 2000, 1998, 1996; Rokach & Brock, 1998, 1997); therefore they are unlikely to make successful leaders. The loneliness literature suggests that the people who are most likely to feel lonely are those who report shyness, low social competence, emotional instability, and low self-esteem (Ernst & Cacioppo, 1998). The traits required to achieve seniority in an organization typically include having high self and social confidence, emotional maturity, self-awareness, and social adeptness (Goleman, 2004; Yukl, 1998). Effective leaders are typically highly interconnected in their social relationships, and these relationships are precisely what make them powerful and respected (Lee & Tiedens, 2001). For these reasons, it suggests that if an effective leader or manager does experience loneliness, the reasons for it are likely to be a complex hybrid of personal, social, and contextual factors, rather than seniority alone. Relationships outside of the work environment may be a powerful determinant in the experience of loneliness and an explanation for the nonsignificant findings. However previous research has shown that lack of supervisor and coworker support are more predictive of work-related loneliness than a lack of nonwork support, suggesting that work-related loneliness may be experienced differently than loneliness more generally.

The results from the present research concur with previous research and provide further strength to the argument that alternative influences drive loneliness at work rather than purely organizational status and hierarchy. These influences could come from the factors related to the individual (which are traditionally what most loneliness research focuses on) or from factors within the environment. For example, loneliness experienced in organizations could be related to the responsibility and isolation of decision making, particularly in relation to personnel decisions. Thus, the intensity and frequency of loneliness experienced by people at work will vary and will largely depend on the qualitative aspects of the person's work environment rather than being determined by an objective environmental condition such as position in the hierarchy.

Both loneliness and organizations are complex phenomena. This research calls for further studies into the complexity of organizational life and the effect this complexity can have on an individual's experience of loneliness. By definition, loneliness experienced because of social deficits implicates the social environment. As with the transaction model of occupational stress (originally Lazarus & Folkman, 1984), loneliness in the workplace is likely to be experienced as a transaction between the person and his or her environment. From several decades of research, a significant body of knowledge has developed on the personal characteristics leading to loneliness. Further research on the contextual reasons that can cause or exacerbate loneliness in organizational settings is warranted in order to better understand the interaction between the employee and his or her work environment.

REFERENCES

Adamson, B., & Axmith, M. (2003). The CEO disconnect: Finding consistency between personal values and the demands of leadership. *Ivey Business Journal, May/June*, 1–6.

Beckman, T. (2004). *British business leaders battle against office politics and loneliness*. Retrieved on January 24, 2011, from http://www.heartmathreport. com/index.php/weblog/2004/06/.

Bell, R. A., Roloff, M. E., Van Camp, K., & Karol, S. H. (1990). Is it lonely at the top? Career success and personal relationships. *Journal of Communication*, *40*(1), 9–23.

Cooper, C. (1981). *The stress check*. Englewood Cliffs, CA: Prentice-Hall.

Cooper, C., & Quick, J. (2003). The stress and loneliness of success. *Counselling Psychology Quarterly*, *16*(1), 1–7.

Cubitt, S., & Burt, C. (2002). Leadership style, loneliness and occupational stress in New Zealand primary school principals. *New Zealand Journal of Educational Studies*, *37*(2), 159–169.

Deng, S., Hassan, L., & Jivan, S. (1995). Female entrepreneurs doing business in Asia. *Journal of Small Business Management, 12*(2), 60–80.
Donadio, R. (2004). *It's lonely at the top*. Retrieved on January 28th, 2011, from http://www.theatlantic.com/doc/200411/donadio.
Earle, W., Giuliano, T., & Archer, R. (1983). Lonely at the top: The effect of power on information follow in the dyad. *Personality and Social Psychology Bulletin, 9*(4), 629–637.
Ernst, J., & Cacioppo, J. (1998). Lonely hearts: Psychological perspectives on loneliness. *Applied & Preventative Psychology, 8*, 1–22.
Goleman, D. (2004). What makes a leader? *Harvard Business Review, 82*(1), 82–91.
Hawkley, L. C., Browne, M. W., & Cacioppo, J. T. (2005). How can I connect with thee? Let me count the ways. *Psychological Science, 16*, 798–804.
Jones, D. (2005). *It's not just lonely at the top: It can be "disengaging," too*. Retrieved on January 24, 2011, from http://www.usatoday.com/money/companies/management/2005-06-20-bummed-execs_x.htm.
Kearns, K. (2005). *Top 7 ways to combat being lonely at the top*. Retrieved on January 22, 2011, from http://www.top7business.com/?id=1199.
Lazarus, R. S., & Folkman, S. (1984). *Stress, appraisal and coping*. New York: Springer.
Lee, F., & Tiedens, L. (2001). Who's being served? Self-serving attributions in social hierarchies. *Organizational Behavior and Human Decision Processes, 84*(2), 254–287.
Lindorff, M. (2001). Are they lonely at the top? Social relationships and social support among Australian managers. *Work and Stress, 15*(3), 274–282.
Longnecker, J., Moore, C., Petty, W., & Palich, L. (2006). *Small business management*. Mason, OH: Thomson.
McIntyre, D. (2009, October 21). Lessening loneliness of life at top. *New Zealand Herald*, p. D6.
McWhirter, B. (1990). Loneliness: A review of current literature, with implications for counselling and research. *Journal of Counselling and Development, 68*, 417–422.
Murphy, K., & Myors, B. (2004). *Statistical power analysis*. Mahwah, NJ: LEA.
Page, R., & Cole, G. (1991). Demographic predictors of self-reported loneliness in adults. *Psychological Reports, 68*, 939–945.
Reinking, K., & Bell, R. (1991). Relationships among loneliness, communication competence, and career success in a state bureaucracy: A field study of the "lonely at the top" maxim. *Communication Quarterly, 39*(4), 358–373.
Rokach, A. (1996). The causes of loneliness. *Psychology: A Journal of Human Behavior, 33*, 1–11.
Rokach, A. (1998). The relation of cultural background to the causes of loneliness. *Journal of Social and Clinical Psychology, 17*(1), 75–88.
Rokach, A. (2000). Loneliness and the life cycle. *Psychological Reports, 86*(2), 629–642.
Rokach, A. (2001). Strategies of coping with loneliness throughout the lifespan. *Current Psychology: Developmental, Learning, Personality, Social, 20*(1), 3–18.
Rokach, A. (2007). The effect of age and culture on the causes of loneliness. *Social Behaviour and Personality, 35*(2), 169–186.
Rokach, A., & Brock, H. (1997). Loneliness and the effects of life changes. *Journal of Psychology, 131*(3), 284–298.
Rokach, A., & Brock, H. (1998). Coping with loneliness. *Journal of Psychology, 132*(1), 107–121.

Russell, D., Peplau, L. A., & Cutrona, C. E. (1980). The revised UCLA loneliness scale: Concurrent and discriminant validity evidence. *Journal of Personality and Social Psychology, 39*, 472–480.

Sala, F. (2001). *It's lonely at the top: Executive's emotional intelligence self [mis] perceptions*. Retrieved on January 20th, 2011, from www.eiconsortium.org/pdf/executive_emotional_intelligence360.pdf.

Seidenberg, R. (1980). The lonely marriage in corporate America. In J. Hartog, J. Audy, & Y. Cohen (Eds.), *The anatomy of loneliness* (pp. 186–203). New York: International Universities Press.

Slater, P. (1976). *The pursuit of loneliness: American culture at the breaking point*. Boston, MA: Beacon.

Stokes-Berry, F. (2010). Understanding the role of the manager in organizational performance and community engagement. *Public Administration Review, 70*, 153–155.

Turner, C. (2006). Ungagged: Executives on executive coaching. *Ivey Business Journal*, (May/June), 1–5.

Wallington, P. (2005). *You're the new boss, but it's lonely at the top*. Retrieved on January 24, 2011, from http://www.cio.com/article/11868/Career_You_re_the_New_Boss_But_It_s_Lonely_At_The_Top.

Weinstein, L. (2007). *Lonely at the top for Yahoo CEO Yang*. Retrieved on January 24, 2011, from http://www.newser.com/story/10127/lonely-at-the-top-for-yahoo-ceo-yang.html.

Wright, S. (2008). *Loneliness in the workplace*. Saarbrücken, Germany: VDM Verlag.

Wright, S., Burt, C., & Strongman, K. (2006). Loneliness in the workplace: Construct definition, scale development and validation. *New Zealand Journal of Psychology, 35*(2), 59–68.

Yukl, G. (1998). *Leadership in organizations*. Englewood Cliffs, NJ: Prentice Hall.

PART II: LONELINESS THROUGH THE LIFE CYCLE

Children's Loneliness, Sense of Coherence, Family Climate, and Hope: Developmental Risk and Protective Factors

ADI SHARABI
Kibbutzim College and Tel Aviv University

UZI LEVI
Peres Academic Center

MALKA MARGALIT
Tel Aviv University and Peres Academic Center

ABSTRACT. The study examined the contributions of individual and familial variables for the prediction of loneliness as a developmental risk and the sense of coherence as a protective factor. The sample consisted of 287 children from grades 5–6. Their loneliness, sense of coherence, hope, effort, and family climate were assessed. Separate hierarchical multiple regression analyses revealed that family cohesion and children's hope contributed to the explanation of the risk and protective outcomes. Yet, the contribution of the family adaptability was not significant. Cluster analysis of the family climate dimensions (i.e., cohesion and adaptability) was performed to clarify the interactive roles of family adaptability together with family cohesion. The authors identified 4 separate family profiles: Children in the 2 cohesive families' clusters (Cohesive Structured Families and Cohesive Adaptable Families) reported the lowest levels of loneliness and the highest levels of personal strengths. Children within rigid and noncohesive family cluster reported the highest levels of loneliness and the lowest levels of children's sense of coherence. The unique role of the family flexibility within nonsupportive family systems was demonstrated. The results further clarified the unique profiles' characteristics of the different family clusters and their adjustment indexes in terms of loneliness and personal strengths.

RELATIONS WITH PEERS play a critical role in children's and adolescents' well-being, and thus the experience of loneliness has been considered a major source of distress and also a noteworthy developmental risk that can predispose them to immediate and long-term negative consequences (Margalit, 2010). However, not every lonely episode is considered a risk factor, given that most children experience short-term loneliness as a normal consequence of everyday social interactions within different contextual conditions. Nevertheless, for some children, these feelings of loneliness may become a chronic condition and a developmental risk.

Research surveys have already documented the interrelations between chronic and high levels of loneliness and various aspects of social and emotional maladjustment during childhood and adolescence, such as physical health problems, depression, social anxiety, low self-esteem, low social status, peer rejection, victimization, aggression and social withdrawal, focusing attention on the different roots of this social distress (Bakkaloglu, 2010; Besevegis & Galanaki, In press). Loneliness studies also pinpointed attention at the protective roles of personal strengths such as high sense of coherence, and hopeful thinking style (Lackaye & Margalit, 2008). Research uses a variety of terms in discussing variables that increase the likelihood of negative outcomes, including risk and vulnerability, in addition to adapted terms such as *protective*, salutogenic and *resilience* to describe variables and processes that decrease the likelihood of a negative outcome (Gabalda, Thompson, & Kaslow, 2010; Luthar & Brown, 2007; Luthar, Cicchetti, & Becker, 2000). In the current study, we use the term *risk* to refer to factors that increase children's odds of experiencing emotional and behavioral problems and protective as factors that reduce the likelihood at all levels of risk.

The current study was also guided by Blatt's dual model of personality (Blatt & Homann, 1992) that proposed two fundamental personality and developmental dimensions, namely the interpersonal relatedness and the self-definition. This model of personality posits that personality development proceeds through complex transactions between two developmental lines: the "interpersonal relatedness" line, involving the development of the capacity to establish increasingly mature, reciprocal, and satisfying interpersonal relationships; and the "self-definition" line, involving the development of a consolidated, realistic, essentially positive self-definition (Blatt, Zohar, Quinlan, & Luthar, 1996; Guisinger & Blatt, 1994). Within the models of risk and protective factors (Margalit, 2010), the goals of the current study were to examine the contribution of individual and familial variables for the prediction of the risk factor loneliness as a measure of interpersonal relatedness, and the protective factor—the sense of coherence as a measure of self-definition. We shall start our research survey by clarifying individualistic developmental aspects—i.e., the loneliness and the sense of coherence –before clarifying their documented relations with the family systemic dimensions and summarizing the role of future expectations as complementary to children's past and present experiences.

Loneliness

Loneliness as a complex set of feelings and cognitions reflects the distressing and negative emotional experience emanating from the individual's perceived deficiencies in intimate and social relationships (Cacioppo & Patrick, 2008). Childhood loneliness has been characterized as a perceived dissatisfaction with various aspects of social relationships. Many times, the loneliness emerged from frustrations related to struggles of peer rejection versus acceptance that reflected the collective liking versus disliking by the group of children or adolescents towards an individual member (Margalit, 2010). However, in addition to the peer relations' status, research focused attention on the importance of the subjective perception of social alienation as a major developmental risk factor for well-being (Qualter, Brown, Munn, & Rotenberg, 2010), and identified personal factors that predicted increased levels of loneliness (Sharabi & Margalit, in press).

Qualter et al. (2010) demonstrated in a longitudinal study from childhood to adolescence that childhood loneliness is more likely to be associated with several factors and processes. They examined the relations between depression and loneliness, and concluded that loneliness has cognitive, affective, and behavioral components that reflected an unfulfilled desire to have closer contacts with people. In addition to a genetic deficit in the appreciation of relationships, the mechanisms by which the children's loneliness could predict symptoms of depression during adolescence include the development of maladaptive cognitive biases and coping strategies that predispose an individual to social desperation, separateness and depression (Flora & Segrin, 2000; Qualter & Munn, 2002).

In conclusion, loneliness reflects the perception of a discrepancy between the interpersonal relationships that one wishes to have and those that one currently has (Qualter, 2004). It is an unpleasant experience related to social relations. Yet, it is not synonymous with social isolation or peer rejection, but the result of perceived quantitative or qualitative deficiencies in one's social relations (Peplau & Perlman, 1982). Studies indicated the existing of dynamic reciprocal relations between perceptions of the self and loneliness, and children whose lonely feelings increased over a year period, reported lower peer acceptance and fewer friendship relations at the second assessment, but in addition, they also became more self-blaming and reported lower self-perceptions (Renshaw & Brown, 1993; Stoeckli, 2009). Yet, several children reported positive self-perceptions, disclosing the important role of protective factors such as the sense of coherence.

Sense of Coherence

The sense of coherence as a measure of global self-appraisal and self-perception has been considered in research as a protective factor for adjustment of children and adults (Antonovsky, 1987; Margalit, 2010). Antonosky (1987) presented the sense of coherence *as* the key variable to promoting well-being and salutogenesis and for understanding people's inner resources and strengths

(Lundman et al., 2010; Schueller, 2009). As an alternative to the pathogenic model of health, and the dual model that differentiated between health and illness as two separate states, the salutogenic model proposes a dynamic conceptualization of the well-being experience. This dynamic construct considers health as constantly moving along a continuum, with illness and dysfunction at one end and wellness and personal strengths at the other (Antonovsky, 1987). Salutogenesis provides a global and dynamic understanding why individuals manage to stay healthy and experience well-being, despite many stresses in their life. Antonovsky (1987) stated that disease and stress could occur everywhere for everybody. The critical question is not why people become ill, but how they can survive in spite of high levels of stress. This question inspired extensive research on resistant resources and the development of the sense of coherence concept.

The sense of coherence is consisted of three interrelated factors within a probability model: (a) the *comprehensibility* refers to the belief that the individual can understand and predict most of the occurrences that will happen in one's life; (b) the *manageability* refers to a belief that the individual will be able to manage most of the events within one's control, and (c) the *meaningfulness* refers to the ability to derive satisfaction and purpose from activities, involvements, and personal investments (Antonovsky, 1993). The sense of coherence reflects the extent to which an individual is likely to construe a stressor as comprehensible, and the individual's appraisal that he or she will manage to overcome such stressors. According to this approach, the sense of coherence provides a measure of the individual's resistance abilities and personal strengths in the face of perceived or expected stresses. While conventional coping measures assess preferences for specific coping strategies, the sense of coherence reflects the individual's global capacity to respond to stressors by the successful application of a variety of coping strategies (Antonovsky, 1987).

Longitudinal research supported the conceptualization of the sense of coherence as a protective self-appraisal for the development and the maintenance of mental health (Edbom, Malmberg, Lichtenstein, Granlund, & Larsson, 2010). Developmental research reported that children's sense of coherence mediated the association between maternal negative affect and children's hope and effort (Al-Yagon, 2010), focusing attention on the unique role of families in fostering their children's well-being. The examination of factors that promote the development of children's and adolescents' strong sense of coherence, clarified the importance of ecological conditions at home and in schools and communities (i.e., parental monitoring and care, positive experiences at school, friends that care, community activities) as predictors of high sense of coherence (Evans, Marsh, & Weigel, 2010). Parents were considered vital sources of social support during childhood and adolescence, and the examination of the family environment may provide in-depth understanding of the development of children's personal strengths and social distresses.

Family Environment

Families play an important role in promoting children's social and emotional development, and parental characteristics as well as their parenting style were related to their children's loneliness (Junttila, Vauras, & Laakkonen, 2007). Interactions among family members were considered particularly important for the understanding of the development of children's interpersonal skills, feelings of relatedness and social bonds (Bowlby, 1988). Growing up in a comforting home, experiencing warm, stable and secure relationships with parents and siblings has been considered a valuable aspect of socialization development, and its impact extends far beyond the boundaries of family life (Vandeleur, Perrez, & Schoebi, 2007). Parents can influence the social experiences of their children and their behaviors in several ways, such as parental modeling of behaviors and expression of attitudes towards social connections and friendships in addition to the impact of the family social–emotional climate.

Olson identified two important interrelated dimensions of family systems: Cohesion and Adaptability (Olson & Gorall, 2003):

1. *Cohesion* was defined as the emotional bonding that family members have towards one another.
2. *Adaptability* was defined as the ability of the family system to change its roles, power structure, relations, and rules in response to situational and developmental stress.

Research documented specific associations between the family climate dimensions, parental well-being, and children's personality, adjustment, and behavior. For example, familial cohesion was related with interpersonal well-being and satisfaction (Green, Harris, Forte, & Robinson, 1991). The adaptive family climate facilitates social change by mediating the demands of the larger social environment through the process of socialization (Lee, 1988). In these studies, adaptability was considered as a positive response to stress (Minuchin, 1974). Minuchin was aware that several families in stress situations tended to increase the rigidity of their transactional patterns and boundaries, and to avoid or resist explorations of alternatives. Indeed often psychological flexibility has been proposed as a predicting factor to personal resilience (Kashdan & Rottenberg, 2010), yet we cannot ignore situations when increased rigidity served families in distress as a defense mechanism during challenging periods. Studies on families of disabled children focused attention on families who faced on-going stress and reported increased order as an effective coping style. They emphasized structure within the family system in order to meet the increased control demands reported by parents of children with academic and behavior challenges (Margalit & Heiman, 1986).

Often flexible and cohesive family climate was related to adolescents' higher self-perception and children's feeling of control on their life (Vandeleur et al., 2007; Zdanowicz, Janne, & Reynaert, 2004). Olson (1986) suggested that higher cohesion levels in family climate were related to youngsters' better social functioning, since in a closer, more involved family system, children's needs were better addressed. A longitudinal study that followed the adjustment of children from preschool to the third grade at school (Sturge-Apple, Davies, & Cummings, 2010) revealed that different patterns of family functioning were associated with changes in children's adjustment in the school context.

Olson (1986) proposed the Circumplex Model, suggesting that the optimal family functioning is within balanced systems. In line with this model, research documented that high levels of flexibility in the family were related to self-reported depression, negative mood and anxiety symptoms for several individuals (Fresco, Williams, & Nugent, 2006). Similarly, chaotic and extreme flexible homes were related with children's problem behavior (Lin, Orsmond, Coster, & Cohn, 2011; Valiente, Lemery-Chalfant, & Reiser, 2007). Several studies suggested a different approach to the family dimensions. Since in nonclinical samples, the amount of truly extreme families is rather low, studies proposed treating the family adaptability and cohesion in a linear model (instead of the Circumplex Model) as protective trends (Al-Yagon, 2008; Roest, Dubas, & Gerris, 2009).

Thus, since Cohesion and Adaptability dimensions dynamically and constantly interact within the family contextual and cultural trends with children's distinct characteristics, the current study proposed to examine the joint roles of the family dimensions as well as to examine their expressions in different types of families as related to children's social distress. In addition to the examination of family processes for the prediction of children's adjustment, the hope theory (Snyder, 2002) may provide unique perspectives for clarifying the dynamic interaction of personal and familial current perceptions with children's future expectations.

Hope

As defined by Snyder (2006), the construct of hope comprises both the pathway thinking (the perceived capacity to generate strategies for attaining goals) and the agency thinking (perceptions involving one's capacity to initiate and sustain movement along the chosen pathways). Thus, Snyder proposed that hope comprises two appraisal processes occurring simultaneously:

1. The appraisal that one is capable of executing the means to attain desired goals (agency thinking).
2. The appraisal that one is capable of generating those means (pathways thinking) (Snyder, 2006).

Conceptually, hope is associated with an initiation of action toward goal attainment, and empirical studies have revealed a host of additional positive outcomes associated with hope (Arnau, Martinez, Nino de Guzman, Herth, & Yoshiyuki Konishi, 2010). For example, hope has been found to be related to adaptive coping styles, academic achievement, and athletic performance in college students

(Curry, Snyder, Cook, Ruby, & Rehm, 1997) as well as in adolescents' academic achievements and their sense of coherence (Lackaye & Margalit, 2006). Hope was negatively related to symptoms of depression and anxiety (Arnau, Rosen, Finch, Rhudy, & Fortunato, 2007; Chang & DeSimone, 2001).

Hope is different from optimism. Dispositional optimism has been considered a stable tendency to believe that good rather than bad things will happen (Scheier & Carver, 1985; Scheier & Carver, 1992). In contrast, the hope construct recognized the importance of the reciprocal action of efficacy expectancies and outcome expectancies, in which both types of expectancies are important and influence each other (Snyder, Harris, et al., 1991; Snyder, Irving, & Anderson, 1991). Thus, the optimist may believe that things will turn out as he or she wants, but not possess the pathways necessary to pursue and acquire the goals. A second difference between hope and optimism is that optimism focuses more broadly on the expected quality of future outcome, whereas hope focuses more directly on the personal attainment of specific goals (Bryant & Cvengros, 2004). Thus, it is not surprising that adolescents with high hopes were more ready to invest effort in their goals. *Effort* refers to the individual child's level of investment, intensity, and persistence in task accomplishment (Lackaye & Margalit, 2006).

Effort

Parents and teachers consider effort to be a major variable in predicting children's achievement. Teachers attribute lower motivation and decreased effort to the desire to gain attention or to avoid incompetence manifestations, to the perceived low importance or usefulness of the task, or to lack of enjoyment (Uhlenberg & Brown, 2002). There is comparatively little research on students' effort and its relations with performance (Yeo & Neal, 2004). Children's effortful control and positive teacher–student relationships operate jointly to contribute to future child academic achievement. Longitudinal studies reported that effort in the first grade predicted achievements in the third grade (Liew, Chen, & Hughes, 2010; Liew, McTigue, Barrois, & Hughes, 2008).

The Current Study

In summary, earlier studies have presented loneliness as a developmental risk factor and the sense of coherence as a protective factor. In line with Blatt's personality model, the goals of the current study were to examine the contribution of individual and familial variables for the prediction of the risk factor loneliness as a measure of interpersonal relatedness, and the protective factor—the sense of coherence—as a measure of self-definition. Following earlier studies that documented the joint role of familial factors in predicting adjustment indexes, we also wanted to identify different groups of families in order to explore their relations to children's characteristics. We hypothesized that different profiles of familial cohesion and adaptability will predict children's strengths and risk factors.

Method

Participants

The sample consisted of 287 children (124 boys and 163 girls) from Grades 5–6 (with age range 10–11.6 years) from five elementary schools in central Israel. The comparisons of gender and age proportions between the students using chi square did not yield significant differences. Students with different disabilities such as learning disabilities were not included in the sample.

Instruments

Loneliness. The Hebrew adaptation (Margalit, 1991) of the Loneliness Scale (Asher, Parkhurst, Hymel, & Williams, 1990) consists of 16 primary items (e.g., "I have many friends in my class"; " I have nobody to talk to in my class"; " I am lonely") and 8 filler items (e.g., " I like school") that cover various activity areas rated on a 5-point Likert-type scale, ranging from 1 (*never*) to 5 (*always*). Higher scores reflect frequent feelings of loneliness. In earlier studies, internal consistency for the measure (Cronbach's alpha) was .86. In the current study, a Cronbach's alpha of .92 was obtained.

Children's Sense of Coherence (CSOC) Scale. The children's sense of coherence (CSOC) Scale (Margalit & Efrati, 1995) is an adaptation of the adults' sense of coherence scale (Antonovsky, 1987). This scale reflects personality strengths and consists of 16 items tapping three interrelated dimensions of children's sense of confidence in themselves in their world:

1. Comprehensibility—feelings that one understands one's environment (e.g., "I feel that I don't understand what to do in class").
2. Manageability—feelings of control and confidence that positive rewards are available (e.g., "When I want something I'm sure I'll get it").
3. Sense of meaningfulness—motivation and interest in different tasks (e.g., "I'm interested in lots of things").

The 5-point Likert-type scale ranges from 1 (*never*) to 5 (*always*). The score is the average of the items on the scale. Thus, a higher score reflects a higher level of CSOC. In earlier studies, internal consistency for the measure (Cronbach's alpha) was .78. In the current study, a Cronbach's alpha of .80 was obtained.

The Family Climate Scale (FACES III). The Family Adaptability and Cohesion Evaluation Scale (Olson, 1986) assesses the degree of cohesion and adaptability within the family. The Hebrew adaptation (Teichman & Navon, 1990) of the scale consists of 20 items on a 5-point Likert-type scale, ranging from 1 (*almost never*) to 5 (*almost always*),comprising two subscales of 10 items each:

1. The cohesion subscale refers to emotional bonding, family boundaries, and time spent together (e.g., "family members feel closer to other family members than to people outside the family").
2. The adaptability subscale refers to discipline, roles, negotiation, and flexibility within the family, focusing on how the family system balances stability versus change (e.g., "we shift household responsibilities from person to person").

The score is the average of the items on the relevant subscale. Thus, a higher score reflects a higher level of cohesion and adaptability. In earlier studies, internal consistency for cohesion was .85 and for adaptability .67. In the current study, we obtained a Cronbach's alpha of .82 for cohesion and a Cronbach's alpha of .70 for adaptability.

Hope Scale. The Hope Scale (Snyder, 2002) assesses the belief in one's ability to pursue desired goals and use strategies to achieve them. The Hebrew adaptation of the Children's Hope Scale (Lackaye & Margalit, 2006) consists of 6 statements to which children respond on a 5-point Likert-type scale, ranging from 1 ("almost never") to 5 ("almost always"). The two dimensions in this scale follow:

1. Three agency items (e.g., "I think I am doing pretty well").
2. Three pathway items (e.g., "I can think of many ways to get things in life").

The score is the average of the items on the scale. Thus, a higher score reflects a higher level of hope. Internal consistency (Cronbach's alphas) for the overall scale was .80. In the current study, a Cronbach's alpha of .76 was obtained.

Effort Scale. The Effort Scale (Lackaye & Margalit, 2006) consisted of four items to which children respond on a 5-point Likert-type scale, ranging from 1 (*almost never*) to 5 (*almost always*) with items such as "I don't give up even when it is difficult to me." In earlier studies, internal consistency for the measure (Cronbach's alpha) was .76. In the current study, a Cronbach's alpha of .66 was obtained.

Procedure

Before data collection, we obtained approval from the Israeli Ministry of Education, schools, and parents. Students completed the set of questionnaires as a group in their classrooms during school hours. The students were told that the questionnaires were not a test and that there were not right or wrong answers. They were informed that participating in the study was voluntary and that information would be kept confidential. The questionnaires were anonymous and took less than 1 hr to complete.

Data Analysis

The statistical package for social sciences (SPSS 19.01) was used for computing descriptive statistics, reliability coefficients (Cronbach's alpha) for the research instruments, and bivariate correlations to examine the relations between variables. In addition, in order to compare between boys and girls and between age groups (classes), tests of analyses of variance were performed including Partial Eta^2 as an estimate of effect size. We performed hierarchical multiple regression analyses to examine the predicted factors in the hope model and a K-means cluster analysis to identify unique groups of family climate profiles.

Results

Preliminary Analysis

To decrease the chance of Type 1 errors, a multivariate analysis of variance (MANOVA) was conducted on gender differences (boys, girls), with the following six dependent variables: all four child measures (self-reported loneliness, sense of coherence, hope, and effort) and the two family climate dimensions (Cohesion and Adaptability). The MANOVA yielded a significant main effect for gender, $F(6, 280) = 2.44, p < .01, \eta^2 = .05$.

Table 1 presents the means, standard deviations, and F scores for the univariate analysis of variances. Significant differences emerged for two of the children's self-reported perceptions. Boys viewed themselves as having lower levels of CSOC and higher levels of loneliness. No significant differences were found for the gender comparisons of the personal perceptions: Hope, effort, and—for the family climate dimensions—cohesion and adaptability.

Pearson correlations among all the study's variables are presented in Table 2.

TABLE 1. Gender Differences of the Study Variables

Variable	Boys	Girls	F(1, 278)	Partial η^2
Loneliness	1.76 (0.71)	1.55 (0.62)	7.10**	.025
Hope	4.17 (.66)	4.28 (.55)	2.92	.01
Effort	4.35 (0.57)	4.47 (0.51)	3.56	.012
CSOC	3.90 (0.52)	4.03 (0.49)	4.81*	.017
Cohesion	4.23 (0.61)	4.21 (0.64)	0.79	.000
Adaptation	3.10 (0.68)	3.2 (0.67)	1.7	.006

Note. Numbers in parentheses are standard deviations.
$^*p < .05$; $^{**}p < .01$.
CSOC = Children's Sense of Coherence.

TABLE 2. Pearson Correlation Among Study's Variables ($n = 287$)

Variable	1	2	3	4	5	6
1. Loneliness	—					
2. Hope	−.42**	—				
3. Effort	−.18**	.56**	—			
4. CSOC	−.63**	.65**	.50**	—		
5. Cohesion	−.27**	.38**	.34**	.47**	—	
6. Adaptation	−.13*	.27**	.22**	.23**	.48**	—

*$p < .05$; **$p < .01$.
CSOC = Children's Sense of Coherence.

Significant associations emerged between children's loneliness and levels of CSOC, hope, effort, and the two family climate dimensions. Children's loneliness was negatively associated with children's self-perceptions and family climate dimensions. The CSOC was positively associated with hope, effort, and the two family dimensions: cohesion and adaptability.

Predictors of the Loneliness and the CSOC

Separate hierarchical multiple regression analyses were conducted to investigate the contribution of the family climate dimensions and hope to children's risk and protective factors: loneliness and the sense of coherence. Concerning children's loneliness, the multiple regression analysis yielded a significant contribution of the family and individual characteristics, which explained 21% of the variance. The cohesion in the family climate, gender and hope provided a significant unique contribution to the equation (see Table 3). Children's higher levels of loneliness were explained by their family lower family cohesion and by their lower levels of hope. The contribution of the adaptability to the explanation was not significant.

Concerning children's sense of coherence, the multiple regression analysis reached 49% explanation of the variance. The regression analysis revealed a significant unique contribution for gender, family cohesion, and hope (see Table 3). Children's higher CSOC levels were explained by their family higher cohesion and by higher levels of hope. Similarly, to the analysis of the predictive factors of loneliness, the contribution of the adaptability to the explanation of the CSOC was not significant.

We found a unique and significant contribution of family cohesion to the explanation of children's risk and protective characteristics. Yet, the contribution of the family adaptability was nonsignificant in both regression analyses, and called

TABLE 3. *R*, *R*², and Betas of a Hierarchical Multiple Regression Predicting Loneliness and CSOC as the Dependent Variables

Step and Variable	R	R^2	Beta	F
		Loneliness as the dependent variable		
Step 1	.32	.10		10.69**
Gender			–.16**	
Cohesion			–.29**	
Adaptation			.02	
Step 2	.46	.21		18.36**
Gender			–.13*	
Cohesion			–.16*	
Adaptation			.05	
Hope			–.36**	
		Children's Sense of Coherence as the dependent variable		
Step 1	.49	.24		30.15**
Gender			.14**	
Cohesion			.48**	
Adaptation			–.02	
Step 2:	.46	.21		67.88**
Gender			.08*	
Cohesion			.23**	
Adaptation			–.07	
Hope			.55**	

*p < .05; **p < .01.
CSOC = Children's Sense of Coherence.

for in-depth examination of the differences among these families. Therefore, we identified profiles of family climate, based on both family climate dimensions.

Cluster Analysis

In order to identify subgroups of children with different profiles of family climates, based on their perceptions of family cohesion and adaptability, a K-means cluster analysis was performed with the cohesion and adaptability variables. The cluster analysis was used to objectively illustrate the structure of the data (Hair & Black, 2000). The rationale for this selection was based on earlier results that identified the joint impact of family dimensions on children's adjustment. In the current study, the cohesion contributed significantly to children's self-perceptions, while the contribution of the family adaptability dimension remained nonsignificant. The K-means iterative method makes multiple passes through the data, assigning units to the cluster with the nearest vector or set of means for the two variables, which is called the cluster center or centroid (Aldenderfer & Blashfield, 1984). The final cluster solution identified four distinct profiles of families. Means and standard

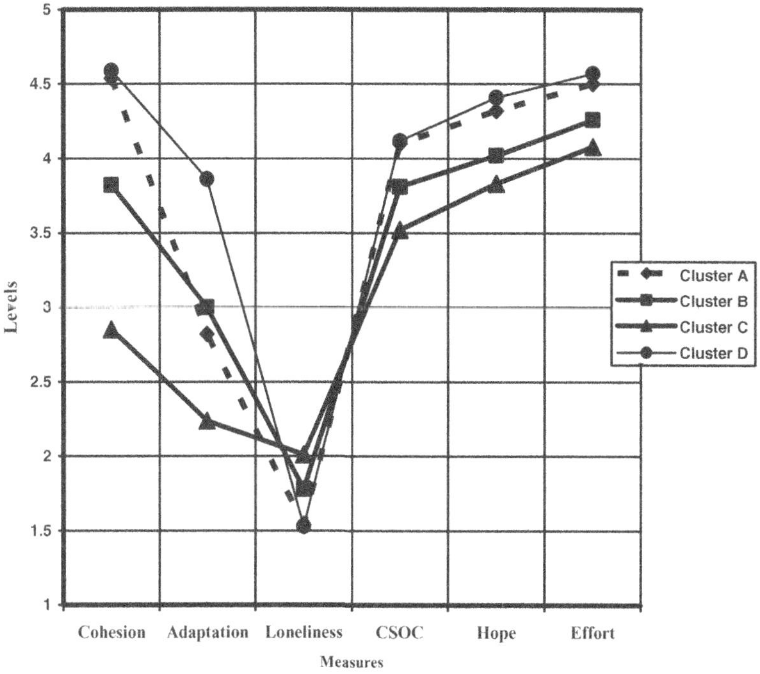

FIGURE 1. Level of study measures for the four clusters. CSOC = Children's Sense of Coherence.

deviations of the scores for each cluster are presented in Table 4 and Figure 1. The four-cluster solution highlighted distinct differences among the groups and provided profiles that separated the groups of children in a meaningful manner.

The four clusters were conceptualized and labeled as follows:

Cluster A: Cohesive structured families. The first cluster ($n = 91$ families of 46 boys [50.5%] and 45 girls [49.5%]) scored high on the family cohesion measure and low on the family adaptability measure.

Cluster B: Adaptable and not cohesive families. The second cluster ($n = 67$ families of 26 boys [38.8%] and 41 girls [61.2%]) scored high on the family adaptability measure and low on the family cohesion measure.

Cluster C: Rigid and not cohesive families. The third cluster ($n = 30$ families of 12 boys [40.0%] and 18 girls [60.0%]) scored very low on both family dimensions: The lowest cohesion and lowest adaptability measures were found in this cluster.

TABLE 4. Clusters' Comparisons

Variable	Cluster A ($n = 91$)	Cluster B ($n = 67$)	Cluster C ($n = 30$)	Cluster D ($n = 99$)	$F(3, 283)$	Group-differences Tukey	Partial η^2
Loneliness	1.54 (0.63)	1.78 (0.63)	2.02 (0.89)	1.53 (0.67)	6.04**	A, D < C;	.06
CSOC	4.1 (0.49)	3.81 (0.38)	3.51 (0.58)	4.11 (0.46)	17.58**	A, D > B, C C < B	.16
Hope	4.32 (0.55)	4.03 (0.54)	3.83 (0.73)	4.41 (0.49)	12.63**	A, D > B, C	.12
Effort	4.5 (0.51)	4.26 (0.56)	4.08 (0.62)	4.57 (0.45)	10.13**	A, D > B, C	.10

Note. Numbers in parentheses are standard deviations.
**$p < .01$.

Cluster D: Cohesive and adaptable families. The fourth cluster (n = 99 families of 40 boys [40.4%] and 59 girls [59.6%]) scored very high (in fact, the highest levels) on the cohesion and adaptability measures.

Comparisons of children's gender proportions and class proportions among the four clusters using chi-square analyses did not reveal significant differences.

Internal Validation

To examine the internal validity of the cluster identification, a MANOVA was performed with the clustering of the families and gender as independent variables and the Cohesion and Adaptability scores as the dependent variables. The MANOVA (using Wilkes's lambda) yielded a significant main effect for the clusters' identification, $F(6, 556) = 221.09$, $p < .001$, $\eta^2 = .695$, but not for the gender or the interactions. As presented in Table 4, significant intergroup differences emerged for the four clusters on both cohesion and adaptability scores indicating that the cluster analysis identified four different clusters according to their defining variables. Cluster A and D were noted for their high levels of cohesion in comparison to Clusters B and C. In addition, Cluster C reported the lowest levels of cohesion than all the remaining families and the lowest levels of adaptability. Cluster D was noted for the highest level of adaptability. In addition, family members of Cluster B reported higher levels of adaptability than did Clusters A and C.

External Validation

To examine whether these four different profiles would be differentially linked to children's characteristics, a MANOVA was performed with the family clusters and gender as the independent variables and with the loneliness, CSOC, hope, and effort ratings as the dependent variables. The MANOVA (using Wilkes's lambda) yielded a significant main effect for the clusters' identification, $F(12, 730.102) = 5.13$, $p < .00$, $\eta^2 = .069$, and for gender differences, $F(4, 276) = 2.53$, $p < .05$, $\eta^2 = .035$, and not for the interactions. The gender differences are already presented in Table 1.

As presented in Table 4, significant intergroup differences (using post-hoc Scheffe) emerged for the four clusters on the four measures indicating that the cluster analysis differed also according to the external variables. Clusters A and D revealed lower levels of loneliness than Cluster C, but Cluster B with a higher level of Adaptability and lower levels of Cohesion did not differ significantly from the clusters of the cohesive families. Yet, children in the cohesive clusters (A and D) reported higher levels of personal coherence than in the lower cohesive clusters (B and C). In addition, children in Clusters C had the lowest levels of coherence (lower than Cluster B). Hope and effort provided a similar differentiation pattern among groups of families, and children in the cohesive family clusters reported a higher level of hope and more effort investment than did children in the less cohesive clusters (B and C).

Pearson correlations were performed separately for each one of the clusters between the loneliness measure and the remaining variables, revealing different sets of relations:

In Cluster A (Cohesive structured families), the loneliness was negatively related with CSOC [$r(n = 91) = -.66$, $p < .01$], hope [$r(n = 91) = -.46$, $p < .01$], and both family dimensions: cohesion [$r(n = 91) = -.23$, $p < .05$], and adaptability [$r(n = 91) = -.21$, $p < .05$].

In Cluster B (Adaptable and not cohesive families), the loneliness measure was negatively correlated with CSOC [$r(n = 67) = -.41$, $p < .01$] and hope [$r(n = 67) = -.25$, $p < .05$]. The correlations with the family dimensions were not significant.

In Cluster C (Rigid and not cohesive families), the experience of loneliness was related negatively only with CSOC [$r(n = 30) = -.58$, $p < .01$].

In Cluster D (Cohesive and adaptable families), the loneliness was negatively related with CSOC [$r(n = 99) = -.68$, $p < .01$], hope [$r(n = 99) = -.51$, $p < .01$], effort [$r(n = 99) = -.31$, $p < .01$], and family cohesion [$r(n = 99) = -.23$, $p < .01$].

Discussion

The goals of the current study were, first, to identify factors that predicted loneliness as a risk factor and the sense of coherence as a protective factor. The second goal was to identify unique family clusters by employing the different family dimensions—cohesion and adaptability—for the classification.

Predictors of Risk and Protective Factors

The factors that predicted children's loneliness as a developmental risk factor were family cohesion and hope. As expected, lower levels of family cohesion and lower levels of hope predicted higher levels of loneliness. The family adaptability did not add significantly to the prediction. Correspondingly, the factors that predicted children's sense of coherence as an expression of their emerging personal strength were family cohesion and hope. Higher family cohesion and increased hope levels predicted higher sense of coherence. Similarly, the family adaptability did not add significantly to the prediction of the sense of coherence. Thus, it can be concluded that family relatedness and support as well as the future expectations predicted the risk and the protective factors. In the current study, similarly to several earlier studies, the family adaptability did not add significantly to these predictions (Al-Yagon & Margalit, 2009; Yahav, 2002). The original definition of adaptability is the family's ability to change its structure in response to situational and developmental stress (Olson, 1986). Adaptive family climate facilitates social change by mediating the demands of the environment (Lee, 1988). Thus, psychological flexibility has been considered a predicting factor to personal resilience (Kashdan & Rottenberg, 2010). In line with the theoretical recognition for the critical role of the joint impact of both family climate dimensions (Dundas, 1994), and the awareness to their dynamic interactive variability (Schrodt, 2005), and since the predictive role of the adaptability dimension was not validated, an in-depth analysis of their interrelations was conducted. We identified four distinctive family clusters that included both dimensions, and we examined their uniqueness within the paradigm of children's risk and protective factors.

Clusters' Summary

Cluster A: Cohesive structured families (n = 91 families). These highly cohesive families were recognized by their low levels of adaptability patterns. The loneliness experience among children in these families was low, and they had high personal strengths. They reported higher hopes and effort than children in Clusters B and C. Their loneliness experience was related to the two family climate dimensions—cohesion as well as adaptability. In addition, it was also related to their personal strengths (Sense of Coherence) and future expectations (Hope). The effort investment was not significantly related with children's loneliness. It seems that within this cohesive and structured family environment, children felt supported and secured.

Cluster B: Flexible and not cohesive families (n = 67 families). These families were open and adaptable to environmental changes and reported low levels of family cohesion. Children in this cluster experienced lower sense of coherence than those in Clusters A and D reported lower levels of hopes and invested less effort in academic studies than expressed by children in cohesive families. Since these families did not provide satisfactory levels of social support and closeness, it seems that the children felt less confident in themselves and developed fewer expectations for their future. However, their reports reflected satisfaction from their existing social network, and did not differ in their loneliness experience from the clusters of cohesive families. Maybe the family flexibility and openness to environmental changes enabled and promoted their independence and their ability to stay alone and to appreciate their interpersonal connections. Different variables were related in this cluster with the loneliness experience. The loneliness was not related to their family cohesion. Yet it was, similarly to the remaining clusters, negatively related with personal strength and future expectations. Within this cluster, those children who achieved higher sense of coherence and competence acquired positive future expectations and experienced lower levels of loneliness.

Cluster C: Rigid and not cohesive families (n = 30 families). This small group of families was noted for their lowest levels of cohesion and adaptability. It is not surprising that in these distanced and rigid family systems, the children reported the highest levels of loneliness and the lowest levels of the sense of coherence. In this cluster of rigid families that were not tuned to environmental changes and did not provide interpersonal closeness, the children were very lonely and had lower confidence in themselves and in their world. For them, the risk factor—the loneliness experience—was related only with the measure of personality strength (CSOC).

Cluster D: Cohesive and adaptive families ($n = 99$ families). These families were noted for their highest levels of family cohesion and flexibility. The children experienced very low levels of loneliness, hold high hopes for the future and were ready to invest effort in academic tasks. In this group of families, the low levels of loneliness were related with family support and cohesion as well as with the individualistic personal strength (CSOC), future expectations (Hope), and effort investment.

As expected, among the four clusters, children of the two cohesive families' clusters reported the lowest levels of loneliness and higher levels of personal strength. It seems that family cohesion provided the children with primary experiences of social support that contributed to their developmental adjustment, their personal strengths, and their relatedness not only to their families but also to their peer group. In flexible families as well as in more structured families, children experienced relatedness and belonging. Yet, the results demonstrated that family cohesion is not the only condition for predicting loneliness. Different family resources may contribute to development of adjustment, and children in flexible but not cohesive families reported higher levels of personal strengths than the noncohesive rigid families, and their loneliness levels were not significantly different from those of the two cohesive families. However, when families did not provide their children with social support in terms of Cohesion or with the flexibility that will promote their independence and flexibility, in terms of the adaptability dimension, the children experienced the highest levels of loneliness and social isolation and the lowest levels of personal strengths.

In conclusion, the results of the study focused attention on the role of family closeness together with personal hope as they may jointly predict the development of positive personal strengths and negatively relate with the experience of social distress. The hope construct provided the unique future perspective that complemented the relations with family characteristic rooted in past developmental processes. Hopes for the future provide empowering options for extending the opportunities' horizons, enhancing effort and well-being and enabling more effective coping with developmental challenges. The cluster analysis further clarified the role of the two-family systemic dimensions, focusing attention not only on the value of support within family in terms of cohesion but also on the possible empowering role of family flexibility and adaptability to changes, which may compensate the risk related to lower family support and personal isolation, and thus contribute to personal strengths.

Special attention should be devoted to the hope construct within the different family clusters. Hope was not significantly related with family dimensions and with personal strengths in the noncohesive and rigid families. Maybe it pointed attention to the option to develop personal strengths even within nonsupportive and rigid families. Future studies may experiment home training for these children, to promote their personal strength through developing perceptions of future opportunities (Cheavens, Feldman, Woodward, & Snyder, 2006; Pretorius, Venter, Temane, & Wissing, 2008). In conclusion, the identification of the four family clusters demonstrated the advantages of moving from global understanding of family relations to in-depth clarification of the relations' variability within families. The differential perspectives drew attention to the distinctive profiles of family climates and their unique relations with children's personal social risks and personal strengths.

The results of the current study offer a unique perspective on relations between the joint impact of two family dimensions and children's characteristics. However, we should be aware of the research limitation. First, this is a correlative study, and in order to disclose the family dynamics, future research may adopt longitudinal approaches to clarify the nature of processes within the family and related children's outcomes. In addition, the present study provided the children's perceptions of the family dimensions. Future studies will have to validate children's perceptions by parental or direct observation. Indeed children's views of their families may differ from their parents' opinions; however, the study of these gaps between parents and children perceptions may provide additional important clarifications to the development of children's risks and strengths. In addition, larger samples in different cultures may clarify the predicting roles of the contextual conditions regarding the relations among variables.

The study has theoretical importance and provides differential understanding to the relations between children's loneliness and familial dimensions. The hope perspective offers the examination of the sources of personal strength not only as rooted in past development but also as related to future expectations. The study confirmed the value of differential examination that reflects differences not only between individuals but also between groups of family systems. In addition, the results have therapeutic values for promoting the development of differential consultation planning adapted to different family supportive styles in order to empower children and to promote their personal strengths, to support their future expectations, and to advance the development of effective coping with social-alienation risks and loneliness.

REFERENCES

Al-Yagon, M. (2008). Maternal personal resources and children's socioemotional and behavioral adjustment. *Child Psychiatry and Human Development, 39*(3), 283–298.

Al-Yagon, M. (2010). Maternal emotional resources and socio–emotional well-being of children with and without learning disabilities. *Family Relations, 59*(2), 152–169.

Al-Yagon, M., & Margalit, M. (2009). Positive and negative affect among mothers of children with intellectual abilities. *British Journal of Developmental Disabilities, 52*(2), 109–127.

Aldenderfer, M. S., & Blashfield, R. K. (1984). *Cluster analysis*. Beverly Hills, CA: Sage.

Antonovsky, A. (1987). *Unraveling the mystery of health*. San Francisco: Jossey-Bass.

Antonovsky, A. (1993). The structure and properties of the sense of coherence scale. *Social Science & Medicine, 36*(6), 725–733.

Arnau, R. C., Martinez, P., Nino de Guzman, I., Herth, K., & Yoshiyuki Konishi, C. (2010). A Spanish–language version of the Herth Hope Scale: Development and psychometric evaluation in a Peruvian sample. *Educational and Psychological Measurement, 70*(5), 808–824.

Arnau, R. C., Rosen, D. H., Finch, J. F., Rhudy, J. L., & Fortunato, V. J. (2007). Longitudinal effects of hope on depression and anxiety: A latent variable analysis. *Journal of Personality, 75*(1), 43–64.

Asher, S. R., Parkhurst, J. T., Hymel, S., & Williams, G. A. (1990). Peer rejection and loneliness in childhood. In S. R. Asher & J. D. Coie (Eds.), *Peer rejection in childhood* (pp. 253–273). Cambridge, England: Cambridge University Press.

Bakkaloglu, H. (2010). A comparison of the loneliness levels of mainstreamed primary students according to their sociometric status. *Procedia—Social and Behavioral Sciences, 2*(2), 330–336.

Besevegis, E., & Galanaki, E. P. (2010). Coping with loneliness in childhood. *European Journal of Developmental Psychology, 7*(6), 653–673.

Blatt, S. J., & Homann, E. (1992). Parent–child interaction in the etiology of dependent and self-critical depression. *Clinical Psychology Review, 12*(1), 47–91.

Blatt, S. J., Zohar, A., Quinlan, D. M., & Luthar, S. (1996). Levels of relatedness within the dependency factor of the depressive experiences questionnaire for adolescents. *Journal of Personality Assessment, 67*(1), 52–71.

Bowlby, J. (1988). *A secure base*. New York: Basic Books.

Bryant, F. B., & Cvengros, J. A. (2004). Distinguishing hope and optimism: Two sides of a coin, or two separate coins? *Journal of Social and Clinical Psychology, 23*(2), 273–302.

Cacioppo, J. T., & Patrick, W. (2008). *Loneliness: Human nature and the need for social connection*. New York: W. W. Norton.

Chang, E. C., & DeSimone, S. L. (2001). The influence of hope on appraisals, coping and dysphoria: A test of hope theory. *Journal of Social and Clinical Psychology, 20*(2), 117–129.

Cheavens, J. S., Feldman, D. B., Woodward, J. T., & Snyder, C. R. (2006). Hope in cognitive psychotherapies: On working with client strengths. *Journal of Cognitive Psychotherapy, 20*(2), 135–145.

Curry, L. A., Snyder, C. R., Cook, D. L., Ruby, B. C., & Rehm, M. (1997). The role of hope in academic and sport achievement. *Journal of Personality and Social Psychology, 73*, 1257–1267.

Dundas, I. (1994). The Family Adaptability and Cohesion Scale III in a Norwegian sample. *Family Process, 33*(2), 191–202.

Edbom, T., Malmberg, K., Lichtenstein, P., Granlund, M., & Larsson, J. O. (2010). High sense of coherence in adolescence is a protective factor in the longitudinal development of ADHD symptoms. *Scandinavian Journal of Caring Sciences, 24*(3), 541–547.

Evans, W. P., Marsh, S. C., & Weigel, D. J. (2010). Promoting adolescent sense of coherence: Testing models of risk, protection, and resiliency. *Journal of Community & Applied Social Psychology, 20*(1), 30–43.

Flora, J., & Segrin, C. (2000). Relationship development in dating couples: Implications for relational satisfaction and loneliness. *Journal of Social and Personal Relationships, 17*(6), 811–825.

Fresco, D. M., Williams, N. L., & Nugent, N. R. (2006). Flexibility and negative affect: Examining the associations of explanatory flexibility and coping flexibility to each other and to depression and anxiety. *Cognitive Therapy & Research, 30*(2), 201–210.

Gabalda, M. K., Thompson, M. P., & Kaslow, N. J. (2010). Risk and protective factors for psychological adjustment among low-income, African American children. *Journal of Family Issues, 31*(4), 423–444.

Green, R. G., Harris, R. N., Forte, J. A., & Robinson, M. (1991). The wives data and FACES IV: Making things appear simple. *Family Process, 30*, 79–83.

Guisinger, S., & Blatt, S. J. (1994). Individuality and relatedness. *American Psychologist, 49*(2), 104–111.

Hair, J. F., & Black, W. C. (2000). Cluster analysis. In L. G. Grimm & P. R. Yarnold (Eds.), *Reading and understanding more multivariate statistics* (pp. 147–206). Washington, DC: APA.

Junttila, N., Vauras, M., & Laakkonen, E. (2007). The role of parenting self-efficacy in children's social and academic behavior. *European Journal of Psychology of Education—EJPE, 22*(1), 41–61.

Kashdan, T. B., & Rottenberg, J. (2010). Psychological flexibility as a fundamental aspect of health. *Clinical Psychology Review, 30*(7), 865–878.

Lackaye, T., & Margalit, M. (2006). Comparisons of achievement, effort and self-perceptions among students with learning disabilities and their peers from different achievement groups. *Journal of Learning Disabilities, 39*(5), 432–446.

Lackaye, T., & Margalit, M. (2008). Self-efficacy, loneliness, effort and hope: Developmental differences in the experiences of students with learning disabilities and their non-LD peers at two age groups. *Learning Disabilities: A Contemporary Journal, 6*(2), 1–20.

Lee, C. (1988). Theories of family adaptability: Toward a synthesis of Olson's Circumplex and the Beavers Systems Models. *Family Process, 27*(1), 73–85.

Liew, J., Chen, Q., & Hughes, J. N. (2010). Child effortful control, teacher–student relationships, and achievement in academically at-risk children: Additive and interactive effects. *Early Childhood Research Quarterly, 25*(1), 51–64.

Liew, J., McTigue, E. M., Barrois, L., & Hughes, J. N. (2008). Adaptive and effortful control and academic self-efficacy beliefs on achievement: A longitudinal study of 1st through 3rd graders. *Early Childhood Research Quarterly, 23*(4), 515–526.

Lin, L. Y., Orsmond, G. I., Coster, W. J., & Cohn, E. S. (2011). Families of adolescents and adults with autism spectrum disorders in Taiwan: The role of social support and coping in family adaptation and maternal well-being. *Research in Autism Spectrum Disorders, 5*(1), 144–156.

Lundman, B., Alex, L., Jonsen, E., Norberg, A., Nygren, B., Santamaki Fischer, R., et al. (2010). Inner strength: A theoretical analysis of salutogenic concepts. *International Journal of Nursing Studies*, *47*(2), 251–260.

Luthar, S. S., & Brown, P. J. (2007). Maximizing resilience through diverse levels of inquiry: Prevailing paradigms, possibilities, and priorities for the future. *Development & Psychopathology*, *19*(3), 931–955.

Luthar, S. S., Cicchetti, D., & Becker, B. (2000). The construct of resilience: A critical evaluation and guidelines for future work. *Child Development*, *71*(3), 543–562.

Margalit, M. (1991). Understanding loneliness among students with learning disabilities. *Behavior Change*, *8*, 167–173.

Margalit, M. (2010). *Lonely children and adolescents: Self perceptions, social exclusion and hope*. New York: Springer.

Margalit, M., & Efrati, M. (1995). Loneliness, coherence and companionship among children with learning disorders. *Educational Psychology*, *16*(1), 69–79.

Margalit, M., & Heiman, T. (1986). Family climate and anxiety of families with learning disabled boys. *Journal of the American Academy of Child Psychiatry*, *25*(6), 841–856.

Minuchin, S. (1974). *Families & family therapy*. Cambridge, MA: Harvard University Press.

Olson, D., & Gorall, D. M. (2003). Circumplex Model of marital and family systems. In F. Walsh (Ed.), *Normal family processes* (3 ed., pp. 514–547). New York: Guilford.

Olson, D. H. (1986). Circumplex model VII: Validation studies and FACES III. *Family Process*, *26*, 337–351.

Olson, D. H. (2000). Circumplex Model of marital and family systems. *Journal of Family Therapy*, *22*(2), 144–167.

Peplau, L. A., & Perlman, D. (1982). Perspectives on loneliness. In L. A. Peplau & D. Perlman (Eds.), *Loneliness: A sourcebook of current theory, research and therapy* (pp. 1–18). New York: Wiley.

Pretorius, C., Venter, C., Temane, M., & Wissing, M. (2008). The design and evaluation of a hope enhancement programme for adults. *Journal of Psychology in Africa*, *18*(2), 301–308.

Qualter, P. (2004). Social and emotional loneliness in childhood. In S. P. Shohov (Ed.), *Advances in psychology research* (Vol. 27, pp. 133–154). Hauppauge, NY: Nova Science Publishers.

Qualter, P., Brown, S., Munn, P., & Rotenberg, K. (2010). Childhood loneliness as a predictor of adolescent depressive symptoms: An 8-year longitudinal study. *European Child & Adolescent Psychiatry*, *19*(6), 493–501.

Qualter, P., & Munn, P. (2002). The separateness of social and emotional loneliness in childhood. *Journal of Child Psychology and Psychiatry and Allied Disciplines*, *43*(2), 233–244.

Renshaw, P. D., & Brown, P. J. (1993). Loneliness in middle childhood: Concurrent and longitudinal predictors. *Child Development*, *64*(4), 1271–1284.

Roest, A. M. C., Dubas, J. S., & Gerris, J. R. M. (2009). Value transmissions between fathers, mothers, and adolescent and emerging adult children: The role of the family climate. *Journal of Family Psychology*, *23*(2), 146–155.

Scheier, M. F., & Carver, C. S. (1985). Optimism, coping, and health: Assessment and implication of generalized outcome expectancies. *Health Psychology*, *4*, 219–247.

Scheier, M. F., & Carver, C. S. (1992). Effects of optimism or psychological and physical well-being: Theoretical overview and empirical update. *Cognitive Therapy and Research*, *16*, 201–228.

Schrodt, P. (2005). Family communication schemata and the Circumplex Model of family functioning. *Western Journal of Communication*, *69*(4), 359–376.
Schueller, S. M. (2009). Promoting wellness: Integrating community and positive psychology. *Journal of Community Psychology*, *37*(7), 922–937.
Sharabi, A., & Margalit, M. (in press). The mediating role of Internet connection, virtual friends, and mood in predicting loneliness among students with and without learning disabilities in different educational environments. *Journal of Learning Disabilities*.
Snyder, C. R. (2002). Hope theory: Rainbows in the mind. *Psychological Inquiry*, *13*(4), 249–275.
Snyder, C. R. (2006). Measuring hope in children. *Adolescent and Family Health*, *4*(1), 26–34.
Snyder, C. R., Harris, C., Anderson, J. R., Holleran, S. A., Irving, L. M., Sigmon, S. T., et al. (1991). The will and the ways: Development and validation of an individual-differences measure of hope. *Journal of Personality & Social Psychology*, *60*(4), 570–585.
Snyder, C. R., Irving, L. M., & Anderson, J. (1991). Hope and health. In C. R. Snyder & D. R. Forsyth (Eds.), *The handbook of social and clinical psychology: The health perspective* (pp. 285–307). Elmsford, NY: Pergamon Press.
Stoeckli, G. (2009). The role of individual and social factors in classroom loneliness. *Journal of Educational Research*, *103*(1), 28–39.
Sturge-Apple, M. L., Davies, P. T., & Cummings, E. M. (2010). Typologies of family functioning and children's adjustment during the early school years. *Child Development*, *81*(4), 1320–1335.
Teichman, Y., & Navon, S. (1990). Family evaluation: The circumplex model. *Psychology*, *2*, 36–46.
Uhlenberg, J., & Brown, K. M. (2002). Racial gap in teachers' perceptions of the achievement gap. *Education and Urban Society*, *34*, 493–530.
Valiente, C., Lemery-Chalfant, K., & Reiser, M. (2007). Pathways to problem behaviors: Chaotic homes, parent and child effortful control, and parenting. *Social Development*, *16*(2), 249–267.
Vandeleur, C. L., Perrez, M., & Schoebi, D. (2007). Associations between measures of emotion and familial dynamics in normative families with adolescents. *Swiss Journal of Psychology*, *66*(1), 5–16.
Yahav, R. (2002). External and internal symptoms in children and characteristics of the family system: A comparison of the linear and circumplex models. *American Journal of Family Therapy*, *30*(1), 39–56.
Yeo, G. B., & Neal, A. (2004). A multilevel analysis of effort, practice, and performance: Effects of ability, conscientiousness, and goal orientation. *Journal of Applied Psychology*, *89*(2), 231–247.
Zdanowicz, N., Janne, P., & Reynaert, C. (2004). Family, health, and adolescence. *Psychosomatics*, *45*(6), 500–507.

The Prevalence of Loneliness Among Adults: A Case Study of the United Kingdom

CHRISTINA R. VICTOR
Brunel University

KEMING YANG
Durham University

ABSTRACT. Within contemporary Western (post) modern societies, loneliness is seen as a problem that is particularly associated with old age. Much less attention has been given to examining variations in loneliness across age groups. We examine patterns of loneliness across adults aged 15 years and older in the United Kingdom using data from the European Social Survey. We first consider the prevalence of loneliness among the adult population; then the relationship between loneliness and a range of key risk factors, and finally the relationship with age for each of our risk factors. Loneliness demonstrates a nonlinear U-shaped distribution, with those aged under 25 years and those aged over 65 years demonstrating the highest levels of loneliness. Depression is associated with loneliness for all age groups. Poor physical health is associated with loneliness in young adult and midlife but not later life. For those in mid and later life, the quality of social engagement is protective against loneliness, while for young adults it is the quantity of social engagement. This indicates that different factors may endow vulnerability (or protect) against loneliness at different stages of life and suggests that preventative strategies or interventions that reflect these variations need to be developed.

WITHIN THE CONTEMPORARY CONTEXT of Western (post) modern societies, loneliness is perceived as a problem that is particularly associated with old age, growing older, and later life. More specifically, within the United Kingdom, loneliness is identified as being one of the particular "problems" of old age (see Rowntree, 1948), and there is a substantial research literature, with a significant historical pedigree, examining the prevalence of loneliness; documenting negative outcomes associated with loneliness; identifying factors that confer vulnerability to or proffer protection against loneliness; and evaluating interventions that aim to reduce loneliness within the United Kingdom and elsewhere (Anderson, 1998; De Jong Gierveld, 1998, 2006; Dykstra, 2009; Heylen, 2010; Johnson and Mullins, 1987; Peplau and Perlman, 1982; Rokach, 2000a; Routaslo and Pitkala, 2002; Scarf and De Jong Gierveld, 2008; Steed, Boldy, & Iredell, 2007; Townsend, 1968; van Tilburg, Havens, & de Jong Gierveld, 2004; Victor, Scambler, Bond, & Bowling, 2000; Victor, Scambler, Bowling, & Bond, 2005; Victor et al., 2002; Weiss, 1973). Researchers focusing on loneliness thus often have an interest in specific population groups such as the young (Rokach and Neto, 2000), the old (Margrett et al., 2011; Victor, Bond, & Scambler, 2009), the childless individuals, and those with specific health problems including mortality (Hawkley and Cacciappo, 2010; Patterson and Veenstra, 2010; Tilvis, Laitala, Routasalo, & Pitkälä, 2011). The predominant focus of attention has been upon examining loneliness among discrete age groups. Few researchers have looked from a comparative perspective at loneliness *across the whole range of adult age groups*, approximating from "young adulthood" to "old age" in nationally representative samples (Perlman, 1988; Rokach, 2001; Schultz and Moore, 1988).

Recently Yang and Victor (2011) suggested that there are two broad theoretical models of the relationship between loneliness and age. If we hypothesize a link between age and loneliness, as the stereotypes and perceptions of old age suggest, then we would expect to see low rates of loneliness for young adults with a progressive age-related increase across the life course with an acceleration in levels of loneliness upon entry to "old age" (for example, 65 years onwards) and a continued increase into very old age. Alternatively, as Yang and Victor (2011) illustrated by drawing on data from 25 European nations, we might hypothesize that the relationship between loneliness and age is, in fact, nonlinear with high rates of loneliness in young adulthood and old age and low rates in early/mid adulthood. What other empirical evidence examines loneliness across the adult age range? Schultz and Moore (1988) studied three age groups—high school students, college students, and older people—and reported that high school students demonstrated the highest levels of loneliness but this study did not include participants in the midlife years. Green et al. (2001) compare young and older adults and report no significant differences in loneliness. Nolen-Hoeksema and Ahrens (2002), in a study focusing upon depression, report that those aged 45–55 years had the highest levels of loneliness, with those aged 65–75 years having the lowest levels of loneliness, and with those aged 25–35 years occupying the intermediate category but this study excludes the youngest adults. Rokach (2000b, 2001) has studied loneliness across four broad age groups—young people (13–18 years); young adults

(19–30 years); adults (31–58 years), and seniors (60–80 years)—focusing upon causes and coping mechanisms in a volunteer population in Canada rather than producing age-specific prevalence rates. More recently, Lauder and colleagues (Lauder, Mummery, Jones, & Caperchione, 2006; Lauder, Mummery, & Sharkey, 2006; Lauder, Sharkey, and Mummery, 2004) have surveyed loneliness for the general adult population in Queensland (Australia) using the de Jong-Gierveld scale. This ranges from 0 (*not lonely*) to 11 (*severely lonely*), with a score of 2 or more being the cut-off point for loneliness. They report that the highest mean loneliness score of 2.6 was recorded by those aged 40–49 years as compared with 1.8 for those 18–19 years and 2.1 for older adults (those aged 60 years and over), although these differences were not statistically significant. This pattern is the inverse of the nonlinear distribution suggested by Yang and Victor (2011).

Table 1 summarizes the evidence from previous studies on the relationship between loneliness, as measured by a self-rating scale (the measure included in our data set) and age. The 2008 New Zealand Quality of Life survey reports rates of loneliness for adults aged 15+ years in the previous year. This reveals that loneliness is highest among the 15–24-year age groups (20%), with rates broadly similar across the 25–65+-year age range at 16%. Using the Household Income and Labour Dynamics in Australia (HILDA) survey data, Flood (2005) computes a social support index (which he argues is the inverse of loneliness) and estimates that the prevalence of loneliness is highest for those aged 15–19 years (16%) and is lowest for those aged 35–54 years (13%), before increasingly slightly to 14% for those aged 65+ years. Franklin and Tranter (2008) report rates of loneliness for adults (aged 18+ years) in Australia using the Australian Survey of Social Attitudes. They report that 30% of those aged 18–24 years report that they had experienced loneliness in the previous week, compared with 15% of those aged 65+ years.

The recent study by the Association of Retired Persons of America (AARP, 2010) measured loneliness for those aged 45+ years. The age groups used in this study do not readily mesh with those in Table 1, thereby rendering direct comparison problematic. They report that 36% of this group were lonely (as defined as a score of 44+ on the UCLA scale devised by Russell, 1996) and that the prevalence of loneliness decreased with age from 43% for those aged 45–49 years, to 25% for those aged 70+ years (with prevalence of 41% for those aged 50–59 years and 35% for those aged 60–69 years). While these rates are much higher than those of the other studies cited in terms of the levels of loneliness reported, they are, like the studies from Australia and New Zealand, suggestive of an inverse relationship between age and loneliness. A similar pattern of an age-related decrease in loneliness is reported by the Mental Health Foundation (Griffin, 2010) survey conducted in the United Kingdom and report that 9% of those aged 55+ years are often lonely, compared with 11% of the 35–54-year age group and 12% of those aged 18–34 years. Unfortunately, the presentation of

TABLE 1. The Prevalence of Loneliness by Age Group: Evidence from Existing Studies (%)

	Flood (2005)		Franklin & Tranter (2008)		New Zealand (2010) Quality of life survey		SLAN–Harrington et al. (2008)	
Age range (years)	Prevalence	F/M ratio	Prevalence	F/M ratio	Prevalence	F/M ratio	Prevalence	F/M ratio
15–19	16	1.4	30****	1.2				
20–24	15	1.1			20*	1.4		
25–34	15	1.1	30	2.9	18	1.3	15**	1.5
35–44	13	1.1	22	2.0	16	1.1	15***	1.2
45–54	13	1.2	23	2.5	16	1.2		
55–64	14	1.1	17	1.9	13	1.1	14	2.3
65+	14	1.4	15	1.1	16	1.4	17	1.6

*19–24 years. **15–29 years. ***30–44 years. ****18–24 years.

the data does not facilitate a more detailed comparison of age groups. The Irish survey (SLAN) (Harrington et al., 2008) used a dichotomous question (yes/no) to evaluate loneliness in the 4 weeks prior to interview. These data suggest that the prevalence of loneliness is stable at approximately 15% until the age of 65+ years, when there is an increase to 17%. This study is at odds with the other studies in being suggestive of a positive relationship between age and loneliness, although the difference is not statistically significant.

It is difficult to establish clear trends as the age groupings used across the range of available studies are often broad and do not facilitate ready comparison and serve to obscure the detail of the relationship between loneliness and age. With the exception of gender, studies have rarely systematically investigated the importance of a range of protective/vulnerability factors across adults of different ages and, therefore, at different stages of the life course. Scrutiny of Table 1 reveals that reported levels of loneliness are markedly higher for females as compared with males across all the studies identified and age groups. This is consistent with most previous research, which demonstrates an association between loneliness and gender, at least for older adults. While the precise magnitude of the differential varies across studies, the excess of reported rates of loneliness among women is consistent across age groups, but there is no consistent pattern of where this excess is most extreme.

Our evaluation of the published literature indicates that there are very few studies looking at loneliness across the whole range of adult age groups. For the small number of studies that do examine multiple age groups (e.g., Griffin, 2010), there is often little systematic examination on how important risk factors, such as the ones we shall study in this article, influence the relationship between age and loneliness. In this article we examine loneliness among adults aged 15 years and older in the United Kingdom using the European Social Survey to examine the relationship between age and loneliness as loneliness is predominantly seen as a "problem" of old age alone (Campaign to End Loneliness; http://www.campaigntoendloneliness.org.uk/). We first consider loneliness among the adult population in order to examine the nature of the relationship with age and consider if loneliness in the United Kingdom is simply a problem of old age. We then focus upon the relationship between loneliness, age and gender as previous univariate research has illustrated the importance of gender (Victor, Scambler, Marston, Bond, & Bowling, 2006). We then consider the relationship between loneliness among adults for a range of key risk factors including household size and marital status, physical and mental health, quality of life and quality of social relationships. Finally, we consider the stability of key vulnerability/protective factors across the whole range of adult age groups to determine if the same factors are important at different ages. This is important not only for our conceptual understanding of loneliness but also for developing "age appropriate" interventions to combat loneliness.

Method

Participants

No available UK data sets include a broad adult population age range, measure loneliness, and follow the participants longitudinally, in the "ideal" study design to examine the relationship between age and loneliness. Thus we employ a cross-sectional survey that fulfils two of these key requirements as follows: (a) targets a population of adults across the whole age range and (b) measures loneliness. The most appropriate data set that fulfils these two criteria is the UK element of the third round of European Social Survey (ESS), which was conducted in 2006 (See ESS website; http://www.europeansocialsurvey.org/). The focus of the ESS is upon tracking social attitudes and values among adults across the 25 participating European countries. The ESS has a strong methodological foundation and focuses upon using common sampling and response-rate calculation algorithms and requires a 70% response rate from each country for the data to be included in the ESS data set (see Yang and Victor, 2011, for more details). In each country the study randomly samples adults aged 15 and older living in the community. As a first step in a program of analysis focusing upon the whole data set that includes all the 25 participating countries, in this article we focus on the United Kingdom sample which included 2393 participants aged 15–97 years of age. The sampling process followed a multistage procedure, with the achieved response rate at 52%.

Measures

Loneliness. The ESS uses a single self-rating scale to measure loneliness. Participants are asked, "Using this card, please tell me how much of the time during the past week you felt lonely," and the options are 1 = "None or almost none of the time," 2 = "Some of the time," 3 = "Most of the time," 4 = "all or almost all of the time," and 8 = "don't know." There have been some concerns over the use of such single item for measuring a subjective and relatively complex concept such as loneliness, especially when used in a cross-national survey (Rook, 1988; Rotenberg & Mackie, 1999). As we are focusing upon a single country, the United Kingdom, where this type of self-rating scale is widely used (see Victor, Grenade, & Boldy, 2005), the issues of cross-national comparison are of less relevance.

Risk factors for loneliness. A plethora of parameters is associated with loneliness among older adults (see Dykstra, 2009). The focus of the ESS on measuring attitudes and values inevitably limits the number of these vulnerability/protective factors associated with loneliness that we can include in our analysis. However, variables indicative of the major vulnerability/protective factors are present as follows: (a) age and gender; (b) perceived physical and mental health; (c) household size and marital status; and (d) perceived and reported social resources including the availability of a confiding relationship.

To facilitate statistical analysis, that is, to increase the number of observations for each factor, we undertook grouping of the values for our selected measures. We used age categories, rather than using age as a continuous variable, because age groups rather than specific age values are predominantly used in the literature when researchers study the prevalence of loneliness. This reflects the focus, as noted earlier, of researchers upon enumerating the prevalence of loneliness among particular age categories, such as the old or the young (Patterson & Veenstra, 2010; Peplau & Perlman, 1982; Rokach and Neto, 2000; Townsend, 1968; Victor, Scambler, Bond, & Bowling, 2000). The classification of ages into specific categories is not, however, consistent across studies and there is no consensus on the threshold ages used to define, for example, old age. Researchers have adopted different schemes reflecting both the specific focus of individual studies and the age ranges included: consequently there a range of classifications and groupings evident in previous studies. Some studies simply use a 10-year range to define each analytical age group (e.g., 20–29 years; 30–39 years; 60–69 years). Others have adopted broader age categories that act as proxies for specific "life stages" (e.g., 40–59 years being "mid life and 60+ years being "old age"). Another approach is to differentiate specific populations into distinct subgroups (e.g., distinguishing the "young old," those aged 65–79 years, from the "old old," those aged 80 years and over). As our aim is to compare the prevalence of loneliness across the whole range of adult age rather than the specific age groups within the old or the young, we have adopted the above simple scheme of three age groups. We created three age groupings for our analysis: "the young" (under 30 years), "the middle-aged" (30–59 years) and "the old" (60 years and above). This classification broadly approximates to those used by Rokach (2000b, 2001), which offers us the opportunity for making direct comparisons with his work, and mirrors the categories used in our previous work examining loneliness across 25 European Countries (Yang and Victor, 2011). Furthermore this three-fold categorization facilitates our statistical analyses with optimal sample size for each age grouping. This is particularly necessary when we study the association between age, loneliness, and selected risk factors (see section on analysis), most of which are variables with multiple categories. A scheme with more categories of age would pose analytical challenges, in terms of generating cells with sparse observations. In terms of the interpretation of our results, the three broad age groups employed in our analyses approximate to broad life stages and enable us to locate our work within the available literature where researchers have typically focused upon youth/young adults, midlife, and old age.

Our category "married" includes both legal marriage and partnership; "divorced/separated" describes a general situation of separation from a spouse, including both legal divorce and separation from a partner; similarly, "widowed" refers to the death of either a legal spouse or a partner. For household size, we defined four categories: single person households, two-person households (mostly couples without children), three or four persons (predominantly families with children), five and more people (large families). Physical health is represented by two variables. Self reported health is classified as "good and very good," "fair," "bad and very bad," and self-reported restrictions in daily activities as a "a lot," "to some extent," and "none." Mental health is measured by the self-reported frequency of depression as "never," "sometimes," and a combined category of "all or most of the times." Three variables measure social engagement: frequency of social contact with friends, relatives, and others (values being grouped into "less than once a month," "once a month or more," and "once a week or more"); having someone to discuss intimate and personal matters with ("yes" and "no"); and perceived evaluation of the level of social engagement compared with others ("more," "about the same," and "less").

Analysis

Our statistical analyses in this article are necessarily exploratory given the preliminary nature of this case study. In addition, we have refrained from employing formal statistical models, such as ordered logistic regression models, for two reasons. First, thus far there are no robust theories of the relationships between the risk factors included in our study and loneliness, therefore making the inclusion of any "causal factors" unfounded or arbitrary. Second, although the sample size (2393) may appear to be quite large it would be overwhelmed by the enormous number of cells (or the combinations of the categories of the risk factors to be used, almost 140 thousand). It is therefore more appropriate and meaningful to investigate the prevalence of loneliness conditioned on each of the risk factors rather than to control all other variables at the same time in a single model. It would require the pan-European sample and a well-justified, more parsimonious model in order to apply formal statistical models, which are clearly beyond the capacity of this preliminary case study.

We first explore the relationship between age and the prevalence of loneliness for both females and males, thereby establishing the context for further analyses and providing a reference framework for comparison with previous research. We then examine the relationship between each of the risk factors and the prevalence of loneliness. We measure the strength and significance of these relationships with the Gamma statistic as, for most pairs of relationships examined, these are ordinal variables. The only exception is marital status, which is a multicategory nominal variable and therefore we have used the chi-square test. Finally, we focus our attention on the prevalence of "severe" loneliness (those who are lonely "all and most of the times") and consider if there is a relationship between age and each vulnerability/protective factor. All statistics were produced with the design weight to increase the representativeness of the sample and hence our findings.

Results

We present our results in three sections: the prevalence of loneliness by age and gender, the examination of factors linked with loneliness in the adult population, and then the importance of these factors across three broad age groups—young adults (those aged under 30 years); midlife adults (those aged 30–59 years), and older adults (those aged 60+ years)—for those with the highest level of reported loneliness.

The Prevalence of Loneliness by Age and Gender

For our initial analysis we have grouped those who reported that they were lonely "almost all of the time" and "most of the time" into a single category defined as lonely "All or most of the time." This group characterizes those with the most severe levels of loneliness and, overall, 6% of adults were so classified; 21% were "sometimes" lonely, and 73% were never lonely (see Figure 1). For the overall sample the relationship with age does not illustrate a linear trend of increasing (or decreasing) loneliness with age. Rather, there is a "nonlinear" U-shaped distribution with loneliness levels high (9% lonely all or most of the time) for those aged under 25 years and those aged 55 years and over and lower rates of 5% for the 25–44-year age group. How does the prevalence of loneliness vary by age and gender? There is a significant relationship between loneliness and gender: 9% of women and 6% of men reported that they were lonely most or all of the time, with a further 25% and 22% respectively reporting that they were sometimes lonely. Thus, 34% of women and 28% of men reported experiencing loneliness. We conclude that, for all age groups, females are more likely to report loneliness than males.

What is the pattern of loneliness across the age groups and does this vary with gender given the importance of the overall relationship between gender and loneliness? If we examine the trend for men and women separately, the high rates

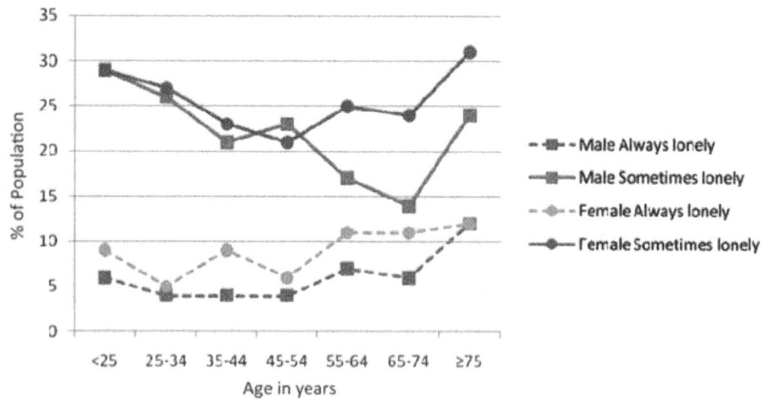

FIGURE 1. Age, gender, and loneliness in the UK (2006). (Color figure available online).

for the less than 25-year age group, the dip in loneliness for those in midlife and then an increase in loneliness in later life is broadly confirmed. For men, severe loneliness rates are broadly stable until the age of 75+ years while for women; severe loneliness rates demonstrate an increase from the age of 55 years onwards. It is clear that across almost all age groups females in the United Kingdom report higher prevalence rates of loneliness than men with the exception of the "sometimes lonely" participants aged 45–54 years. We see a substantially higher percentage of females reporting loneliness after the age of 55 years, while for men the increase is at the age of 75+ years. This suggests that for women and men the timing of the increase in loneliness is differentially distributed, suggesting that this is triggered by either different factors or differential timing of a shared event or experience such as bereavement.

We can consider the relative relationship between loneliness, age, and gender by employing the female-to-male ratio of reported levels of loneliness (Figure 1). For severe loneliness, this fluctuates across the age groups with the highest differentials being for the 35–44-year age group (female-to-male ratio of 2.2) and the 65–74-year age group (ratio of 1.8), while for those aged 75+ years, the prevalence of severe loneliness is equal for men and women. For the sometimes-lonely category, gender differences are less pronounced until the age of 55 years, while there is an excess of males reporting intermediate levels of loneliness among those aged 45–54 years (female-to-male ratio of 0.9).

What Factors Are Associated With Loneliness?

We have already established the importance of the relationship between gender and loneliness. What other factors are associated with loneliness? For our whole sample, the relationship between each factor included in our analysis and loneliness is statistically significant (see Table 2). The variation between the risk factors lies in the level of statistical significance (either 0.05 or 0.01), the strength of the relationship and the direction of the relationship (i.e., positive or negative). In our analysis, we differentiate between two types of "risk factors": vulnerability factors (those that are associated with increased loneliness) and protective factors (those linked with decreased levels of loneliness). In terms of vulnerability factors, depression demonstrates the strongest relationship with lack of an intimate/confiding relationship, poor self rated health, and being female also important. In terms of protective factors, engagement in social activities, good physical health as measured by no reported chronic illnesses, being married, tertiary education, and household size were all important.

Relationships Across the Age Groups

How robust and stable are these relationships across the broad age ranges? Are different vulnerability/protective factors more (or less) important across different age groups? To consider this question we examine the prevalence of severe loneliness (those feeling lonely all or most of the times) for each category of each risk

TABLE 2. Prevalence of Loneliness for Key Sociodemographic and Health Variables: United Kingdom 2006

Variable and range	Lonely all or most of the time	Lonely some of the time	Never lonely	Gamma
Age				−0.09**
<30	6.3	27.5	66.3	
30–59	5.5	19.6	74.9	
60+	7.4	18.4	74.2	
Gender				0.17***
Male	4.6	18.8	76.6	
Female	7.6	22.7	69.7	
Marital status				p-value of
Married/partnership	3.4	14.3	82.3	chi-square < 0.001
Divorced/separated	13.1	31.7	55.2	
Widowed	19.3	33.1	43.6	
Single	6.6	28.8	64.6	
Household size				−0.20***
1	15.4	38.6	46.0	
2	3.1	15.2	81.7	
3 and 4	5.9	17.5	76.6	
5 and above	3.7	24.9	71.4	
Education (highest)				−0.17***
Primary or below	17.6	23.5	58.8	
Secondary	7.4	21.4	71.3	
Tertiary	3.2	19.7	77.1	
Subjective physical health				0.26***
Good or very good	4.5	19.6	75.9	
Fair	8.8	25.9	65.4	
Bad or very bad	17.4	20.6	61.9	
Frequency of feeling depressed				0.66***
Never	1.8	15.7	84.5	
Sometimes	9.2	35.8	55.0	
All or most of the times	39.1	30.5	30.5	
Hampered in daily activity				−0.21***
Yes a lot	14.2	23.0	62.8	
Yes to some extent	7.1	24.7	68.2	
No	4.9	19.4	75.2	
Frequency of being social				−0.11**
Less than once a month	15.2	25.7	59.0	
Once a month or more	5.8	18.3	75.9	
Once a week or more	5.2	21.1	73.8	
Social activities				−0.22***
Less than others	10.8	25.0	64.2	
About the same	2.5	16.9	80.6	
More than others	4.9	20.9	74.2	
Have someone to discuss intimate or personal matters				0.45***
Yes	5.1	20.5	74.4	
No	20.5	26.3	53.2	

Source: ESS.

factor for three broad age groups: young adults, mid life adults and older adults. We employ the Gamma statistic (chi-square for marital status) to summarize the significance, strength, and direction of the relationship between loneliness and each risk factor for each age group (see Table 3).

Only one variable, self-reported depression, is associated with loneliness across all three age groups; moreover, the strength and direction of the relationship is also consistently strong (see Table 4). Those who report that they are depressed all, or most of the time, have the highest reported rates of loneliness at approximately 38%. No other variables are consistently linked with loneliness across all three age groups. The key socio-demographic variables (gender, marital status), household size, level of education, rating of social contact and availability of a confiding relationship are associated with loneliness for middle-aged and older adults but not with the younger adults. The relationship between loneliness and gender and household size appears to be stronger for older adults as compared with those in midlife. Severe loneliness for older and midlife adults is also linked with perceived level of social relationships and having an intimate/confiding relationship. The two measures of physical health status (self-reported health rating and limitations in daily activities) are only associated with loneliness for the young and the middle-aged groups but not with the oldest age groups. This is also true for the frequency of social contact with friends, relatives, and colleagues. All of our risk factors are associated with loneliness in midlife. However for our older participants frequency of social contact and physical health were not linked with loneliness. Conversely, physical health was linked with loneliness for young adults as was the frequency of social contact but not the availability of a confidante or their evaluation of their levels of contact. In terms of social engagement, it was the reported quantity of contacts that was important for this age group.

Discussion

In this article, we have examined patterns of loneliness among adults of differing ages within a single country, the United Kingdom, which may be characterized as a country whose prevalence rate of loneliness is "low" according to the typology of Yang and Victor (2011). We demonstrate that loneliness among adults in the United Kingdom illustrates a broadly U-shaped distribution being higher among those under 25 years and those aged over 65 years as compared with those in middle-age and that this trend is consistent for both men and women. Depression, limited quantity and quality of social engagement and being female were factors that rendered adults vulnerable to loneliness. "Protective factors" against loneliness were being married, good health, having a confidant, larger household size, and tertiary education. However, when we examine "vulnerability and protective" factors for different age groups, only depression is associated with loneliness across our three age groups. While social engagement is linked with loneliness across all three age groups, the perceived quality of social relationships

TABLE 3. The Prevalence of Frequent Loneliness (All and Most of the Times) for Three Age Groups in the UK (2006/7) and Correlation (Gamma) With Each Risk Factor

	Age group (with sample size)		
Variable	<30 years ($n = 495$)	30–59 years ($n = 1209$)	60+ years ($n = 690$)
Gender	0.04	0.16**	0.33***
Male	5.2	3.9	5.8
Female	7.0	6.9	9.1
Marital status		p of chi-square < 0.001	p of chi-square < 0.001
Married/partnership	8.4	3.1	3.0
Divorced/separated	0.0	13.2	14.5
Widowed	0.0	30.0	17.9
Single	6.0	9.4	3.1
Household size	0.06	−0.25***	−0.61***
1	3.3	14.8	17.6
2	1.9	4.2	2.5
3 and 4	7.4	5.2	6.0
5 and above	8.7	1.1	0.0
Education (highest)	0.06	−0.19**	−0.31***
Primary or below	0.0	25.0	18.2
Secondary	6.4	7.0	8.5
Tertiary	6.1	2.9	2.2
Subjective physical health	0.26**	0.42***	0.13
Good or very good	5.3	3.6	5.9
Fair	13.0	8.8	7.6
Bad or very bad	10.0	23.0	14.1
Frequency of feeling depressed	0.62***	0.68***	0.68***
Never	1.6	1.1	2.8
Sometimes	10.7	7.2	11.7
All or most of the times	35.7	40.2	39.0
Hampered in daily activity	−0.33**	−0.34***	−0.14
Yes a lot	23.1	13.6	13.6
Yes to some extent	17.6	6.7	5.5
No	4.9	4.4	6.5
Frequency of being social	−0.20*	−0.12**	−0.14
Less than once a month	29.4	12.6	20.3
Once a month or more	14.1	3.9	6.9
Once a week or more	4.1	5.0	6.2
Social activities	0.03	−0.37***	−0.23***
Less than others	10.9	10.1	11.9
About the same	2.3	1.6	4.4
More than others	7.1	4.4	3.8
Have someone to discuss intimate or personal matters	0.29	0.47***	0.50***
Yes	5.5	4.6	5.5
No	18.2	20.0	21.7

Source: ESS

*p = 0.05. **p = 0.01. ***p = 0.001.

TABLE 4. Summary of Key Factors Associated with Loneliness by Age Group in the United Kingdom (2006)

Risk factor	Young adults (15–29)	Mid life adults (30–59)	Older adults (60+)
Gender		X	X
Marital status		X	X
Education		X	X
Subjective health rating	X	X	
Self-reported limitations in daily activities	X	X	
Self-reported depression	X	X	X
Frequency of social contact	X	X	
Rating of social activities		X	X
Availability of confiding/intimate relationship		X	X

X = statistically significant relationship with severe loneliness.

was important for midlife and older adults, while what was important for young adults was the quantity of relationships. In discussing these findings, we first locate our study within previous work looking at loneliness and age. We then evaluate the strengths and limitations of the European Social Survey and our method of measuring loneliness, as these factors are important for evaluating the robustness and veracity of our findings. We conclude by discussing our key findings and consider the implications of these for both further research and the development of interventions to combat loneliness.

Research studies reporting rates of loneliness among specific age groups, such as young and older adults, have served to raise questions about the relationship between age and loneliness. Yang and Victor (2011) have hypothesized that there are two potential models of the relationship between loneliness and age: either a linear age-related trend or a nonlinear U-shaped distribution with high rates at the extremes of old age and young adulthood and low rates in the middle adult years. Preliminary analysis by Yang and Victor suggests that if we examine all of the 25 countries in the 2006 ESS as a single entity we see an age-related trend for severe loneliness (the always/most of the time category) and a nonlinear trend for the intermediate, sometimes lonely, category. When individual countries are examined separately, three broad groupings based upon the relationship between age and loneliness were identified: an age-related pattern of loneliness exemplified by the countries of Eastern Europe/Soviet Union; a nonlinear relationship of high rates at the youngest and oldest age groups as illustrated by southern European countries such as Spain and Portugal; and a third group of countries with low loneliness prevalence rates which are largely flat but which accelerate from the age of 70 years such as the countries of Northern Europe (e.g., Norway, Sweden, Denmark). In this article, we have extended this analysis by looking in detail at the patterns of loneliness among adults of differing ages within a single country, the United Kingdom, which, with an overall level of reported loneliness for adults of approximately 9%, may be characterized as a "low"-loneliness prevalence-rate country (Yang and Victor).

The link between age and loneliness and a range of vulnerability/protective factors is clearly complex and culturally situated. In this article, we have examined this relationship in depth in the United Kingdom using the ESS as this enables us to take an explicitly comparative approach towards the measurement of loneliness across the whole range of adult age groups within an individual country. There are, inevitably, some limitations of our chosen dataset as with secondary data analysis more generally. First, the ESS uses a single self-rating scale to measure loneliness. Ideally, we might have wished to include an additional method of measuring loneliness such as the scale developed by de Jong-Gierveld and Kamphuis (1985) or the UCLA scale (Russell, 1996). This would both have facilitated additional statistical analysis and provide internal validation for our findings. However, the levels of loneliness enumerated by the ESS mesh with the established literature (Sundström, Fransson, Malmberg, & Davey, 2009) and our age-specific prevalence data for the United Kingdom are very similar to those reported for the Antipodes by Flood (2005). Similarly, the prevalence of loneliness from the ESS data set of 10% for those aged 65 years and over is very similar to that from previous British studies (see Victor et al., 2002). Thus, there is consistency in loneliness prevalence rates across studies that provide external credibility for our findings.

Overall, we demonstrate that loneliness is indeed higher among those under 25 years and those aged over 65 years as compared with those in middle age. This fits with the nonlinear model of the relationship between loneliness and age proposed by Yang and Victor (2011). While this trend is broadly consistent for both men and women, we identified a "break point" at which loneliness rates accelerate for women at the 55+-year age group and at age 75+ years for men. Combined with the observed differences in prevalence rates between men and women, this suggests that either different factors are involved in the increase in loneliness for older men and women and/or that the timing of these events/factors such as widowhood, the on-set of chronic illness or the entry of a spouse into care is experienced differentially by them. This is clearly an area that merits more detailed examination, especially as understanding factors associated with increased rates of loneliness at specific ages for men and women has implications for the development of interventions to prevent/reduce loneliness. The male: female differential is most extreme in relative terms for the 35–44 year age group, where 9% of women and 4% of men report severe loneliness, although the differential for intermediate levels of loneliness is less pronounced (24% of females compared with 21% of males). The similarity of the sometimes lonely prevalence rates for men and women in this age group suggests that the difference in severe loneliness rating is not solely an artifact of men being unwilling to report that they experience loneliness. Furthermore, this intriguing finding meshes with the results of Franklin and Tranter (2008), suggesting that women aged 30–50 years are especially vulnerable to loneliness (or that men are protected). Further investigation is merited here to tease out the factors involved in the generation of this pattern and to establish the generalizability of this observation and our other gender-related relationships between age and loneliness.

It is a limitation of the ESS that, because of its focus upon measuring attitudes and values in a pan-European context, it does not include measures of some key factors associated with loneliness (e.g., expectations of old age, amount of time spent alone, and psychological traits such as self-efficacy and financial and other material resources) and includes only partial measures of some key dimensions such as chronic illness, depression, and psychological well-being. As with other studies we demonstrated a relationship between loneliness and a range of socio-demographic factors in the anticipated direction. Again, this adds external validity to our findings and thus enhances our confidence in the results of our study-in particular the relationship between age and risk factors for loneliness-not previously reported for a UK adult population. Depression, low levels of social contact, perceived low levels of social engagement and being female were factors that rendered adults vulnerable to loneliness. "Protective factors" against loneliness were being married, reporting good physical health and perceived health, having a confiding relationship, living in larger households (i.e., not living alone), and having received tertiary level education. The link with education is less often reported but mirrors the work by Victor, Scambler, Bowling, and Bond (2005) and Victor, Bond, and Scambler (2009). Our results show very clearly that education has a highly significant effect on loneliness: 3% of those with tertiary education report severe loneliness and 20% moderate loneliness compared with 20% and 24% respectively for those with only primary level education. This is an intriguing finding that merits further investigation to determine if education is acting as a proxy for access to material resources more broadly or something intrinsic to the receipt of higher education.

By examining the relationship between these factors and loneliness by age group, we have sought to identify the factors generically linked to loneliness that may underpin the societal background level of loneliness and the factors linked with loneliness as reported by our specific age groups. Depression is the one factor associated with loneliness across our three age groups and thus may well be a key factor in determining the generic level of loneliness in a given adult population. This is clearly an area for further research. Poor physical health status as measured by limitations in daily activity and perceived health rating demonstrates a clear link with loneliness for the young and midlife age groups but not for the older age group. That older people do not demonstrate such a robust link between loneliness and health rating/mobility limitations may reflect the expectations of poor health in later life: older people may anticipate health limitations and thus "cope" with the consequences better than those in youth or midlife for whom poor physical health is both unanticipated and non "normative." The relationship between age, loneliness, and social engagement is similarly intriguing. For our midlife and older populations, having a confident and the perception of their level of social engagement is protective against loneliness, while for young adults it is *the quantity* of social contact that is protective. This may link with the hypothesis of Perlman (1988), who proposed that loneliness at different stages of the life span was associated with deficits in different domains of social engagement: younger people being focused upon friendship networks (i.e., the quantity of relationships), while midlife and older adults derive their "protection" from loneliness from kinship and marital relationships as reflected in our measures of engagement quality and the importance of a confiding relationship.

These findings mesh with the conceptualization of loneliness advanced by Weiss (1973), who argued that loneliness was a relational deficit: the lack of relationships of the desired quantity and/or quality. Furthermore, Weiss distinguishes between emotional loneliness resulting from the deficit of "close" relationships and social loneliness resultant from the lack of a supportive social network. Our data suggest that younger adults experienced social loneliness as they value the size rather than quality of their social networks. Midlife and older adults illustrate a more emotional form because their sense of loneliness derives from deficits in the quality of their social engagements and loss of a confiding relationship, which links to the loss of spouse/partner, the death or entry into care of friends, or the "empty nest" syndrome when adult children leave the parental home.

These results suggest a number of avenues for more detailed investigation and further research. First, within the group of low-loneliness prevalence countries identified by Yang and Victor (2011), including Belgium, Denmark, Finland, Germany, Ireland, Netherlands, Norway, Sweden, Switzerland, and the United Kingdom, we need to examine age-related loneliness in more detail by focusing upon "finer grained" age groupings and using age as a continuous variable to established a more complete and nuanced understanding of this complex relationship. We can also extend this investigation to those countries characterized by both age-related and nonlinear patterns of loneliness and consider the similarity (or otherwise) of those in greater detail to see if they replicate the pattern of relationships observed in the United Kingdom. Second, we need to consider, in more detail, the importance, timing, and impact of the factors/events linked to loneliness by both age and gender. While loneliness is not exclusively a female issue, rates of loneliness are consistently higher among females, and the onset of late-life loneliness occurs earlier for women as compared with men. One explanation is linked to the differential age of widowhood for men and women, a hypothesis that requires further investigation. There are also potentially important areas for further research examining the factors associated with loneliness in both young adulthood and midlife. While the experience of loneliness may be universal at the individual level, it is clear that there are differences across the age groups in terms of "risk/vulnerability" factors, the triggers linked to loneliness onset, and the likelihood of recovering from loneliness. As Rook (1988) suggested, we need to develop a more nuanced and differentiated understanding of loneliness across the adult life course as a basis for developing more appropriate "age specific" interventions to prevent and mediate loneliness and in order to advance our conceptual and theoretical understanding of this complex but quintessentially human experience.

REFERENCES

American Association of Retired People (AARP). (2010). *Loneliness among older adults: A national survey of adults 45+*. Washington, DC: AARP.

Anderson, L. (1998). Loneliness research and interventions: A review of the literature. *Aging & Mental Health*, *2*, 264–274.

De Jong Gieveld, J. (1998). A review of loneliness: Concepts and definitions, causes and consequences. *Reviews in Clinical Gerontology*, *8*, 73–80.

De Jong Gierveld, J., & Kamphuis, F. (1985). The development of a Rasch-type loneliness scale. *Applied Psychological Measurement*, *9*, 289–299.

Dykstra, P. A. (2009). Older adult loneliness: Myths and realities. *European Journal of Ageing*, *6*, 91–100.

Flood, M. (2005). *Mapping loneliness in Australia*. Canberra, Australia: The Australia Institute.

Franklin, A., & Tranter, B. (2008). *Loneliness in Australia*. Research Paper 13, Housing and Community Research Unit. Hobart, Tasmania: University of Tasmania.

Green, L. R., Richardson, D. S., Lago, T., & Schatten-Jones, E. C. (2001). Network correlates of social and emotional loneliness in young and older adults. *Personality and Social Psychology Bulletin*, *27*(3), 281–288.

Griffin, J. (2010). *The lonely society?* London: The Mental Health Foundation.

Harrington, J., Perry, I., Lutomski, J., Morgan, K., McGee, H., Shelley, E., . . . Barry, M. (2008). *SLÁN 2007: Survey of lifestyle, attitudes and nutrition in Ireland*. Dublin, Ireland: The Stationery Office.

Hawkley, L., & Cacioppo, J. T. (2010). Loneliness matters: A theoretical and empirical review of consequences and mechanisms. *Annals of Behavioural Medicine*, *40*(2), 218–227.

Heylen, L. (2010). The older, the lonelier? Risk factors for social loneliness in old age. *Ageing & Society*, *30*, 1177–1196.

Hopkins, D., & King, G. (2010). Improving anchoring vignettes: Designing surveys to improve interpersonal incomparability. *Public Opinion Quarterly, 74*, 201–222.

Johnson, D. P., & Mullins, L. C. (1987). Growing old and lonely in different societies: Toward a comparative perspective. *Journal of Cross-Cultural Gerontology, 2*, 257–275.

King, G., Murry, C., Salomon, J., & Tandon, A. (2004). Enhancing the validity and cross-cultural comparability of measurements in survey research. *American Political Science Review, 98*, 191–207.

Lauder, W., Mummery, K., Jones, M., & Caperchione, C. (2006). A comparison of health behaviours in lonely and non-lonely populations. *Psychology, Health, & Medicine, 11*, 233–245.

Lauder, W., Mummery, K., & Sharkey, S. (2006). Social capital, age and religiosity in people who are lonely. *Journal of Clinical Nursing, 15*, 334–340.

Lauder, W., Sharkey, S., & Mummery, K. (2004). A community survey of loneliness. *Journal of Advanced Nursing, 46, 1*, 88–94.

Margrett, J. A., Daugherty, K., Martin, P., Macdonald, M., Davey, A., Woodard, J. L., ... & Poon, L. W. (2011). Affect and loneliness among centenarians and the oldest old: The role of individual and social resources. *Aging & Mental Health, 15*(3), 385–396.

New Zealand. (2010). *New Zealand social report 2008*. Available from http://socialreport.msd.govt.nz/social-connectedness/loneliness.html (accessed August 31, 2011).

Nolen-Hoeksema, S., & Ahrens, C. (2002). Age differences and similarities in the correlates of depressive symptoms. *Psychology and Ageing, 17*(1), 116–124.

Patterson, A. C., & Veenstra, G. (2010). Loneliness and risk of mortality: A longitudinal investigation in Alameda County, California. *Social Science and Medicine, 71*, 181–186.

Peplau, L., & Perlman, D. (Eds.). (1982). *Loneliness: A sourcebook of current theory, research and therapy*. New York: Wiley.

Perlman, D. (1988). Loneliness: A life-span, family perspective. In R. M. Milardo (Ed.), *Families and social networks* (pp. 190–220). Newbury Park, CA: Sage Publications.

Rokach, A. (2000a). Loneliness and the life cycle. *Psychological Reports, 86*, 629–642.

Rokach, A. (2000b). Perceived causes of loneliness in adulthood. *Journal of Social Behaviour and Personality, 15*(1), 67–84.

Rokach, A. (2001). Strategies of coping with loneliness throughout the lifespan. *Current Psychology: Developmental, Learning, Personality, Social, 20*, 3–18.

Rokach, A., & Neto, F. (2000). Causes of loneliness in adolescence: A cross-cultural study. *International Journal of Adolescence and Youth, 8*, 65–80.

Rokach, A., & Neto, F. (2005). Age, culture, and the antecedents of loneliness. *Social Behaviour and Personality, 33*, 477–494.

Rook, K. S. (1988). Toward a more differentiated view of loneliness. In S. Duck (Ed.), *Handbook of personal relationships: Theory, research, and interventions* (pp. 57–589). New York: Wiley.

Rotenberg, K. J., & MacKie, J. (1999). Stigmatization of social and intimacy loneliness. *Psychological Reports, 84*, 147–148.

Rowntree, S. (Chairman). (1947). *Old people : Report of a survey committee on the problems of ageing and the care of old people*. London: Oxford University Press. For the Trustees of The Nuffield Foundation.

Russell, D. (1996). UCLA Loneliness Scale (version 3): Reliability, validity, and factor structure. *Journal of Personality Assessment, 66*, 20–40.

Scharf, T., & de Jong Gierveld, J. (2008). Loneliness in urban neighbourhoods: An Anglo-Dutch comparison. *European Journal of Ageing, 5*,103–115.

Schultz, N., & Moore, D. (1988). Loneliness: Differences across three age groups. *Journal of Social and Personal Relationships, 5*, 275–284.

Steed, L., Boldy, D., & Iredell, H. (2007). The demographics of loneliness among older people in Perth, Western Australia. *Australasian Journal on Ageing*, *26*(2), 81–86.
Sundström, G., Fransson, E., Malmberg, B., & Davey, A. (2009). Loneliness among older Europeans. *European Journal of Ageing*, *6*(4), 267–275.
Tilvis, R. S, Laitala, V., Routasalo, P. E., & Pitkälä, K. H. (2011). Suffering from loneliness indicates significant mortality risk of older people. *Journal of Aging Research*. doi: 10.4061/2011/534781
Townsend, P. (1968). Isolation and loneliness. In E. Shanas, P. Townsend, D. Wedderburn, H. Friis, P. Milhoj, & J. Stehouwer (Eds.), *Old people in three industrial societies* (pp. 258–287). London: Routledge and Kegan Paul.
van Tilburg, T., Havens, B., & de Jong Gierveld, J. (2004). Loneliness among older adults in the Netherlands, Italy, and Canada: A multi-faceted comparison. *Canadian Journal on Aging*, *23*, 2, 169–180.
Victor, C. R., Bond, J., & Scambler, S. (2009). *The social world of older people*. Maidenhead, UK: Open University Press.
Victor, C. R., Grenade, L., & Boldy, D. (2005). Measuring loneliness in later life: A comparison of different measures. *Reviews in Clinical Gerontology*, *15*, 63–70.
Victor, C. R., Scambler, S. J., Bond, J., & Bowling, A. (2000). Being alone in later life: Loneliness, isolation and living alone in later life. *Reviews in Clinical Gerontology*, *10*, 407–417.
Victor, C. R., Scambler, S. J., Bowling, A., & Bond, J. (2005) The prevalence of, and risk factors for, loneliness in later life: A survey of older people in Great Britain. *Ageing and Society*, *25*(3), 357–376.
Victor, C. R., Scambler, S. J., Shah, S., Cook, D. G., Harris, T., Rink, E., & de Wilde, S. (2002). Has loneliness amongst older people increased? An investigation into variations between cohorts. *Ageing and Society*, *22*(5), 585–597.
Victor, C., Scambler, S., Marston, S., Bond, J., & Bowling, A. (2006). Older people's experiences of loneliness in the UK: Does gender matter? *Social Policy and Society*, *5*, 27–38.
Weiss, R. S. (1973). *Loneliness: The experience of emotional and social isolation*. Cambridge, MA: MIT Press.
Yang, K., & Victor, C. (2011). Age and Loneliness in 25 European nations. *Ageing & Society*, *31*, 1–21.

Association Between Loneliness and Suicidality During Middle Childhood and Adolescence: Longitudinal Effects and the Role of Demographic Characteristics

KATHERINE C. SCHINKA
MANFRED H. M. VAN DULMEN
Kent State University

ROBERT BOSSARTE
University of Rochester

MONICA SWAHN
Georgia State University

ABSTRACT. The association between loneliness and suicidality has been documented in many studies, but these studies have been limited by cross-sectional designs and the use of adult-only populations. The purpose of the current study was to overcome these limitations by (a) investigating whether the link between loneliness and suicidal thoughts and behaviors occurs cross-sectionally, longitudinally, or both and (b) investigating how the link between loneliness and suicidality might be influenced by different demographic variables, including gender, ethnicity, and socioeconomic status. Logistic regression analyses were used to analyze data from a large sample ($N = 937$) of youth from the NICHD Study of Early Child Care. Results indicated that loneliness at age 15 years was concurrently associated with both suicidal ideation and suicidal behavior at age 15 years. Loneliness in middle childhood was longitudinally associated with suicidal behaviors at age 15 years, but not with suicidal ideation at age 15 years. None of the demographic characteristics influenced these associations.

This study was conducted by the NICHD Early Child Care Research Network supported by NICHD through a cooperative agreement that calls for scientific collaboration between the grantees and the NICHD staff. This project was supported by funding from the Centers for Disease Control and Prevention (R01 CE001395).

SUICIDE is the third leading cause of death in youth between the ages of 10 and 14 years, resulting in more than 4000 adolescent deaths per year (Centers for Disease Control and Prevention [CDC], 2008). Suicide represents an important health crisis around the world, and many researchers have tested various factors that may help us understand risk for suicide. Researchers and psychologists have most commonly used demographic characteristics to understand and predict suicidality. This research provided much needed knowledge about certain groups, such as minorities and low-income people, who might be more at risk for suicide. However, the recent trend in suicide research has been to focus on psychosocial factors by themselves and in conjunction with demographic factors. Loneliness may be one psychosocial risk factor that varies across different social groups and helps explain some of the differences between them. This study aims to investigate one important risk factor for suicide, loneliness, across different demographic characteristics both cross-sectionally and longitudinally.

Loneliness in Middle Childhood and Adolescence

Loneliness results from the perception that one's interpersonal relationships do not meet personal expectations and thus are deficient (Peplau & Perlman, 1982). Although loneliness is considered a normal part of development, it can cause considerable distress. Loneliness interferes with an innate human need for belongingness in social groups (Heinrich & Gullone, 2006; Joiner, 2005). Chipuer explored this definition in a study of fifth and sixth graders (2004). Chipuer found that loneliness in middle childhood is conceptualized mainly as a combination of deficits in social relationships and distressing emotions. These children described loneliness as being left out of activities or having no one to play with, and they generally reported low to moderate levels of loneliness on the Loneliness and Social Dissatisfaction Questionnaire. Adolescents, on the other hand, tend to experience loneliness more intensely than persons of other age groups. Some studies concluded that loneliness peaks in adolescence (Brennan, 1982; Hawthorne, 2008; Goossens, 2006; van Roekel, Scholte, Verhagen, Goossens, & Engels, 2010). A recent study of a large sample of adolescents found that 36.1% of participants experienced increases in loneliness from middle childhood into adolescence (Schinka, van Dulmen, Mata, Swahn, & Bossarte, 2011). Adolescents likely report high levels of loneliness for two reasons. First, as young people enter the teenage years, peers become an increasingly important form of social support and their needs for intimacy, attachment, and acceptance are met more by peers than by family (Goossens, 2006; Parkhurst & Hopmeyer, 1999). In addition, some adolescents start spending more time alone, and they tend to perceive aloneness as negative instead of a time for quiet solitude (Koenig & Abrams, 1999).

Loneliness has consistently been associated with negative mental health outcomes. Adolescents who suffer from chronic loneliness are more likely to experience more psychopathology, including internalizing and externalizing problems

(Goossens, 2006; Koenig & Abrams, 1999; Schinka, van Dulmen, Mata, Swahn, & Bossarte, 2011). We recently found that children and adolescents who experience chronically high levels of loneliness are more likely to report depression, suicidality, aggression, and social-skills deficits in adolescence (Schinka, van Dulmen, Mata, Swhan, & Bossarte, 2011). Further, children who perceive themselves to become lonelier throughout middle childhood and adolescence display more depression and externalizing problems compared to those children who do not become lonelier over time (Jones, Schinka, van Dulmen, Bossarte, & Swahn, in press). Other researchers found that loneliness predicts depression even when controlling for baseline depression symptoms (Koenig & Abrams, 1999). Last, loneliness is associated with poorer general health (Hawthorne, 2008; Qualter & Brown, 2010).

Loneliness can be severe enough to lead to death by suicide (Heinrich & Gullone, 2006; Trout, 1980). In general, the perception of a lack of satisfying interpersonal relationships can be so damaging to adolescents that it predicts suicidality (Jeglic, Pepper, Vanderhoff, & Ryabchenko, 2007). One study of Asian adolescents found a positive association between loneliness and suicide attempts in the past 12 months and lifetime suicide attempts (Page, Yanagishita, Suwanteerangkul, Zarco, Mei-Lee, & Maio, 2006). Roberts and colleagues (1998) found that adolescents with a high degree of loneliness were two times as likely to exhibit suicidal ideation. In an effort to parse out the differences in these associations, Negron and colleagues (1997) compared a group of adolescent suicide ideators and a group of adolescent suicide attempters between the ages of 12 and 17 years. They found that, as compared to suicide ideators, suicide attempters were more likely to report more isolation.

Loneliness and Suicide Across Demographic Groups

Ethnicity. In regards to suicide, there are clear ethnic differences. Across all ages, American Indian and Alaskan Native males have the highest suicide rates with Caucasian males falling close behind (CDC, 2008). Lower suicide rates in adult minority populations have been attributed to increased social support and religious connections in certain subpopulations, such as Hispanics (Joiner, 2005). There is some evidence that the same mechanism may be at work in adolescents. In a clinical sample, African American adolescents reported more social support than Caucasian participants, and those adolescents who reported less social support also had higher depression scores and reported more suicidal ideation (Joe, Clarke, Ivey, Kerr, & King, 2007). However, in the past decade minority suicide rates (Hispanics, African Americans, Native Americans) have increased overall (Rutter & Behrendt, 2004). African American adolescents have a significantly higher attempt rate than Caucasian adolescents, and African American males have experienced the greatest rate increase in suicidality in recent decades (Joe & Marcus, 2003). Furthermore,

African American adolescents have both the highest number and the highest percentage of suicides in all of the African American population, and cohort studies have shown them to be more at risk than older generations (Crosby & Molock, 2006; Joe, 2006).

In regards to loneliness, some researchers suggest that ethnic minority status may lead to loneliness because of discrimination and differences in social expectations (King & Merchant, 2008; van Bergen, Smit, van Balkom, van Ameijden, & Saharso, 2008). Despite this conjecture, many studies have found no differences in loneliness across ethnic groups (Brennan & Auslander, 1979; Page & Cole, 1991), or at least the variables that predict loneliness are similar across ethnic groups (Jones, Carpenter, & Quintana, 1985).

Gender. It is clear that males and females exhibit differences in loneliness, but the direction of the differences is debated. While some studies reported no statistical differences in loneliness between males and females (Koenig & Abrams, 1999; Marcoen, Goosens, & Caes, 1987), other studies directly contradict each other. Some say females report more loneliness in adolescence (Brennan, 1982; Brennan & Auslander, 1979; Hawthorne, 2008) while others claim males report more loneliness (Koenig, Isaacs, & Schwartz, 1994; Rich, Kirkpatrick-Smith, Bonner, & Jans, 1992). In the most recent study on prevalence rates of loneliness in a community sample, Hawthorne and colleagues (2008) found that females were more likely than males to experience chronic loneliness across all ages, but that these differences were not statistically significant. Meanwhile, one longitudinal study on loneliness lent results which suggest that the level of loneliness for adolescent females remains fairly stable across time while males exhibit a slight decrease across the same time period (van Roekel, Scholte, Verhagen, Goossens, & Engels, 2010). The goal of the current study is to parse out some of these findings by investigating the moderating effect of gender on the loneliness-suicide link. In regards to suicide, it has been well documented that females tend to ideate more often than males; however, males attempt suicide at four times the rate of their female counterparts (CDC, 2008).

Socioeconomic status. In regards to socioeconomic status and loneliness, there is a surplus of research concerning retired and elderly people but few studies regarding how economic strain may impact children and adolescents. Overall, there is a significant relationship between economic standing and loneliness. Poorer and less educated males and females generally report the highest rates of isolation and loneliness (Chen & Chung, 2007; Fischer & Phillips, 1982; Ozdemir & Tuncay, 2008). In a study of adults 18 years and older, Lauder, Mummery, and Sharkey (2006) found that participants with the lowest reported income also reported the highest rates of loneliness. Participants in this study reported decreases in loneliness with higher income. Hawthorne (2008) also assessed income in his study of prevalence rates of loneliness. He found income to be negatively correlated with loneliness and unemployed participants to be 11 times more likely to be isolated. Mullins (1991) also found inadequate income to be associated with increased loneliness in a sample of 16–65-year-olds. One study of adolescents in a rural, farming community found that economic strain in the family is directly linked to a factor consisting of depression and loneliness (Lempers, Clark-Lempers, & Simone, 1989).

Experiences of economic strain are also associated with increased suicidality. Economic strains may include job loss, demotion, loss of home, or receiving government assistance (Rojas & Stenberg, 2010; Stack & Wasserman, 2007). One qualitative study, for instance, found that medical records of suicide victims indicated unemployment almost half of the time (Stack & Wasserman, 2007). In addition, Chinese researchers found an inverse association between economic growth and suicide rates for both males and females (Zhang et al., 2010). As gross domestic product and average income increased, suicide rates decreased. Even children can be influenced by economic strain. Rojas and Stenberg (2010) found that poverty in childhood predicted suicide in adolescence and young adulthood.

Summary and Goals of Current Study

The above studies clearly delineate an association between loneliness and suicide. They also implicate associations between ethnicity, gender, and socioeconomic status with loneliness and suicidality. These studies have significant shortcomings that limit their generalizability to children and adolescents. First, the research on loneliness and suicide is limited by cross-sectional designs. More research is needed to see if loneliness impacts suicidality over the long-term. Second, many studies concerning demographic factors, specifically socioeconomic status, are limited by using adult samples. The implications for risk in children and adolescents are largely unknown. Last, studying the above demographic factors is important for epidemiological purposes because it is informative about *who* is at risk, but it does not inform us *why* these subgroups may be at risk (Rutter & Behrendt, 2004). The current research aims to investigate the combined effects of demographic factors and loneliness in order to give a more complete picture of who is at risk for suicide; this may prove helpful in tailoring invention for youth at risk.

The current study has three goals. First, we want to see if the effect of loneliness on suicidality is time-limited (cross-sectional) or longitudinal (from middle childhood to adolescence). Second, we will test whether loneliness predicts suicidality differently across ethnicity, gender, and socioeconomic status. Third, since previous studies indicate psychosocial risk factors may differ for suicidal thoughts and suicidal behaviors (Negron, Piacentini, Graae, Davies, & Shaffer, 1997), we conducted analyses separately for these two outcomes. Based on previous research in adult samples, we expect that loneliness will be associated with suicidal ideation and suicidal behavior concurrently and longitudinally. We also expect that minority status, female gender, and lower income status will interact with loneliness score to predict more suicidality in these groups.

Method

Participants

Data for this study came from 937 study participants with complete data from the NICHD Study of Early Child Care (NICHD SECC, NICHD Early Child Care Research Network, 2000). This national, multisite study followed children from birth through age 15 years and gathered information during four phases. Data was collected from multiple informants, including mothers, fathers, and the study children themselves. This sample was 80.4% Caucasian and almost equally distributed among genders (51.7% male, 48.3% female).

The current study used data from Phases 3 and 4 of this dataset. Phase 3 took place during middle childhood when the study children were in grades three through six. Phase 4 took place when participants were 15 years old.

Measures

Demographic characteristics. Gender, ethnicity, and socioeconomic status were the included demographic variables. Socioeconomic status was measured using an income-to-needs ratio. The income-to-needs ratio variable was created by the NICHD SECC using an equation reflecting total family income and the number of persons in the family. Higher income-to-needs ratios indicate higher affluence. Income-to-needs ratios lower than 1 indicate families living below poverty line.

Loneliness. Loneliness was measured in middle childhood at grades three and five using the Loneliness and Social Dissatisfaction Questionnaire (Asher, Hymel, & Renshaw, 1984). Sixteen items from this self-report measure examine the study child's perception of his or her peer relationships. Item examples include "I feel alone," "I don't have anyone to play with," "There's nobody I can go to when I need help," and "I'm lonely." Each item was scored on a Likert scale from 1 (*not at all true*) to 5 (*always true*). Higher scores indicate higher levels of loneliness.

The highest loneliness score, regardless of whether it is in grade three or five, was used for each study child. The correlation between the scores in these two grades was moderate ($r = .41, p < .001$). The Loneliness and Social Dissatisfaction Questionnaire has been tested with African American and Hispanic American children and has been found to be a psychometrically valid measure for use in minority populations (Bagner, Storch, & Roberti, 2004).

Suicidal ideation. Suicidal ideation was measured at age 15 years using mother report from The Child Behavior Checklist and the Youth Self-Report (Achenbach, 1991, 1992). Items included "Child talks about killing self" (CBCL) and "I think about killing myself" (YSR). Item responses were dichotomized into "yes" and "no" responses. Endorsement of either of these items by the mother or study youth constituted suicidal ideation. At age 15 years, 5.1% reported suicidal thoughts ($N = 69$).

Suicidal behavior. Suicidal behavior was measured at age 15 years using mother report from the Child Behavior Checklist and the Youth Self-Report (Achenbach, 1991, 1992). Items included "Child harms self/attempts suicide" (CBCL) and "I deliberately try to hurt or kill myself" (YSR). Item responses were dichotomized into "yes" and "no" responses. Similar to the suicidal ideation construct, endorsement of either item from either informant constituted suicidal behavior. At age 15 years, 2.8% of the current sample reported suicidal behavior ($N = 38$).

Analysis Plan

Binary logistic regressions were used in this study because dichotomous group membership (suicidal behavior or no suicidal behavior; suicidal ideation or no suicidal ideation) was predicted from a continuous independent variable. Several sets of logistic regression analyses were conducted. The first model tested the cross-sectional link between loneliness and suicidal ideation at age 15 years. The second model tested the cross-sectional link between loneliness and suicidal behaviors at age 15 years.

The next two logistic regressions tested these same relationships, but longitudinally instead of cross-sectionally. We tested the link between loneliness in middle childhood and suicidal ideation at age 15 years and the link between loneliness in middle childhood and suicidal behaviors at age 15 years. In all of the above analyses, ethnicity, gender, and socioeconomic status were considered controls. Next, we added interaction terms to investigate whether demographic variables (ethnicity, gender, income-to-needs ratio) moderated the association between loneliness and suicidal ideation and suicidal behaviors.

Results

We first wanted to establish whether loneliness was cross-sectionally associated with suicidal behavior and thoughts after control for demographic factors (see Table 1). The first model indicated that loneliness at age 15 years was concurrently related to suicidal thoughts at age 15 years ($e^B = 1.94$, $p < .001$). The second model indicated that adolescent loneliness at age 15 years was also concurrently related to suicidal behavior at age 15 years ($e^B = 1.86$, $p < .001$). In other words, risk for suicidal thoughts and suicidal behavior increased by 94% and 86% respectively for each 1-point increase in loneliness at age 15 years.

Next, we investigated whether the effect of loneliness on suicidal behavior and thoughts extends across time (see Table 1). We found that higher levels of loneliness in middle childhood were associated with suicidal behavior at age 15 years ($e^B = 1.37$, $p < .05$), suggesting that with each one point increase in loneliness in middle childhood, risk for suicidal behavior at age 15 years increased by 37%. However, loneliness in middle childhood was not significantly associated with suicidal thoughts at age 15 years.

TABLE 1. Results of Logistic Regression Analyses Predicting Adolescent Suicidal Behavior and Suicidal Ideation from Loneliness During Middle Childhood and Adolescence (N = 937)

	Adolescent Suicidal Behavior				Adolescent Suicidal Ideation			
	Middle Childhood Predictors		Adolescent Predictors		Middle Childhood Predictors		Adolescent Predictors	
Variable	B (SE B)	e^B	B (SE B)	e^B	B (SE B)	e^B	B (SE B)	e^B
Gender	.24 (.33)	1.27	.22 (.35)	1.25	.27 (.26)	1.31	.36 (.27)	1.43
Income-to-Needs Ratio	.03 (.04)	1.03	.03 (.04)	1.03	−.07 (.04)	.94	−.06 (.05)	.94
Ethnicity	.54 (.38)	1.71	.32 (.40)	1.37	.12 (.26)	1.13	−.05 (.27)	.96
Loneliness	.31* (.16)	1.37	.62** (.14)	1.86	.18 (.12)	1.19	.66** (.11)	1.94
$\chi^2(4)$	6.26		18.73**		6.86		38.78**	

*$p < .05$. **$p < .001$.

A second set of analyses was run separately using the different demographic variables—gender, ethnicity, and income-to-needs ratio—as moderators. None of these analyses produced statistically significant results. These statistics indicate that gender, ethnicity, and socioeconomic status do not moderate the association between loneliness and suicidal ideation or the association between loneliness and suicidal behavior.

Discussion

The purpose of the current study was to investigate how loneliness in middle childhood and adolescence is related to suicidal thoughts and suicidal behaviors cross-sectionally and longitudinally. In addition, we investigated differences in these connections among different demographic factors: gender, ethnicity, and socioeconomic status. We found loneliness to be related to suicidality. Specifically, we found a longitudinal link between loneliness in middle childhood and suicidal behaviors at age 15 years. However, the link between loneliness and suicidal thoughts did not hold up across time and was only cross-sectional in nature. Further, there were no differences in the association between loneliness and suicidality among different demographic groups. Ethnicity, gender, and socioeconomic status did not moderate the association between loneliness and suicidality.

The findings in the current study are consistent with previous research on loneliness and suicide (Heinrich & Gullone, 2006) and offer several important extensions. First, the loneliness and suicide link has primarily been studied in adult populations. Extending this association to children and adolescents is important because loneliness is likely more prevalent during the non-adult years (Heinrich & Gullone, 2006). Hawthorne (2008) found participants between the ages of 15 years and 30 years to be specifically at risk for loneliness. In a study of second, fourth, and sixth graders, Luftig (1987) found that the younger children reported the highest levels of loneliness.

Second, these findings suggest a longitudinal element in the link between loneliness and suicidal behavior. Past studies have been limited by cross-sectional designs that do not allow prediction across time. While loneliness does impact immediate psychological functioning, the current study is important because it shows that loneliness also has serious long-term effects on psychological functioning. Namely, loneliness in middle childhood longitudinally influenced suicidal behavior at age 15 years.

Third, previous studies focused on suicidality as either a broad construct or as consisting of only suicidal thoughts or suicidal behaviors. We eliminated this drawback by differentiating between suicidal ideation, or thoughts about suicide, and suicidal behaviors. This differentiation is important since Negron and colleagues (1997) found differences in isolation between suicide attempters and suicide ideators. This distinction was salient in the current study since we found a longitudinal link with only suicidal behaviors and not suicidal thoughts. Given the lack of specificity in longitudinal research in this area, this finding is important as it raises the question of how predictors of suicidal thoughts and behaviors differ longitudinally. Perhaps psychosocial risk factors are more important as distal predictors for suicidal behaviors.

Fourth, a large proportion of suicide research has been based solely on demographic factors, and studies using only minority populations have been mostly qualitative in nature or have only reported on prevalence rates (e.g., Joe, 2006; Joe & Marcus, 2003). The current study built off these studies by investigating demographic factors in conjunction with psychosocial factors. According to the current results, demographic factors did not moderate the relationship between loneliness and suicidal thoughts or suicidal behaviors. This finding shows that, although demographic characteristics are informative about prevalence rates, psychosocial factors are important in predicting suicidality and should be the focus of prevention efforts.

Implications for Research and Practice

The results of current study serve as further evidence that demographic factors alone cannot tell us who is at risk for suicidal thoughts and behaviors. Instead, psychosocial factors—specifically those concerning peer relationships—are important for understanding suicidality. In this case, loneliness influenced both concurrent and future suicidality.

The longitudinal association between loneliness and suicidal behavior is particularly meaningful in that it shows the serious long-term effects of deficits in interpersonal relationships. This knowledge can inform approaches to intervention by emphasizing the importance of interpersonal relationships on long-term psychological functioning. Prevention efforts could focus on recognizing children who lack meaningful peer relationships and on ameliorating this problem through either social-skills training or facilitation of building relationships with other children.

Limitations of the Current Study

Suicide is a low base rate phenomenon, and the data in this study are no exception. The current national rate of suicidal ideation is 13.8%, and the rate of suicide attempt is 6.3% (Youth Risk Behavior Survey; Eaton et al., 2010). From our community low-risk sample, our rates of suicidal ideation and behavior were lower than national averages: 5.1% and 2.8%, respectively. In addition, it is possible that the null demographic results were the product of a fairly highly functioning, homogeneous sample. The sample was mostly Caucasian, with only a small percentage of families living on the threshold of poverty.

Further, valid measurement of loneliness is often debated. Researchers have argued that loneliness should be investigated in a multidimensional way, or by researching multiple informants, multiple contexts, and different affinities for loneliness (Marcoen, Goossens, & Caes, 1987). The Loneliness and Social Dissatisfaction Questionnaire (Asher, Hymel, & Renshaw, 1984) is a unidimensional measure since it reflects loneliness only in the peer context. Thus, we can only generalize these findings and the important relationship between loneliness and suicidality to peer relationships. Future research on the link between loneliness and suicide would be remiss not to include measure of loneliness in several contexts. In particular, it would be interesting to investigate to what extent loneliness in family contexts contributes to mental health functioning.

Conclusions

In conclusion, this study illustrated the importance of studying how psychosocial factors, specifically loneliness, are associated with suicidality. Loneliness at age 15 years was concurrently associated with suicidal thoughts and suicidal behavior at age 15 years, and loneliness in middle childhood was longitudinally associated with suicidal behaviors at age 15 years. This is one of the first studies to link loneliness in childhood with suicidal behavior in adolescence, thus establishing a longitudinal association. Further, we found that this association did not differ across ethnicity, gender, or socioeconomic status.

REFERENCES

Achenbach, T. M. (1991). *Manual for the Youth Self-Report and 1991 Profile*. Burlington, VT: University of Vermont, Department of Psychiatry.

Achenbach, T. M. (1992). *Manual for the Child Behavior Checklist 2–3 and 1992 Profile*. Burlington, VT: University of Vermont, Department of Psychiatry.

Asher, S. R., Hymel, S., & Renshaw, P. (1984). Loneliness in children. *Child Development*, *55*, 1456–1464.

Bagner, D. M., Storch, E. A., & Roberti, J. W. (2004). A factor analytic study of the Loneliness and Social Dissatisfaction Scale in sample of African-American and Hispanic-American children. *Child Psychiatry & Human Development*, *34*, 237–250.

Brennan, T. (1982). Loneliness at adolescence. In L. A. Peplau & D. Perlman (Eds.), *Loneliness: A sourcebook of current theory, research, and therapy* (pp. 269–290). New York: Wiley.

Brennan, T., & Auslander, N. (1979). *Adolescent loneliness: An exploratory study of social and psychological predispositions and theory* (Vol. 1). Bethesda, MD: National Institute of Mental Health, Juvenile Problems Division.

Centers for Disease Control and Prevention (CDC), National Center for Injury Prevention and Control. (2008). *Suicide: Facts at a glance*. Atlanta, GA: CDC, National Center for Injury Prevention and Control. Retrieved January 4, 2010, from http://www.cdc.gov/ncipc/dvp/Suicide/SuicideDataSheet.pdf.

Chen, L. J. & Chung, S. K. (2007). Loneliness, social connectedness, and family income among undergraduate females and males in Taiwan. *Social Behavior and Personality, 35*, 1353–1364.

Chipuer, H. M. (2004). Australian children's understanding of loneliness. *Australian Journal of Psychology, 56*, 147–153.

Crosby, A. E. & Molock, S. D. (2006). Introduction: Suicidal behaviors in the African American community. *Journal of Black Psychology, 32*, 253–261.

Eaton, D. K., Kann, L., Kinchen, S., Shanklin, S., Ross, J., Hawkins, J., Harris, W. A., Lowry, R., McManus, T., Chyen, D., Lim, C., Whittle, L., Brener, N. D., & Wechsler, H. (2010). Youth risk behavior surveillance : United States, 2009. *MMWR Weekly, 59*(SS 5), 1–36.

Fischer, C. S. & Phillips, S. L. (1982). Who is alone? Social characteristics of people with small networks. In L. A. Peplau & D. Perlman (Eds.), *Loneliness: A sourcebook of current theory, research, and therapy* (pp. 269–290). New York: Wiley.

Goossens, L. (2006). Affect, emotion, and loneliness in adolescence. In S. Jackson & L. Goossens (Eds.), *Handbook of adolescent development* (pp. 51–70). Hove, Great Britain: Psychology Press.

Hawthorne, G. (2008). Perceived social isolation in a community sample: Its prevalence and correlates with aspects of peoples' lives. *Social Psychiatry and Psychiatric Epidemiology, 43*, 140 150.

Heinrich, L. M. & Gullone, E. (2006). The clinical significance of loneliness. *Clinical Psychology Review, 26*, 695–718.

Jeglic, E. L., Pepper, C. M., Vanderhoff, H. A., & Ryabchenko, K. A. (2007). An analysis of suicidal ideation in a college sample. *Archives of Suicide Research, 11*, 41–56.

Joe, S. (2006). Explaining changes in the patterns of Black suicide in the United States from 1981 to 2002: An age, cohort, and period analysis. *Journal of Black Psychology, 32*, 262–284.

Joe, S., Clarke, J., Ivey, A. Z., Kerr, D., & King, C. A. (2007). Impact of familial factors and psychopathology on suicidality among African American adolescents. *Journal of Human Behavior in the Social Environment, 15*, 199–218.

Joe, S. & Marcus, S. C. (2003). Data points: Trends by race and gender in suicide attempts among U.S. adolescents, 1991–2001. *Psychiatric Services, 54*, 454.

Joiner, T. E. (2005). *Why people die by suicide*. Cambridge, MA: Harvard University Press.

Jones, A. C., Schinka, K. C., van Dulmen, M. H. M, Bossarte, R., & Swahn, M. (in press). Changes in loneliness during middle childhood predict risk for adolescent suicidality indirectly through mental health problems. *Journal of Clinical Child and Adolescent Psychology*.

Jones, W. H., Carpenter, B. N., & Quintana, D. (1985). Personality and interpersonal predictors of loneliness in two cultures. *Journal of Personality and Social Psychology, 48*, 1503–1511.

King, C. A., & Merchant, C. (2008). Social and interpersonal factors relating to adolescent suicidality: A review of the literature. *Archives of Suicide Research, 12*, 181–196.

Koenig, L. J., & Abrams, R. F. (1999). Adolescent loneliness and adjustment: A focus on gender differences. In K. J. Rotenberg & S. Hymel (Eds.), *Loneliness in childhood and adolescence* (pp. 296–322). Cambridge, UK: Cambridge University Press.

Koenig, L. J., Isaacs, A. M., & Schwartz, J. A. J. (1994). Sex differences in adolescent depression and loneliness: Why are boys lonelier if girls are more depressed? *Journal of Research in Personality, 28*, 27–43.

Lauder, W., Mummery, K., & Sharkey, S. (2006). Social capital, age, and religiosity in people who are lonely. *Journal of Clinical Nursing, 15*, 334–340.

Marcoen, A., Goossens, L., & Caes, P. (1987). Loneliness in pre- through late adolescence: Exploring the contributions of a multidimensional approach. *Journal of Youth and Adolescence, 16*, 561–577.

Negron, R., Piacentini, J., Graae, F., Davis, M., & Shaffer, D. (1997). Microanalysis of adolescent suicide attempters and ideators during the acute suicidal episode. *Journal of the American Academy of Child and Adolescent Psychiatry, 36*, 1512–1519.

NICHD Early Child Care Research Network. (2000). The relation of child care to cognitive and language development. *Child Development, 71*, 958–978.

Ozdemir, U., & Tuncay, T. (2008). Correlates of loneliness among university students. *Child and Adolescent Psychiatry and Mental Health, 2*, 29.

Page, R. M., & Cole, G. E. (1991). Demographic predictors of self-reported loneliness in adults. *Psychological Reports, 68*, 939–945.

Page, R. M., Yanagishita, J., Suwanteerangkul, J., Zarco, E. P., Mei-Lee, C., & Miao, N. (2006). Hopelessness and loneliness among suicide attempters in school-based samples of Taiwanese, Philippine, and Thai adolescents. *School Psychology International, 27*, 583–598.

Parkhurst, J. T., & Hopmeyer, A. (1999). Developmental change in the sources of loneliness in childhood and adolescence: Constructing a theoretical model. In K. J. Rotenberg & S. Hymel (Eds.), *Loneliness in childhood and adolescence* (pp. 56–79). Cambridge, UK: Cambridge University Press.

Peplau, L. A., & Perlman, D. (1982). *Loneliness: A sourcebook of current theory, research, and therapy*. New York: Wiley.

Qualter, P., & Brown, S. L. (2010, March). *Trajectories of loneliness during childhood and adolescence*. Paper presented at the meeting of the Society for Research on Adolescence, Philadelphia, PA.

Rich, A. R., Kirkpatrick-Smith, J., Bonner, R. L., & Jans, F. (1992). Gender differences in the psychosocial correlates of suicidal ideation among adolescents. *Suicide and Life-Threatening Behavior, 22*, 364–373.

Roberts, R. E., Roberts, C. R., & Chen, R. Y. (1998). Suicidal thinking among adolescents with a history of attempted suicide. *Journal of the American Academy of Child & Adolescent Psychiatry, 37*, 1294–1300.

Rojas, Y., & Stenberg, S.-A. (2010). Early life circumstances and male suicide: A 30-year follow-up of a Stockholm cohort born in 1953. *Social Sciences and Medicine, 70*, 420–427.

Rutter, P. A., & Behrendt, A. E. (2004). Adolescent suicide risk: Four psychosocial factors. *Adolescence, 39*, 295–302.

Schinka, K. C., van Dulmen, M. H. M., Mata, A. D., Swahn, M., & Bossarte, R. (2011, April). *Predictors and outcomes of loneliness trajectories from middle childhood to adolescence*. Paper presented at the meeting of the Society for Research on Child Development, Montreal, Canada.

Stack, S., & Wasserman, I. (2007). Economic strain and suicide risk: A qualitative analysis. *Suicide and Life-Threatening Behavior, 37*, 103–112.

Trout, D. (1980). The role of social isolation in suicide. *Suicide and Life-Threatening Behavior, 10*, 10–23.

van Bergen, D. D., Smit, J. H., van Balkom, A. J. L. M., van Ameijden, E., & Saharso, S. (2008). Suicidal ideation in ethnic minority and majority adolescents in Utrecht, The Netherlands. *Crisis, 29*, 202–208.

van Roekel, E., Scholte, R. H. J., Verhagen, M., Goossens, L., & Engels, R. C. M. E. (2010). Loneliness in adolescence: Gene x environment interactions involving the serotonin transporter gene. *Journal of Child Psychology and Psychiatry, 51*, 747–754.

Zhang, J., Ma, J., Jia, C., Sun, J., Guo, X., Xu, A., & Li, W. (2010). Economic growth and suicide rate changes: A case in China from 1982 to 2005. *European Psychiatry, 25*, 159–163.

Family of Origin Environment and Adolescent Bullying Predict Young Adult Loneliness

CHRIS SEGRIN
NATALIE NEVAREZ
ANALISA ARROYO
JAKE HARWOOD
University of Arizona

ABSTRACT. This study tested parental loneliness, family of origin environment, and a history of being bullied as predictors of loneliness in young adults. The role of social skills in young adults' loneliness was also examined. Participants were 111 young-adult–parent dyads who completed measures of loneliness and the family communication environment. In addition, young adults completed measures of social skills and history of being bullied. Predictions were tested with structural equation modeling, path analysis, and multiple regression analysis. Results showed that parental loneliness and a history of being bullied were each significant predictors of young adult loneliness. A family environment that supported open communication was negatively associated with young adults' loneliness. Parental loneliness and a history of being bullied each had direct effects on young adults' loneliness as well as indirect effects through reduced social skills.

LONELINESS is a pervasive psychosocial problem that can affect people throughout the lifespan with impaired quality of life. For example, loneliness tends to be strongly associated with psychological problems such as depression (Cacioppo, Hawkley, & Thisted, 2010; Segrin, 1998) and social anxiety (Stednitz & Epkins, 2006). Loneliness also appears to have deleterious effects on physical health (Hawkley & Cacioppo, 2003; Segrin & Passalacqua, 2010). As the serious consequences of loneliness are beginning to be documented and understood, researchers are attempting to understand the origins or risk factors for loneliness as well as the implications of loneliness for interpersonal well-being. Toward that end, the primary aims of this investigation were to examine family and peer contributions to loneliness in young adults, to examine the association between loneliness and poor social skills in young adults, and to examine how loneliness and social skills might be directly or indirectly affected by family of origin and peer experiences.

Recent evidence has showed that loneliness tends to run in families and other social networks (e.g., Cacioppo, Fowler, & Christakis, 2009; Distel et al., 2010). The agglomeration of loneliness within families suggests that many people may be predisposed to experience loneliness by factors inherent in their family of origin. Indeed Rokach (2003) argued that one's family of origin can contribute significantly to the experience of loneliness. This prediction was supported in a large scale descriptive analysis in which participants often cited cold or maladaptive family environments as playing an important role in their experience of loneliness (Rokach, 1989). Theoretically, there are several mechanisms that could contribute to family resemblance for loneliness. One possibility is social learning. Environmental, psychological, and skills deficits that cause parents to be lonely impact the child directly and indirectly though dysfunctional modeling by the lonely parent. Presumably a lonely parent would not be an effective model for behaviors such as conversation initiation, conflict resolution, greeting and meeting strangers, and so forth. Absent an effective role model for these crucial communication behaviors, children may not readily acquire the behaviors and therefore be at risk for loneliness. Experimental research shows that social learning of effective communication skills in children is dependent upon observation of a competent adult model (Sonnenschein & Whitehurst, 1981). Another theory of nonindependence of loneliness among family members centers on genetic contributions (Distal et al.). Distal et al. documented heritable components of loneliness and estimated that 37% of the variance in loneliness is explainable by genetic factors. In either case, it appears that parent loneliness may be an important predictor of child loneliness.

Parents may have relatively direct effects on their offspring's loneliness though corrupted modeling and genetic transmission. At the same time, they may contribute to their children's loneliness more indirectly though creation of dysfunctional family environments. A substantial theme in the accounts of loneliness offered by the adult participants in the Rokach (1989) investigation was a poor family of origin environment marked by coldness, inhibited expression of feelings, and feeling misunderstood by parents. Adolescents' loneliness is similarly predicted by interparental conflict and low family cohesion (Johnson, LaVoie, & Mahoney, 2001). When people do not feel supported and free to express their thoughts and feelings in the family of origin, they may consequently feel alienated, disconnected, and misunderstood—the very components of loneliness. Parental loneliness may increase the propensity to create a family environment that increases the potential for offspring loneliness. Lonely parents tend to have low parenting self-efficacy (indicated by problems with nurturance, discipline, and supporting the child's socialization with peers) that can contribute to a family environment that promotes loneliness in their children (Junttila, Vauras, & Laakkonen, 2007).

Naturally, the experience of loneliness is not just predicted by parent and family factors but by peer relations as well. Another theme that is common in descriptions of loneliness experiences is aversive social experiences in which people had negative or hurtful interactions with friends and peers (Rokach, 1989). One such aversive peer experience that is emerging as an important predictor of loneliness is bullying (e.g., Woods, Done, & Kalsi, 2009). Two massive international surveys with sample sizes in excess of 100,000 each showed that being the victim of bullying is significantly and positively associated with loneliness in young people (Due et al., 2005; Fleming & Jacobsen, 2009). Due et al. specifically estimated that bullying increased the odds of victims' loneliness by a factor of 2–4 times. A history of aversive social experiences is assumed to impact people's readiness to relate to others and to get close to them (Rokach, 1989). Inhibitions of these interpersonal processes could predispose people to loneliness.

An additional factor that may play a role in both parental transmission and bullying effects on loneliness is social skill. People who are lonely often exhibit problems with social skills (Riggio & Kwong, 2009). However, the relationship between loneliness and poor social skills is somewhat complex. Some theoretical models specify poor social skills as an antecedent of loneliness. According to the "skills deficit" model (e.g., Jones, 1982), people with poor social skills would find it difficult to achieve their interpersonal goals and to connect with others in effective and meaningful ways. Consequently, loneliness would follow from this state of affairs. There is empirical evidence in the literature supportive of the skills deficit model (e.g., Segrin, 1993, 1999; Segrin & Flora, 2000). An alternative model, sometimes referred to as the "atrophy model," specifies social skills deficits as a consequence of loneliness (e.g., Spitzberg & Hurt, 1989; Young, 1982). In this model, people who become lonely are thought to have few opportunities to cultivate and practice their social skills. Over time, the skills deteriorate from lack of use.

It is plausible that the skills deficit model could be useful for explaining situational impacts on loneliness through poor social skills. For example, an impoverished family environment in which children do not learn good social skills could make them vulnerable to subsequent loneliness, as indicated in the skills deficit model. The atrophy model might provide a plausible account of how factors that readily precipitate loneliness (e.g., separation, loss, bullying/alienation) could eventually lead to deterioration in people's social skills as they have less practice with social interactions.

The present investigation tests parental loneliness, family of origin environment, and a history of being bullied as potential predictors of young adults' loneliness. We conceptualized a functional family environment as one in which family members feel free to express their thoughts and feelings and feel supported in doing so. Such functional family environments leave family members feeling satisfied with their interactions and content with the family's communication patterns. This type of family of origin environment is assumed to protect against loneliness. We felt that it was important to assess the family of origin environment from the perspectives of both the young adult and his/her parents to get a more comprehensive and accurate picture of the family's functioning. After assessing the association between parental loneliness and family of origin environment and young adults' loneliness, we sought to test two models that explained the relationships between parental loneliness, bullying, and young adults' social skills and loneliness. One was guided by the atrophy model, and the other was guided by the skills deficit model.

Method

Participants

Participants were 111 students enrolled at a large university in the Southwestern United States and 1 of their parents. Students' ages had an average of M = 20.77 years (SD = 2.93 years), with 45 male and 75 female respondents. Their race/ethnicity was 83% White/Caucasian, 7% Latino, 4% other, 3% Black/African American, and 3% Asian. The majority (76%) of the parents were mothers, and they had a mean age of 52.10 years (SD = 5.09 years). The parent participants were 86% White/Caucasian, 6% Latino, 4% Asian, 3% Black/African American, and 1% American Indian. Parents' highest levels of education completed were 1% some high school, 7% high school, 27% some college/associate's degree, 35% bachelor's degree, 7% some postgraduate school, and 24% a postgraduate degree (MA or PhD).

Procedure

Young adult participants were recruited through oral announcements made in their university classes. They were offered extra credit toward their final course grade in exchange for their participation. Young adults completed a 30–45 min online survey with measures described in the following section and provided the e-mail address of the parent selected to participate with them. They were free to choose their mother or father. Parents completed a 15–20 min online survey that was a shortened version of the young adult survey. Participation was voluntary and not required for the course in which the young adults were enrolled.

Measures

All measures were adapted to be answered on 5-point Likert-type scales and appeared on both the parent and child surveys, unless otherwise noted.

Loneliness. Loneliness was measured with the 20-item UCLA Loneliness Scale (version 3; Russell, 1996). This instrument contains items that assess feelings indicative of loneliness without ever using the term "lonely." Sample items include "How often do you feel you lack companionship?" and "How often do you feel there are people who really understand you?" (reverse scored). The UCLA Loneliness Scale has an extensive history of use throughout the social sciences and has excellent psychometric properties (e.g., Hartshorne, 1993). In the present investigation, the scale had an internal consistency reliability of $\alpha = .91$ for young adults and .92 for parents.

Family environment. The assessment of young adults' family of origin environment was carried out with two measures, each completed by both young adults and their parents. The first measure was the conversation orientation subscale of the revised Family Communication Patterns instrument (Ritchie & Fitzpatrick, 1990). This 15-item measure contains statements about the extent to which the family engages in frequent discussion and promotes the free and open expression of ideas and feelings. Sample items include "My parents often ask my opinion when the family is talking about something" and "In our family we often talk about our feelings and emotions." The wording was changed slightly for the parent version to make it appropriate for parent respondents. The internal consistency reliability of this instrument was $\alpha = .93$ for young adults and .90 for parents. The second family of origin environment measure was the Family Satisfaction Scale (Olson & Wilson, 1982). The scale has 10 items and asks participants to rate the degree to which they are satisfied with various aspects of the family's communication. Sample items include "The quality of communication between family members," "Your family's ability to resolve conflicts," and "The way problems are discussed." The internal consistency reliability of this instrument was $\alpha = .96$ for young adults and .92 for parents.

Social skills. Young adults' social skills were assessed with two instruments. The first was a shortened version of the Communication Competence Scale (Wiemann, 1977). Communicative competence is defined as the ability to select and enact appropriate communication behaviors that help people achieve their interpersonal goals (Wiemann, 1977). Seven items that reflect this conceptualization were selected from the scale, including, for example, "I am easy to talk to," "I am an effective conversationalist," and "I am a good listener." The internal consistency reliability of this measure was $\alpha = .74$. The second measure of young adults' social skills was the social control subscale of the Social Skills Inventory (SSI; Riggio, 1986, 1989). This 15-item scale measures respondents' comfort and ease in social settings along with their self-perceived impression management skills. Sample items included "I find it very difficult to speak in front of a large group of people" (reverse scored) and "I am usually very good at leading group discussions." The internal consistency reliability of this scale was $\alpha = .86$.

Bullying. Bullying was measured using The Revised Olweus Bully/Victim Questionnaire (OBVQ; Olweus, 1996; Solberg & Olweus, 2003). The OBVQ was shortened to include only victim items, and answer choices were modified into yes/no options that were summed to form a composite index. Young adult participants were instructed to focus on their high school years when responding to these items. OBVQ has a record of psychometric quality, including validity, for the assessment of bully as well as victim behaviors (Kyriakides, Kaloyirou, & Lindsay, 2006). Examples of the 13 victim items include "Other students left me out of things on purpose, excluded me from their group of friends, or completely ignored me" and "I was called mean names, was made fun of, or teased in a hurtful way." The internal consistence reliability of this measure was $\alpha = .75$.

Data Analysis

The prediction that both parental loneliness and family environment would be associated with young adult loneliness was tested with structural equation modeling in AMOS 18. For this analysis, family environment was analyzed as a latent variable, with parental and young adult loneliness treated as observed variables. Path analysis was used to test associations between parental loneliness and a history of bullying to young adults' loneliness, and subsequently young adults' social competence (atrophy model), also with AMOS 18. A comparable path analysis was used to test associations between parental loneliness and a history of bullying to young adults' social competence, and subsequently young adults' loneliness (skills deficit model). Multiple regression analysis was used to test specific indirect effects that are specified in the atrophy and skills deficit models.

Results

Correlations among all study variables as well as their means and standard deviations are presented in Table 1. The first analysis focused solely on family of origin predictors of young adult loneliness. Specifically, parental loneliness and a family of origin environment characterized by low levels of conversation orientation and low levels of satisfaction with family communication patterns were predicted to contribute to loneliness experienced by young adults. As a prelude to testing these predictions, a measurement model was examined for its adequacy in representing the four observed family environment variables (i.e., family conversation orientation and family communication satisfaction, assesses from both parent and young adult child) as a single latent variable. The results showed that this measurement model, which is depicted as part of Figure 1, fit the sample data well, $\chi^2 = 0.43$, $df = 1$, $p = .51$, $\chi^2/df = 0.43$, CFI = 1.00, RMSEA = $.00_{(.00–.22)}$. The test of the structural model specified a path from this family environment latent variable to young adult loneliness. It also specified a path from parental loneliness to both the family environment latent variable and the young adult loneliness observed variable. Results of this analysis are depicted in Figure 1.

Initial results indicated that the proposed model only had a marginally acceptable fit, but modification indices showed that with specification of correlations between two pairs of error terms (i.e., parent family conversation orientation and parent family communication satisfaction, parent family communication satisfaction and parent loneliness) model fit could be improved. With these two additional specifications, the resultant model provided a good fit to the sample data, $\chi^2 = 11.96$, $df = 6$, $p = .06$, $\chi^2/df = 1.99$, CFI = .97, RMSEA = $.09_{(.00–.17)}$.

TABLE 1. Correlations, Means, and Standard Deviations of Major Study Variables

Variable	1	2	3	4	5	6	7	8	9
1. Young adult loneliness	—								
2. Young adult family conversation orientation	−.25	—							
3. Young adult family communication satisfaction	−.31	.55	—						
4. Young adult communication competence	−.56	.33	.30	—					
5. Young adult social control	−.58	.22	.23	.52	—				
6. Young adult bullying	.22	−.03	−.16	−.15	−.09	—			
7. Parent loneliness	.30	−.10	−.19	−.22	−.23	−.05	—		
8. Parent family conversation orientation	−.22	.36	.30	.18	.21	−.01	−.29	—	
9. Parent family communication satisfaction	−.12	.36	.36	.14	.10	.09	−.41	.74	—
M	2.32	3.52	3.65	4.04	3.72	1.82	2.28	3.91	3.65
SD	0.45	0.81	0.90	0.58	0.63	0.16	0.45	0.63	0.71

Note. With the sample size of this study, minimum r significant at $p = .05$ is .19. Minimum r significant at $p = .01$ is .24. Minimum r significant at $p = .001$ is .31.

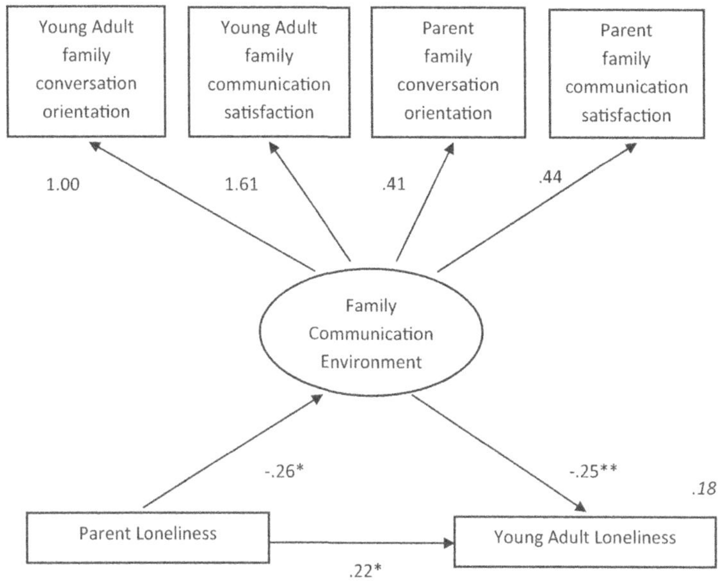

FIGURE 1. Structural model of parent loneliness, family environment, and young adult loneliness. Values in italics are R^2.

As evident from Figure 1, parental loneliness was significantly and positively associated with young adult loneliness. At the same time, parental loneliness was significantly and negatively associated with the family environment latent variable, and family environment variable was significantly and negatively associated with young adult loneliness. These later two results suggest that parental loneliness may have an indirect effect on young adult loneliness through a less open and functional family environment. A bootstrapping procedure was used in AMOS 18 to estimate this indirect effect at $\beta = .07$, $p < .01$. Accordingly, this structural model suggests that parental loneliness has both direct and indirect effects on young adult loneliness through a family environment that is less open and conversational in nature. Collectively, parental loneliness and the family environment latent variable explained 18% of the variance in young adult loneliness.

The second set of predictions focused on the relationship between family and peer interaction antecedents to young adult loneliness and social skills. Within this set of observed variables, there were two specific models tested. The first was the atrophy model. According to this model, parental loneliness and a history of adolescent bullying are specified as antecedent to young adult loneliness. Young adult loneliness in turn is predicted to be associated with lower social skills. Path analysis was used to test this model and the results are depicted in Figure 2. This

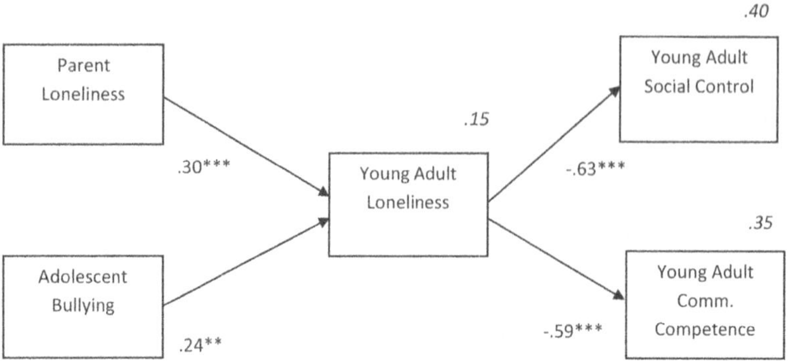

FIGURE 2. Structural model of parental loneliness, bullying, young adult loneliness, and social skills (atrophy model). Values in italics are R^2.

model exhibited an excellent fit to the sample data, $\chi^2 = 6.42$, $df = 6$, $p = .38$, $\chi^2/df = 1.07$, CFI = .99, RMSEA = $.03_{(.00–.13)}$. As evident from Figure 2, both parental loneliness and a history of being bullied were significantly associated with higher levels of young adult loneliness. Young adult loneliness in turn was significantly and strongly associated with lower self-reported social skills. Between 35 and 40% of the variance in young adults' social skills was explained by parental loneliness, a history of bullying, and young adults' loneliness.

The second model tested within this domain was the skills deficit model. In this model, parental loneliness and a history adolescent bullying were specified as antecedent to poor social skills (i.e., communication competence and social control) in young adults. These observed social skills variables were in turn specified as predictors of young adult loneliness. This path model and its associated path coefficients are depicted in Figure 3. Initial results for this model indicated a less than adequate fit, and modification indices suggested that the fit could be improved by specification of a correlation between the error terms of the parent and young adult loneliness variables, and between the error terms of the two young adult social skills variables. With these additional specifications, the resultant model exhibited an excellent fit to the sample data, $\chi^2 = 2.13$, $df = 2$, $p = .34$, $\chi^2/df = 1.06$, CFI = .99, RMSEA = $.03_{(.00–.19)}$. Parental loneliness was significantly associated with one of the young adult social skills variables (communication competence) and had a marginal ($p = .09$) association with the other (social control). Similarly, bullying had a significant association with communication competence and a marginal ($p = .06$) association with social control. Between 6 and 8% of the variance in young adults' social skills was explained by the combination of parental loneliness and a history of being bullied. The two young adult social skills variables were each significantly associated with young adult loneliness. All of

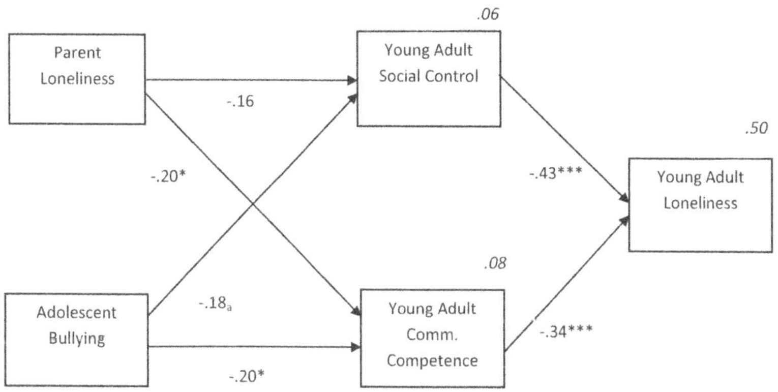

FIGURE 3. Structural model of parental loneliness, bullying, young adult loneliness, and social skills (skills deficit model). Values in italics are R^2. $_a$ $p = .06$. Comm. = communication.

the antecedent variables in the model (i.e., parental loneliness, history of being bullied, young adult social skills) explained 50% of the variance in young adults' loneliness.

Comparison of the atrophy and skill deficits model indicated no superiority in the fit of one model versus the other, $\Delta\chi^2 = 4.29$, $df = 4$, *ns*. Because both models exhibited an adequate fit, and the parsimony of each of the two is comparable in terms of observed variables, it must be concluded that both models provide a plausible account of the association between parent loneliness and a history of being bullied as contributors to young adult loneliness and poor social skills.

To further deconstruct the effects in Figure 2 and Figure 3, their indirect effects were evaluated. Both the atrophy and skills deficit models imply four indirect effects. These were individually estimated and tested with multiple regression analyses using bootstrapping techniques described by Preacher and Hayes (2004). Results of the tests of indirect effects appear in Table 2. As evident in Table 2, all of the indirect effects of parental loneliness and history of being bullied on young adults' social skills, through young adults' loneliness were significant, although the effect in one case was borderline ($p = .054$). In contrast, only one of the four indirect effects was significant for the association between parent loneliness and history of being bullied on young adults' social skills through young adults' loneliness.

TABLE 2. Indirect Effects of Parental Loneliness and History of Being Bullied on Young Adult Loneliness and Social Skills

Effect of	On	Through	*B*	*z*	*p*
Parent Loneliness	Comm. Competence	Young Adult Loneliness	–.20	–2.62	.009
Parent Loneliness	Social Control	Young Adult Loneliness	–.27	–2.96	.003
History of Bullying	Comm. Competence	Young Adult Loneliness	.44	2.34	.019
History of Bullying	Social Control	Young Adult Loneliness	.42	1.93	.054
Parent Loneliness	Young Adult Loneliness	Comm. Competence	.12	2.05	.043
Parent Loneliness	Young Adult Loneliness	Social Control	.10	1.75	.081
History of Bullying	Young Adult Loneliness	Comm. Competence	–.20	–1.46	.144
History of Bullying	Young Adult Loneliness	Social Control	–.11	–0.77	.440

Discussion

The purpose of this investigation was to test theoretically specified associations between family of origin (i.e., parent loneliness, family environment) and peer (i.e., bullying) influences on loneliness along with potential social skills deficits that could be associated with loneliness. The results confirmed that parental loneliness and a history of being bullied were predictive of higher levels of loneliness in young adults. At the same time, a family environment that supported the open expression of ideas and feelings was negatively associated with young adults' loneliness. Last, the findings provide some support for both the skills deficit and atrophy models of loneliness and poor social skills.

It is becoming apparent that there are a number of different mechanisms that link family of origin factors to loneliness, even in people who no longer reside with that family (Distel et al., 2010; Rokach, 1989). The results of this investigation provide further evidence of family resemblance for loneliness. Parent loneliness consistently emerged as a significant predictor of young adults' loneliness. The structural model of parental loneliness, family of origin environment, and young adult loneliness in Figure 1 indicates that there is both a direct effect and an indirect effect of parent loneliness on young adult loneliness. The indirect effect appears to occur, in part, through a less open and functional family of origin environment. In other words, lonely parents appear to have a hand in creating an environment that is not as conversational, supportive, and effective in nature as the family environment that nonlonely parents help to construct. The family environment in which communication patterns are more restrictive and less effective is itself associated with young adults' loneliness. These findings suggest that lonely parents have a dual influence on their offspring's loneliness: though direct means (e.g., genetic transmission) and indirect means (e.g., by creating a family environment that is less supportive and functional).

The results of this investigation show that a history of being bullied is a significant predictor of young adult loneliness. Although an association between being bullied and loneliness has been shown concurrently in adolescents (e.g., Woods et al., 2009), findings from the present investigation suggest that the effects of bullying persist into young adulthood. It is remarkable that participants in this investigation who reported being the victim of bullying while in high school also reported higher levels of loneliness while attending a university, several years after successfully completing high school. Rokach (1989) argued that a history of aversive interpersonal experiences could corrode people's readiness to interact and connect with other people in a meaningful way. Findings from this investigation suggest that these aversive experiences may have a scarring effect that could persist beyond the immediate exposure to such experiences. The findings also show that bullying is associated with loneliness, not just among adolescents who presumably have a more fragile self-concept, but even among young adults who have otherwise had some vocational successes in life (e.g., graduating from high school, successful admission into a university).

A history of bullying not only exhibited a direct effect on loneliness, but an indirect effect as well through lower social skills in the young adult victims of the bullying. Although it is as plausible to assume that bullying can damage the social skills of victims as it is to assume that people with poor social skills are targeted for bullying (Fox & Boulton, 2005), in either case the combination of bullying and poor social skills in the victim appears to create a risk for loneliness. One obvious mechanism by which bullying could lead to decrements in social skills is through social anxiety. A history of being bullied could make the victim reticent and fearful of others. Social anxiety may play a prominent role in the etiology of loneliness as well as poor social skills (Segrin & Kinney, 1995).

The results of this investigation provide some support for both the skills deficit model of loneliness and the skill atrophy model of loneliness. Poor social skills were significant predictors of loneliness, and loneliness predicted poor social skills. Each model fit the sample data equally well. However, one difference between the two was that virtually all of the indirect effects in the skills deficit model were significant, and most were not in the atrophy model. In the skills deficit model, the exogenous factors (i.e., parent loneliness, history of being bullied) had significant effects on loneliness through lower social skills. Therefore, the skills deficit model, as tested in this study, has additional utility for identifying what may be antecedents to skills deficits. When juxtaposed with the atrophy model, the possible antecedents to skills deficits (i.e., parental loneliness, history of being bulled) identified in the skills deficit model do not appear to be associated with deficient social skills because they are also associated with loneliness.

There are several limitations inherent in this investigation that must be considered when interpreting its findings. First, the cross-sectional nature of the data do not allow for conclusive evaluation of causal ordering. For example, it was noted that bullying may lead to poor social skills and that poor social skills may also lead to bullying. The same can be said for associations between poor social skills and loneliness. One important implication of assessing a history of being bullied concurrently with loneliness is the possibility for recall bias. People who are lonely might be more likely to recall prior victimization experiences. With that said, it is important to bear in mind that loneliness is an inherently perceptual phenomenon. Whether people were actually bullied or not, have friends or not, and so forth, is not as important as how lonely people see these issues from their own vantage point. Another potential limitation concerns restriction of range in both family of origin environment and young adults' social skills. Perhaps the nature of the sample (people who have successfully been admitted into a university) and procedure (the requirement of a parent who would also participate) explains why the average participant had scores above the scale midpoint on social skills and family of origin environment. It is therefore unlikely that the findings documented in this study are overstating the associations between such factors as family of origin environment, young adults' social skills, and young adults' loneliness.

In conclusion, this investigation shows that parental loneliness and a history of being bullied as an adolescent are significant predictors of young adults' loneliness. Parental loneliness had several indirect effects on young adults' loneliness through a less open and supportive family environment and through lower social skills in young adults. A history of being bullied also had indirect effects on young adults' loneliness through lower young adult social skills. These findings highlight the pivotal role of poor social skills in young adults as potential consequents of parental loneliness and a history of being bullied that, in turn, put young adults at risk for experiencing loneliness.

REFERENCES

Cacioppo, J. T., Fowler, J. H., & Christakis, N. A. (2009). Alone in the crowd: The structure and spread of loneliness in a large social network. *Journal of Personality and Social Psychology*, *97*, 977–991.

Cacioppo, J. T., Hawkley, L. C., & Thisted, R. A. (2010). Perceived social isolation makes me sad: 5 year cross-lagged analyses of loneliness and depressive symptomatology in the Chicago Health, Aging, and Social Relations study. *Psychology and Aging*, *25*, 453–463.

Distel, M. A., Rebello-Mesa, I., Abdellaoui, A., Derom, C. A., Willemsen, G., Cacioppo, J. T., & Bloomsma, D. I. (2010). Familial resemblance for loneliness. *Behavior Genetics*, *40*, 480–494.

Due, P., Holstein, B. E., Lynch, J., Diderichsen, F., Gabhain, S. N., Scheidt, P., ... The Health Behaviour in School-Aged Children Bullying Working Group. (2005). Bullying and symptoms among school-aged children: International comparative cross sectional study in 28 countries. *European Journal of Public Health*, *15*, 128–132.

Fleming, L. C., & Jacobsen, K. H. (2010). Bullying among middle-school students in low and middle income countries. *Health Promotion International*, *25*, 73–84.

Fox, C. L., & Boulton, M. J. (2005). The social skills problems of victims of bullying: Self, peer and teacher perceptions. *British Journal of Educational Psychology*, *75*, 313–328.

Hartshorne, T. S. (1993). Psychometric properties and confirmatory factor analysis of the UCLA Loneliness Scale. *Journal of Personality Assessment*, *61*, 182–195.

Hawkley, L. C., & Cacioppo, J. T. (2003). Loneliness and pathways to disease. *Brain, Behavior, and Immunity*, *17*(Suppl. 1), S98–S105.

Johnson, H. D., LaVoie, J. C., & Mahoney, M. (2001). Interparental conflict and family cohesion: Predictors of loneliness, social anxiety, and social avoidance in late adolescence. *Journal of Adolescent Research*, *16*, 304–318.

Jones, W. H. (1982). Loneliness and social behavior. In L. A. Peplau & D. Perlman (Eds.), *Loneliness: A sourcebook of current theory, research, and therapy* (pp. 238–252). New York: Wiley.

Junttila, N., Vauras, M., & Laakkonen, E. (2007). The role of parenting self-efficacy in children's social and academic behavior. *European Journal of Psychology of Education, 22*, 41–61.

Kyriakides, L., Kaloyirou, C., & Lindsay, G. (2006). An analysis of the Revised Olweus Bully/Victim Questionnaire using the Rasch measurement method. *British Journal of Education Psychology, 76*, 781–801.

Olson, D. H., & Wilson, M. (1982). Family inventories: Inventories used in a national survey of families across the family life cycle. In D. H. Olson, H. I. McCubbin, H. Barnes, A. Larsen, M. Muxen, & M. Wilson (Eds.), *Family social science* (pp. 25–31). St. Paul, MN: University of Minnesota.

Olweus, D. (1996). *The Revised Olweus Bully/Victim Questionnaire*. Unpublished manuscript, University of Bergen.

Preacher, K. J., & Hayes, A. F. (2004). SPSS and SAS procedures for estimating indirect effects in simple mediation models. *Behavior Research Methods, Instruments, & Computers, 36*, 717–731.

Riggio, H. E., & Kwong, W. Y. (2009) Social skills, paranoid thinking, and social outcomes among young adults. *Personality and Individual Differences, 47*, 491–497.

Riggio, R. E. (1986). Assessment of basic social skills. *Journal of Personality and Social Psychology, 51*, 649–660.

Riggio, R. E. (1989). *Manual for the Social Skills Inventory*. Palo Alto, CA: Consulting Psychologists Press.

Ritchie, L. D., & Fitzpatrick, M. A. (1990). Family communication patterns: Measuring intrapersonal perceptions of interpersonal relationships. *Communication Research, 17*, 523–544.

Rokach, A. (1989). Antecedents to loneliness: A factorial analysis. *Journal of Psychology, 123*, 369–384.

Rokach, A. (2003). Loneliness among loved ones: Alienation in the family. *Psychology and Education, 40*, 1–18.

Russell, D. W. (1996). UCLA Loneliness Scale (Version 3): Reliability, validity, and factor structure. *Journal of Personality Assessment, 66*, 20–40.

Segrin, C. (1993). Social skills deficits and psychosocial problems: Antecedent, concomitant, or consequent? *Journal of Social and Clinical Psychology, 12*, 336–353.

Segrin, C. (1998). Interpersonal communication problems associated with depression and loneliness. In P. A. Anderson & L. A. Guerrero (Eds.), *The handbook of communication and emotion* (pp. 215–242). New York: Academic Press.

Segrin, C. (1999). Social skills, stressful life events, and the development of psychosocial problems. *Journal of Social and Clinical Psychology, 18*, 14–34.

Segrin, C., & Domschke, T. J. (in press). Social support, loneliness, recuperative processes and their direct and indirect effects on health. *Health Communication*.

Segrin, C., & Flora, J. (2000). Poor social skills are a vulnerability factor in the development of psychosocial problems. *Human Communication Research, 26*, 489–514.

Segrin, C., & Kinney, T. (1995). Social skills deficits among the socially anxious: Loneliness and rejection from others. *Motivation and Emotion, 19*, 1–24.

Segrin, C., & Passalacqua, S. (2010). Functions of loneliness, social support, and health behaviors in association with poor health. *Health Communication, 25*, 312–322.

Solberg, M. E., & Olweus, D. (2003). Prevalence estimation of school bullying with the Olweus Bully/Victim Questionnaire. *Aggressive Behavior, 29*, 239–268.

Sonnenschein, S., & Whitehurst, G. J. (1980). The development of communication: When a bad model makes a good teacher. *Journal of Experimental Child Psychology, 29*, 371–390.

Spitzberg, B. H., & Hurt, T. (1989). The relationship of interpersonal competence and skills to reported loneliness across time. In M. Hojat & R. Crandall (Eds.), *Loneliness: Theory, research, and applications* (pp. 157–172). Newbury Park, CA: Sage.
Stednitz, J. N., & Epkins, C. C. (2006). Girls' and mothers' social anxiety, social skills, and loneliness: Associations after accounting for depressive symptoms. *Journal of Clinical Child and Adolescent Psychology*, *35*, 148–154.
Wiemann, J. M. (1977). Explication and test of a model of communication competence. *Human Communication Research*, *3*, 195–213.
Woods, S., Done, J., & Kalsi, H. (2009). Peer victimization and internalizing difficulties: The moderating role of friendship quality. *Journal of Adolescence*, *32*, 293–308.
Young, J. E. (1982). Loneliness, depression, and cognitive therapy: Theory and application. In L. A. Peplau & D. Perlman (Eds.), *Loneliness: A sourcebook of current theory, research, and therapy* (pp. 379–405). New York: Wiley.

"When It's Just Me at Home, It Hits Me That *I'm Completely Alone*": An Online Survey of Adolescents in Self-Care

MÓNICA RUIZ-CASARES
McGill University
CSSS de la Montagne

ABSTRACT. The present study examined adolescents' experiences of loneliness and solitude in their responses to an online survey on self-care. Both quantitative ($n = 272$) and qualitative ($n = 150$) responses were coded for these feelings when home alone. Results indicate that adolescents experience the duality of aloneness, including both positive solitude and negative loneliness. Adolescents' responses range from embraced solitude and self-care to feelings of loneliness and rejection of time by themselves. Adolescents reporting loneliness were significantly less likely to enjoy being home alone during the day and at night ($p \leq .001$). Also, gender, age, and emotions such as fear, boredom, and separation anxiety are associated with loneliness among adolescents in self-care. Interventions to increase connectedness and combat loneliness during out-of-school hours are recommended.

My major regret in life is that my childhood was unnecessarily lonely.
—Truman Capote

ACROSS HISTORY AND CULTURAL SETTINGS, children and adolescents have spent time alone as a result of daily practices (e.g., sleeping arrangements; Latz, Wolf, & Lozoff, 1999) and to mark important transitions towards full community involvement. Among the Chimbu of Papua New Guinea and the Nharo people of Botswana, for example, female initiation rites have involved the isolation of the pubescent girl in a hut for days or weeks, during which she is instructed in proper behavior (Barnard, 1980; Ross, 1965). Whereas sometimes time alone has been found to be a source of creativity, wisdom, and learning, at other times it has

Thanks to Kids Help Phone/Jeunesse J'Écoute staff for their support with this study and to Cécile Rousseau for early discussions on the conceptualization of this article.

been linked to isolation, abandonment, and exclusion. In both industrialized and nonindustrialized countries, many children spend time home alone on a regular basis before or after school or on weekends (Ruiz-Casares & Heymann, 2009; Vandell & Posner, 1999). Various contributing factors (e.g., parents' availability, children's age and perceived risk) and negative outcomes linked to longer periods of time in self-care have been identified (Colwell, Pettit, Meece, Bates, & Dodge, 2001; Vandivere, Tour, Zaslow, Calkins, & Capizzano, 2003). Despite initial evidence that many children and adolescents experience loneliness when they are home alone or living in isolated areas (Cummins, 2009; Ruiz-Casares & Rousseau, 2010), little attention has been paid to date to their experiences of aloneness when in self-care.

Scholars have distinguished two sides to aloneness—loneliness and solitude (Tillich, 1963)—with young children generally being able to distinguish between them (Corsano, Majorano, & Champretavy, 2006; Galanaki, 2004; Hymel, Tarulli, Hayden Thomson, & Terrell-Deutsch, 1999). Closely related yet distinct experiences, time alone to reflect, rest, question, and discover who we are (i.e., solitude) can be "renewing and creative" (Potthoff, 1976, pp. 13), while loneliness may be deeply distressing. In the words of Moustakas (1972), "solitude is as much an intrinsic desire in man as his gregariousness," and in it there is peace, joy, a sense of wonder, and self-renewal (p. 41–53). In contrast, loneliness entails a sense of isolation, abandonment, misunderstanding, and/or rejection. "Loneliness involves the feeling that there is no one and no thing responsive to our deep hunger for support and caring. We are really alone" (Potthoff, 1976, pp. 13–14).

Loneliness can be particularly difficult in adolescence (Larson, 1990; Margalit, 2010). A time of individuation and possibility, adolescence is also a time of search—and often (re)definition—of one's own identity and relationships. In the midst of change, "because the adolescent is not sure who and what and where he is, it is a time involving deep loneliness" too (Potthoff, 1976, p. 38). Whereas aloneness is necessary for development, loneliness can interfere with adolescents' psychosocial development and physical health (Buchholz & Catton, 1999; Krause-Parello, 2008). Among children and adolescents, loneliness is associated with factors such as boredom (Kirova, 2004), low self-esteem (Brage, Meredith, & Woodward, 1993), and problems in interpersonal relationships (Doman & Roux, 2010; Klarin, 2004) among others (Mahon, Yarcheski, Yarcheski, Cannella, & Hanks, 2006). Research further suggests that enduring childhood loneliness may predispose to depressive symptoms later in life (P. Qualter, Brown, Munn, & Rotenberg, 2010). To what extent the regular use of self-care arrangements may turn transient or situational loneliness into a more stressful enduring condition is unknown.

Loneliness in childhood and adolescence has mostly been studied in the context of specific health and developmental conditions such as autism (Bauminger, Shulman, & Agam, 2003; Kaminsky & Dewey, 2002; White & Roberson-Nay,

2009), developmental coordination disorder (Poulsen, Ziviani, Cuskelly, & Smith, 2007; Poulsen, Ziviani, Johnson, & Cuskelly, 2008), attention deficit hyperactivity disorder (ADHD) (Hurt, Hoza, & Pelham, 2007), depression (Baskin, Wampold, Quintana, & Enright, 2010; de Minzi, 2006; Lau, Chan, & Lau, 1999; P. Qualter et al., 2010), obsessive-compulsive disorder (OCD) (Storch et al., 2006), learning disorders (Al-Yagon & Mikulincer, 2004; Coleman, Mcham, & Minnett, 1992; Lackaye, Margalit, Ziv, & Ziman, 2006), specific language impairment (SLI) (Brinton & Fujiki, 1999), cancer (Moody, Meyer, Mancuso, Charlson, & Robbins, 2006), Barth Syndrome (Storch et al., 2009), overweight (Mériaux, Berg, & Hellström, 2010; Storch et al., 2007), short stature (Storch et al., 2005), endocrine disorders (Storch et al., 2004), deafness (Most, 2007), craniofacial anomalies (CFA) (Pope & Ward, 1997), and gifted children (Kaluger & Martin, 1960). Also, it has been investigated in regards to homelessness (Kidd, 2007; Rew, 2000), peer victimization (Storch & Masia-Warner, 2004), and suicide (Cui, Cheng, Xu, Chen, & Wang, 2011). In contrast, little attention has been paid to the relationship between adolescents' aloneness when in self-care and their feelings of loneliness and solitude. Interviews with children who regularly spent time home alone suggest that children experience both the enjoyment of independence and a sense of responsibility as well as feelings of fear, boredom, and loneliness when they are by themselves (Kaplan, 2004, 2006; Ruiz-Casares & Rousseau, 2010). Indeed, in the words of one of the participants in Ruiz-Casares and Rousseau's study (2010), "you learn what loneliness is" by being home alone (p. 2567).

In the current global youth culture, the fear of loneliness leads children to reach out to family, friends, and neighbors through phone or Internet. The contribution of the Internet and new social media to enhancing feelings of connectedness has been questioned (Kraut et al., 1998). On the one hand, Internet users may have the impression of being always "connected"; on the other, there may actually not be a "real" bonding and excessive Internet use may generate increased psychosocial distress, including loneliness, depression, and self-harm (Kelleci & İnal, 2010; Kim, LaRose, & Peng, 2009; Lam, Peng, Mai, & Jing, 2009; Park, 2009). In consequence, whereas for some, time alone with online access may be comforting, for others it is a source of distress, including feelings of loneliness.

This article reports on one of the few studies to explore adolescents' experiences of aloneness when in self-care and their feelings of loneliness and solitude in that context. I analyzed responses to an online survey administered by Kids Help Phone/Jeunesse J'Écoute (KHP/JJ) to understand young people's experiences home alone and how they cope with the feelings and needs that emerge while unsupervised. This article contributes a deeper understanding of the dynamics of aloneness and the duality of feelings among children who spend time regularly home alone.

Method

Sample

This study is a secondary analysis of data collected by Kids Help Phone/Jeunesse J'Écoute (KHP/JJ) through an online survey to document children's and youths' experiences home alone. KHP/JJ is a not-for-profit organization that provides toll-free, bilingual, confidential, and anonymous professional phone and web counseling, referral, and information for children and youth across Canada. Results included in this article concern 272 respondents aged 10–17 years (Median = 15 years, $SD = 1.812$ years) who lived in Canada and had spent time home alone. Home alone comprised both times when respondents were completely alone as well as when they were with other children (e.g., brothers and sisters or a young babysitter), and there was no adult around. Most respondents were female (78.7%, $n = 267$) and lived in medium-sized and large cities (70.4%, $n = 189$). I excluded from the analysis cases that did not answer more than 3 items or did not provide information on their date of birth, country of residence, or whether they spent time home alone. I calculated age based on self-reported year of birth. I use the expressions "home alone" and "self-care" interchangeably throughout this article.

Procedure

Through its web counseling sites, KHP/JJ invited users to participate in an online survey about their experiences home alone. The survey was open in the English and French sites during 4 weeks in fall 2009. Respondents were assured anonymity and required to agree to the purpose and conditions of the study before they could proceed to the survey. Once assent was given, participation was voluntary for all other items. KHP/JJ did not collect IP addresses nor provide any compensation to those participating in the study. KHP/JJ invited respondents throughout the survey to contact their counselors if needed. After manually screening all qualitative information to remove any identifying information, I assigned respondents a code and alias for analysis and publication. Aliases take into account information provided on gender and cultural background. The research ethics office at McGill University gave ethics approval for analysis of data collected by KHP/JJ.

Measure

The questionnaire contained two types of questions: 25 close-ended and 6 open-ended questions. Close-ended questions covered socio-demographic characteristics, living conditions, and activities, emotions, and satisfaction when home alone during the past year. Open-ended questions invited respondents to further describe their needs, positive and negative feelings, and coping mechanisms when home alone as well as to share any advice they may have to other children and adolescents who stay home alone. The questionnaire was pilot tested and refined in both English and French before administration. The secondary analysis presented here focuses on the key questions about respondents' feelings when home alone and their circumstances and coping responses to loneliness and solitude.

Analysis

I obtained descriptive statistics of quantitative responses (frequency tables and chi-square tests) for the whole sample (N = 272) using SPSS® 17. Given the focus of the study, I did not consider for the quantitative analyses participants who did not respond to the question of loneliness (n = 71). I analyzed qualitative data (n = 150) using content analysis procedures (Patton, 1990), with a focus on spontaneous disclosures of loneliness and solitude. Using Atlas-ti 5.0, I first coded responses to the 6 open-ended questions for key words or phrases, in both English and French. I noted all instances of loneliness, (social and geographical) isolation, abandonment, as well as enjoyment of being alone. Following this, I used open coding to identify complementary themes (e.g., family conflict and coping mechanisms). I selected and developed into narratives three cases to illustrate adolescents' positive, negative, and ambiguous experiences of aloneness; I used information from their responses to all items in the survey to sketch their profiles. Direct quotes are weaved into the narratives and throughout the article and presented in italics. I have translated into English and proofread quotes selected for inclusion in this manuscript.

Results

Loneliness in the Overall Sample

When asked about their most salient feelings when they are home alone, the majority of respondents did not select loneliness (63.7%). Nonetheless, over a third (36.3%) of respondents indicated they felt lonely and would rather be with people (Table 1). Significant differences emerged for sex and age, with females (p = .015) and the youngest and oldest respondents (p = .011) reporting more loneliness (Table 1 and Figure 1 and Figure 2). Similarly, differences were significant for satisfaction with home alone, with fewer lonely respondents enjoying spending time home alone both during the day and night time (p = .000). Although lonely respondents were less likely to make the decision to be home alone or to spend more than 20 hr a week in self-care, differences were not significant based on who made the decision or the duration of this care arrangement. Likewise, adolescents seem to engage in a similar range of activities regardless of whether they feel lonely.

Not surprisingly, respondents who were not allowed to go out (14.4%) were less likely to meet with friends while in self-care than those who did not have that restriction, 9.1% vs. 55.3%, $X^2(1, n = 229) = 23.940$, p = .000 Similarly, respondents who were not allowed to invite friends home when they were alone (22.3%) were less likely to do it than those without that prohibition, 11.8% vs.

TABLE 1. Characteristics of Participants Who Are Home Alone by Feelings of Loneliness ($N = 201$)

	Feels lonely when home alone[a]					
	Yes		No			
Characteristic	n	%	n	%	χ^2	df
Gender ($n = 198$)					5.919**	1
Male	6	8.5	28	22.0		
Female	65	91.5	99	78.0		
Age ($n = 197$)					8.937**	2
10–12 years	16	22.9	16	12.6		
13–15 years	24	34.3	71	55.9		
16–17 years	30	42.9	40	31.5		
Residence ($n = 187$)					.880	2
Rural	5	7.1	13	11.1		
Small town	15	21.4	22	18.8		
Urban	50	71.4	82	70.1		
Family composition ($n = 180$)[b]					.085	1
Two parents	42	63.6	75	65.8		
Single-parent	24	36.4	39	34.2		
Decision to stay home alone ($n = 198$)					2.524	2
Parents/caretakers	36	49.3	49	39.2		
Child	9	12.3	24	19.2		
Negotiated	28	38.4	52	41.6		
Frequency (hours/week) ($n = 200$)					3.883	4
<2	10	13.7	12	9.4		
2–5	17	23.3	41	32.3		
5–10	19	26.0	36	28.3		
10–20	13	17.8	23	18.1		
>20	14	19.2	15	11.8		
Activities home alone ($n = 200$)[c]						
Do homework	53	72.6	94	74.0	.048	1
Read	40	54.8	59	46.5	1.289	1
Watch TV	65	89.0	110	86.6	.250	1
Play	55	75.3	93	73.2	.108	1
Talk on phone	39	53.4	68	53.5	.000	1
Internet	65	89.0	109	85.8	.423	1
Care for sibs	15	20.5	37	29.1	1.776	1
Meet friends	30	41.1	60	47.2	.708	1
Invite friends	22	30.1	40	31.5	.040	1
Fight with sibs	27	37.0	32	25.2	3.098	1
Have sex	10	13.7	27	21.3	1.758	1
Cook	25	34.2	54	42.5	1.328	1
Enjoy home alone[d]						
Day time	46	63.0	120	93.8	30.539***	1
Night time ($n = 195$)	14	20.0	71	56.8	24.713***	1

[a]Overall, lonely = 73; not lonely = 128. [b]Does not include 4 cases of not living with either parent. [c]Activities: 1 = *engages in activity*, 0 = *does not engage in activity*. [d]Includes *most of the time* and *usually* (4-point scale).
$*p \leq .05$. $**p \leq .01$. $***p \leq .001$.

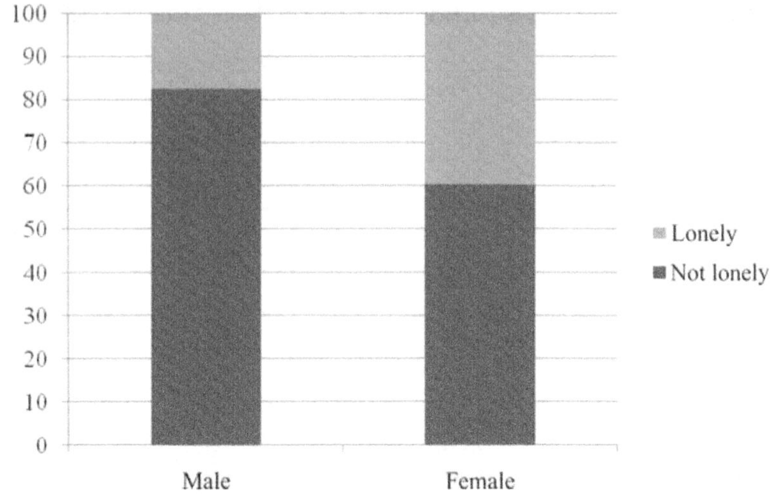

FIGURE 1. Sex by loneliness status when home alone.

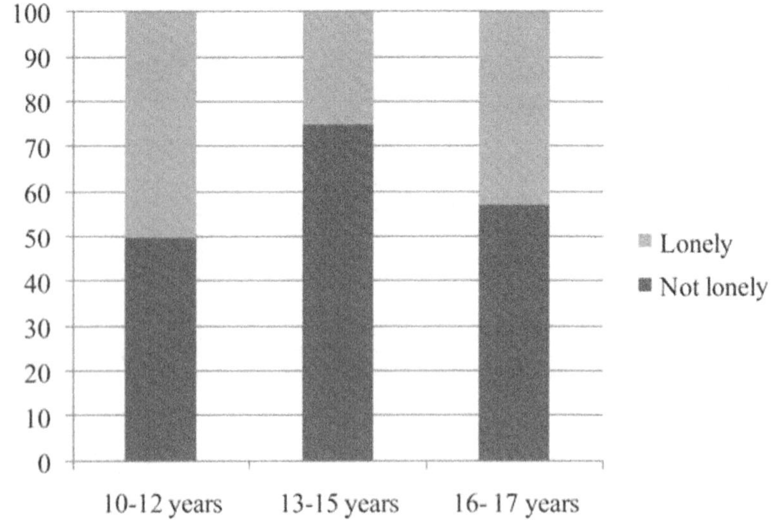

FIGURE 2. Age groups by loneliness status when home alone.

39.9%, $X^2(1, n = 229) = 14.048$, $p = .000$ (data not presented). There was no significant association between loneliness and all of these groups.

Circumstances and Coping Strategies Through Adolescents' Narratives

Silence and Darkness: A Portrayal of Loneliness

Grace, 17 years old

> *I first stayed home at the age of 8 because my mom ... worked all the time then after work she would go out partying. I never knew my father and I grew up taking care of myself ..., My mother has bipolar and border line personality disorder; she used to beat me. ... I have gotten pretty used to staying home by myself. I would rather be home alone then getting the crap beat out of me. When I am home alone, I feel abandoned like no one cares. I feel sad. I feel hurt. I feel angry. I feel like I could just disappear and no one would notice.*

It was Grace's mother[1] who decided that her daughter should stay home alone, which she did frequently (>20 hours per week). During that time, she watched TV, went online to find out information about things that are hard to talk about with other people (she usually had a computer in her room), did household chores, and went out with friends. Her mother did not know where she was or what she was doing; she was not reachable nor did she call Grace at least once. In fact, Grace believes that she did not care much. Grace often felt lonely and bored.

Like Grace, many adolescents experienced heightened feelings of loneliness when home alone. *I don't like being alone,* explained 14-year old Rosalie, *because I am a social person and I am very afraid of loneliness.* Usually looked after by their parents, she and her sibling have been spending 5–10 hr per week alone for the last few years. She is usually all right during the day—but not at night. Similarly, 16-year-old Ava confessed that she *can't barely handle* being home alone at night and that she does not *get much sleep because I'm too scared of what will happen like who will come into the house, when my parents are getting home, etc.* For some, loneliness was accompanied by *lack of motivation to do work, feelings of being unwanted,* sadness, and fear, particularly as respondents' spent longer periods of time alone. Kaitlyn's mother worked until late and often slept at her boyfriend's house: *If there's a patch of days where I* [Kaitlyn] *don't spend time with my mom, I do get depressed. Some days I'll come home from school, turn on the TV and not talk to anyone till school the next day.* In fact, some of these feelings persisted in the company of others. For the previous 5 years, Hannah had been spending quite a lot of time home alone as both parents worked outside of the house. During that time, she experienced *difficulty dealing with my* [her] *parents being gone, and feeling like they don't care ... what I* [she] *do*[es] *and don't bother to pay attention to me* [her] *when they get home ... even though I* [she] *just spent 6 hours home alone. It makes me* [her] *really sad.* Well aware of the hardships of depression and the difficulties of facing it alone, a 15-year-old from Prince Edward Island recommended KHP/JJ that they *just keep letting them* [other children] *know, they're never alone. It's the one thing my friends could never stop saying to me. "You're never alone, don't ever think you're alone in this fight," and it helps.*

Unknown noises, darkness, and uncertainty as to when caretakers would come back often triggered fear and even panic reactions while home alone. Noemie, a 12-year-old female from Quebec, did not enjoy being home alone when her father left *without telling me* [her] *when he is going to come back*. Separation anxiety and fear of abandonment were highlighted by other respondents too. Thus, Ava normally needs *help with not feeling very alone* even if she *said to her parents that it's fine* to leave her by herself: *If I am home alone for more than 12 hours at a time I get very panicky because I have trust issues and I'm always scared that one day they ... will never come back home again and I won't have my mom anymore.* And, as 11-year-old William put it, some are afraid that they *will be alone forever*. Feelings of loneliness seemed to intensify in situations of bullying or conflict with boyfriend, girlfriend, siblings, or peers. In the words of 16-year-old Olivia, *I feel lonely and upset like my worlds crumbling around me specially when I just had a fight with a boyfriend or a friend and then I come home to an empty house. It's the worse feeling ever.*

Other respondents, like 14-year-old Maria, were *scared that something bad will happen to me, and nobody will be there to save me or stop me from doing something stupid*. For her, *being home alone is always a struggle* and *makes me* [her] *feel more alone then what I* [she] *already am* [is]. Adolescents admitting to using drugs or engaging in self-harming behaviors were particularly graphic in their descriptions—*I'm scared I'll overdose on something and no one will be there*, said Alisa [17-year-old female]. Although some might seek to numb their pain or escape their emotions this way, these behaviors did not seem to ease adolescents' difficulty in being alone. In fact, after describing spiraling episodes of bulimia and self-hitting, Camille admitted she was undertaken by *a strong feeling of emptiness* that she is *not capable to endure*.

Neither Black Nor White: Weighting Separateness

Marianne, 17 years old

> [When I am home alone] *I love the fact that I am with myself and precisely that I can work just on that ... Basically, my schedule is very different from my parents' and I end up alone very often. I take advantage of that to learn more about myself, to question myself (which is not always easy (...) and surf* [the net] *to satisfy my curiosity. I remember when I was young searching about sexuality. (...) Sometimes I feel terribly lonely and I have the impression that, precisely, I am isolated from the world. (...) At first, I met people on the net, but I quickly*

> *saw it was a bad idea. I try now to enjoy the moments I spend with people who are close to better endure my moments of aloneness. I don't avoid those moments.*

> At age 11–12 years, Marianne and her parents agreed that she would start spending time home alone because her mother was taking on a job outside of the house and there was no one else to look after her or her parents were going out. Last year, for example, she was by herself about 5–10 hours per week. Her parents never left her alone at night and Marianne enjoyed being by herself most of the time, any time of the day. Loneliness was often present, though. She indicated that all the help she needed when home alone, she got it online. She would also talk on the phone, meet with friends inside or outside of the house, read a book, watch TV, or play games. She did not do homework or any household tasks when she was home alone.

Like Marianne, 15-year-old Andrea enjoyed *being home alone sometimes because I can just relax and be alone with my thoughts, or I can blast the music up and won't have to worry about disturbing anyone. I like being alone usually but if my younger brothers are there with me then I'm cool with that ... so I don't get bored. Also sometimes I need a break from my parents ... and being alone is fun, cause I can talk to guys on the phone without my mothering asking who it is and who I like ... she's really embarrassing. I do homework too and work better when I'm alone because there are no distractions so I don't usually bring friends over because we wont do any work at all anyway.* At the same time, she admitted that *if I'm having one of those days ... when I feel really lonely and there's no one around sometimes I just drop by my neighbors ... or just go outside ride my bike and take my mind off stuff ... or I just call up a friend on the phone or facebook something, and just do something to keep me busy.* Indeed, many respondents held both positive and negative emotions about being home alone, particularly describing feelings of loneliness and actions to combat it while commending the time they spend by themselves. Another eloquent example came from 13-year-old Ai-li, who got homework done and enjoyed the freedom of being alone: *NO ONE KNOWS WHAT I'M DOING! I can do stuff that would be very embarrassing if I did it in front of my family. I have lots of privacy and I feel more laid back.* However, she suffered from loneliness, fear, and boredom too: *I start turning on all the lights in my house so I will know what's in front of me and that my home will be less gloomy and that I'll have a sense of safeness. I also move around the house faster because I feel uneasy staying in one place for too long, fearing that I something bad may happen.*

In the case of other respondents, their dual emotions stem from their conflictive relationships with their caretakers or peers; thus, their time home alone emerge as an opportunity to avoid such stress. When asked about the things that they feel really good or happy about staying home alone, 15-year-old Anna mentioned: *I don't have to hear my parents fight.* Similarly, Laura, a 12-year-old female from British Columbia, shared how *probably just getting away from my parents is the best part* [of being home alone], *since there is no fights and its peaceful and quiet, its just my emotions go wild when I'm alone, however.*

To confront loneliness, boredom, and fear, adolescents read a book, watched a movie, went on msn or Facebook, talked on the phone, or, like Emily, *just wait*ed *by the phone for my mom to call.* Thirteen-year-old Arianne would *invite a friend over or rent a film, because occasionally we find the time long*:). They kept their minds off worrying by singing, dancing, playing music loud, or raising the volume of the TV *as if there were really people in the house* and *without any worry about disturbing anyone.* They closed curtains, switched on all the lights, locked all the windows and doors, and ignored the phone and doorbell when they rang. Ava, for instance, would *also check all the doors and locks like 10 times in the hour if I feel afraid that someone will brake in.* They played (or fought) with their siblings, walked and played with their dog, or reached out to neighbors, friends, or counseling lines like KHP/JJ. Those respondents with clear symptoms of distress used dysfunctional coping strategies such as using substances or self-cutting when home alone.

Relishing Solitude

Gabrielle, 16 years old

I am quite a solitary girl by nature. So, when I have the chance to stay home alone, I love it. I like not having anyone to bother me. That allows me to reflect and to relax. (. . .) I manage my feelings very well. I am not afraid of being alone because if anything happened, I know how to get help (. . .) When I have questions for my parents (for instance, I want to go to my friend's place and I must ask for their permission and obviously tell them where I am), I just have to call them [on their cell phone] *and they will* [always] *answer. (. . .) Also, I know how to defend myself and I make sure that all is safe (for instance, lock the doors). (. . .) Being home alone has really never been a problem for me.*

Gabrielle and her parents lived in the countryside. Except for approximately 5–10 hours/week when she stayed home alone, Gabrielle was usually looked after by her parents. She started spending time home alone regularly when she was 11–12 years of age. Her parents decided she would stay on her own while they went out, but they did not leave her alone at night. Gabrielle enjoyed being home alone although she was often hungry. She did not cook when she was alone, but she did other household chores and also passed her time doing homework, reading, watching TV, playing, talking on the phone, doing email, chatting online, or surfing the net in search for information on health issues or on things that are hard to discuss with others. She sometimes went out with friends or invited them over.

Like Gabrielle, many respondents did not feel lonely when they were home alone; in fact, they liked it *because I can get some peace and quiet* (13-year-old Heidi) *and do my things quietly, undisturbed* (12-year-old Amelie). Several adolescents praised the independence and the quietness of being by themselves. For Sasha, what matters is that *no one is yelling at me, or tell me what to do, I'm kind of free to do what I want, and I manage my time as I wish. That's what I like so much: the fact of having a moment to myself, a moment of freedom.* Time home alone is equally welcomed in the midst of a busy schedule of school and extra-curricular activities. For example, Lucy, a 14-year-old female living in Ontario, enjoyed being home alone in grade 7 and 8 after school *after a day busy in the classroom and a night of skating ahead of me!* In the privacy of their own space, they might call KHP/JJ to seek advice, or just do things that they would not do in a social context. Azlina, for example, enjoyed being home alone *because I get to do things I normally wouldn't do in front of people for fear of embarrassment. Like singing (really badly) to music I like, or playing dress up (yes, I'm 14).* Even if they might sometimes get scared at night if they heard noises or bored if they are alone for too long, these respondents emphasized that they enjoyed being by themselves and undisturbed, making most productive and even creative use of time, and that they had no problem being home alone.

Discussion

Along with Larson (1990, 1997), who has paid significant attention to adolescent's time alone, the findings of this study provide evidence of adolescents' dual perceptions of aloneness, including both constructive solitude and painful loneliness. Furthermore, their coping response to loneliness when in self-care ranged from embraced, to engaged, and to confronted (Carter, 2000). Whereas some respondents indicated choosing self-care and appreciating time alone, others only tolerated it within the context of lack of viable alternatives or dissatisfaction with their family or peer relationships, and yet others saw this care arrangement as solitary confinement often leading to depression and self-harm. The latter was often the case of adolescents with disclosed psychological distress or who engaged in risk behaviors. In line with other studies (Moore & Schultz, 1983), fear, boredom, separation anxiety emerged as emotions associated with loneliness. In contrast, like others have found (Kaplan, 2006; Kealey et al., 2009; Ruiz-Casares & Rousseau, 2010), adolescents who enjoyed being alone rather emphasized the satisfaction of learning and accomplishing work when in self-care.

The distinction between involuntary aloneness (loneliness) and voluntary aloneness (solitude) does not hold well with this sample, though. Whereas the decision of staying home alone was made by children, caretakers, or both does not seem to make a difference on adolescents' appreciation for being alone. One possible explanation is that respondents hold ambivalent feelings about being alone (i.e., may not always desire to be alone when in self-care) or may have chosen self-care among other less attractive alternatives (e.g., child care with much younger children or boring after-school programs). Since parental views on the decision-making process were not ascertained, it is possible that respondents overestimated their role in the actual process. Additional research should be done to describe the process by which decisions are made to leave children home alone, incorporating the perspectives of both children and caregivers. Future studies should examine how loneliness is influenced by sociocultural context as significant differences have been reported on views and causes of loneliness in different ethnocultural communities (Chen et al., 2004; Rokach, Bauer, & Orzeck, 2003; Rokach & Neto, 2000; Rokach, Orzeck, Moya, & Expósito, 2002).

Age and gender differences in the experience of loneliness have already been reported in the literature (Besevegis & Galanaki, 2010; Klarin, 2004; Lau et al., 1999). In the current study, respondents at both ends of the age range reported more loneliness. Other studies have documented pre-adolescents (10–12 years) less frequent desire to be alone when compared with older adolescents (Larson, 1997). Genetic studies are showing that loneliness is highest in early adolescence (Van Roekel, Scholte, Verhagen, Goossens, & Engels, 2010). For this age group, Galanaki (2004) speculated that their difficulty in perceiving aloneness as something beneficial and desirable rather than negative or simply tolerable, may be due to their underdeveloped capacity to be alone or the common belief that equates aloneness with loneliness (e.g., isolation is often used as a form of punishment by parents). As for older adolescents, there is evidence that they are more likely to spend time home alone and to be lonelier than younger adolescents (Brage et al., 1993; Vandivere et al., 2003). Their higher prevalence of loneliness suggests the presence of other psychological distress or risk behaviors. Further research is needed on children and adolescent's ability to be alone, both in the general population and in subgroups that may be especially vulnerable (e.g., children with depression). More reported loneliness among females coincides with findings from some studies (Galanaki, 2004) yet contrasts with others (Brage et al., 1993). Female respondents provided more narratives, disclosing both loneliness and solitude. Possible explanations provided include socialization practices (i.e., girls rather than boys are often encouraged to express their emotions, nurture social relationships, and engage in indoor, solitary activities), and girls' greater (cognitive) maturity (i.e., developmental ability to identify their feelings as loneliness) (Galanaki, 2004). Given that our study involved what may be considered a clinical sample (as visitors to the KHP/JJ site are mostly children and youth with mental health concerns), the observed gender differences resonate with overall patterns of mental health distress and help-seeking behaviors during adolescence (Brooks, Harris, Thrall, & Woods, 2002).

Adolescents described engaging in different activities while home alone. The fear of loneliness lead many to keep busy, to escape silence and poorly lighted rooms, and, when possible, to get together with friends or reach out to family and peers through phone or Internet. Recent studies have found positive social outcomes resulting from online communications for adolescents who experience feelings of loneliness or anxiety (Bonetti, Campbell, & Gilmore, 2010; Burns, Durkin, & Nicholas, 2009). Similarly, adolescents' responses point at phone and

Internet–based counseling and information lines as promising sources of support, helping adolescents confront loneliness and fear (Ruiz-Casares & Rousseau, 2010). Nonetheless, there is a lack of strong evidence on regards to the costs and benefits of Internet use and the usefulness of interventions to combat loneliness (Kim et al., 2009; Pamela Qualter, 2003). For example, although comprehensive self-care training programs for parents and children have proven effective in other regards (e.g., increasing children self-confidence and home safety), they have not been consistently successful in combating loneliness (Koblinsky & Todd, 1989). Similarly, there is evidence that suggests that lonely adolescents avoid instant online communications (van den Eijnden, Meerkerk, Vermulst, Spijkerman, & Engels, 2008). The role of schools should not be ignored (Krause-Parello, 2008; Pamela Qualter, 2003). Also, extra-curricular school activities as well as neighborhood and community centers may provide a space for adolescents to gather after school and develop useful social and cognitive skills to alleviate loneliness. Leisure activities such as participation in team sports may contribute to overcoming loneliness and improving mental health by creating opportunities for social interaction, promoting positive moods, and diverting stress (Coleman & Iso-Ahola, 1993; Sabo, Miller, Melnick, Farrell, & Barnes, 2005). Nonetheless, mere company will not necessarily end loneliness as "loneliness is caused not by being alone but by being without some definite needed relationship or set of relationships" (Weiss, 1973, p. 17). In fact, some respondents praised home alone as an opportunity to avoid conflictive relationships with their caretakers. In consequence, future interventions should pay more attention to parent–child and peer relations as a way to address emotional and social isolation and better equip adolescents for dealing with self-care (Hall Lande, Eisenberg, Christenson, & Neumark-Sztainer, 2007).

There are several limitations to this study. First, the present analyses are based on self-reports of loneliness. It is possible that respondents who refused to provide more detailed accounts of their emotions in a narrative form experienced more or less loneliness. Younger and male respondents, for example, are under-represented in the sample and provided few narrative responses, hence limiting our ability to better understand their experiences. Despite the anonymity offered by the data collection method, some adolescents may have hesitated to self-reveal loneliness. Second, small sample size may explain the lack of significance for some associations (e.g., physical isolation due to place of residence). Third, respondents to the survey were self-selected and constituted a clinical sample therefore preventing generalization of results to the overall population. Similarly, the cross-sectional nature of the data prevents us from drawing cause–effect conclusions. Last, respondents were the only ones to assess contextual circumstances having an impact on adolescents' feelings of loneliness (e.g., relationships with parents and peers).

Through participation in an online survey and voluntary narrative disclosure, this study has documented adolescents' feelings of loneliness and solitude when in self-care. If, as Potthoff (1976) posited, "there is hope for the person who can admit his loneliness, who is free to express the pain of it, and who then acknowledges that there may be some first steps he can take in dealing with it," many survey respondents seem to be on the right track to an optimistic embracement or engagement with aloneness.

REFERENCES

Al-Yagon, M., & Mikulincer, M. (2004). Socioemotional and academic adjustment among children with learning disorders: The mediational role of attachment-based factors. *Journal of Special Education*, *38*(2), 111–123.

Barnard, A. (1980). Sex roles among the Nharo Bushmen of Botswana. *Africa: Journal of the International African Institute*, *50*(2), 115–124.

Baskin, T. W., Wampold, B. E., Quintana, S. M., & Enright, R. D. (2010). Belongingness as a protective factor against loneliness and potential depression in a multicultural middle school. *Counseling Psychologist*, *38*(5), 626–651.

Bauminger, N., Shulman, C., & Agam, G. (2003). Peer interaction and loneliness in high-functioning children with autism. *Journal of Autism and Developmental Disorders*, *33*(5), 489–507.

Besevegis, E., & Galanaki, E. P. (2010). Coping with loneliness in childhood. *European Journal of Developmental Psychology*, *7*(6), 653–673.

Bonetti, L., Campbell, M. A., & Gilmore, L. (2010). The relationship of loneliness and social anxiety with children's and adolescents' online communication. *Cyberpsychology, Behavior, and Social Networking*, *13*(3), 279–285.

Brage, D., Meredith, W. M., & Woodward, J. (1993). Correlates of loneliness among Midwestern adolescents. *Adolescence*, *28*(111), 685–693.

Brinton, B., & Fujiki, M. (1999). Social interactional behaviors of children with specific language impairment. *Topics in Language Disorders*, *19*(2), 49–69.

Brooks, T. L., Harris, S. K., Thrall, J. S., & Woods, E. R. (2002). Association of adolescent risk behaviors with mental health symptoms in high school students. *Journal of Adolescent Health*, *31*(3), 240–246.

Buchholz, E. S., & Catton, R. (1999). Adolescents' perceptions of aloneness and loneliness. *Adolescence*, *34*(133), 203.

Burns, J. M., Durkin, L. A., & Nicholas, J. (2009). Mental health of young people in the United States: What role can the Internet play in reducing stigma and promoting help seeking? *Journal of Adolescent Health*, *45*(1), 95–97.

Capote, T. Quotes by Truman Capote. Retrieved from http://www.quotesarchive.com/authors/c/truman-capote/quotes/page-2

Carter, M. A. (2000). Abiding loneliness. An existential perspective on loneliness. *Second Opinion*, *3*, 37–54.

Chen, X., He, Y., Oliveira, A. M. D., Coco, A. L., Zappulla, C., Kaspar, V., et al. (2004). Loneliness and social adaptation in Brazilian, Canadian, Chinese and Italian children: A multi-national comparative study. *Journal of Child Psychology and Psychiatry, 45*(8), 1373–1384.

Coleman, D., & Iso-Ahola, S. E. (1993). Leisure and health: The role of social support and self-determination. *Journal of Leisure Research, 25*, 111–128.

Coleman, J. M., Mcham, L. A., & Minnett, A. M. (1992). Similarities in the social competences of learning-disabled and low achieving elementary-school-children. *Journal of Learning Disabilities, 25*(10), 671–677.

Colwell, M. J., Pettit, G. S., Meece, D., Bates, J. E., & Dodge, K. A. (2001). Cumulative risk and continuity in nonparental care from infancy to early adolescence. *Merrill-Palmer Quarterly, 47*(2), 207–234.

Corsano, P., Majorano, M., & Champretavy, L. (2006). Psychological well-being in adolescence: The contribution of interpersonal relations and experience of being alone. *Adolescence, 41*(162), 341–353.

Cui, S., Cheng, Y., Xu, Z., Chen, D., & Wang, Y. (2011). Peer relationships and suicide ideation and attempts among Chinese adolescents. *Child: Care, Health and Development, 37*(5), 692–702.

Cummins, H. (2009). Rural children's perceptions of life on the land in Southwestern Ontario. *Canadian Geographer-Geographe Canadien, 53*(1), 63–83.

de Minzi, M. A. C. R. (2006). Loneliness and depression in middle and late childhood: The relationship to attachment and parental styles. *Journal of Genetic Psychology: Research and Theory on Human Development, 167*(2), 189–210.

Doman, L. C. H., & Roux, A. (2010). The causes of loneliness and the factors that contribute towards it: A literature review. *Tydskrif Vir Geesteswetenskappe, 50*(2), 216–228.

Galanaki, E. (2004). Are children able to distinguish among the concepts of aloneness, loneliness, and solitude? *International Journal of Behavioral Development, 28*(5), 435–443.

Hall-Lande, J. A., Eisenberg, M. E., Christenson, S. L., & Neumark-Sztainer, D. (2007). Social isolation, psychological health, and protective factors in adolescence. *Adolescence, 42*(166), 265.

Hurt, E. A., Hoza, B., & Pelham, W. E. (2007). Parenting, family loneliness, and peer functioning in boys with attention-deficit/hyperactivity disorder. *Journal of Abnormal Child Psychology, 35*(4), 543–555.

Hymel, S., Tarulli, D., Hayden Thomson, L., & Terrell-Deutsch, B. (1999). Loneliness through the eyes of children. In K. J. Rotenberg & S. Hymel (Eds.), *Loneliness in childhood and adolescence* (pp. 80–106). Cambridge, UK: Cambridge University Press.

Kaluger, G., & Martin, R. (1960). The loneliness of the gifted-child. *Elementary School Journal, 61*(3), 127–132.

Kaminsky, L., & Dewey, D. (2002). Psychosocial adjustment in siblings of children with autism. *Journal of Child Psychology and Psychiatry and Allied Disciplines, 43*(2), 225–232.

Kaplan, S. B. (2004, August). *"The best thing is I can eat as many cookies as I want": Children's views of self-care during the after-school hours*. Paper presented at the annual meeting of the American Sociological Association, San Francisco, CA.

Kaplan, S. B. (2006, October). *Children's views of self-care: Concepts of autonomy and risk*. Paper presented at the annual meeting of the American Sociological Association, Montreal, Quebec, Canada. Retrieved from http://www.allacademic.com/meta/p104117_index.html

Kealey, K. A., Ludman, E. J., Marek, P. M., Mann, S. L., Bricker, J. B., & Peterson, A. V. (2009). Design and Implementation of an effective telephone counseling intervention for adolescent smoking cessation. *Journal of the National Cancer Institute, 101*(20), 1393–1405.

Kelleci, M., & İnal, S. (2010). Psychiatric symptoms in adolescents with Internet use: Comparison without Internet use. *Cyberpsychology, Behavior, and Social Networking, 13*(2), 191–194.
Kidd, S. A. (2007). Youth homelessness and social stigma. *Journal of Youth and Adolescence, 36*(3), 291–299.
Kim, J., LaRose, R., & Peng, W. (2009). Loneliness as the cause and the effect of problematic Internet use: The relationship between Internet use and psychological well-being. *CyberPsychology & Behavior, 12*(4), 451–455.
Kirova, A. (2004). Lonely or bored: Children's lived experiences reveal the difference. *Interchange, 35*(2), 243–268.
Klarin, M. (2004). The role of peer's social support and peer's relationships in preadolescents' and adolescents' loneliness. *Drustvena Istrazivanja, 13*(6), 1081–1097.
Koblinsky, S. A., & Todd, C. M. (1989). Teaching self-care skills to latchkey children: A review of research. *Family Relations, 38*(4), 431–435.
Krause-Parello, C. A. (2008). Loneliness in the school setting. *Journal of School Nursing, 24*(2), 66–70.
Kraut, R., Patterson, M., Lundmark, V., Kiesler, S., Mukophadhyay, T., & Scherlis, W. (1998). Internet paradox: A social technology that reduces social involvement and psychological well-being? *American Psychologist, 53*(9), 1017–1031.
Lackaye, T., Margalit, M., Ziv, O., & Ziman, T. (2006). Comparisons of self-efficacy, mood, effort, and hope between students with learning disabilities and their non-LD-matched peers. *Learning Disabilities Research & Practice, 21*(2), 111–121.
Lam, L. T., Peng, Z., Mai, J., & Jing, J. (2009). The association between Internet addiction and self-injurious behaviour among adolescents. *Injury Prevention, 15*, 403–408.
Larson, R. W. (1990). The solitary side of life: An examination of the time people spend alone from childhood to old age. *Developmental Review, 10*(2), 155–183.
Larson, R. W. (1997). The emergence of solitude as a constructive domain of experience in early adolescence. *Child Development, 68*(1), 80–93.
Latz, S., Wolf, A. W., & Lozoff, B. (1999). Cosleeping in context: Sleep practices and problems in young children in Japan and the United States. *Archives of Pediatrics & Adolescent Medicine, 153*(4), 339–346.
Lau, S., Chan, D. W. K., & Lau, P. S. Y. (1999). Facets of loneliness and depression among Chinese children and adolescents. *Journal of Social Psychology, 139*(6), 713–729.
Mahon, N. E., Yarcheski, A., Yarcheski, T. J., Cannella, B. L., & Hanks, M. M. (2006). A meta-analytic study of predictors for loneliness during adolescence. *Nursing Research, 55*(5), 308–315.
Margalit, M. (2010). *Lonely children and adolescents: Self-perceptions, social exclusion, and hope*. New York: Springer.
Mériaux, B. G., Berg, M., & Hellström, A.-L. (2010). Everyday experiences of life, body and well-being in children with overweight. *Scandinavian Journal of Caring Sciences, 24*(1), 14–23.
Moody, K., Meyer, M., Mancuso, C. A., Charlson, M., & Robbins, L. (2006). Exploring concerns of children with cancer. *Supportive Care in Cancer, 14*(9), 960–966.
Moore, D., & Schultz, N. R. (1983). Loneliness at adolescence: Correlates, attributions, and coping. *Journal of Youth and Adolescence, 12*(2), 95–100.
Most, T. (2007). Speech intelligibility, loneliness, and sense of coherence among deaf and hard-of-hearing children in individual inclusion and group inclusion. *Journal of Deaf Studies and Deaf Education, 12*(4), 495–503.
Moustakas, C. E. (1972). *Loneliness and love*. Englewood Cliffs, NJ: Prentice-Hall.
Park, S. (2009). The association between Internet use and depressive symptoms among South Korean adolescents. *Journal for Specialists in Pediatric Nursing, 14*(4), 230–238.

Patton, M. Q. (1990). *Qualitative evaluation and research methods* (2nd ed.). Newbury Park, CA: Sage.

Pope, A. W., & Ward, J. (1997). Factors associated with peer social competence in preadolescents with craniofacial anomalies. *Journal of Pediatric Psychology, 22*(4), 455–469.

Potthoff, H. H. (1976). *Loneliness: Understanding and dealing with it.* Nashville, TN: Abingdon.

Poulsen, A. A., Ziviani, J. M., Cuskelly, M., & Smith, R. (2007). Boys with developmental coordination disorder: Loneliness and team sports participation. *American Journal of Occupational Therapy, 61*(4), 451–462.

Poulsen, A. A., Ziviani, J. M., Johnson, H., & Cuskelly, M. (2008). Loneliness and life satisfaction of boys with developmental coordination disorder: The impact of leisure participation and perceived freedom in leisure. *Human Movement Science, 27*(2), 325–343.

Qualter, P. (2003). Loneliness in children and adolescents: What do schools and teachers need to know and how can they help? *Pastoral Care in Education, 21*(2), 10–18.

Qualter, P., Brown, S. L., Munn, P., & Rotenberg, K. J. (2010). Childhood loneliness as a predictor of adolescent depressive symptoms: An 8-year longitudinal study. *European Child & Adolescent Psychiatry, 19*(6), 493–501.

Rew, L. (2000). Friends and pets as companions: Strategies for coping with loneliness among homeless youth. *Journal of Child and Adolescent Psychiatric Nursing, 13*(3), 125–132.

Rokach, A., Bauer, N., & Orzeck, T. (2003). The experience of loneliness of Canadian and Czech youth. *Journal of Adolescence, 26*(3), 267–282.

Rokach, A., & Neto, F. (2000). Coping with loneliness in adolescence: A cross-cultural study. *Social Behavior and Personality, 28*(4), 329–342.

Rokach, A., Orzeck, T., Moya, M. C., & Expósito, F. (2002). Causes of loneliness in North America and Spain. *European Psychologist, 7*(1), 70–79.

Ross, J. A. (1965). The puberty ceremony of the Chimbu girl in the Eastern Highlands of New Guinea. *Anthropos, 60*(1–6), 423–432.

Ruiz-Casares, M., & Heymann, J. (2009). Children home alone unsupervised: Modeling parental decisions and associated factors in Botswana, Mexico, and Vietnam. *Child Abuse and Neglect, 33*(5), 312–323.

Ruiz-Casares, M., & Rousseau, C. (2010). Between freedom and fear: Children's views on home alone. *British Journal of Social Work, 40*, 2560–2577.

Sabo, D., Miller, K. E., Melnick, M. J., Farrell, M. D., & Barnes, G. M. (2005). High school athletic participation and adolescent suicide: A nationwide US survey. *International Review for the Sociology of Sport, 40*(1), 5–23.

Storch, E. A., Keeley, M., Merlo, L. J., Amant, J. B., Jacob, M., Storch, J. F., et al. (2009). Psychosocial functioning in youth with Barth Syndrome. *Children's Health Care, 38*(2), 137–156.

Storch, E. A., Ledley, D. R., Lewin, A. B., Murphy, T. K., Johns, N. B., Goodman, W. K., et al. (2006). Peer victimization in children with obsessive-compulsive disorder: Relations with symptoms of psychopathology. *Journal of Clinical Child and Adolescent Psychology, 35*(3), 446–455.

Storch, E. A., Lewin, A. B., Silverstein, J. H., Baumeister, A., Strawser, M. S., & Geffken, G. R. (2005). Psychological adjustment of children with short stature: A comparison of clinic-referred children with short stature and Type 1 diabetes mellitus. *Journal of Pediatric Endocrinology & Metabolism, 18*(4), 395–401.

Storch, E. A., Lewin, A. B., Silverstein, J. H., Heidgerken, A. D., Strawser, M. S., Baumeister, A., et al. (2004). Social-psychological correlates of peer victimization in children with endocrine disorders. *Journal of Pediatrics, 145*(6), 784–789.

Storch, E. A., & Masia-Warner, C. (2004). The relationship of peer victimization to social anxiety and loneliness in adolescent females. *Journal of Adolescence*, *27*(3), 351–362.

Storch, E. A., Milsom, V. A., DeBraganza, N., Lewin, A. B., Geffken, G. R., & Silverstein, J. H. (2007). Peer victimization, psychosocial adjustment, and physical activity in overweight and at-risk-for-overweight youth. *Journal of Pediatric Psychology*, *32*(1), 80–89.

Tillich, P. (1963). *The eternal now: Sermons*. New York: Scribner.

van den Eijnden, R. J. J. M., Meerkerk, G.-J., Vermulst, A. A., Spijkerman, R., & Engels, R. C. M. E. (2008). Online communication, compulsive Internet use, and psychosocial well-being among adolescents: A longitudinal study. *Developmental Psychology*, *44*(3), 655–665. doi:10.1037/0012-1649.44.3.655.

Van Roekel, E., Scholte, R. H. J., Verhagen, M., Goossens, L., & Engels, R. C. M. E. (2010). Loneliness in adolescence: Gene × environment interactions involving the serotonin transporter gene. *Journal of Child Psychology and Psychiatry*, *51*(7), 747–754.

Vandell, D. L., & Posner, J. K. (1999). Conceptualization and measurement of children's after-school environments. In S. L. Friedman & T. D. Wachs (Eds.), *Measuring the environment across the lifespan* (pp. 167–196). Washington, DC: American Psychological Association Press.

Vandivere, S., Tour, K., Zaslow, M., Calkins, J., & Capizzano, J. (2003). *Unsupervised time: Family and child factors associated with self-care* (Occasional Paper Number 71). Washington, DC: The Urban Institute. Retrieved from The Urban Institute website: http://www.urban.org/uploaddpdf/310894_OP71.pdf

Weiss, R. S. (Ed.). (1973). *Loneliness: The experience of emotional and social isolation*. Cambridge, MA: Massachusetts Institute of Technology.

White, S. W., & Roberson-Nay, R. (2009). Anxiety, social deficits, and loneliness in youth with autism spectrum disorders. *Journal of Autism and Developmental Disorders*, *39*(7), 1006–1013.

Loneliness, Depression, Social Support, and Quality of Life in Older Chronically Ill Appalachians

LAURIE A. THEEKE
R. TURNER GOINS
JULIA MOORE
HEATHER CAMPBELL
West Virginia University

ABSTRACT. This study's purpose was to describe loneliness and to examine the relationships between loneliness, depression, social support, and QOL in chronically ill, older Appalachians. In-person interviews were conducted with a convenience sample of 60 older, chronically ill, community-dwelling, and rural adults. Those with dementia or active grief were excluded. The UCLA Loneliness Scale (Russell, Peplau, & Cutrona, 1985), Geriatric Depression Scale (Shiekh & Yesavage, 1986), Katz ADL scale (Katz, Down, & Cash, 1970), MOS Social Support Scale (Sherbourne & Stewart, 1991), and a visual analog scale for Quality of Life (Spitzer et al., 1981) scale were used. Diagnoses were obtained through chart reviews. SPSS was used for data analyses. The majority of the 65% female sample (*M* age = 75 years) were married and impoverished. Participants' number of chronic illnesses averaged more than 3. Over 88% of participants reported at least 1 area of functional impairment. Loneliness was prevalent with UCLA loneliness scores indicating moderate to high loneliness, ranging from 39 to 62 (possible scores were 20–80). Higher loneliness scores correlated with depression, lower Qol, and lower social support, particularly lower emotional support. This study provides evidence that loneliness is a significant problem for older chronically ill Appalachian adults and that it may be related to low emotional support. Further, it provides evidence that this population may be significantly lonely and may not self-identify as lonely. Screening for loneliness and designing interventions that target the emotional aspects of loneliness could be important in this population.

LONELINESS HAS BEEN STUDIED worldwide by multiple disciplines as a significant problem for older adults. Its prevalence is reported to be 35% or higher in older adult U.S. samples (Holmen, Ericsson, Andersson, & Winblad, 1992; C.

Wilson & Moulton, 2010). As a phenomenon of interest in social science and healthcare literature, loneliness has been conceptualized and defined in varied ways and from various theoretical perspectives, but a consistent theme in these definitions is that loneliness, as a perceived deficit of affective or social need, is a significant psychosocial stressor associated with negative psychological, social, and health consequences.

Multiple sociodemographic, psychological, and health-related correlates of loneliness have been reported in the literature. Sociodemographic correlates have included advancing age (Dykstra, van Tilburg, & Gierveld, 2005), low socioeconomic status (Mullins, Elston, & Gutkowski, 1996), rurality (Liu & Guo, 2007), low educational attainment, widowhood (Savikko, Routasalo, Tilvis, Strandberg, & Pitkala, 2005), and lack of religious affiliation (Kirkpatrick, Shillito, & Kellas, 1999). Loneliness has been associated with diminished social contact and social support, depression (Cacioppo, Hughes, Waite, Hawkley, & Thisted, 2006), low self-efficacy beliefs (Fry & Debats, 2002), increased tobacco use (Theeke, 2010), and cognitive impairment (R. S. Wilson et al., 2007). Health-related correlates have consistently included poor health perception, poor functional status (Dykstra et al., 2005), and increased use of the healthcare system (Geller, 2000).

Loneliness is predictive of negative health outcomes in older adults. It is a predictor for depression (Cacioppo et al., 2006), negative health behaviors (Theeke, 2010), fewer positive health practices (Yarcheski, Mahon, Yarcheski, & Cannella, 2004), and lower quality of life (QoL) for older adults and their caregivers (Ekwall, Sivberg, & Hallberg, 2005).

Culture is recognized as being a significant contributor to loneliness (Jylha, 2004). Older adults in Appalachia experience a unique culture and they are a recognized health disparity group (Behringer, 2006; Halverson, Ma, & Harner, 2004). Older Appalachians experience many determinants and sequelae that have been associated with loneliness in the health and social science literature. Older Appalachians have described a multidimensional holistic conceptualization of health that includes maintaining functional ability, absence of disease, spirituality, and positive psychological state with emotional meaning (Goins, Spencer, & Williams, 2011).

Appalachia comprises 410 counties that span 205,000 square miles from southern New York to northern Mississippi, including all of West Virginia and parts of 12 other states. A disproportion of the region's population is rural compared to the national population (Haaga, 2004). Appalachia is an area with increased poverty rates, increased physical illness, and lower educational attainment (Halverson, Ma, & Harner, 2004). In addition, it has been theorized that the implementation of welfare reform in the early 1990s has resulted in further inequities in the Appalachian region due to rurality and limited employment opportunities, leaving older adults in this region with no support, even more impoverished, and unable to meet basic needs (Henderson & Tickamyer, 2008). These characteristics of Appalachia make it likely that loneliness is a problem for older adults living in this region.

The geographic rural nature of Appalachia coupled with the lack of public transportation, may limit social contacts. Though there is a stereotypical view of Appalachians living rurally with close extended family, it has been reported that, for Appalachians, other forms of social support may be more important than family proximity in predicting mental health outcomes (McCulloch, 1985). Particularly for women, emotional support from friends has been reported to enhance affect (Patrick, Cottrell, & Barnes, 2001). Knowing that older adults who live rurally may experience illness with a sense of quiet pride (Davis & Magilvy, 2000) makes it even more important that health care providers address problems that may be associated with negative social stigma, such as loneliness and depression.

Thus, the purpose of this research was to describe self-identification and scale measures of loneliness and to examine the relationships between loneliness and specific sociodemographic, psychosocial, and health-related variables in a sample of older chronically ill Appalachians. Three research questions were posed for this study:

1. What is the relationship between self-identification of loneliness and scale measure of loneliness in the context of Appalachian culture?

   Hypothesis: Self-identification of loneliness will relate positively to scale measure of loneliness.

2. What sociodemographic, psychosocial, and health related variables are associated with loneliness in a sample of older, chronically ill Appalachians?

   Hypothesis: Age, female gender, widowhood, lower education, lower income, higher number of chronic diseases, impaired functional status, poorer self-report of health, depression, lower social support, and poorer quality of life would be associated with loneliness, both by a single-item self-identification measure and by scale measure.

3. What are the differences between very lonely persons and less lonely persons on the psychosocial and health-related variables?

   Hypothesis: Participants with higher loneliness scores will have higher depression scores, lower social support scores, lower quality of life scores, more functional impairment, lower cognitive scores, and higher numbers of chronic illnesses when compared to those with lower loneliness scores.

Method

This descriptive, cross-sectional study took place in a university family medicine center in northern West Virginia. It reports analyses from data that were gathered between January and March of 2009. The convenience sample of 60 older adults was recruited using newspaper advertisements in the local newspaper serving a tristate Appalachian area of West Virginia, Pennsylvania, and Maryland, and through flyers and posters placed in a University Health Sciences Center. The sample included adults who were aged 65 years or older, community-dwelling, living in Appalachia, and living with chronic illness. Older adults diagnosed with dementia or psychotic illness by medical chart reviews and those grieving the loss of a spouse in the 2 years before the interviews were excluded.

Data were gathered in face-to-face meetings where the participants completed pen and paper surveys. The principal investigator and research assistant were available to facilitate data collection, read questions to the participants if needed, and to answer logistical questions about the surveys. There were no refusals to complete any parts of the surveys, leaving the principal investigator with complete data on all surveys. Chronic illness diagnoses were obtained from medical chart reviews. The study was approved by the West Virginia University Institutional Review Board.

Measurements

Loneliness. Two measures were used to operationalize loneliness: the 20-item UCLA loneliness scale (D. Russell, Peplau, & Cutrona, 1980) and the single-item measure from the Center for Epidemiologic Studies Depression Scale (CESD) (Radloff, 1977). The 20-item UCLA Loneliness scale has been reported to have high internal consistency ($\alpha = 0.890.94$) and adequate test–retest reliability ($r = .73$) (D. W. Russell, 1996). Radloff (1977) reported good internal consistency for the CESD with alpha coefficients of .84 and .85 in white community samples. Further, the CESD has been reported to have good internal consistency ($\alpha = 0.90$) in community-dwelling older adults (Arean & Miranda, 1997). To assess loneliness using the single item, respondents are asked whether they have been "feeling lonely" for most of the past week. It is recognized that use of the single-item is not the same as use of the scale but this single-item measure of loneliness has been widely used in the literature and past research indicates that this single-item measure of loneliness has a significant correlation with the UCLA Loneliness Scale ($r = 0.79$, $p < 0.001$) (D. Russell, Peplau, & Ferguson, 1978). Two measures were used so that the first study aim could be answered.

Sociodemographics. Age, gender, marital status, education level, annual household income, employment status, and living situation were collected. Age was measured as years at the time of the interviews. Gender was self-reported and dichotomous, coded as male = 0, female = 1. Marital status was operationalized categorically as *never married, widowed, separated or divorced, married with spouse absent from home, married with spouse living at home.* Education was assessed categorically for completion of: *grade school, middle school, high school, some college, Associates Degree, Bachelors Degree, Masters Degree, and Doctoral Degree.* Annual household income was measured per annum using \$10,000 incremental categories beginning with *less than or equal to \$20,000* up to the final category of *greater than \$100,000.* Employment status was operationalized categorically as: *retired, working part-time, working full-time, working more than full-time, and unemployed.* Living situation was operationalized with two variables including the number of persons living in the home and the relation of those living in the home to the participant.

Psychosocial variables. Psychosocial variables included depression, social support, and QoL. Depression was operationalized with the 5-item Geriatric Depression Scale (GDS) (Sheikh & Yesavage, 1986). This version of the GDS has been tested in older adults in multiple settings and is reported to have a sensitivity of 0.94, a specificity of 0.81, a positive predictive value of 0.81, a negative predictive value of 0.94, a positive likelihood ratio of 4.92, and a negative likelihood ratio of 0.07 with high test–retest reliability ($\kappa = 0.84$) (Rinaldi et al., 2003). Social Support was measured with the Medical Outcomes Survey (MOS) Social Support Scale which includes four different subscales of social support; tangible support (the provision of material aid or behavioral assistance), affection support (involving expressions of love and affection), positive social support (the availability of other persons to do fun things with you), and emotional support (the expression of positive affect, empathetic understanding, and the encouragement of expressions of feelings) (Sherbourne & Stewart, 1991). The MOS Social Support Survey has adequate psychometric properties with high internal consistency ($\alpha = 0.97$) with alpha coefficients > 0.90 for each subscale as well (Sherbourne & Stewart, 1991). QoL was measured with the visual analog scale (VAS) (Spitzer et al., 1981) where a value of 0 was "as bad as it can be" and 10 was "as good as it can be." This VAS has established to correlate significantly with multi-item scales (de Boer et al., 2004). In addition, participants were asked if they believed they had an emotional problem on a single item, coded as no = 0 and yes = 1.

Health-related variables. Four health-related variables that were previously reported in the literature as correlates of loneliness were collected: self-rated health, functional status, number of chronic illnesses, and cognitive status. Self-rated health was measured with a single-item self-report question with response options being *excellent, very good, good, fair,* and *poor.* Functional status was assessed by self-report of difficulty with the Katz activities of daily living scale and instrumental activities of daily living assessment which assesses independence in bathing, dressing, toileting, transferring, elimination, eating, telephone use, travel beyond walking distance, grocery shopping, housework, cooking, handyman work, laundry, medicine management, stair climbing, and money management (Katz,

Downs, & Cash, 1970). There is limited literature reporting the reliability and validity of the Katz ADL instrument though it has been used extensively to indicate functional ability of older persons. Number of chronic illnesses was measured as the sum number of eight possible chronic illness diagnoses; *arthritis, heart disease, hypertension, stroke, lung disease, diabetes, cancer,* or *psychiatric illness*, which were obtained through medical chart review. Cognitive status was assessed using the minimental status exam (MMSE) (Folstein, Folstein, & McHugh, 1975).

Data Analysis

To answer the first research question, univariate analysis was completed for descriptive information on the two loneliness measures, and correlations were examined to evaluate relationships between the two lonely measures.

To answer the second research question, univariate descriptive analysis for each variable was followed by correlations and ANOVA testing, and independent samples *t* tests were used to evaluate mean differences on the continuous or discrete variables. Chi-square testing was completed for categorical variables to evaluate independence from the loneliness variable. Multivariate logistic regression analysis was then used to evaluate the significant correlates of loneliness for explanation of self-identification of loneliness. The single-item self-identification of loneliness variable was regressed on the significant independent variables through the use of the multivariate binary logistic regression procedure in SPSS version 18.0 using the forward conditional selection procedure. Entry and exit criterion for the analysis was set at 0.1, and the cutoff value was set at 0.10 to reflect the prevalence of self-identification of loneliness in the sample and to minimize Type 1 errors.

To answer the third research question, the UCLA scale scores, which were normally distributed with a mean of 51.5 and a median of 51, were used to divide the participants into two groups: less lonely participants (those with scores less than 51) and lonelier participants (those with scores greater than or equal to 51). Mean comparisons were completed using independent-sample *t* tests to evaluate mean differences between the lonely and not lonely and between the less lonely and lonelier for both measures for depression, social support, all social support subscales, and quality of life. All instruments were evaluated for reliability estimates using the study sample, and for all statistical analyses, the alpha level was set at 0.05.

Results

The sample included 60 older chronically ill Appalachian adults who were community-dwelling. Table 1 reports the sociodemographic and health-related characteristics of the sample. Psychometric property testing of each scale was conducted and is presented in Table 2.

TABLE 1. Sample Characteristics

Variable	Category	N (%)
Gender	Female	39 (65)
	Male	21 (35)
Age	65–84 years	58 (97)
$M = 75.2$ years (SD = 6.42 years)	85 years and more	2 (3)
Marital Status	Married	39 (65)
	Married, spouse absent	1 (2)
	Separated/divorced	2 (3)
	Widowed	17 (28)
	Never married	1 (2)
Education	Less than high school	4 (7)
	High school diploma	26 (43)
	Some college	12 (20)
	College degree and higher	18 (30)
Household Income ($/year)	1st quartile ($0–20,000)	14 (23)
	2nd quartile ($20,001–30,000)	16 (27)
	3rd quartile ($30,001–50,000)	16 (27)
	4th quartile ($50,001 and more)	14 (23)
Relation of Others in Home	Spouse	39 (65)
	Nobody, lives alone	15 (25)
	Sibling, children or grandchildren	6 (10)
Employment Status	Retired	52 (87)
	Working part-time	4 (7)
	Working full-time	3 (5)
	Working more than full-time	1 (2)
Perceived Health	Excellent	5 (8)
	Very good	16 (27)
	Good	21 (35)
	Fair	15 (25)
	Poor	3 (5)
Basic ADLs	No impairment	53 (88)
	Impaired in one basic activity	7 (12)
Instrumental ADLs	No impairment	27 (45)
	Some assistance, one activity	7 (12)
	Some assistance, two activities	3 (5)
	Some assistance, three activities	5 (8)
	Some assistance, four or more activities	18 (30)
Loneliness by single-item measure	Lonely	54 (90)
	Not lonely	6 (10)
Loneliness by UCLA Scale Measure	Less lonely (score < 51)	35 (57)
Mean score 51.5 years ($SD = 6.45$ years)	Lonelier (score ≥ 51)	26 (43)
Number of chronic illnesses	Two or fewer	8 (2)
	Three	12 (13)
	Four	11 (18)
	Five or more	29 (48)

Note. ADLs = activities of daily living. Totals may not exactly be 100% due to rounding.

TABLE 2. Psychometric Properties of Instruments Based on Study Sample ($N = 60$)

Instrument	Cronbach's alpha	*M*	*SD*	Study range	Scale range
UCLA Loneliness Scale (20-Item)	.83	37.08	9.21	39–62	20–80
Geriatric Depression Scale (5 Item)	.47	0.833	1.01	0–5	0–5
Katz Instrumental ADL Scale (10 Items)	.79	12.34	2.96	10–22	10–30
Basic ADL Scale (4 Items)	–.12	4.11	0.32	6–7	6–18
MOS Social Support Total Scale (18 Items)	.93	80.1	14.43	21–90	18–90
MOS Social Support Total Scale (7 Items)	.93	80.1	14.43	21–90	18–90
MOS Tangible Support Subscale (4 Items)	.91	17.35	4.72	4–20	4–20
MOS Tangible Support Subscale (3 Items)	.91	17.35	4.72	4–20	4–20
MOS Positive Social Support Subscale (4 Items)	.91	18.23	3.79	4–20	4–20

Note. There was zero variance in two items on the Basic ADL Scale (Toileting and Eating), so they were removed from the scale analysis.

Loneliness

Descriptive analysis indicated that study participants were moderately lonely with a mean UCLA Loneliness Scale score of 51.1 (*SD* = 4.7) and that 95% of participants had scores of 44 or higher. Of the sample, 10% self-identified as being lonely on the CES–D single item, and one third of the sample self-identified as having an emotional problem. Participants who self-identified as having an emotional problem had an average of 12 of 20 positive items on the UCLA Loneliness Scale. Those who self-identified as lonely had an average of 3 positive items on the UCLA scale, most commonly reporting that they were feeling left out, isolated and alone. The UCLA scale scores did not significantly correlate with the single-item measure of loneliness from the CES–D.

Descriptors of Depression, Social Support, and Quality of Life

The mean depression score on the 5-item GDS was 0.83 (*SD* = 1.01), indicating that the sample did not have significant depressive symptoms. The majority of the sample (66.7%) answered yes to one specific GDS question, indicating that they prefer to stay at home, which affected the depression scores. The mean total score for the MOS social support scale was 4.21 (*SD* = 0.76) with subscale means of 4.33 (*SD* = 1.18) for tangible support, 4.39 (*SD* = 0.93) for emotional support, 4.58 (*SD* = 0.95) for affective support, and 4.55 (*SD* = 0.94) for positive social support. Overall mean QOL scores were 8.2 (*SD* = 2.1) on the visual analog scale.

Sociodemographic, Psychosocial, and Health-Related Correlates of Loneliness

Age and gender. Advancing age correlated negatively with the total UCLA loneliness scale scores ($r = .293$, $p < 0.05$) and affective support ($r = .262$, $p < 0.05$). Males and females did not differ on marital status, education, relation to those living in the household, income, or employment status. Also, mean comparison testing indicated that men and women differed on loneliness ($t = 2.21$, $p < 0.05$), total social support ($t = 2.21$, $p < 0.05$), and QOL ($t = 2.66$, $p = 0.01$), but did not differ on depression scores ($t = .666$, $p = 0.51$), with men having higher mean scores for loneliness, total social support, and QoL.

Marital status. One-way ANOVA testing was used to compare means for loneliness, depression, social support, and QOL based on marital status. There were no mean differences based on marital status for loneliness, depression, or QOL. Total social support [F (4,55) = 6.556, p <0.001)], emotional support [(F (4,55) = 5.778, $p < 0.01$)], positive social support [(F (4, 55) = 4.510, $p < 0.01$)], affective support [(F(4, 55) = 2.335, $p < 0.05$)], and tangible support [(F(4, 55) = 4.815, $p < 0.01$)] all differed significantly based on marital status. The participant with the highest loneliness score (56) was married, but the spouse was not living in the home.

Education, income, living situation, and employment. Mean scores for loneliness, depression, social support, or QoL did not differ based on education levels, employment status, or living situation. Actual number of persons living in the home did not correlate with advancing age, either measure of loneliness, functional status, social support, depression, or quality of life. Annual household income was not associated with loneliness, depression, QoL, or total social support, emotional support, tangible support, or positive social support. Income was divided into quartiles for even distribution and still did not differ on means for loneliness, depression, QoL, or social support measures.

Depression, social support, quality of life, and health-related variables. Correlation coefficients are reported in Table 3. Depression negatively correlated with QoL, total social support, emotional support, and positive social support. QoL correlated with total social support, emotional support, tangible support, affective support, and positive social support.

Loneliness, when measured by the UCLA scale, did not correlate with depression, diminished QoL, or social support. Self-identification of loneliness did correlate with lower QoL, higher depression scores, lower total social support, and lower emotional support. Neither measure of loneliness was associated with self-rated health, number of chronic illnesses, functional status, or MMSE score. Self-identification of loneliness correlated negatively with the emotional support subscale ($r = .459, p < 0.001$), total social support ($r = .274, p < 0.05$), depression ($r = .388, p < .0.01$), quality of life ($r = .272, p < 0.05$) and MMSE scores ($r = 0.285, p < 0.05$). Those who self-identified as lonely did not differ significantly by age but the group that self-identified as lonely had a lower mean age of 71.8 years ($SD = 5.3$) when compared to the group that reported as nonlonely ($m = 75.5, SD = 6.4$). Chi-square analysis revealed that the self-identified lonely person did not differ from the self-identified nonlonely person on gender, marital status, educational level, income category, employment status, or self-rated health.

Age, gender, total social support, subscales of social support, depression, and QoL were entered into the logistic regression analyses as potential variables explanatory of self-identification of loneliness, given their significant relationship to the single-item measure of self-identification of loneliness. Age, tangible support, and emotional support remained in the model as explanatory of self-identification of loneliness with high age indicating that participants were approximately 22% less likely to report loneliness. Those with less emotional support were 2.5 times more likely to self-identify as being lonely. Table 4 displays the logistic regression statistics.

Mean Comparisons Based on Loneliness Status

Mean comparisons were evaluated for differences between the high loneliness scores (51 or higher) and lower loneliness scores (less than 51) based on the UCLA measure. Comparisons between the less lonely and the lonelier (based on the UCLA scale groups), revealed no difference on functional status, cognitive status, total social support, number of chronic illnesses, depression scores, or QoL

TABLE 3. Correlation Coefficients for Psychosocial and Health-Related Variables

Variable	1	2	3	4	5	6	7	8	9	10	11	12	13	14
1. UCLA Loneliness Scale	1													
2. Single-Item Lonely Measure	.073	1												
3. Depression Score	.005	.388**	1											
4. Total Social Support	.007	−.274*	−.346**	1										
5. Emotional Support	−.067	−.459**	−.312*	.896**	1									
6. Affective Support	.059	−.031	−.230	.726**	.539**	1								
7. Tangible Support	−.012	−.013	−.218	.813**	.558**	.671**	1							
8. Positive Social Support	.060	−.213	−.334**	.701**	.586**	.244	.379**	1						
9. Visual Analog QOL	.118	−.272*	−.596**	.608**	.541**	.405**	.444**	.522**	1					
10. Perceived Health	.050	−.083	.318	−.059	.033	.008	−.210	−.028	−.197	1				
11. Basic ADLs	.101	.052	.319*	−.039	−.098	.048	−.005	−.009	−.185	.278*	1			
12. Instrumental ADLs	−.150	−.114	.305	−.113	.012	−.237	−.176	−.052	−.401**	.490**	.328*	1		
13. Number of Chronic Illnesses	.238	.245	.235	−.160	−.137	.012	−.147	−.199	−.247	.478**	.112	.150	1	
14. Mini-Mental Status Exam	.162	.144	−.213	.049	.016	.080	−.080	−.198	.285*	−.045	−.298*	−.495**	.101	1

TABLE 4. Logistic Regression for Explanatory Variables of Self-Reported Loneliness, $N = 60$

				95% CI		
Variable	B	SE	OR	Lower	Upper	p
Age	–0.218	0.129	0.804	0.625	1.036	0.092
Tangible Support Subscale	1.051	0.599	2.860	0.883	9.260	0.080
Emotional Support Subscale	–2.450	0.913	0.086	0.014	0.517	0.007

Note. CI = Confidence Interval; Initial −2 log likelihood = 39.010; Final −2 log likelihood 21.309. Cox & Snell $R^2 = 0.255$; Nagelkerke's $R^2 = 0.534$. Hosmer-Lemeshow statistic remained significant at 8 iterations with chi square of 17.701, $df = 3$, $p = .001$.

scores. The groups did differ on mean scores for emotional support, with the lonelier group reporting a lower mean for emotional support [$F(2, 58) = 5.23$, $p < 0.05$].

Discussion

The primary aim of this study was to better understand the relationships between loneliness and depression, social support, and quality of life for older adults living with chronic illness in Appalachia. The study had three study questions, which were answered by the analyses. The first question sought the relationship between self-identification of loneliness and scale measure in this specific population. It was hypothesized that the two measures would significantly correlate as they have in other populations. This hypothesis was not supported, and that result was surprising and has further implications for studies of loneliness in Appalachia.

It is important to note in this study that older Appalachians had moderately high UCLA Loneliness Scale scores but did not self-identify as lonely. Simple self-identification of loneliness does not elaborate on specific emotional or psychological characteristics that each participant associates with loneliness, but it is considered, in the literature, to still be a valid assessment of identification of lonely individuals and continues to be used in scientific studies (Ekwall et al., 2005; Fry & Debats, 2002; Paul, Ayis, & Ebrahim, 2006; Routasalo, Savikko, Tilvis, Strandberg, & Pitkala, 2006; Victor, 2005). Self-identification of loneliness was the original standard against which the UCLA scale was validated (D. Russell et al., 1978) and it was reported to correlate highly with self-identification of loneliness ($r = 0.79$, $p < 0.01$). The lack of correlation in this particular sample could relate to a social stigma associated with loneliness (Lau & Gruen, 1992) in a culture that values belonging to a community (Davis & Magilvy, 2000). This finding makes it important to consider the method of measurement of loneliness in the context of Appalachian culture. The low self-identification of loneliness in the face of high loneliness scale scores may be an indication that older adults living in Appalachia will also continue to suffer loneliness with quiet pride and will not report loneliness as a problem to healthcare providers. Use of an abbreviated measure of loneliness in Appalachia could result in significant underreporting of loneliness. Also, it is potentially true, given the links between loneliness and emotional support, that loneliness may be conceptualized as more of an emotional problem in Appalachia and that it may be necessary to use a measure that reflects this conceptualization.

The second question sought to understand how loneliness related to sociodemographics and specific psychosocial and health-related variables that have been linked to loneliness in larger broader samples. Based on the literature, it was hypothesized that widowhood, lower education, lower income, higher number of chronic diseases, impaired functional status, poorer self-report of health, depression, lower social support, and poorer quality of life would be associated with loneliness. This hypothesis was only marginally supported. The positive correlations between loneliness, depression, and some components of social support are consistent with what has been reported in many samples of lonely persons. It was surprising that loneliness did not correlate with these specified variables since marital status, poverty, high numbers of chronic illness, impaired function, and self-report of health have been predictive of loneliness in national samples (Theeke, 2009) and since loneliness has been predictive of depression (Cacioppo, Hawkley, & Thisted, 2010) and poor quality of life (Ekwall et al., 2005) in other studies. Future studies with more complex analyses testing a model of predictors of loneliness in this population would add to the current knowledge of loneliness in Appalachia.

The third question explored differences between self-identified lonely persons and not lonely persons and between high- and low-loneliness scorers. It was hypothesized that participants with high lonely scores would have higher depression, lower social support, and lower quality of life scores when compared to those with lower lonely scores. This hypothesis was supported, and there was a new finding of a significant difference on the emotional support subscale between those who report loneliness and those who did not. Since Sherbourne and Stewart (1991) defined *emotional support* as "the expression of positive affect, empathetic understanding, and the encouragement of expressions of feelings" (707), it may be logical that interventions for loneliness could be developed to target different aspects of this definition, addressing the psychological problems that arise from low emotional support.

Loneliness and Demographic Variables

It was not expected that advancing age would be a negative correlate of loneliness, depression, and QOL or that those who self-identified as lonely would have a lower mean age. This finding may be illustrative of the developmental phase of the older old adults participating in the study. More recent literature indicates that loneliness may be a problem that is more prevalent in the middle age group than in older adult samples (C. Wilson & Moulton, 2010).

Another surprising finding was that men had higher loneliness scores and higher QoL scores, and that result is inconsistent with literature that reported women with higher scores (Holmen et al., 1992) and that reported that loneliness negatively correlates with QoL (Ekwall et al., 2005).

Limitations

The cross-sectional design of this study eliminates the possibility of establishing causal relationships between the psychosocial variables under study. The study examined loneliness, social support, depression, and QOL in a homogenous vulnerable rural older adult sample which limits the generalizability of the findings. Data was gathered based on a small convenience sample and self-report methods for psychosocial variables, and that situation carries with it the possibility of sample bias or self-report errors and limits generalizability.

Conclusions

This study provides evidence that loneliness is a significant problem for older chronically ill Appalachian adults and that it may be related to low emotional support. Further, it provides evidence that this population may be significantly lonely and may not self-identify as lonely. The value of functional independence coupled with the stigma associated with loneliness may be leading older Appalachians to maintain a quiet sense of pride in the face of experiencing significant loneliness. In addition, knowing that this population may not self-identify as being lonely may mean that healthcare providers will have to be proactive in the assessment of loneliness.

If loneliness is conceptualized as more of an emotional problem in Appalachia, then it will be necessary to consider interventions that target this aspect of loneliness. Measuring loneliness in this population may require special attention to the emotional aspect of loneliness as well. Since participants of this study reported relatively high QoL scores in the face of loneliness, poverty, and prevalent chronic illness, it could be considered that lower life or cultural expectations may exist for those who bear witness to the health disparities experienced in Appalachia.

Implications for Future Practice and Research

It may be important for healthcare providers to initiate the conversation about loneliness since it has been reported that community-dwelling adults with subsyndromal depressive and anxiety symptoms may not report a need (Garrido, 2009). Considering loneliness as a reimbursable diagnosis could fuel these conversations between providers and patients. Future longitudinal studies evaluating interventions aimed at diminishing the emotional pain of loneliness could diminish loneliness and the negative outcomes associated with loneliness, which include multiple chronic illnesses and increased use of the healthcare system.

REFERENCES

Arean, P. A., & Miranda, J. (1997). The utility of the Center for Epidemiological Studies Depression Scale in older primary care patients. *Aging & Mental Health*, *1*(1), 9.

Behringer, B. F., & Freidell, G. H. (2006). Appalachia: Where place matters in health. *Preventing Chronic Disease*, *3*(4), 1–14.

Cacioppo, J. T., Hawkley, L. C., & Thisted, R. A. (2010). Perceived social isolation makes me sad: 5–year cross-lagged analyses of loneliness and depressive symptomatology in the Chicago Health, Aging, and Social Relations Study. *Psychology and Aging*, *25*(2), 453–463. doi: 2010–11857–019 [pii]10.1037/a0017216

Cacioppo, J. T., Hughes, M. E., Waite, L. J., Hawkley, L. C., & Thisted, R. A. (2006). Loneliness as a specific risk factor for depressive symptoms: Cross-sectional and longitudinal analyses. *Psychology and Aging*, *21*(1), 140–151. doi: Doi 10.1037/0882–7974.21.1.140

Davis, R. A., & Magilvy, J. (2000). Quiet pride: The experience of chronic illness by rural older adults. *Journal of Nursing Scholarship*, *32*(4), 6.

de Boer, A. G. E., van Lanschot, J. J. B., Stalmeier, P. F. M., van Sandick, J. W., Hulscher, B. F., de Haes, J. C. J., & Sprangers, M. A. G. (2004). Is the Single-Item Visual Analogue Scale as valid, reliable and responsive as multi-item scales in measuring quality of life? *Quality of Life Research*, *13*(2), 9.

Dykstra, P. A., van Tilburg, T. G., & Gierveld, J. D. (2005). Changes in older adult loneliness: Results from a seven-year longitudinal study. *Research on Aging*, *27*(6), 725–747. doi: Doi 10.1177/0164027505279712

Ekwall, A. K., Sivberg, B., & Hallberg, I. R. (2005). Loneliness as a predictor of quality of life among older caregivers. *Journal of Advanced Nursing*, *49*(1), 23–32.

Folstein, M. F., Folstein, S. E., & McHugh, P. R. (1975). Minimental state: A practical method for grading the cognitive state of patients for the clinician. *Journal of Psychiatric Research*, *12*, 9.

Fry, P. S., & Debats, D. L. (2002). Self-efficacy beliefs as predictors of loneliness and psychological distress in older adults. *International Journal of Aging & Human Development*, *55*(3), 233–269.

Garrido, M. K. R.; Kaas, M.; & Kane, R. (2009). Perceived need for mental health care among community-dwelling older adults. [Research descriptive]. *Journals of Gerontology Series B: Psychological Sciences and Social Sciences*, *64B*(6), 8. doi: 10.1093/geronb/gbp073

Geller, J. (2000). Loneliness: an overlooked and costly health risk factor. *Minnesota Medicine*, *83*(4), 48–51.

Goins, R. T., Spencer, S. M., & Williams, K. (2011). Lay meanings of health among rural older adults in Appalachia. *Journal of Rural Health, 27*, 7.
Haaga, J. (2004). *The aging of Appalachia: Demographic and socioeconomic change in Appalachia*. Washington, DC: Appalachian Regional Commission.
Halverson, J. A., Ma, L., & Harner, E. J. (2004). *An analysis of disparities in health status and access to care in the Appalachian region*. Washington, DC: Appalachian Regional Commission.
Henderson, D., & Tickamyer, A. (2008). Lost in Appalachia: The unexpected impact of welfare reform on older women in rural communities. *Journal of Sociology & Social Welfare, XXXV*(3), 19.
Holmen, K., Ericsson, K., Andersson, L., & Winblad, B. (1992). Loneliness among elderly people living in Stockholm: A population study. *Journal of Advanced Nursing, 17*(1), 43–51.
Jylha, M. (2004). Old age and loneliness: Cross-sectional and longitudinal analyses in the tampere longitudinal study on aging. *Revue Canadienne Du Vieillissement [Canadian Journal on Aging], 23*(2), 157–168.
Katz, S., Downs, T., & Cash, H. (1970). Progress in development of the index of ADL. *Gerontologist, Spring, 10*(1), 20–30.
Kirkpatrick, L. A., Shillito, D. J., & Kellas, S. L. (1999). Loneliness, social support, and perceived relationships with God. *Journal of Social and Personal Relationships, 16*(4), 513–522.
Lau, S., & Gruen, G. E. (1992). The social stigma of loneliness: Effect of target persons and perceivers' sex. *Personality and Social Psychology Bulletin, 18*(2), 182–189.
Liu, L. J., & Guo, Q. (2007). Loneliness and health-related quality of life for the empty nest elderly in the rural area of a mountainous county in China. *Quality of Life Research, 16*(8), 1275–1280. doi: DOI 10.1007/s11136–007–9250–0
McCulloch. (1985). The relationship of family proximity and social support to the mental health of older rural adults: The Appalachian context. *Journal of Aging Studies, 9*(1), 17.
Mullins, L. C., Elston, C. H., & Gutkowski, S. M. (1996). Social determinants of loneliness among older Americans. *Genetic Social and General Psychology Monographs, 122*(4), 453–473.
Patrick, J. H., Cottrell, L. E., & Barnes, K. A. (2001). Gender, emotional support, and well-being among rural elderly. *Sex Roles, 45*(1/2), 15.
Paul, C., Ayis, S., & Ebrahim, S. (2006). Psychological distress, loneliness and disability in old age. *Psychology, Health, & Medicine, 11*(2), 221–232. doi: NKP4H48802610027 [pii]10.1080/13548500500262945
Radloff, L. S. (1977). The CES–D scale: A self-report depression scale for research in the general population. *Applied Psychological Measurement, 1*, 16.
Rinaldi, P., Mecocci, P., Benedetti, C., Ercolani, S., Bregnocchi, M., Menculini, G., . . . Cherubini, A. (2003). Validation of the Five-Item Geriatric Depression Scale in elderly subjects in three different settings. *Journal of the American Geriatrics Society, 51*, 5.
Routasalo, P. E., Savikko, N., Tilvis, R. S., Strandberg, T. E., & Pitkala, K. H. (2006). Social contacts and their relationship to loneliness among aged people: A population-based study. *Gerontology, 52*(3), 181–187. doi: Doi 10.1159/000091828
Russell, D., Peplau, L. A., & Cutrona, C. E. (1980). The revised UCLA Loneliness Scale: Concurrent and discriminant validity evidence. *Journal of Personality and Social Psychology, 39*(3), 472–480.
Russell, D., Peplau, L. A., & Ferguson, M. L. (1978). Developing a measure of loneliness. *Journal of Personality Assessment, 42*(3), 290–294.
Russell, D. W. (1996). UCLA Loneliness Scale (Version 3): Reliability, validity, and factor structure. *Journal of Personality Assessment, 66*(1), 20–40.

Savikko, N., Routasalo, P., Tilvis, R. S., Strandberg, T. E., & Pitkala, K. H. (2005). Predictors and subjective causes of loneliness in an aged population. *Archives of Gerontology and Geriatrics*, *41*(3), 223–233. doi: DOI 10.1016/j.archger.2005.03.002

Sheikh, J., & Yesavage, J. (1986). Geriatric Depression Scale (GDS): Recent evidence and development of a shorter version. *Clinical Gerontologist: The Journal of Aging and Mental Health*, *5*(1–2), 8.

Sherbourne, C., & Stewart, A. (1991). The MOS social support survey. *Social Science Medicine*, *32*, 9.

Spitzer, W. O., Dobson, A. J., Hall, J., Chesterman, E., Levi, J., Shepherd, R., Catchlove, B. R. (1981). Measuring the quality of life of cancer patients: A concise QL–index for use by physicians. *Journal of Chronic Disease*, *34*(12), 585–597.

Theeke, L. A. (2009). Predictors of loneliness in US adults over age sixty-five. *Archives of Psychiatric Nursing*, *23*(5), 387–396. doi: DOI 10.1016/j.apnu.2008.11.002

Theeke, L. A. (2010). Sociodemographic and health-related risks for loneliness and outcome differences by loneliness status in a sample of U.S. older adults. *Research in Gerontolological Nursing*, *3*(2), 113–125. doi: 10.3928/19404921–20091103–99

Victor, C. (2005). Do self-reported levels of loneliness amongst older people change over time? A two year follow-up. *Gerontologist*, *45*, 319–319.

Wilson, C., & Moulton, B. (2010). Loneliness among older adults: A national survey of adults 45+ (Special report). In *Knowledge networks and insight policy research.*Washington, DC: AARP.

Wilson, R. S., Krueger, K. R., Arnold, S. E., Schneider, J. A., Kelly, J. F., Barnes, L. L., … Bennett, D. A. (2007). Loneliness and risk of Alzheimer disease. *Archives of General Psychiatry*, *64*(2), 234–240. doi: 64/2/234 [pii] 10.1001/archpsyc.64.2.234

Yarcheski, A., Mahon, N. E., Yarcheski, T. J., & Cannella, B. L. (2004). A meta-analysis of predictors of positive health practices. *Journal of Nursing Scholarship, Second Quarter*, *7*, 102–108.

Life Events and Personality Predicting Loneliness Among Centenarians: Findings From the Georgia Centenarian Study

BOB HENSLEY
The College of Saint Scholastica

PETER MARTIN
JENNIFER A. MARGRETT
Iowa State University

MAURICE MACDONALD
Kansas State University

ILENE C. SIEGLER
Duke University

LEONARD W. POON
University of Georgia

THE GEORGIA CENTENARIAN STUDY[1]

ABSTRACT. Regarding the purpose of this study, the researchers analyzed the roles that both life events (life-time positive events and life-time negative events) and personality (Neuroticism, Extraversion, Trust, Competence, and Ideas) played in participants of the Georgia Centenarian Study. The researchers analyzed these variables to determine whether they predicted loneliness. Analyses indicated that life-time negative events significantly predicted loneliness. In essence, the higher was the number of life-time negative life events, the higher was the loneliness score. Moreover, Neuroticism, Competence, and Ideas were all significant predictors of loneliness. The higher was the level of Neuroticism and intellectual curiosity, the higher was the level of loneliness, whereas the lower was the level

[1]*Additional authors include S. M. Jazwinski, R. C. Green, M. Gearing, J. L. Woodard, M. A. Johnson, J. S. Tenover, W. L. Rodgers, D. B. Hausman, C. Rott, A. Davey, and J. Arnold.*

of Competence, the higher was the level of loneliness. In addition, both life-time positive and life-time negative life events were significant predictors of Neuroticism. The higher was the number of life-time positive events, the lower was the level of Neuroticism, and the higher was the number of life-time negative events, the greater was the level of Neuroticism. These results indicated that life-time negative events indirectly affect loneliness via Neuroticism. Last, our results indicated that the Competence facet mediated the relationship between life-time negative life events and loneliness. Life-time negative life events significantly affected centenarians' perceived competence, and Competence in turn significantly affected the centenarians' loneliness. These results as a whole not only add to our understanding of the link between personality and loneliness, but also provide new insight into how life events predict loneliness.

LONELINESS IS A PHENOMENON that can affect people at various ages throughout the lifespan. It can be defined as the pain of feeling alone (Tillich, 1959), is a disabling condition characterized by a fundamental sense of emptiness, worthlessness, and a lack of control (Cacioppo & Patrick, 2008). From a developmental perspective, loneliness has been linked to elevated vascular resistance in younger adults and increased blood pressure in older adults (Hawkley & Cacioppo, 2007) and has been shown to predict changes in depressive symptoms above and beyond social isolation, neuroticism, stress, and social support (Cacioppo, Hawkley, & Thisted, 2010). In addition, both visual and auditory impairment have been found to contribute to loneliness (Savikko, Routasalo, Tilvis, Strandberg, & Pitkälä, 2005). One particular developmental period that has been studied regarding the effects of loneliness is late adulthood (Bishop & Martin, 2007; Fees, Martin, & Poon, 1999; Hensley, Martin, MacDonald, & Poon, 2010; Long & Martin, 2000; Martin, Hagberg, & Poon, 1997).

Within late adulthood, one group of importance to gerontologists when studying loneliness is centenarians. Research has demonstrated that a key issue that centenarians face in their day-to-day lives, more so than in any other period in the lifespan, is social isolation (Hawkley & Cacioppo, 2007) and that this isolation is connected with a loss of social support (Martin et al., 1997). In addition, both visual and auditory impairment, conditions more prominent on average in late adulthood (especially in centenarians) than in other developmental periods, can contribute to loneliness, as these impairments hinder communication with family members and friends (Savikko et al., 2005). Moreover, the functional limitations of centenarians can inhibit opportunities for these individuals to socially interact with others, which can contribute to the experience of loneliness.

One area of interest upon which scholars have focused is how personality affects loneliness in late adulthood. Regarding personality variables, anxiety, extraversion, and neuroticism have been shown to predict loneliness (Fees, Martin, & Poon, 1999; Hensley et al., 2010; Long & Martin, 2000; Martin, Hagberg, & Poon, 1997), whereas Cacioppo et al. (2010) concluded that neuroticism did not influence loneliness across time. However, less is known of the effect of other personality variables (e.g., Conscientiousness) on loneliness. Beyond proximal influences (those present-day influences, such as personality) that can predict loneliness, researchers have studied the role in loneliness of distal variables (those variables from the distant past, such as childhood life events), including childhood health (Hensley et al., 2010), educational attainment (Bishop & Martin, 2007), and stressful life events (Cacioppo et al., 2010). However, less is known about whether and how these distal variables (and other ones, including positive life events) influence loneliness in centenarians. Hensley et al. (2010) found that after control for personality, both childhood health and number of children were still significant predictors of loneliness. Regarding the purpose of this study, the researchers analyzed the role that both life events (life-time positive events and life-time negative events) and personality (Neuroticism, Trust, Competence, and Ideas) played in participants of the Georgia Centenarian Study. The researchers analyzed these variables to determine whether they predicted loneliness.

The current research is of value because it provides further understanding of the roles that both life events and personality play in later life regarding loneliness. This research not only provides insights into the direct effects that proximal variables (e.g., personality) have on loneliness in late life, but also illustrates the potential indirect effects of distal variables (e.g., life-time negative life events) on loneliness via personality.

Theoretical Orientations

When investigating the role that distal influences play in these critical variables in late adulthood, two theoretical perspectives are most appropriate to utilize. The key theoretical model used in our study is the developmental adaptation model (Martin & Martin, 2002), and embedded in this model is another influential theoretical framework, the life course perspective (Crosnoe & Elder, 2002; Elder, 1994).

The developmental adaptation model (Martin & Martin, 2002) can help explain the role of distal experiences on personality and well-being in older adults. The model serves to provide an understanding of how potential developmental trajectories based on life histories as well as present resources influence successful adaptation. The model includes distal developmental influences, proximal developmental influences, behavioral coping mediators, and developmental outcomes. This model has two central components found in other models of adult development: a stress and coping component and a life-span/life course time frame.

Regarding stress and coping, one model in the literature was introduced by Taylor and Aspinwall (1996), who argued that there are several mediators and moderators of psychosocial stress. Important moderators of psychosocial stress include familial influences, individual difference factors, and external resources. The key mediator between psychosocial stress and the developmental outcome (i.e., loneliness) is coping. In essence, the effects of personal, social, and external resources are mediated extensively via coping. Moreover, personal (e.g., early negative life events) and social resources may operate earlier in the causal chain of events and not just at the time of psychosocial stress experience (e.g., high levels of loneliness) (Taylor & Aspinwall).

In addition to the stress and coping focus, the life-course perspective (Crosnoe & Elder, 2002; Elder, 1994) is also a crucial component in the developmental adaptation model. Because the life course perspective focuses on transitions and periods in one's life and poses the question to what extent early experiences exert an influence on later life development (Elder), this paradigm seems appropriate when investigating how distal influences affect various critical outcomes during the various transitions from childhood to late adulthood.

Life Events and Loneliness in Late Adulthood

Previous research has investigated the link between distal variables (e.g., life events) and loneliness in older adults. Hensley et al. (2010), in studying both octogenarians and centenarians, concluded that both childhood health and number of children, even after controlling for personality, significantly predicted loneliness. In addition, Bishop and Martin (2007), in studying unmarried older adults, found that past educational attainment had a negative indirect effect on loneliness through neuroticism. Moreover, Hawkley and Cacioppo (2007) stated that lonely adults reported a greater number of childhood adversities (e.g., childhood hospitalization, parental divorce, physical abuse) than their nonlonely counterparts. Lonely participants also perceived the present-day negative effects of these events as more potent than the nonlonely participants. In contrast, Cacioppo et al. (2010), via longitudinal analysis, suggested that the relationship between loneliness and depressive symptoms was not attributable to stressful life events influencing either one of these variables. Unlike Bishop and Martin (2007) and Hensley et al. (2010), who studied life events as distal variables, Cacioppo et al. (2010) analyzed life events as a proximal variable, with participants indicating the stressful life events that occurred in their lives within the previous year. Despite the research presented here, additional research on the role that life events from the distant past play in loneliness in centenarians is needed, given the paucity of research (Hensley et al., 2010) on the topic.

Personality and Loneliness in Late Adulthood

Several studies have addressed the role that one's personality plays in experiencing loneliness in later life. In their research with participants from the Georgia Centenarian Study, Hensley et al. (2010) found that both Extraversion and Neuroticism significantly predicted loneliness, whereas Bishop and Martin (2007) found not only that Neuroticism directly affected loneliness, but also that educational attainment indirectly affected loneliness via Neuroticism. Long and Martin (2000), in studying personality, relationship closeness, and loneliness of the oldest old and their children, reported that Anxiety (neuroticism) positively predicted loneliness in the oldest old, whereas Extraversion negatively predicted children's loneliness. Moreover, Fees et al. (1999), in their research on loneliness and physical health status, stated that Anxiety directly influenced loneliness when loneliness was used as both an outcome variable and a mediator. Last, Martin et al. (1997), in a parallel study regarding the predictors of loneliness between participants in the United States and Sweden, found differential predictions in the experience of loneliness between the two samples. In their American sample, high neuroticism served as the most important predictor of loneliness, whereas in the Swedish sample, both cognition and social support served as the key predictors. However, in results obtained from the Chicago Health, Aging, and Social Relations Study, Cacioppo et al. (2010) concluded that the longitudinal effect of loneliness on depressive symptoms was significant above and beyond neuroticism. Despite the existing literature on the connection between personality and loneliness in later life, more research is needed on the role that other personality traits (e.g., Conscientiousness, Openness, Agreeableness) play in the experience of loneliness, especially in centenarians. Thus far, few researchers (Hensley et al.; Long and Martin) have studied other personality traits (Extraversion) beyond neuroticism, and none have addressed the role that aforementioned traits play in loneliness.

Research Questions

Regarding the purpose of this study, we analyzed the role that both life events (both life-time positive and life-time negative ones) and personality (i.e., Neuroticism, Extraversion, Trust, Competence, and Ideas) played in determining whether they predicted loneliness. In addition, we wanted to determine whether personality served as a mediator between life events and loneliness. From the review of the literature, a few research questions can be posed. These questions include the following: (a) What direct effects do life events and personality have on a centenarian's experience of loneliness? Regarding previous research, we predicted that neuroticism would be positively related to loneliness. (b) What direct effects do life events have on personality? (c) Does personality act as a mediating variable between life events and loneliness? (d) Does personality act as moderating variable between life events and loneliness?

Method

Participants

This study consisted of 137 centenarians of the Georgia Centenarian Study (Poon et al., 2007). These participants constituted part of the interview segment assessing their mental status, ADL functioning, depression, and family history. Of the total sample, women comprised 78.8% of the group, and men comprised 21.2% of sample. The majority of participants (83.2%) classified themselves as Caucasian, and 39% of the sample had completed either high school or 1–3 years of college. Investigators recruited participants via voter registration rolls from the state of Georgia and from calls to a random subset of care facilities. The sampling frame for the current study consisted of 44 counties in Northeast Georgia within a two-hour drive from the University of Georgia campus. Investigators first recruited participants by telephone and mail, and then face-to-face interviews followed. The researchers either left questionnaire packets with the participants or mailed them to a close family member or care provider in order to receive information regarding centenarians.

Measures

Life events. The distal variables included 23 life events, from which a series of summary scores was created. The life events were based on common life events, such as those used in the PERI Life Events Scale (Dohrenwend, Krasnoff, Askenasy, & Dohrenwend, 1978) and included items such as marriage, death of a spouse, birth of children, change of employment, serious financial problems, and residential change. If these life events had happened at any point in their life, investigators requested that participants indicate whether the event had been a positive or negative influence on their life. Participants also indicated when the event had happened. The summary scores utilized for the present study consisted of total life-time negative events as well as total life-time positive events.

Personality. Regarding personality, we used selected domains and facets from the Revised NEO Personality Inventory (NEO-PI-R; Costa & McCrae, 1992) in the present study. The NEO-PI-R contains five domains (Neuroticism, Extraversion, Openness, Conscientiousness, and Agreeableness), and within each domain are six respective subsets, or facets, of personality items.

Most personality studies have assessed the major Big Five traits, whereas the assessment of more specific personality facets has not received sufficient attention (Siegler & Brummett, 2000). Because the entire NEO assessment battery would have been too taxing for centenarians, we asked centenarians to respond to scales from the Five-Factor Model of personality based on versions of the NEO PI-R system. The NEO Five-Factory Inventory (FFI) was used as a validated short form of the domains Neuroticism and Extraversion and trait-level indicators from three factors representing Openness to Ideas (i.e., O5—Ideas), Conscientiousness (i.e., C1—Competence), and Agreeableness (i.e., A1—Trust). We based the selection of domains and traits on earlier work on personality among centenarians (Martin, 2007; Martin et al., 2002).

Moreover, previous research has shown the extent to which both Neuroticism and Extraversion mediate health outcomes in stress-and-coping paradigms (Adler & Mathews, 1994; Taylor & Aspinwall, 1996). Moreover, Neuroticism and Extraversion account for much of the explained variability in psychosocial development and adjustment (Barrera, 1988; Wheaton, 1985).

Therefore, with these considerations in mind, we reduced the number of personality factors investigated in the current analyses from five to two (i.e., Neuroticism and Extraversion). Items are scored on a 3-point scale (-1 = *disagree*, 0 = *in between*, and 1 = *agree*), and high scores on these scales are indicative of both high Neuroticism and Extraversion. In addition, we used the more specific personality facets of Trust, Competence, and Ideas (these facets correspond to the Agreeableness, Conscientiousness, and Openness domains, respectively) from the NEO-PI-R. We also scored these items on a three-point scale, and high scores on these facets are indicative of Trust, Competence, and Ideas as well. Martin et al. (2006) obtained the following reliabilities from the respective scales: Extraversion, $\alpha = .81$; Neuroticism, $\alpha = .87$; Trust, $\alpha = .86$; Competence, $\alpha = .80$, and Ideas, $\alpha = .84$.

Loneliness. The researchers measured loneliness by using the UCLA Loneliness Scale (Russell, 1996). The UCLA Loneliness Scale (Version 3) is a highly reliable 20-item instrument with a high test–retest reliability over 1 yr ($r = .73$) and internal consistency ranging from .89 to .94. Out of 10 items on the short version of the scale, 5 are worded positively (e.g., "How often do you feel close to people?"), and the remaining 5 are worded negatively (e.g., "How often do you feel left out?"). Each question is responded to using a 4-point scale where "1" corresponds to "never" and "4" corresponds to "always." A total score on the loneliness scale is created by recoding responses to the positively worded items and then summing together scores on the 10 items. Cronbach's alpha for our pilot sample on the 10-item version of the scale was $\alpha = .81$.

Analyses

The investigators conducted several analyses in this study. First, we computed descriptive analyses to assess the means and standard deviations of the measures used in this investigation. Second, we computed multiple regression analyses to determine whether both the aforementioned personality factors (i.e., Neuroticism and Extraversion) and facets (i.e., Trust, Competence, and Ideas) and the life events variables (i.e., life-time negative and life-time positive life events) predicted the loneliness. Moreover, we used additional regression analyses to determine whether personality acted as a mediating variable between life events and loneliness.

Results

Means, standard deviations, and frequencies of each measure used in this study are presented in Table 1. Some noteworthy results were evident. Regarding life events, participants experience more negative life events ($M = 7.19$) than positive life events ($M = 4.12$). In addition, participants did not display, on average, high levels of Neuroticism ($M = -7.30$) and loneliness ($M = 14.13$), but reported high levels of trust in their world ($M = 6.26$). Moreover, the bivariate correlations of all the variables used in the present study are presented in Table 2. Significant correlations (among others) existed between life-time negative life events and Competence, $r = -.22, p < .05$, as well as between Neuroticism and loneliness, $r = .59, p < .01$.

TABLE 1. Means and Standard Deviations of Measures Used in the Present Study on Life Events, Personality, and Loneliness

Variable	*M*	*SD*
Life Events		
Life-time Negative Events Summary Score	7.19	2.59
Life-time Positive Events Summary Score	4.12	1.62
Personality		
Extraversion Summary Score (Range −11 to 11)	1.95	4.13
Neuroticism Summary Score (Range −12 to 10)	−7.30	5.43
Trust Facet (Range 1–8)	6.26	2.02
Ideas Facet (Range −8 to 8)	−1.54	4.13
Competence Facet (Range −3 to 7)	5.60	2.23
Loneliness		
Loneliness Summary Score (Range 10–29)	14.13	4.32

TABLE 2. Bivariate Correlations for Variables Used in the Present Study

Variables	1	2	3	4	5	6	7	8
Life Events								
1. Life-time Negative Life Events Summary Score	1							
2. Life-time Positive Life Events Summary Score	.44**	1						
Personality								
3. Extraversion Summary Score	.08	−.02	1					
4. Neuroticism Summary Score	.13	−.12	−.15	1				
5. Trust Facet	−.18*	.10	.11	−.24**	1			
6. Ideas Facet	.11	.10	.13	−.01	−.10	1		
7. Competence Facet	−.22*	−.11	.26**	−.39**	.17	.09	1	
Loneliness								
8. Loneliness Summary Score	.17	−.01	−.27**	.59**	−.29**	.26*	−.49**	1
M	7.19	4.12	1.95	−7.30	6.26	−1.54	5.60	14.13
SD	2.59	1.62	4.13	5.43	2.02	4.13	2.23	4.32

$^{*}p < .05$. $^{**}p < .01$.

TABLE 3. Summary of Regression Analyses for Life Events and Personality Variables Predicting Loneliness

	Loneliness (n = 104)		
Variable	B	SE	β
Life-time Negative Events	.38	.18	.22*
Life-time Positive Events	−.30	.29	−.11
Extraversion Summary Score	−.16	.08	−.15+
Neuroticism Summary Score	.35	.06	.44**
Trust Facet	−.18	.16	−.08
Competence Facet	−.56	.16	−.29*
Ideas Facet	.31	.08	.30**
R^2		.55	

*$p < .05$. **$p < .01$. +$p = .052$.

Our first research question focused on whether life events (both life-time positive and life-time negative events) as well as personality directly affected the centenarians' loneliness. Analyses indicated that life-time negative events significantly predicted loneliness, $\beta = .22, p < .05$ (Table 3). In essence, the higher was the number of life-time negative life events, the higher was the loneliness score. Moreover, several personality variables predicted loneliness as well. These personality variables included one factor (Neuroticism) as well as two facets (Competence and Ideas). Neuroticism, Competence, and Ideas were all significant predictors of loneliness: $\beta = .44, p < .01$; $\beta = -.29, p < .05$; $\beta = .30, p < .01$, respectively. The higher was the level of Neuroticism and intellectual curiosity, the higher was the level of loneliness (the finding with Neuroticism supported our hypothesis), whereas the lower was the level of Competence, the higher was the level of loneliness (Table 3). Moreover, a statistical trend was evident for Extraversion predicting loneliness, $\beta = -.15, p = .052$. The higher was the level of Extraversion, the lower was the level of loneliness.

The second research question investigated the direct effects of the distal variables (life-time negative and positive life events) on personality. Our analyses suggested that both life-time positive and life-time negative life events were significant predictors of Neuroticism, $\beta = -.22$, $p < .05$; $\beta = .23$, $p < .05$; and Trust, $\beta = .23$, $p < .05$; $\beta = -.29$, $p < .05$, respectively. The higher was the number of life-time positive events, the lower was the level of Neuroticism, and the higher was the number of life-time negative life events, the greater was the level of Neuroticism. In addition, the higher was the number of life-time positive life events, the higher was the level of Trust, whereas the higher was number of life-time negative life events, the lower was the level of Trust. Last, life-time negative life events significantly predicted Competence, $\beta = -.22$, $p < .05$. The higher was the number of life-time negative life events, the lower was the level of Competence.

The third research question focused on whether personality acted as a mediating variable between life events and loneliness. In addition to computing the direct effects presented in Table 3, meditational analyses were run by computing additional multiple regression analyses linking life events to all the personality factors and facets and linking these personality variables and life events variables to loneliness. Analyses indicated that of all the personality variables examined, only the Competence facet mediated the relationship between life-time negative life events and loneliness (Figure 1). Applying the Sobel test supported the meditational effect, $z = 2.12$, $p < .05$. Life-time negative life events significantly affected centenarians' perceived competence, and Competence in turn significantly affected the centenarians' loneliness. The direct effect from life-time negative life events and loneliness was nonsignificant.

Our fourth research question dealt with whether personality acted as a moderator variable in relation to life events and loneliness. Regression analyses, after centering the appropriate independent variables, yielded results that were not significant. Thus, we concluded that personality did not serve as a moderator variable in this investigation.

Discussion

Regarding the purpose of this study, we analyzed the role that both life events and personality played in participants of the Georgia Centenarian Study. We analyzed these variables to determine whether they predicted loneliness. Previous research has demonstrated the significance in studying loneliness in centenarians, especially in how the loss of friends and family can create social isolation (Hawkley

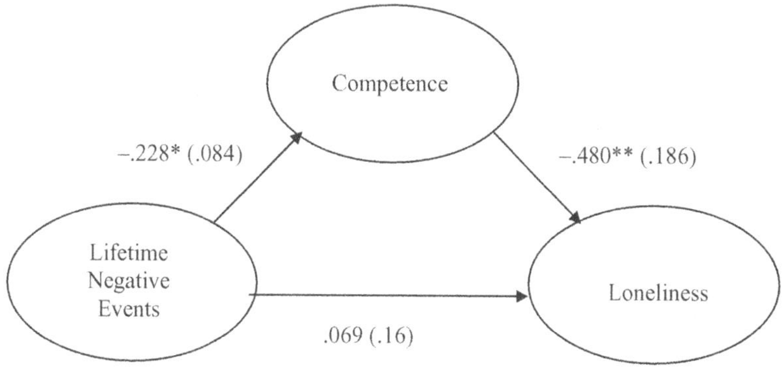

FIGURE 1. Lifetime negative events, Competence, and loneliness.

& Cacioppo, 2007), and this social isolation can decrease the social support centenarians receive (Martin et al., 1997). At the key time when social support is needed to assist centenarians with the challenges of advanced age, social support is often lacking (Long & Martin, 2000), and this lack of social support can be predictive of loneliness (Fees et al., 1999).

Our first research question focused on whether life-time positive and negative life events as well as personality directly affected the centenarians' experience of loneliness. We found that life-time negative life events as well as Neuroticism, Competence, and Ideas were all significant predictors of loneliness. The finding that the higher number of negative life events increases the level of loneliness, first and foremost, makes intuitive sense. Experiencing certain life events, like the death of a spouse, can create a void in one's life in terms of social support and emotional connectedness that could foster loneliness. In addition, the findings regarding life events as well as neuroticism influencing loneliness are supported in the literature. The link between life events and loneliness is established, especially with life events being a distal variable. Hawkley and Cacioppo (2007) stated that not only did lonely adults report a greater number of childhood adversities (e.g., childhood hospitalization, parental divorce, physical abuse) than their nonlonely counterparts, but these individuals also perceived the present-day negative effects of these events as more potent than the nonlonely participants. Moreover, Hensley et al. (2010) found that after controlling for personality, childhood health and number of children still predicted loneliness. However, this study is the only one to the best of our knowledge to find a significant link between a life events summary score and loneliness. Viewing life events in this manner can add to our understanding of the collective, enduring influence of these events across the lifespan.

Regarding the role that neuroticism plays in loneliness in older adults, our results indicated that the higher were the levels of emotional instability, the higher was the level of loneliness. Like the previous finding linking negative life events and loneliness, this finding regarding neuroticism also makes intuitive sense. For instance, individuals displaying consistent emotional instability could behave in such a way as to compromise (if not harm) existing relationships with others, and these strained relationships could contribute to older adults' feeling lonely. This result also adds to a body of literature (Bishop & Martin, 2007; Fees et al., 1999; Hensley et al., 2010; Long & Martin, 2000; Martin et al., 1997) that supports the link between these two variables.

Our second research question dealt with the effect of these distal variables (life events) on personality. Our analyses suggest that both life-time positive and life-time negative events were significantly associated with Neuroticism, Trust, and Competence. The higher was the number of life-time positive events, the lower was the level of Neuroticism, and the higher was the number of life-time negative events, the greater was the level of Neuroticism. In addition, the higher was the number of life-time positive events, the higher was the level of Trust, whereas the higher was the number of life-time negative events, the lower was the level of Trust. Last, the higher was the number of life-time negative events, the lower was the level of Competence. Regarding neuroticism, it would make sense that the higher is the amount of unpleasant life events that one experiences across the lifespan, the greater is the likelihood that one would be more "on edge" and possibly less emotionally stable about what is happening to one in the world around oneself than a person who experiences a greater amount of positive life events. In addition, the same effect that these life events have with neuroticism could also apply to one's trust in the world. Having experienced many negative life events might make an older individual trust his or her everyday world less than one who interprets more life events in a positive light. Last, the link between negative life events and competence is a particularly intriguing one because it is part of a more comprehensive meditational model to be discussed in the next section. According to Costa and McCrae (1992), adults with higher scores on the Competence facet feel well-prepared to deal with life, whereas low scorers often admit they feel unprepared and inept in dealing with life's challenges. Our finding regarding this facet suggests that the greater amount of life events interpreted as negative, the more unprepared and inept participants feel in terms of dealing with other life events as well. Even though some negatively interpreted life events (e.g., a divorce) can make one more resilient, the loss of a spouse via divorce could also affect one's feeling of being interpersonally capable, and negatively influence other intimate relationships in the future.

Empirically speaking, little research has been done on how distal variables (like life events) affect personality in older adults. Bishop and Martin (2007) found that the distal variable in their study, educational attainment, was significantly associated with Neuroticism. In essence, the greater was the educational attainment, the lower was the amount of Neuroticism. However, unlike the present study, Bishop and Martin did not exclusively study centenarians. These results on how distal variables affect personality add to our understanding on how life events can shape present-day functioning, much like the conclusions of Hawkley and Cacioppo (2007).

Our third research question dealt with whether personality acted as a mediating variable between life events and loneliness. We found that the Competence facet mediated the relationship between life-time negative life events and loneliness. In short, life-time negative life events significantly affected loneliness through Competence. A greater amount of negative life events experienced by centenarians was linked to a lower amount of perceived effectiveness in the world, and this lower amount of perceived effectiveness was linked to higher levels of loneliness.

This meditational relationship offers further empirical support for our theoretical underpinning, the developmental adaptation model (Martin & Martin, 2002). A central feature of this theoretical model is the interplay between distal and proximal variables and their respective effects on a selected developmental outcome variable. In this instance, the distal variable of life-time negative events indirectly affected loneliness (the developmental outcome) through Competence (a proximal influence). Even though in the meditational model, life-time negative events did not directly affect loneliness, our results suggest that this variable's effect on the developmental outcome was mediated by Competence.

Our results here support previous research by both Bishop and Martin (2007) and Hawkley and Cacioppo (2007) on the long-term effects of variables from the distant past on older adults. Bishop and Martin stated that the distal variable used in their study, educational attainment, indirectly affected loneliness through Neuroticism. In addition, greater educational attainment reduced loneliness in the presence of Neuroticism or stress, but the indirect effect was most pronounced when mediated by Neuroticism. Even though Hawkley and Cacioppo did not discuss the role that mediating variables played in their research, they did state that lonely participants regarded the current negative effects of childhood adversities (e.g., childhood hospitalization and parental divorce) as more potent than their nonlonely counterparts. In other words, these distal variables had a more powerful "reach" across the lifespan for lonely adults than for nonlonely adults. Our findings that support the developmental adaptation model contribute to the scientific literature by representing one of the few studies to indirectly link life events to loneliness via personality in centenarians.

The fourth research question investigated whether personality served as a moderator variable in relation to life events and loneliness. Our analyses indicated no significant interactions between the life events and personality variables, and therefore we concluded that neither the Neuroticism and Extraversion factors, nor the Trust, Competence, and Ideas facets were moderators in the present study. Even though our current investigation did not find evidence of personality acting as a moderator, future research could examine this role with different variables (e.g., stress and coping, social support) than the ones used in this study to determine if any noteworthy interactions exist between this proximal variable and other variables of interest.

When taken as a whole, these findings are significant because they add to our knowledge of the day-to-day functioning of centenarians. As previously stated, although research has been done regarding the impact of life events and personality in older adults, little if any work has addressed the role that all three variables play with centenarians. Not only does this investigation add to our knowledge of this rapidly growing segment of our population, but more specifically it adds to the minimal research done regarding the role that life events play in personality in older adults. In essence, this study makes a substantive contribution to the research literature on centenarians.

There are a few noteworthy limitations of the present study. First and foremost, the study is cross-sectional in nature, and thus the changes in aforementioned variables across time cannot be determined, and the causal order cannot be established. In addition, the life events variables rely on the recall of information via the centenarians. Thus, these results need to be interpreted with caution. Future research utilizing short-term interval longitudinal designs with these selected variables could provide a greater insight into the developmental effects of distal and proximal variables on physical health in centenarians. Second, rather than relying on information on personality gleaned from five domains, the present study yielded findings on personality from two domains and three facets. Perhaps collecting data on all five personality domains utilized by the NEO-PI-R (Costa & McCrae, 1992) would have yielded a more distinctive personality configuration in centenarians than the one we obtained. Nonetheless, we argue that the respective domains and facets used in our investigation made both practical and logical sense. Third, our sample, drawn from the Southeast United States, might not be truly representative of centenarians in other parts of the United States or across various cultures.

Although several limitations in this study exist, our study does have practical value for professionals. Gerontologists, geriatric counselors, educators, and aging service providers should use this information to develop educational programs and extension services that focus on the importance of life events (including those that happened decades ago) and personality as key factors in contributing to loneliness in the aging population. In light of previous research that states that higher levels of social support relate to lower levels of loneliness (Martin et al., 1997), these programs, in part, could utilize social support as a way to reduce loneliness in centenarians. In addition, retirement community and care center coordinators could develop voluntary social networks among residents to provide the support to fellow residents that might reduce the level of loneliness in them. By understanding the interplay between distant and recent variables, professionals could help enhance the quality of life for the oldest old.

In conclusion, this investigation contributes to the research on how distal (life events) and proximal (personality) variables influence the present-day experience of loneliness in centenarians, and this investigation can serve as a catalyst for additional research on the interplay of distal and proximal variables in other developmental outcomes (e.g., spirituality, perceived optimism). Additional research on the role that both life events and personality variables play in current functioning is needed to help us understand the complexities in the world of the centenarian.

REFERENCES

Adler, N., & Matthews, K. (1994). Health psychology: Why do some people get sick and some stay well? *Annual Review of Psychology*, *45*, 229–259. doi:10.1146/annurev.ps.45.020194.001305

Barrera, M. (1988). Distinctions between social support concepts, measures, and models. *American of Journal of Community Psychology*, *14*, 413–445.

Bishop, A., & Martin, P. (2007). The indirect influence of educational attainment on loneliness among unmarried older adults. *Educational Gerontology*, *33*, 897–917. doi:10.1080/03601270701569275

Cacioppo, J. T., Hawkley, L. C., & Thisted, R. A. (2010). Perceived social isolation makes me sad: 5-year cross-lagged analyses of loneliness and depressive symptomatology in the Chicago Health, Aging, and Social Relations Study. *Psychology and Aging*, *25*(2), 453–463. doi:10.1037/a0017216

Cacioppo, J. T., & Patrick, B. (2008). *Loneliness: Human nature and the need for social connection*. New York: Norton.

Costa, P. T., & McCrae, R. R. (1992). *NEO-PI-R Professional manual*. Lutz, FL: Psychological Assessment Resources.
Crosnoe, R., & Elder, G. (2002). Successful adaptation in the later years: A life course approach to aging. *Social Psychology Quarterly*, *65*(4), 309–328. doi:10.2307/3090105
Dohrenwend, B. S., Krasnoff, L., Askenasy, A. R., & Dohrenwend, B. P. (1978). Exemplification of a method for scaling life events: The PERI Life Events Scale. *Journal of Health and Social Behavior*, *19*, 205–229. doi:10.2307/2136536
Elder, G. (1994). Time, human agency, and social change: Perspectives on the life course. *Social Psychological Quarterly*, *57*, 4–15.
Fees, B. S., Martin, P., & Poon, L. (1999). A model of loneliness in older adults. *Journal of Gerontology: Psychological Sciences*, *54B*(4), P231–P239.
Hawkley, L. C., & Cacioppo, J. T. (2007). Aging and loneliness: Downhill quickly? *Current Directions in Psychological Science*, *16*(4), 187–191. doi:10.1111/j.1467-8721.2007.00501.x
Hensley, R., Martin, P., MacDonald, M., & Poon, L. (2010). Family history and adaptation among centenarians and octogenarians. *Gerontology*, *56*, 83–87. doi:10.1159/000271955
Long, M. V., & Martin, P. (2000). Personality, relationship closeness, and loneliness of oldest old adults and their children. *Journal of Gerontology: Psychological Sciences*, *55B*(5), P311–P319.
Martin, P. (2007). Personality and coping among centenarians. In L. W. Poon & T. T. Perls (Eds.), *Annual review of gerontology and geriatrics. Vol. 27. Biopsychosocial approaches to longevity* (pp. 89–106). New York: Springer.
Martin, P., da Rosa, G., Siegler, I. C., Davey, A., MacDonald, M., & Poon, L. (2006). Personality and longevity: Findings from the Georgia Centenarian Study. *Age*, *28*, 343–352. doi:10.1007/s11357-006-9022-8
Martin, P., Hagberg, B., & Poon, L. (1997). Predictors of loneliness in centenarians: A parallel study. *Journal of Cross-Cultural Gerontology*, *12*, 203–224. doi:10.1023/A:1006587502257
Martin, P., Long, M. V., & Poon, L. (2002). Age changes and differences in personality traits and states of the old and very old. *Journal of Gerontology: Psychological Sciences*, *57B*, P144–P152. doi:10.1023/A:1006587502257
Martin, P., & Martin, M. (2002). Proximal and distal influences on development: The model of developmental adaptation. *Developmental Review*, *22*, 78–96. doi:10.1006/drev.2001.0538
Russell, D. W. (1996). UCLA Loneliness Scale (Version 3): Reliability, validity, and factor structure. *Journal of Personality Assessment*, *66*, 20–40. doi:10.1207/s5327752jpa6601-2
Savikko, N., Routasalo, P., Tilvis, R. S., Strandberg, T. E, & Pitkälä, K. H. (2005). Predictors and subjective causes of loneliness in an aged population. *Archives of Gerontology and Geriatrics*, *41*, 223–233. doi:10.1016/j.archger.2005.03.002
Siegler, I. C., & Brummett, B. H. (2000). Associations among NEO personality assessments and well-being at midlife: Facet-level analyses. *Psychology and Aging*, *15*, 710–714. doi:10.1037/0882-7984.15.4.710
Taylor, S. E., & Aspinwall, L. G. (1996). Mediating and moderating processes in psychosocial stress: Appraisal, coping, resistance, and vulnerability. In H. B. Kaplan (Ed.), *Psychosocial stress: Perspectives on structure, theory, life-course, and methods* (pp. 71–110). New York: Academic Press.
Tillich, P. (1959). The eternal now. In H. Feifel (Ed.), *The meaning of death* (pp. 30–38). New York: McGraw-Hill.
Wheaton, B. (1985). Models for the stress-buffering functions of coping resources. *Journal of Health and Social Behavior*, *26*, 352–364. doi:10.2307/2136658

No Place Like Home? Potential Pathways to Loneliness in Older Adults Under the Care of a Live-In Foreign Home Care Worker

LIAT AYALON
Bar Ilan University

SHARON SHIOVITZ-EZRA
The Hebrew University of Jerusalem

YUVAL PALGI
University of Haifa

ABSTRACT. The arrangement in which frail older adults from the developed world are cared for in their homes by individuals from the developing world has become increasingly prevalent worldwide. In Israel, this arrangement is termed *foreign home care*. In this article, the authors first describe the global phenomenon of foreign home care of frail older adults as well as the more local characteristics of this arrangement in Israel. The authors then describe the concept of loneliness. Based on empirical and theoretical knowledge in the field of loneliness, the authors argue that older adults under live-in foreign home care may be particularly prone to feelings of loneliness for several reasons: some that are general to older adults with cognitive or physical disability and others that are specific to this particular caregiving arrangement. The authors conclude by providing ideas for future practice and research on this highly vulnerable group that, to date, has received only minimal research attention.

THIS ARTICLE OUTLINES THE MANY POTENTIAL pathways to loneliness in older adults, under the care of a live-in foreign home care worker. Although, in many ways, this caregiving arrangement is perceived as ideal, as it maintains the older adult in his or her natural environment (Ayalon, Kaniel, & Rosenberg,

2008), we argue that this arrangement may, at times, predispose the older care recipient to intense feelings of loneliness. To date, there has been no formal evaluation of loneliness in older adults under the care of a live-in foreign home care worker. Therefore, we cannot comment on the magnitude of loneliness, its origins, or consequences in this already highly vulnerable population. In order to account for current lack of research on the topic, we synthesize existing literature on foreign home care and loneliness. We first describe the global phenomenon of foreign home care of frail older adults as well as the more local characteristics of this phenomenon in Israel. Next, we describe the concept of loneliness. We then discuss specific characteristics of older adults under live-in foreign home care that may predispose this group to intense feelings of loneliness. Finally, we provide ideas for future practice and research.

The care of frail older adults from the developed world by individuals from the developing world represents one form of globalization (Ehrenreich & Hochschild, 2000). This global social phenomenon is aimed at addressing the shortage of available family members as carers (Prochazkova & Schmid, 2009; Yeoh, Huang, & Gonzalez, 1999). This shortage is due to multiple demographic changes that have been taking place in the past century. These include the increase in lifespan, the decrease in childbirth, the fragmentation and nuclearization of the family system, and the entrance of women into the workforce (Ehrenreich & Hochschild, 2000; Popenoe, 1993). The shortage of family members as caregivers is further intensified by the low status assigned to caregiving in the developed world (Feldbaum & Feldbaum, 1981).

Financial considerations also contribute to the popularity of this caregiving arrangement. Given the low financial costs associated with home care relative to institutional care (Aronson & Neysmith, 1996), this is often the preferred alternative not only among family members and older adults, but also among governments (Ayalon et al., 2008; Heller, 2003). The fact that foreign home care workers receive attractive salaries relative to the salaries in their home country, yet these salaries are much lower than the salaries that would have been paid for locals for the same job, further contributes to the popularity of this arrangement. In fact, in some countries, such as the Philippines, the export of women carers has become the Number 1 source of revenue from export to the country (Ehrenreich & Hochschild, 2000).

Finally, the fact that home care is perceived as the best alternative for frail older adults further contributes to its popularity (Ayalon, 2009b). It is considered to represent the wishes of many older adults and frail individuals to stay in their home environment for as long as they possibly can (Keysor, Desai, & Mutran, 1999). This favorable perception of foreign home care is prevalent not only among older care recipients, but also among their family members and social workers, who are in charge of this caregiving arrangement (Ayalon et al., 2008). In fact, many believe that foreign home care is not only a preferred alternative relative to institutional care, but also a preferred alternative relative to care by locals, as foreign workers are perceived to have caring qualities, such as compassion, obedience, and patience that locals are lacking (Ayalon et al., 2008).

Although, foreign home care is a global phenomenon, we use the Israeli case as an example. In Israel, there are 54,000 documented foreign home care workers and at least 40,000 undocumented workers (Nathan, 2008b). The government partially subsidizes the foreign home care arrangement in an attempt to maintain older adults and frail individuals in the community for as long as possible. Because only the most impaired individuals are eligible for a foreign home care worker, most care recipients are physically and/or cognitively impaired older adults, and a minority are younger individuals who suffer from severe functional and/or cognitive limitations (Heller, 2003). Given their severe limitations, many care recipients require round-the-clock care, which is provided almost exclusively by foreign home care workers and not by Israelis (Nathan, 2008a). These workers are responsible for providing personal care, such as assistance in grooming or feeding (Heller, 2003). The majority of these workers are from the Philippines, but others come from India, Nepal, Sri Lanka, Romania, Moldavia, or Hungary. These workers are not considered new immigrants as their stay in the country is expected to be temporary, and they are expected to leave the country after several years or when their care recipient dies (Ofir et al., 2001). In order to assure their limited stay in the country, workers are not allowed to bring their family members with them, and their prospects of becoming Israeli citizens are almost nonexistent. Nonetheless, despite efforts of the Israeli government to restrict the number of foreign workers in the country (Borowski & Yanay, 1997), their numbers have been steadily increasing, because permits are given solely based on need, which continues to increase with the aging of the Israeli population (Heller, 2003; Klein-Zeevi, 2003; Ofir et al., 2001).

Loneliness in Care Recipients of Foreign Home Care

To date, there has been no research on the phenomenon of loneliness in care recipients of live-in foreign home care. Given lack of research on this phenomenon, we cannot comment on the magnitude, manifestation, origins, or consequences of loneliness in this population. Instead, we synthesize existing literature on the topic of foreign home care and loneliness. Based on the unique circumstances of older adults under live-in foreign home care and current research on loneliness, we suggest that there are multiple potential pathways for loneliness in this population of older adults. These potential pathways include loss of roles, friends and significant others, the presence of physical and cognitive disability, and the provision of care by formal carers, who are also foreigner. Whereas some of these pathways concern older adults or older adults with disability in general, others, such as the provision of care by paid live-in foreign workers are unique to the present caregiving arrangement. We discuss both general and unique potential pathways, because they both characterize this caregiving arrangement.

The subjective nature of loneliness is its most salient aspect. Even though subjective aspects of loneliness may correlate with objective social situations, such as number of friends or frequency of contact, they represent a separate realm. Therefore, a distinction should be made between loneliness and aloneness (Andersson, 1998; Marangoni & Ickes, 1989). As Peplau and Perlman (1982) argued, "Loneliness is a subjective experience, it is not synonymous with objective social isolation. People can be alone without being lonely or lonely in the crowd" (Peplau & Perlman, 1982, p. 3).

There is a common distinction between two forms of loneliness: emotional loneliness and social loneliness. The former emphasizes the absence of an intimate figure. This type of emotional loneliness is common following the divorce or death of a partner. Social loneliness, on the other hand, relates to the absence of valued social networks. For instance, losing a job due to retirement also means losing social contacts with colleagues and peers, who share similar activities and interests, and, thus, has the potential of generating feelings of social loneliness (Weiss, 1973, 1987). Following this perspective, we argue that older adults under foreign home care may be exposed to both types of loneliness due to multiple reasons, some related to old age and disability in general, such as loss of roles, friends, and significant others, disability, and cognitive impairment; whereas others are more specific to their particular caregiving arrangement, which consists of a live-in paid foreigner who provides their most intimate care.

Loss of Roles, Friends, and Significant Others

In old age, many individuals likely have experienced losses of roles, responsibilities, and social ties. These losses have shown to be directly related to loneliness (Lantz, 2006). One such loss, quite common in old age, is the loss of a spouse. Research has shown that marriage is one of the best protective factor against loneliness in old age, whereas living alone or widowhood serve as risk factors for loneliness (Theeke, 2009). Although not unique to older adults under the care of a foreign home care worker, it does characterize this particular population of foreign home care recipients as they tend to be relatively old, sick, and disabled. Many of them are widows and have lost not only their spouse but also social relations with other family members and friends. In addition, given the fact that in Israel, the presence of physical dependency or a need for supervision constitute an eligibility criterion for having a foreign worker (Heller, 2003), the majority of older adults under this caregiving arrangement is likely retired and does not hold formal positions. We expect both emotional and social loneliness to prevail, given multiple losses of roles and activities inflicted upon this population of frail older adults.

The Presence of Physical Disability

Physical disability is considered to be one of the main risks for loneliness (Korporaal, Broese van Groenou, & van Tilburg, 2008), as it appears to influence one's experiences of both social and emotional loneliness (Weiss, 1973, 1987). Disability is thought to have a direct association with social loneliness through its influence on one's social interaction. This can be due to deteriorated senses, such as hearing or vision that in return, cause communication problems with others, as in the case of cerebral palsy, which affects verbal communication (Balandin, Berg, & Waller, 2006).

Alternatively, loneliness may also be attributed to physical disability, which affects performance of activities such as walking, bathing, and eating (Buchman et al., 2010). This may result in loss of independence and autonomy (Lyons, 1995), which may also influence one's sense of self-worth and self-esteem, by inducing feelings of shame, guilt, and inferiority (Bondevik & Skogstad, 1998).

These negative feelings induced by disability may also take their toll in social interactions with friends and family members. For instance, research has shown that relative to living with one's spouse, living alone or with children or extended family members is related to greater loneliness. The magnitude of these differences is greater for older adults with physical disability (Russell, 2009). Because older adults under the care of a foreign home care worker most likely suffer from some type of disability, one would expect high levels of loneliness in this group.

Finally, the tendency of loneliness to spread in social circumstances, primarily among women (Cacioppo, Fowler, & Christakis, 2009) should also be taken into consideration when considering the potential association of disability with loneliness. In line with this idea, researchers found that wives' disability was related to higher levels of social loneliness in their husbands, whereas for women, mainly their own disability was related to higher levels of social loneliness (Korporaal et al., 2008). Given this finding, it is expected that loneliness is prevalent not only among older recipients of foreign home care with disability but also among the people who care for them, either their paid carers or their partners.

The Presence of Cognitive Disability

Another factor that may be responsible for increased sense of loneliness in older care recipients of live-in foreign home care is cognitive disability. Cognitive disability has the potential to narrow one's social world, which may result in social isolation and feelings of loneliness. When, for example, an individual experiences a memory decline, this can lead to negative feelings such as shame and embarrassment that subsequently result in social withdrawal (Ballard, 2010). Presenting signs and symptoms of cognitive impairment or dementia and having a diagnosis of dementia can also affect other people in one's social cycle, who may move away from this person sometimes simply because they do not know how to act in his or her presence, and at other times because of the stigma associated with dementia (Werner, Goldstein, & Buchbinder, 2010).

To date, there has been only limited research concerning the association of cognitive functioning and loneliness. We identified only three articles written by Holmen and her colleagues. All three were based on the Kungsholmen longitudinal project, which involved individuals who were 75 years old or older, living in Stockholm. In these articles, a comparison was made between two groups based on their cognitive functioning (e.g., cognitively impaired vs. intact persons). Results showed that feelings of loneliness were more prevalent among the cognitively impaired group relative to the cognitively intact group (Holmen, Ericsson, & Winblad, 1999; Karin, Kjerstin, & Bengt, 2000). However, when the authors differentiated between the two types of loneliness, emotional and social loneliness, only social loneliness was significantly correlated with impaired cognitive status, whereas no significant correlation was found with regard to emotional loneliness (Holmen, Ericsson, & Winblad, 2000). Unfortunately, our knowledge of the topic is restricted by the fact that the only three studies evaluating loneliness in this unique group of cognitively impaired older adults were carried out in a single city by a single research group. Thus, the external validity of these findings is low.

It is important to note however, that more studies, though still limited in number, explored loneliness as a risk factor for cognitive dysfunction. These studies were carried out in different countries and found somewhat inconsistent results. In the Helsinki Aging Study, a longitudinal project conducted in Finland, loneliness at baseline predicted a 10-year cognitive decline (Tilvis et al., 2004). Loneliness was also inversely associated with cognitive functioning among randomly selected noninstitutionalized Irish people, aged 65 years and more (Conroy, Golden, Jeffares, O'Neill, & McGee, 2010). In accordance with these studies, loneliness was found to be a robust risk factor for developing clinical Alzheimer's disease after controlling for the effect of potential confounders, including social isolation (Wilson, et al., 2007). In the only qualitative research found in this field, Latino family caregivers of patients with Alzheimer's disease made an association between loneliness and the onset/worsening of their relatives' Alzheimer's disease (Hinton & Levkoff, 1999). On the other hand, a longitudinal study, conducted in Zutphen in the Netherlands among men, found that changes in cognitive function were not related to loneliness (Tijhuis, De Jong-Gierveld, Feskens, & Kromhout, 1999).

The Provision of Care by Live-In Paid Foreign Home Carers

One aspect that makes older care recipients of live-in foreign home care particularly vulnerable to loneliness is the unique circumstances of this caregiving arrangement. In Israel, the majority of foreign home care workers comes from Asia or East Europe (Nathan, 2007). These workers come from a very different cultural background and usually do not speak the local language upon their arrival. Hence, we expect communication difficulties between workers and older adults. In fact, research has shown that the cultural and linguistic division between the older adults and their foreign home care workers is at times so pronounced that family members have to serve as mediators (Ayalon, 2009b). Nevertheless, even when family members successfully serve as mediators, at times cultural and linguistic gaps may prevent satisfactory communication between the older adult and the carer (Ayalon, 2009b). The fact that most foreign home care workers are substantially younger than the older adults they care for serves as yet another barrier for satisfactory communication between the involved parties (Ayalon & Shiovitz-Ezra, 2010).

Ageist attitudes (i.e., discrimination based on age) held by the worker may be another mechanism responsible for pervasive loneliness among older adults under this caregiving arrangement. The majority of foreign home care workers comes from the developing world and holds completely different attitudes and perceptions of old age and older adults. Although research has shown that attitudes towards older adults in some Asian countries are substantially more favorable than the attitudes held by Western society (Jones, Zhang, Jaceldo-Siegl, & Meleis, 2002), others have argued that because the life span in these countries is much shorter and because of their constant encounter with sickness and disability in the host country, foreign home care workers tend to hold some unfavorable opinions with regard to the older adults they care for (Ayalon, 2009a). The finding that loneliness spreads across individuals (Cacioppo, et al., 2009) may also dispose some older care recipients of live-in foreign home care to increased sense of loneliness. Past research has documented the profound loneliness experienced by foreign home care workers, who often leave their entire family behind in order to work abroad in a country that regards them as a temporary workforce (Ayalon & Shiovitz-Ezra, 2010). Thus, it is expected that the entire social interaction between the parties is colored by loneliness, which is being mutually fueled by both parties.

Another potential mechanism responsible for loneliness in this group of older adults is the fact that their personal care is provided by a paid worker. Research has shown that formal (paid) care does not replace informal care (unpaid, provided by family and friends) (Daatland, 1997). However, the nature of the relationship does appear to change. Apparently, as a foreign home care worker moves into the family, he or she is eventually expected to perform not only physical tasks, but also emotional and social tasks. Family members, in contrast, resort to performing more administrative and managerial tasks and less emotional tasks, especially as the physical and cognitive functioning of the older adult deteriorates and the presence of the foreign home care worker becomes an acceptable fact (Ayalon, 2009b). We argue that although the presence of a live-in foreign worker may alleviate some of the loneliness experienced by frail older adults, the tendency of the family to disconnect emotionally and socially may result in increased feelings of emotional loneliness in the older care recipient.

Implications for Health Care Professionals

The present review suggests that many factors, such as loss of roles, relationship, and physical and cognitive abilities, are not unique to older care recipients of foreign home care, yet may place them at a disadvantaged position with regard to loneliness. Although a live-in foreign home care worker may potentially alleviate some of the loneliness experienced by older care recipients, it is highly likely that many older care recipients of live-in foreign home care are still subjected to severe emotional and social loneliness. Acknowledging the fact that a foreign home care worker does not necessarily alleviate emotional and social loneliness is an important step in promoting the well-being of older care recipients. By realizing this, family members and social workers in charge of this caregiving arrangement may be less inclined to designate the responsibility for social and emotional care to the foreign home care worker. We argue that greater social and emotional involvement of family members in this caregiving arrangement is essential. Family members should be encouraged to maintain their social and emotional roles, in addition to their more administrative roles, even once a foreign home care worker has entered the family.

It is also important to address cultural and linguistic barriers that may prevent satisfactory interactions between the involved parties. In doing so, it is important to keep in mind that the use of family members as mediators may hamper the social interaction between the older adult and his or her foreign home care worker and may impair the development of emotional relationship between the two. It is also important to address cultural beliefs and practices that may serve as barriers for successful social interactions.

Although workers usually receive some training prior to entering the home of the older adult, this training is not necessarily geared towards meeting the emotional needs of the older adult. Educational efforts should help workers to maintain more accurate views of older adults and aging that are not necessarily connected with illness and disability. Finally, given the contagious nature of loneliness, interventions to alleviate loneliness in foreign home care workers may also alleviate loneliness in their care recipients.

Implications for Researchers

First and foremost, the present synthesis serves as an urgent call to researchers to further study the extent and nature of loneliness in this highly vulnerable population of older adults. To date, there has been no research on loneliness in older care recipients of live-in foreign home care. In light of the circumstances that surround this caregiving arrangement and our knowledge concerning loneliness, in this article we argued that this population might be particularly prone to loneliness, and we discussed several potential pathways to loneliness in this group of older adults.

There is a need to continue to explore factors that are related to loneliness in older adults in general as well as more specific factors related to loneliness in older adults under a live-in foreign home care worker. Our review identified several areas that have received only limited research attention so far. For instance, the relationship between loneliness and cognitive functioning has received only limited attention, despite the high prevalence of both loneliness and cognitive impairment in old age (de Jong-Gierveld, Kamphuis, & Dykstra, 1987; Hendrie, 1998) and the mutual associations of loneliness and cognitive impairment with depression (Cacioppo, Hughes, Waite, Hawkley, & Thisted, 2006; Emery & Oxman, 1997). In addition, the role of ageism as a source of loneliness in older adults has not received adequate attention and has not been evaluated in a cross-cultural context. Finally, the particular caregiving arrangement, which involves an encounter between a vulnerable older adult from a developed country and a vulnerable caregiver from the developing world, should receive increased attention in its own rights. The potential clash between cultures and world views, the high interdependence between the involved parties, and the low status of both caregivers and care recipients may all contribute to a high sense of loneliness in older adults and their foreign home caregivers under this caregiving arrangement.

Nevertheless, the present caregiving arrangement may also be a source of friendship and companionship both to the older care recipient and—even more so—to his or her partner (Ayalon, 2009b). Hence, in accordance with the view of so many older adults and their family members (Ayalon, 2009b), we agree that this caregiving arrangement also encompasses many potential benefits including the opportunity to maintain old connections in the community and to develop new ones with one's caregiver. Future research will benefit from integrating negative and positive aspects of this arrangement with regard to loneliness.

REFERENCES

Andersson, L. (1998). Loneliness research and interventions: A review of the literature. *Aging & Mental Health*, *2*(4), 264–274.

Aronson, J., & Neysmith, S. M. (1996). The work of visiting homemakers in the context of cost cutting in long-term care. *Canadian Journal of Public Health*, *87*(6), 422–425.

Ayalon, L. (2009a). Beliefs and practices regarding Alzheimer's disease and related dementias among Filipino home care workers in Israel. *Aging & Mental Health*, *13*(3), 456–462.

Ayalon, L. (2009b). Family and family-like interactions in households with round-the-clock paid foreign carers in Israel. *Ageing and Society*, *29*, 671–686.

Ayalon, L., Kaniel, M., & Rosenberg, L. (2008). Social workers' perspectives on care arrangements between vulnerable elders and foreign home care workers: Lessons from Israeli/Filipino caregiving arrangements. *Home Health Care Services Quarterly*, *27*(2), 121–142.

Ayalon, L., & Shiovitz-Ezra, S. (2010). The experience of loneliness among live-in Filipino homecare workers in Israel: implications for social workers. *British Journal of Social Work*, *40*(8), 2538–2559.

Balandin, S., Berg, N., & Waller, A. (2006). Assessing the loneliness of older people with cerebral palsy. *Disability and Rehabilitation, 28*(8), 469–479.

Ballard, J. (2010). Forgetfulness and older adults: Concept analysis. *Journal of Advanced Nursing, 66*(6), 1409–1419.

Bondevik, M., & Skogstad, A. (1998). The oldest old, ADL, social network, and loneliness. *Western Journal of Nursing Research, 20*(3), 325–343.

Borowski, A., & Yanay, U. (1997). Temporary and illegal labour migration: The Israeli experience. *International Migrant, 35*(4), 495–511.

Buchman, A. S., Boyle, P. A., Wilson, R. S., James, B. D., Leurgans, S. E., Arnold, S. E., Bennet, D.A. (2010). Loneliness and the rate of motor decline in old age: The Rush Memory and Aging Project, a community-based cohort study. *BMC Geriatrics, 10*(1), 77–84.

Cacioppo, J. T., Fowler, J. H., & Christakis, N. A. (2009). Alone in the crowd: The structure and spread of loneliness in a large social network. *Journal of Personality and Social Psychology, 97*(6), 977–991.

Cacioppo, J. T., Hughes, M. E., Waite, L. J., Hawkley, L. C., & Thisted, R. A. (2006). Loneliness as a specific risk factor for depressive symptoms: Cross-sectional and longitudinal analyses. *Psychology and Aging, 21*(1), 140–151.

Conroy, R. N. M., Golden, J., Jeffares, I., O'Neill, D., & McGee, H. (2010). Boredom-proneness, loneliness, social engagement and depression and their association with cognitive function in older people: A population study. *Psychology, Health & Medicine, 15*(4), 463–473.

Daatland, S. (1997). Family solidarity, popular opinion and the elderly: Perspectives from Norway. *Ageing International, 24*(1), 51–62.

de Jong-Gierveld, J., Kamphuis, F., & Dykstra, P. (1987). Old and lonely? *Comprehensive Gerontology B, 1*(1), 13–17.

Ehrenreich, B., & Hochschild, A. R. (2000). *Global woman: Nannies, maids, and sex workers in the new economy*. New York: Metropolitan Books.

Emery, V. O., & Oxman, T. E. (1997). Depressive dementia: A "transitional dementia"? *Clinical Neuroscience, 4*(1), 23–30.

Feldbaum, E. G., & Feldbaum, M. B. (1981). Caring for the elderly: Who dislikes it least? *Journal of Health Politics Policy and Law, 6*(1), 62–72.

Heller, E. (2003). The treatment of older adults in Israel. The topic of foreign home care workers in Israel and Israeli nursing care workers: Needs and available solutions. Jerusalem, Israel: Haknesset Research and Information Center.

Hendrie, H. C. (1998). Epidemiology of dementia and Alzheimer's disease. *American Journal of Geriatric Psychiatry, 6*(2, Suppl. 1), S3–18.

Hinton, W. L., & Levkoff, S. (1999). Constructing Alzheimer's: Narratives of lost identities, confusion and loneliness in old age. *Culture, Medicine and Psychiatry, 23*(4), 453–475.

Holmen, K., Ericsson, K., & Winblad, B. (1999). Quality of life among the elderly: State of mood and loneliness in two selected groups. *Scandinavian Journal of Caring Science, 13*(2), 91–95.

Holmen, K., Ericsson, K., & Winblad, B. (2000). Social and emotional loneliness among non-demented and demented elderly people. *Archives of Gerontology and Geriatrics, 31*(3), 177–192.

Jones, P. S., Zhang, X. E., Jaceldo-Siegl, K., & Meleis, A. I. (2002). Caregiving between two cultures: An integrative experience. *Journal of Transcultural Nursing, 13*(3), 202–209.

Karin, H. N., Kjerstin, E., & Bengt, W. (2000). Social and emotional loneliness among non-demented and demented elderly people. *Archives of Gerontology and Geriatrics, 31*(3), 177–192.

Keysor, J. J., Desai, T., & Mutran, E. J. (1999). Elders' preferences for care setting in short- and long-term disability scenarios. *Gerontologist, 39*(3), 334–344.
Klein-Zeevi, N. (2003). *[Foreign workers in Israel: Current status]*. Jerusalem, Israel: Haknesset Research and Information Center.
Korporaal, M., Broese van Groenou, M. I., & van Tilburg, T. G. (2008). Effects of own and spousal disability on loneliness among older adults. *Journal of Aging & Health, 20*(3), 306–325.
Lantz, M. S. (2006). Loneliness and boredom: A psychiatric disorder or late-life challenge? *Clinical Geriatrics, 14*(12), 12–14.
Lyons, R. F., Sullivan, M. J. L., Ritvo, P. G., & Coyne, J. C. (1995). *Relationships in chronic illness and disability*. Thousand Oaks, CA: Sage.
Marangoni, C., & Ickes, W. (1989). Loneliness: A theoretical review with implications for measurement. *Journal of Social and Personal Relationships, 6*(1), 93–128.
Nathan, G. (2007). *Supervision of the relationship between older care recipients and their foreign home care workers*. Jerusalem, Israel: Haknesset Research and Information Center.
Nathan, G. (2008a). *An automatic approval to employ a foreign home care worker*. Jerusalem, Israel: Haknesset Research and Information Center.
Nathan, G. (2008b). *Examining the reform of foreign home care workers*. Jerusalem, Israel: Haknesset Research and Information Center.
Ofir, Y., Deskel, H., Dror, N., Holzman, B. G., Hirshfeld, O., & Salomon, H. (2001). *Foreign workers in the field of home care*. Jerusalem, Israel: Ministry of Work and Welfare.
Peplau, L. A., & Perlman, D. (1982). Perspectives on loneliness. In L. A. Peplau & D. Perlman (Eds.), *Loneliness: A sourcebook of current theory, research and therapy* (pp. 1–18). New York: Wiley-Interscience.
Popenoe, D. (1993). American family decline, 1960–1990: A review and appraisal. *Journal of Marriage and the Family, 55*, 527–555.
Prochazkova, L., & Schmid, T. (2009). Homecare aid: A challenge for social policy and research. In S. R. a. D. Zavirsek (Ed.), *Critical edge issues in social work and social policy: Comparative research perspective*. Ljubljana, Slovenia: University of Ljubljana.
Russell, D. (2009). Living arrangements, social integration, and loneliness in later life: The case of physical disability. *Journal of Health and Social Behavior, 50*(4), 460–475.
Theeke, L. A. (2009). Predictors of loneliness in U.S. adults over age sixty-five. *Archives of Psychiatric Nursing, 23*(5), 387–396.
Tijhuis, M. A., De Jong-Gierveld, J., Feskens, E. J., & Kromhout, D. (1999). Changes in and factors related to loneliness in older men: The Zutphen Elderly Study. *Age & Ageing, 28*(5), 491–495.
Tilvis, R. S., Kahonen-Vare, M. H., Jolkkonen, J., Valvanne, J., Pitkala, K. H., & Strandberg, T. E. (2004). Predictors of cognitive decline and mortality of aged people over a 10-year period. *Journal of Gerontol A: Medical Sciences, 59*(3), 268–274.
Weiss, R. S. (1973). *Loneliness: The experience of emotional and social isolation*. Cambridge, MA: MIT Press.
Weiss, R. S. (1987). Reflections on the present state of loneliness research. *Journal of Social Behavior and Personality, 2*, 1–16.
Werner, P., Goldstein, D., & Buchbinder, E. (2010). Subjective experience of family stigma as reported by children of Alzheimer's disease patients. *Quality of Health Research, 20*(2), 159–169.
Wilson, R. S., Krueger, K. R., Arnold, S. E., Schneider, J. A., Kelly, J. F., Barnes, L. L., Tang, Y., & Bennet, D. A. (2007). Loneliness and risk of Alzheimer disease. *Archives of General Psychiatry, 64*(2), 234–240.
Yeoh, B. S., Huang, S., & Gonzalez, J. (1999). Migrant female domestic workers: Debating the economic, social and political impacts in Singapore. *International Migration Review, 33*(1), 114–136.

Cross-National Differences in Older Adult Loneliness

TINEKE FOKKEMA
Netherlands Interdisciplinary Demographic Institute

JENNY DE JONG GIERVELD
Netherlands Interdisciplinary Demographic Institute
VU University

PEARL A. DYKSTRA
Erasmus University

ABSTRACT. Loneliness concerns the subjective evaluation that the number of relationships is smaller than the individual considers desirable or that the intimacy that the individual wishes for has not been realized. The aim of this study was to assess variations in levels of late-life loneliness and its determinants across Europe. Data came from the SHARE surveys, Wave 2 (Börsch-Supan et al., 2008), encompassing adults aged 50 years and over in Austria, Belgium, the Czech Republic, Denmark, France, Germany, Greece, Ireland, Italy, the Netherlands, Poland, Spain, Sweden, and Switzerland ($N = 12{,}248$). Loneliness was measured by a single item derived from the CES-D (depression) scale. Using logistic models, the present authors tested several types of explanations for country differences: differences in demographic characteristics, wealth and health, and social networks. Older adults in the southern and central European countries were generally lonelier than their peers in the northern and western European countries. In the southern and central European countries, loneliness was largely attributable to not being married, economic deprivation,

---

The SHARE data collection has been primarily funded by the European Commission through the 5th framework program (project QLK6-CT-2001-00360 in the thematic program Quality of Life). The present authors are grateful for further support by the European Commission through the 6th framework program (projects SHARE-I3, RII-CT-2006-062193, as an Integrated Infrastructure Initiative, COMPARE, CIT5-CT-2005-028857, as a project in Priority 7, Citizens and Governance in a Knowledge Based Society, and SHARE-LIFE [CIT4-CT-2006-028812]) and through the 7th framework program (SHARE-PREP [211909]) and SHARE-LEAP [227822]). Also, the present authors are grateful for additional funding by the U.S. National Institute on Aging (grant numbers U01 AG09740-13S2; P01 AG005842; P01 AG08291; P30 AG12815; Y1-AG-4553-01; OGHA 04-064; R21 AG025169; IAG BSR06-11) and by various national sources (see http://www.share-project.org for a full list of funding institutions).

and poor health. Frequent contacts with parents and adult children, social participation, and providing support to family members were important in preventing and alleviating loneliness in almost all countries. To combat loneliness among older adults, the findings suggest both (a) generic approaches aimed at improving social embeddedness and (b) country-tailored approaches aimed at improving health and wealth.

SOCIAL INTEGRATION and feeling socially well embedded in the context of one's community and family are important determinants of quality of life in late adulthood. Policy makers assembled in the United Nations International Conference on Population and Development, Cairo, September 1994, formulated their objectives in this respect as "To enhance, through appropriate mechanisms, the self-reliance of elderly people, and to create conditions that promote quality of life and enable them to work and live independently in their own communities as long as possible or as desired" (6.17, p. 39). An indication of the extent to which these objectives have been achieved is the absence of social integration in the form of loneliness. Loneliness is considered to be the outcome of the evaluation of the match between the quantity and quality of existing relationships and one's relationship desires (Peplau & Perlman, 1982).

Levels of loneliness have been found to differ across societies. A series of studies carried out by Rokach and associates has repeatedly shown that cultural heritage is significantly related to the manner in which people express and cope with loneliness experiences (e.g., Rokach, 2008; Rokach & Neto, 2005; Rokach, Orzeck, & Neto, 2004). Those researchers observed, for instance, that Croatians scored lower than Canadians on all loneliness subscales under study, a finding that possibly reflected increased interdependence on primary group members in Croatia in connection with the war and ensuing social and economic malaise (Rokach, Orzeck, Cripps, Lackovic-Grgin, & Penezic, 2001). In a study enquiring into perceived causes of loneliness, Canadian seniors were less likely to attribute loneliness to personal inadequacies than their Czech peers, possibly because the latter feel more doubtful about their personal abilities and coping resources, having lived most of their lives under communist rule (Rokach, 2007). Studies examining cross-national differences in loneliness in western European countries (e.g., Jylhä & Jokela, 1990; Sundström, Fransson, Malmberg, & Davey, 2009; Walker, 1993) have, without exception, observed a clear North–South gradient. This gradient, however, is in reverse order to the rates of institutionalization and solitary living, factors that are generally believed to contribute to loneliness. On average, older residents of northern European countries are less lonely than their peers in southern European countries.

As noted by Tesch-Römer and Von Kondratowitz (2006), current comparative aging research is characterized by little theorizing. We aim to contribute to theoretical development by viewing the emergence of loneliness as an interplay of personal factors and environmental conditions and constraints (Rokach & Brock, 1997). In our view, it is important to explore the division and intersection of broad modes of state, regional, and community provisions underlying social integration. Although the intersections of modes differ between countries, it is the total organization of activities oriented towards social integration that is decisive for the specific loneliness situation in a country. These state, regional, and community provisions shape the conditions for individual older adults to participate in the community and to be involved in social activities with kin and nonkin network members and consequently lead to varying country-level outcomes in loneliness.

The goal of this study was to investigate older adult loneliness in a country-comparative perspective by not only measuring variations in the prevalence of loneliness between European countries but also identifying some of the determinants of these variations. We improve on the literature in two ways. Contrary to the customary focus on North versus South, we include countries from four different regions: North, West, South, and Central Europe. Rather than restricting ourselves to a short list of determinants, we include a wide range of explanatory factors encompassing demographic, socioeconomic, and health indicators, in addition to characteristics of the social network.

The investigation of loneliness in the European context is important now that several societal trends potentially have a negative effect on the social embeddedness of older women and men. First, most European countries are confronted with a sharp increase in the proportion of older adults living alone. Western and northern European countries are forerunners in this respect, but in more and more other countries, older adults, after widowhood or divorce, are deciding to continue living independently for as long as possible. While marriage can help maintain social well-being, living alone is one of the main risk factors for loneliness (De Jong Gierveld, Van Tilburg, & Dykstra, 2006; Wenger, Davies, Shahtahmasebi, & Scott, 1996). Waite and Lehrer (2003) view marital support as the key channel through which marriage leads to mental and physical well-being and alleviation of loneliness. Older adults living alone have to contact people outside the household for support and help. Maintaining contact with network members living elsewhere requires more time, more initiative, and perseverance, although faster methods of communication (telephone, electronic mail) and travel (car, air) have facilitated contact among network members who do not live close to each other (Ajrouch, Akiyama, & Antonucci, 2007). In this context, one needs to take into account that widowhood is more frequently a woman's experience than a man's experience, suggesting gender differences in the risks of loneliness.

Although partner relationships are important vehicles for instrumental and emotional support exchanges, with increasing age more help and care are needed, that is, people outside the nuclear household are expected to step in and provide additional support, regardless of whether it is informal help (from siblings and children) or formal help. Nowadays, the question is raised if this additional support by family members will be available and will be sufficient to guarantee optimal social embeddedness of older women and men. The integrative functioning of the family seems to be at risk as a consequence of the trends towards increasing rates of divorce and remarriage after marital break up, in combination with the forming of complex new forms of stepfamilies.

These concerns are related to changes in attitudes as summarized in the ideas of the Second Demographic Transition (Van de Kaa, 1987). Cultural changes that have taken place in Europe since the 1960s have influenced the system of values and norms cherished by young and older adults: the past decades have seen a decline in normative control on behavioral patterns, enabling people to fulfill their personal wishes and preferences to a much greater extent than their peers were able to do in the past. Not only has the authority to exert normative control declined in recent decades, but the wish to exert such control has diminished as well (Liefbroer, 1999). These changes are linked to processes such as secularization and individualization, which affect the opportunities of individuals to decide how they wish to organize their lives.

In addition, the level of social participation and social embeddedness is related to the health situation of older adults. Those in good health, without ADL or IADL limitations, are better positioned to be in contact with family and nonfamily members of their social network. However, the increase in life expectancy in most European countries for both women and men, the related increase in the number of years with disabilities, and the death of peers at later age increase the risks for shrinking social networks and feelings of loneliness. Studies have repeatedly shown that older adults who are in poor health are most prone to loneliness (for reviews see De Jong Gierveld, Van Tilburg, & Dykstra, 2006; Pinquart & Sörensen, 2001; Victor, Scrambler, Bond, & Bowling, 2000).

Differences in socioeconomic position, and especially in old age income levels, as related to the availability and level of state and (obligatory) company pension schemes and to appropriate social welfare policies for those in need, form additional determinants of older adults' conditions to realize a certain quality of life and alleviate loneliness. Each of these determinants represents opportunities for or obstacles to rewarding social involvements (Hawkley et al., 2008). More generous old age pension schemes, social security systems, and health care systems are mechanisms helpful for enhancing self-reliance of older people and for guaranteeing appropriate conditions for optimal health, quality of life, social integration, and alleviation of loneliness.

The aforementioned processes of increasing life expectancy, changing characteristics of the family structure, and trends in familial support systems differ between European countries, both in pace and in impact. Moreover, the socioeconomic characteristics of countries and the ins and outs of the health care and social security systems differentially affect older adults. In certain aspects, the northern European countries can be viewed as forerunners (acceptance and realization of divorce and the forming of nonmarriage living arrangements), whereas in other aspects the southern European countries are taking the lead (postponement of family formation and leaving the parental home). It is reasonable to expect that differences in the composition and functioning of the familial system (exchange of instrumental support, e.g., as related to coresident living arrangements), the connected cultural values and norms, and the socioeconomic characteristics of countries continue to differently affect the social embeddedness in varying countries of Europe. Hence, in investigating country differences in loneliness, we looked at the following broad groups of explanatory factors (Dykstra, 2009): differences in the population composition, differences in health and wealth, and differences related to the size, composition, and functioning of older adults' social networks. Data came from the Survey of Health and Retirement in Europe (SHARE), Wave 2. Using logistic models, we tested several subsets of factors related to country differences in older adults' loneliness. Fourteen countries from North, West, South, and Central Europe were included in the analyses.

Background and Hypotheses

The concept of loneliness. Loneliness is a subjective and negative experience, the outcome of the evaluation of the match between the quantity and quality of existing relationships and one's relationship desires or standards. Some people with a restricted social network feel lonely, whereas others do not. Loneliness needs to be differentiated from social isolation. The latter is an objective situation and refers to the absence of relationships with other people (Cornwell & Waite, 2009; De Jong Gierveld, Van Tilburg, & Dykstra 2006).

Country-level variations in loneliness: Refraining from simple typologies. An often-heard assumption is that countries in Mediterranean Europe, where care and support arrangements are embedded more or less exclusively within the family and frequently materialized via co-residence arrangements, are better equipped to guarantee social integration of older adults than countries in Northern Europe, characterized by residential autonomy of older adults (Manzi, Vignoles, Regalia, & Scabini, 2006; Reher, 1998). In investigating country-level differences in loneliness, we nevertheless refrain from ordering the countries into a priori simple subsets such as the dichotomy individualistic country versus family-oriented country. Such a dichotomy suggests homogeneity among countries belonging to a particular subset. Recent research has indicated that a simple typology does not do justice to the complexity of regional- and country-level family patterns (Attias-Donfut, Ogg, & Wolff, 2005; Dykstra & Fokkema, 2011; Glaser, Tomassini, & Grundy, 2004; Hank, 2007).

Country-level differences in the demographic composition of populations. In investigating country-level differences in loneliness, this study takes into consideration the demographic circumstances of countries, more specifically the age, gender, and marital status composition. Among older adults, loneliness increases with age, especially after the age of 75 years (Dykstra, 2009; Jylhä, 2004). In addition, loneliness is more common among older women than among older men. However, what makes the oldest old and older women more socially vulnerable is not age and gender per se. Higher levels of loneliness among these population groups are generally linked to—besides deteriorating health, low income and shrinking networks—widowhood. Loneliness research has repeatedly demonstrated the protective role of marriage (e.g., De Jong Gierveld, Broese van Groenou, Hoogendoorn, & Smit, 2009; Dykstra & De Jong Gierveld, 2004; Pinquart, 2003; Stevens & Westerhof, 2006), simultaneously underlining the increased risks of loneliness for divorced and widowed men and women (Dykstra & Fokkema, 2007; Guiaux, Van Tilburg, & Broese van Groenou, 2007).

Country-level differences in marriage among older adults are to a certain extent related to differences between men and women in life expectancy and the related sex ratio in older age. Comparing female and male life expectancies of the European countries under investigation (Table 1), the female life expectancy at age 65 years varies between two years higher than that for men in Greece to more than 4 years higher in France and Poland. Per 100 women aged 60 years and over, Table 1 shows the lowest ratio of men in Poland (66) and the Czech Republic (73) as compared to Denmark, Sweden, the Netherlands, and Ireland with a ratio of more than 80. The proportions of married females aged 60 years and over are lowest in Austria (41.3) and especially Poland (40.6). The resulting discrepancies between countries as presented in Table 1—for example, Poland with low proportions of married older females, a low sex ratio, and a high female–male discrepancy in life expectancy at age 65 years—need careful attention.

In sum, having a higher age, being female, and being unmarried are main determinants of older adults' loneliness. Given the high discrepancy in life expectancy of women and men, the low share of men aged 60 years plus as compared to women aged 60 years plus, and the rather low share of married older female adults in Poland, we expect that this country has a relatively high proportion of lonely older adults (H1).

Country-level differences in wealth. Recent research has shown that low socioeconomic status (captured by, for instance, level of education and income) is associated with a high level of loneliness (Hawkley et al., 2008). Quite often these more distal predictors are linked to proximal factors such as having greater difficulties in maintaining optimal get-togethers with network members, a small number of friends, or relationships of poor quality. Research by Scharf and Smith (2004) and by O'Rand (2001) has shown that people living in economically deprived regions and confronted with income levels that restrict making ends meet are prone to experiencing social exclusion and more intense loneliness.

Countries within Europe differ significantly as far as socioeconomic indicators are concerned. Table 1 shows that especially Poland and the Czech Republic are characterized by lower Gross Domestic Product (GDP) levels compared to other countries. Low-GDP countries face difficulties in guaranteeing basic social protection and an old age pension above the local poverty level and consequently have to refrain from supporting older adults in independent living and maintaining

TABLE 1. Country-Level Indicators: Countries in Alphabetical Order

	Country													
Variable	Austria ($N = 517$)	Belgium ($N = 1055$)	Czech Rep. ($N = 1117$)	Denmark ($N = 965$)	France ($N = 1090$)	Germany ($N = 920$)	Greece ($N = 1037$)	Ireland ($N = 382$)	Italy ($N = 987$)	Netherlands ($N = 930$)	Poland ($N = 975$)	Spain ($N = 744$)	Sweden ($N = 1018$)	Switzerland ($N = 511$)
Female–male discrepancy in life expectancy at age 65 years[a]	3.3	3.7	3.4	2.9	4.4	3.4	2.1	3.1	3.8	3.6	4.2	3.9	3.2	3.5
Sex ratio per 100 women 60+ years[b]	75.3	77.7	72.7	83.5	76.3	77.4	82.2	85.7	76.1	83.4	66.4	77.9	83.8	79.4
% married females 60+ years[c]	41.3	48.8	44.6	48.8	46.7	49.1	52.4	46.6	49.2	51.7	40.6	48.6	45.6	49.0
GDP PPP in US$[a]	33495	32049	20362	33214	29809	31378	24928	38596	28144	35105	13784	27377	32319	35733
Social protection expenditures as % of GDP[a]	28.0	28.2	18.5	29.4	29.5	28.6	23.9	16.9	25.4	26.0	19.2	20.4	30.9	27.1
Poverty rates at age 66–75 years[d]	7.6	10.7	1.3	3.8	9.9	9.7	22.2	14.6	14.6	1.5	4.0	14.8	4.6	10.4
Public health expenditures as % of GDP[a]	7.9	7.4	6.3	8.0	8.8	8.2	5.7	5.7	6.8	5.9	4.3	5.9	7.5	6.7
Female life expectancy at age 65 years[a]	20.2	20.2	17.8	19.0	22.0	20.1	19.2	19.7	21.3	20.0	18.5	21.1	20.6	21.6
Female healthy life expectancy at age 60 years (HALE)[e]	18.4	18.0	15.8	16.5	19.4	17.6	17.7	16.9	18.8	17.8	13.8	18.3	18.7	19.7

[a]Generations and Gender Surveys, Contextual Database; data 2005.
[b]United Nations (2010), World Ageing Report; data 2009.
[c]United Nations (2010), World Ageing Report; data vary between 1991 (Spain) and 2008 (Denmark and the Netherlands).
[d]Michael Förster & Marco Mira d'Ercole (2005).
[e]Generations and Gender Surveys, Contextual Database; data 2000.

a certain level of social integration. Besides Poland and the Czech Republic, Ireland is also characterized by a relatively low percentage of GDP expenditures on social protection. Looking at the income situation of Europe's older adults, poverty rates among the population aged 66–75 years are especially high in Greece, Spain, Italy, and Ireland.

Based on their less favorable social status, we expect relatively high proportions of lonely older adults in the central and southern European countries of Poland, the Czech Republic, Greece, Spain, and Italy (H2).

Country-level differences in health. Research has shown a strong negative interrelationship between the health condition of older adults and loneliness (Halleröd, 2009; Havens & Hall, 2001; Kramer, Kapteyn, Kuik, & Deeg, 2002; Mullins, Elston, & Gutkowski, 1996; Penninx et al., 1999; Savikko, Routasalo, Tilvis, Strandberg, & Pitkala, 2005; Steverink, Westerhof, Bode, & Dittman-Kohli, 2001; Wilson et al., 2007). Loneliness not only has adverse outcomes on physical and mental health because of a reluctance to engage in exercise behavior and see a doctor, or because of difficulties in remembering to take medications (Cacioppo et al., 2002; Ó Luanaigh & Lawlor, 2008; Pérodeau & du-Fort, 2000; Wilson et al., 2007). There is also empirical evidence that the causal relation runs in the opposite direction, that is, that deteriorating own or spousal health increases emotional and social loneliness of both partners (Korporaal, Broese van Groenou, & Van Tilburg, 2008).

Countries differ in the levels of public health expenditures and medical services made available for (frail) older adults as shown in Table 1, with Poland at one end of the continuum and France at the other, resulting in differences in mental and physical health conditions of older adults (Lehtinen, Sohlman, & Kovess-Masfety, 2005; Mackenbach et al., 2008). Table 1 also shows that female life expectancy at age 65 years and female healthy life expectancy at age 60 years lag in Poland and the Czech Republic.

In view of the above findings, we expect that loneliness is more prevalent amongst older adults in the central European countries Poland and the Czech Republic and that the situation is partly due to a higher risk of poor health conditions (H3).

Country-level differences in the size and composition of social networks. Research has shown that the size and composition of the family network, in particular the bonds with children, are strongly associated with the likelihood of loneliness among older adults (De Jong Gierveld & Dykstra, 2008; Kaufman & Uhlenberg, 1998; Kitson & Morgan, 1990; Pinquart, 2003). However, the mechanisms that connect the family network to loneliness differ by the cultural contexts of the countries (Van Tilburg & Dykstra, 2008). According to Jylhä and Jokela (1990) older adults in Scandinavian countries have fewer expectations about community and frequent and close contacts with family and friends than do older adults in Mediterranean countries. In more collectivist cultures, expectations of communality are likely to be higher than in a more individualistic type of culture (Johnson

& Mullins, 1987). Similarly, contacts with friends and participation in volunteer work and clubs are lower in collectivistic societies than in individualistic societies (Pilusuk & Minkler, 1980; Väänänen, Buunk, Kivimäki, Pentti, & Vahtera, 2005; Van Tilburg, De Jong Gierveld, Lecchini, & Marsiglia, 1998; Wagner, Schütze, & Lang, 1999). For this reason, differences in the size and composition of kin and nonkin networks will be taken into account in investigating varying patterns of loneliness of older adults across European countries. Given the absence of country-level information about the size and composition of social networks, we refrain from formulating specific hypotheses for this field of research. We will investigate the interrelationships from an exploratory perspective.

Country-level differences in the functioning of social networks. Exchanges of support within the network of social relationships are generally considered to be the building stones of social integration. However, countries differ in the value assigned to the type and frequency of support exchanges. In countries where the independence of aging parents and adult children is valued and financially feasible, such as in Sweden and Denmark, receiving instrumental informal support is culturally associated with greater older adult loneliness. In these countries, the preferred life-style is "intimacy at a distance" (Rosenmayr & Köckeis, 1963) with frequent get-togethers between adult children and their parents and exchanges of emotional support. In other societies such as Greece, where familial intergenerational bonds are close and are the traditional institutional arrangement for exchanges of support and help, instrumental support is consistent with normative ideas about family responsibilities and family cohesiveness and contributes to feelings of social integration (Adams, Anderson, & Adonu, 2004; see also Höllinger & Haller, 1990). Again we refrain from formulating specific hypotheses and consider country differences in the type and frequency of support exchanges from an exploratory perspective.

Method

Data Source

To test the hypotheses, we used data from the second wave of the Survey of Health, Ageing and Retirement in Europe (SHARE), which was collected in 2006–2007 in 14 European countries: Austria, Belgium, the Czech Republic, Denmark, France, Germany, Greece, Ireland, Italy, the Netherlands, Poland, Spain, Sweden, and Switzerland (for details see Börsch-Supan & Jürges, 2005; Börsch-Supan et al., 2008). This survey has longitudinal data among the noninstitutionalized population aged 50 years and over, including extensive information on living conditions, health, financial situation, social embeddedness, support exchanges, and well-being. Face-to-face, computer-assisted personal interviews were conducted, supplemented by a self-completion paper and pencil questionnaire. We decided to use the second wave of SHARE because of the wider country coverage compared to the first wave (including two new EU member states—the

Czech Republic and Poland—as well as Ireland) and, more importantly, because of the inclusion of the loneliness question in the interview rather than in the self-completion section (which would result in a smaller sample) and the incorrect Dutch translation of the loneliness question in Wave 1; in the Dutch version, loneliness was translated as being alone. After excluding those with missing data on key variables, our pooled multinational sample contains 12,248 individuals.

Measurements

Loneliness, the dependent variable, was measured by a direct, single item derived from the CES-D (depression) scale. Respondents were asked whether or not (0 = no, 1 = yes) they felt lonely much of the time during the past 1 week.

Demographic characteristics. Three variables measured demographic characteristics: (a) *age* (in years; range: 50–104 years), (b) *gender* (coded 0 = male, and 1 = female), and (c) *marital status*, distinguishing the categories of married (reference group), widowed, divorced, and never married individuals.

Socioeconomic status. Three variables refer to the respondent's socioeconomic status. The first is level of *education*, reflecting the highest level the respondents had completed by obtaining a qualification or diploma, coded into the 1997 International Standard Classification of Education (ISCED-97) with three levels: low (preprimary education, primary education or first stage of basic education, and lower secondary or second stage of basic education), intermediate ([upper] secondary education, and postsecondary nontertiary education), and high (first stage of tertiary education and second stage of tertiary education). The second is being currently *employed* (0 = no, 1 = yes). The third is *perceived difficulties with current income*, running from 0 = comfortable (reference group) to 3 = great difficulties. In case of "level of education" and "perceived difficulties with current income," a separate category for missing cases was created as both measures had more missing data than other variables.

Health. Numerous indicators for respondent's health status were included: perceived health, functional limitations, and problems with seeing or hearing. *Perceived health*, *seeing*, and *hearing* were measured by asking the respondents to rate their own health, seeing (with the use of glasses or contact lenses if usually wearing them) and hearing (with the use of hearing aids if usually wearing them), respectively, on a 5-point scale ranging from excellent to poor. Functional limitations were measured using a 6-item list of Activities of Daily Living (ADLs) and a 7-item list of Instrumental Activities of Daily Living (IADLs), respectively. The respondents were asked whether or not they had any difficulty in doing each of these activities. The variables *ADLs* and *IADLs* were dichotomized: difficulties with none (= 0) versus one or more (I)ADLs (= 1).

Social embeddedness. With regard to social embeddedness, we constructed three variables. The variable *children* pertained to whether the respondent had children and if so, how often they had contact, either in person, by telephone, or by mail contact, with at least one of them, distinguishing four categories ranging from 1 = almost daily contact to 4 = less than weekly contact with one or more children, with childless respondents as the reference group. The same construction was used for the variable *parents*, with a further breakdown of the fourth category along parent's health (good versus poor health). *Social participation* was measured as a count of four activities in which the respondent could participate in the last month.

Support exchange. With regard to support exchange, we constructed the following four variables. The first is *regular help with personal care given inside the household* (0 = no, 1 = yes), that is, whether the respondent had given personal care (e.g., dressing, bathing or showering, eating, getting in or out of bed, using the toilet) to one or more household members. The second is *informal help given outside the household*, based on the question of whether the respondent had given practical household help (e.g., with home repairs, gardening, transportation, shopping, household chores) and/or help with paperwork (e.g., filling out forms, settling financial or legal matters) to someone outside the household and if so, to whom, distinguishing the following categories: to at least one family member, only to one or more nonfamily members, and none (reference group). The third is *informal help received*, that is, whether the respondent had received practical household help and/or help with paperwork from (a) at least one family member or (b) one or more nonfamily members outside the household, with (c) none as reference group. The fourth is *looking after grandchildren*: how often the respondent had looked after the grandchildren from outside the household in the last 12 months, ranging from 1 = daily to 4 = never, with "no grandchildren" as the reference group.

Results

Descriptives

Table 2 shows descriptive characteristics per country. Mean age per country differs between 64.0 years (the Netherlands) and 67.7 years (Spain), and the percentage that is female varies between 52.5% (Sweden) and 59.3% (France). The proportions of married older respondents vary between countries: high levels of married respondents in the Netherlands, Italy, Germany, Poland, Sweden, and Spain; high levels of widowhood in Austria and Greece; and high levels of divorce in Denmark, the Czech Republic, and Switzerland. Experiencing (some or great) difficulties in making ends meet is most frequent among respondents in Poland, Greece, Italy, the Czech Republic, and Italy. Table 2 shows that mean levels of subjective health and of ADL and IADL limitations are not evenly distributed across the countries under investigation: Poland, Italy, Spain, and the Czech Republic are among the countries with relatively high levels of health problems.

Social embeddedness differs between countries. Older childless people are more common in Ireland and Greece. Daily contacts with at least one of the children differ sharply, from 22% in Switzerland to more than 60% in Italy and

TABLE 2. Descriptive Statistics (Unweighted); Countries Ordered by Rate of Loneliness ($N = 12248$)

Variable	Country														Significance test
	Denmark ($N = 965$)	Switzerland ($N = 511$)	Netherlands ($N = 930$)	Germany ($N = 920$)	Sweden ($N = 1018$)	Austria ($N = 517$)	Ireland ($N = 382$)	Belgium ($N = 1055$)	Czech Rep. ($N = 1117$)	Greece ($N = 1037$)	Spain ($N = 744$)	France ($N = 1090$)	Poland ($N = 975$)	Italy ($N = 987$)	
Demographic															
Age (mean; 50–104)	64.2	65.2	64.0	64.8	66.4	66.8	64.6	65.2	64.4	67.0	67.7	65.4	64.7	67.1	$F = 13.66$***
Female	54.3	54.6	54.0	55.7	52.5	57.3	56.8	56.3	55.3	55.7	53.9	59.3	56.1	56.3	$\chi 2 = 14.09$
Marital status															$\chi 2 = 394.66$***
Married	70.1	73.0	78.8	77.9	76.5	59.8	72.3	74.5	68.1	67.5	75.4	67.5	76.8	78.7	
Widowed	13.2	11.9	11.5	11.6	10.9	24.4	17.0	15.3	18.7	21.8	15.9	17.7	17.2	13.9	
Divorced	10.7	10.0	5.5	5.7	8.2	7.7	2.6	6.7	10.7	4.1	2.2	8.3	2.6	1.4	
Never married	6.0	5.1	4.2	4.8	4.4	8.1	8.1	3.5	2.5	6.6	6.9	6.5	3.4	6.0	
Socioeconomic															
Level of education															$\chi 2 = 2365.89$***
Low	23.2	32.3	52.5	15.5	51.9	30.0	40.3	48.4	57.2	63.5	84.9	49.0	50.0	77.9	
Medium	43.0	57.1	23.0	59.1	26.4	49.7	17.3	24.8	32.7	21.4	6.9	30.1	41.5	18.2	
High	33.0	9.2	23.2	24.9	20.2	19.9	41.6	25.6	9.0	10.3	7.1	19.4	7.4	3.7	
Missing	0.8	1.4	1.3	0.5	1.5	0.4	0.8	1.2	1.1	4.8	1.1	1.5	1.1	0.2	
Paid job	39.5	38.4	30.2	28.0	35.7	14.5	32.2	22.1	27.6	24.0	15.6	25.0	13.2	11.9	$\chi 2 = 479.86$***
Perceived income															$\chi 2 = 2307.52$***
Comfortable	36.2	36.5	32.4	20.0	35.1	22.9	22.5	27.2	6.2	5.7	6.5	18.9	2.8	4.0	
Fair easily	23.6	23.7	29.0	28.8	28.5	36.8	29.1	24.0	23.4	14.3	18.8	28.8	13.9	21.4	
Some difficulties	7.3	10.4	7.5	14.1	8.5	13.2	17.0	15.7	30.3	31.8	25.4	18.8	33.6	27.3	
Great difficulties	1.3	2.2	2.8	3.7	2.9	5.0	7.3	4.5	9.0	18.4	12.1	7.4	19.5	13.3	
Missing	31.6	27.2	29.1	33.4	25.0	22.1	24.1	28.6	31.1	29.8	37.2	26.1	30.2	34.0	
Health															
Subjective health															$\chi 2 = 1919.57$***
Excellent	20.2	14.9	11.7	5.8	17.8	8.1	21.5	8.6	2.9	6.4	2.8	6.3	1.0	6.5	
Very good	32.1	29.5	14.1	16.1	21.7	19.1	29.8	20.2	16.2	26.0	7.1	13.6	5.3	11.3	
Good	24.2	37.6	44.8	42.2	30.5	38.5	30.4	43.0	39.2	38.3	41.3	43.5	29.6	31.7	
Fair	17.9	14.9	25.2	27.2	23.3	25.7	13.6	22.3	29.7	23.7	34.5	26.5	29.5	35.1	
Poor	5.5	3.1	4.2	8.8	6.8	8.5	4.7	5.9	12.0	5.6	14.2	10.1	34.5	15.4	
ADL (1 or more limitations)	7.4	4.9	5.9	8.8	8.2	11.8	11.5	10.5	8.8	7.8	12.4	10.2	24.7	11.9	$\chi 2 = 287.01$***
IADL (1 or more limitations)	12.3	8.4	13.0	11.2	12.1	19.9	15.7	16.7	16.7	19.2	19.8	16.0	28.0	19.5	$\chi 2 = 193.84$***

Seeing															$\chi2 = 2045.34$***
Excellent	40.9	28.4	23.2	16.1	43.9	20.9	24.1	17.8	19.0	16.0	2.8	29.4	7.9	13.9	
Very good	36.7	38.2	19.7	36.2	24.1	41.2	30.4	29.7	27.3	39.2	16.4	25.0	17.9	19.4	
Good	15.5	28.6	48.0	40.1	25.1	28.6	31.2	39.1	41.7	33.1	55.9	32.7	40.6	43.3	
Fair	4.0	3.9	6.5	5.2	4.3	7.2	11.3	10.5	8.0	9.8	18.5	8.4	16.3	17.6	
Poor	2.8	1.0	2.7	2.4	2.6	2.1	3.1	2.8	4.0	1.9	6.3	4.4	17.2	5.9	
Hearing															$\chi2 = 928.70$***
Excellent	25.4	20.5	14.6	14.0	26.3	20.1	27.0	15.2	20.1	21.8	3.5	18.7	7.4	15.6	
Very good	34.1	33.7	18.1	30.7	23.4	31.3	30.6	26.3	28.2	38.2	17.7	20.1	23.1	19.5	
Good	24.1	33.3	47.2	39.0	41.1	31.5	26.4	38.5	37.6	28.3	53.5	38.7	43.4	41.8	
Fair	14.0	11.5	18.5	13.9	7.6	14.5	13.9	16.0	10.6	10.5	21.0	16.5	16.7	18.4	
Poor	2.4	1.0	1.6	2.4	1.7	2.5	2.1	4.1	3.6	1.3	4.3	6.0	9.4	4.7	
Social embeddedness															
Children															$\chi2 = 1321.38$***
Childless	7.0	13.1	8.9	11.2	7.4	13.6	15.2	10.5	5.8	14.8	13.5	12.6	6.6	11.5	
≥1 children almost daily contact	24.7	21.7	32.6	31.4	29.7	35.4	49.7	36.3	35.2	60.9	45.3	30.4	45.9	64.2	
≥1 children more than weekly contact	46.0	37.6	41.8	28.3	41.9	26.9	22.3	35.0	32.6	19.1	25.7	34.3	21.6	17.9	
≥1 children almost weekly contact	16.4	19.4	12.7	17.5	16.8	13.3	8.6	12.3	14.8	4.2	9.9	15.3	14.8	3.7	
≥1 children less than weekly contact	5.9	8.2	4.0	11.6	4.2	10.8	4.2	5.9	11.6	1.0	5.6	7.4	11.1	2.7	
Parents															$\chi2 = 341.33$***
Both parents died	71.3	67.3	73.3	72.9	70.4	81.8	81.4	73.3	73.5	78.3	83.5	68.2	78.5	79.9	
≥1 parents almost daily contact	3.2	3.7	3.2	4.9	4.8	5.0	6.0	6.1	4.6	8.5	5.4	5.5	4.6	9.2	
≥1 parents more than weekly contact	10.3	9.4	8.8	6.6	9.5	4.6	5.0	8.4	6.3	5.6	4.6	8.4	3.7	4.9	
≥1 parents almost weekly contact	6.8	9.4	5.5	7.0	6.4	3.9	3.4	5.9	5.7	3.9	2.0	6.6	4.6	2.0	
≥1 parents less than weekly contact, parents poor health	5.8	6.7	7.0	6.3	7.0	4.3	3.9	4.4	7.7	2.3	4.0	8.4	7.4	3.5	

(Continued on next page)

TABLE 2. Descriptive Statistics (Unweighted); Countries Ordered by Rate of Loneliness ($N = 12248$) *(Continued)*

Variable	Denmark ($N = 965$)	Switzerland ($N = 511$)	Netherlands ($N = 930$)	Germany ($N = 920$)	Sweden ($N = 1018$)	Austria ($N = 517$)	Ireland ($N = 382$)	Belgium ($N = 1055$)	Czech Rep. ($N = 1117$)	Greece ($N = 1037$)	Spain ($N = 744$)	France ($N = 1090$)	Poland ($N = 975$)	Italy ($N = 987$)	Significance test
≥1 parents less than weekly contact, parents good health	2.6	3.5	2.2	2.3	1.9	0.4	0.3	1.9	2.2	1.4	0.5	2.9	1.2	0.5	
Social participation (mean; 0–4)	0.8	0.7	0.7	0.5	0.6	0.4	0.8	0.6	0.2	0.4	0.2	0.5	0.1	0.2	$F = 81.29^{***}$
Support exchange															
Regular help with personal care given to hhmember(s)	4.9	2.7	3.2	4.9	3.3	5.2	7.1	4.9	5.5	5.9	8.7	4.6	9.1	7.9	$\chi 2 = 81.73^{***}$
Informal help given to:															
Family members	38.9	25.8	37.3	27.0	37.1	22.4	27.2	36.5	25.4	15.5	9.3	23.2	13.3	20.2	$\chi 2 = 545.97^{***}$
Nonfamily members	7.4	5.1	6.9	5.0	5.9	2.7	2.4	5.7	2.4	1.0	0.4	2.0	2.1	2.0	$\chi 2 = 172.50^{***}$
Informal help received by:															
Family members	22.2	10.8	15.5	21.2	16.8	17.8	14.4	17.6	33.7	20.3	14.1	11.7	19.4	12.9	$\chi 2 = 283.73^{***}$
Nonfamily members	4.2	2.2	3.2	3.0	3.4	3.1	1.0	1.9	4.1	0.9	0.7	1.1	2.3	1.1	$\chi 2 = 78.25^{***}$
Looking after grandchildren															$\chi 2 = 1517.23^{***}$
No grandchildren	27.4	42.9	37.0	37.4	30.1	34.0	41.0	29.6	17.6	38.2	32.5	34.2	14.6	30.1	
Daily	1.5	1.2	1.5	3.8	1.3	5.0	7.9	7.8	5.0	14.3	8.7	3.5	17.2	16.2	
At least weekly	9.2	13.9	18.8	11.3	10.3	8.9	13.1	19.1	11.4	8.3	7.3	10.6	9.0	9.1	
Less than weekly	30.3	12.5	17.1	12.6	26.4	12.2	17.3	15.8	15.7	7.4	7.5	18.8	10.9	6.5	
Never	31.6	29.5	25.6	34.9	31.9	38.9	20.7	27.7	50.3	31.8	44.0	32.9	48.3	38.1	
Feelings of loneliness	6.3	8.0	8.3	8.5	10.1	11.2	11.8	13.4	15.6	15.6	15.9	17.8	20.0	25.4	$\chi 2 = 287.17^{***}$

$^{***}p < .001$.

hhmember(s) = household member(s).

Greece. The majority of seniors in all countries under investigation are in weekly or almost weekly contact with adult children. The majority no longer having living parents, with the highest percentage observed in Spain (84%), Austria (82%), and Ireland (81%), and for those who have one or two parents alive, frequencies of contact are especially high in Italy and Greece. Social participation in clubs, volunteer organizations, and so on is highest in Denmark, Ireland, Switzerland, and the Netherlands. Rates of help with personal care given to household members are higher in southern European populations than in most of the northern and western European countries. Providing informal help to noncoresidential family members is highest in northern and western European countries, reflecting differences in living arrangements.

The final row of Table 2 shows that the prevalence of loneliness runs from 6.3% for Denmark to 25.4% for Italy. Countries with the highest reports of loneliness are the Czech Republic, Greece, Spain, France, Poland, and Italy, indicating that countries in the Mediterranean region and in Central Europe and France have the highest prevalences of loneliness.

Multivariate Analysis

Table 3 shows the results of multivariate logistic regression analysis, providing insight into the sources of country-level differences in loneliness. Model 1 provides the basic differences in loneliness between countries, with Denmark, Switzerland, the Netherlands, Germany, and Sweden located significantly on the lower side of the loneliness continuum, and the Czech Republic, Greece, Spain, France, Poland, and Italy on the other side.

As expected, Model 2 shows that a higher incidence of loneliness at the country level is attributable to having an older population, a population with a higher proportion of women, and a population with a higher proportion of never and formerly married older adults. The prevalences of loneliness in the Czech Republic and Greece are no longer significantly higher than the 14-country mean after control for age, sex, and marital status composition. Contrary to H1, however, the relatively high rate of loneliness in Poland is not attributable to the demographic make-up of the country.

In Model 3, differences in socioeconomic status are taken into consideration. In line with previous studies, higher levels of education are negatively related, and income levels that are evaluated as difficult are positively related, to the country level of loneliness. Socioeconomic factors account for the higher level of loneliness in the central European countries Poland and the Czech Republic and in the southern European countries Greece, Spain, and Italy, offering support for H2. While rates of loneliness in Poland and Italy are still above the 14-country mean after control for the less favorable socioeconomic status of their older adult population, the levels of loneliness in the Czech Republic, Greece, and Spain no longer differ from the 14-country mean.

TABLE 3. Hierarchical Logistic Regression on Loneliness ($N = 12248$)

	Model						
Variable	1	2	3	4	5	6	7
Country (compared to grand mean):							
Denmark	0.47***	0.43***	0.66**	0.61***	0.51***	0.48***	0.64**
Switzerland	0.60**	0.59**	0.77	0.82	0.62**	0.61**	0.83
Netherlands	0.63***	0.70**	0.74*	0.67***	0.68**	0.68**	0.81
Germany	0.64***	0.70**	0.77*	0.63***	0.63***	0.61***	0.66**
Sweden	0.78*	0.84	0.93	0.94	0.83	0.83	1.12
Austria	0.88	0.64**	0.89	0.86	0.81	0.83	0.64**
Ireland	0.92	0.90	0.99	1.15	0.98	1.00	1.20
Belgium	1.07	1.10	1.14	1.10	1.10	1.17	1.23*
Czech Republic	1.28**	1.18	1.13	1.16	1.22*	1.10	0.95
Greece	1.28**	1.12	0.94	1.36***	1.29**	1.21*	0.92
Spain	1.31**	1.38**	1.04	0.98	1.17	1.21	1.00
France	1.50***	1.39***	1.48***	1.48***	1.49***	1.56***	1.35**
Poland	1.73***	1.99***	1.24*	1.01	1.60***	1.66***	0.99
Italy	2.36***	2.98***	1.85***	1.96***	2.30***	2.47***	2.48***
Demographic							
Age		1.01**					0.98***
Female		1.35***					1.28***
Marital status (ref. married):							
Widowed		6.36***					5.89***
Divorced		4.73***					3.81***
Never married		4.05***					2.49***

Socioeconomic				
Level of education (ref. low):				
Medium	0.81**			1.05
High	0.69***			0.98
Missing	1.17			0.86
Paid job	0.57***			0.77**
Perceived income (ref. comfortable):				
Fair easily	1.42***			1.19
Some difficulties	2.09***			1.58***
Great difficulties	3.91***			2.50***
Missing	0.72**			1.08
Health				
Subjective health (excellent to poor)		1.50***		1.45***
ADL (1 or more limitations)		1.18		1.10
IADL (1 or more limitations)		1.62***		1.25**
Seeing (excellent to poor)		1.18***		1.10**
Hearing (excellent to poor)		1.02		1.05
Social embeddedness				
Children (ref. childless)				
≥1 children almost daily contact			0.48***	0.56***
≥1 children more than weekly contact			0.53***	0.65**
≥1 children almost weekly contact			0.59***	0.70*
≥1 children less than weekly contact			0.71**	0.70*

(Continued on next page)

TABLE 3. Hierarchical Logistic Regression on Loneliness ($N = 12248$) *(Continued)*

	Model						
Variable	1	2	3	4	5	6	7
Parents (ref. both parents died):							
≥1 parents almost daily contact					0.63**		0.96
≥1 parents more than weekly contact					0.73**		1.17
≥1 parents almost weekly contact					0.49***		0.83
≥1 parents less than weekly contact, parents poor health					1.06		1.40*
≥1 parents less than weekly contact, parents good health					0.83		1.32
Social participation (low to high)					0.75***		0.87**
Support exchange							
Regular help with personal care given to hhmember(s)						0.97	1.35*
Informal help given to:							
Family members						0.64***	0.82*
Nonfamily members						1.07	1.21
Informal help received by:							
Family members						2.07***	1.21*
Nonfamily members						1.18	0.94
Looking after grandchildren (ref. no grandchildren)							
Daily						0.54***	0.61**
At least weekly						0.58***	0.78*
Less than weekly						0.60***	0.72**
Never						1.09	1.05

***$p < .001$. **$p < .01$. *$p < .05$.
hhmember(s) = household member(s).

Subjective health is known to be significantly associated with loneliness, as is also indicated in Model 4: subjective health, IADL limitations, and problems in seeing are significantly related to loneliness. Somewhat surprising and contrary to prior research, ADL limitations and hearing problems are not related to increased loneliness. Population differences in health account for country-level differences in loneliness. Congruent with H3, after we took health factors into consideration, loneliness levels in the Czech Republic and Poland did not significantly differ from the 14-country mean. Our findings show furthermore that a substantial part of the high level of loneliness among Spanish older adults is attributable to their relatively poor health.

More frequent get-togethers with children and parents and higher levels of social participation are inversely related to the prevalence of loneliness, as is shown in Model 5 of Table 3. With regard to children, the largest differences in the prevalence of loneliness are found between older adults with and without children; the frequency of contact with their children seems to be of less importance. With regard to parents, older adults with weekly or more contact with their parents are less likely to be lonely; there are no substantial differences between older adults whose parents died and those who meet their parents less than once a week, regardless of parents' health. The frequencies of get-togethers with children and parents, as well as the levels of involvement in the community via social participation do not differ between countries in affecting the level of loneliness, except for in Spain, where the rate of loneliness no longer deviates from the 14-country mean once social participation is controlled for.

Support exchanges within the family and with network members outside the family were entered into Model 6. Informal help given to family members and regularly providing grandparental care are inversely related to loneliness intensity. In contrast, receiving informal support from family members is positively associated with loneliness. Countries differ as to whether support exchanges mediate the onset and continuation of loneliness. In the Czech Republic and Spain, in particular, support exchanges within the family are strongly associated with loneliness. After taking into account the exchange of familial support, the levels of loneliness in the Czech Republic and Spain no longer differ from the 14-country mean. Apparently, high levels of loneliness at the country level are only partially attributable to differences in the functioning of the kin and nonkin social network. These indicators account for the relatively high levels of loneliness in the Czech Republic and Spain, but not for those in Greece, France, Poland, and Italy.

Model 7 of Table 3 provides an overview of the loneliness rate in the 14 European countries after we took into account country-level differences in demographic characteristics, wealth, health, social embeddedness, and support exchange. In contrast to the basic Model 1, with six countries characterized by a significantly higher level of loneliness, in Model 7 only two countries have significantly higher levels of loneliness: Italy and France. Whereas the higher loneliness levels in the

Czech Republic, Poland, Greece, and Spain can be attributed to varying combinations of factors such as a high age, a high proportion of women, a high proportion of unmarried individuals, unfavorable socioeconomic circumstances, poor health, and limited social networks, the relatively high loneliness levels in Italy and France cannot be fully accounted for.

Discussion

Previous studies on cross-national differences in older adult loneliness have reported a North–South divide in Europe (Jylhä & Jokela, 1990; Sundström, Fransson, Malmberg, & Davey, 2009; Walker, 1993). In the northern European countries, there is a lower prevalence of loneliness among the elderly than in the southern European countries. Our study largely confirmed this pattern, showing low rates of loneliness in Denmark, Switzerland, and the Netherlands and high rates of loneliness in Greece, Spain, and Italy. Contrary to expectations, France was among the high-loneliness countries. We extended the range of countries beyond the North–South divide. The second wave of SHARE offered the opportunity to include former communist countries. Results showed high prevalences of loneliness in the Czech Republic and Poland.

To understand cross-national differences in loneliness, we focused on differences in population composition, examining four sets of factors: demographic, socioeconomic, health, and social networks. Findings showed that the relatively high levels of loneliness in the Czech Republic and Greece were largely attributable to high proportions of unmarried men and women among the elderly. Marriage generally serves to protect against loneliness (Dykstra & De Jong Gierveld, 2004; Stack, 1998), and the Czech Republic and Greece have relatively many older adults who lack this protective bond. Limited socioeconomic means and poor health contributed to the relatively high levels of loneliness in Spain, Italy, the Czech Republic, and Poland. Social (support) network characteristics, though important determinants of loneliness at the individual level, did not strongly contribute to an explanation of cross-national differences in loneliness. At the individual level, those who maintained frequent contacts with their parents and adult children and those who provided support to noncoresident family members were less prone to loneliness. These findings are consistent with earlier research (De Jong Gierveld, Van Tilburg, & Dykstra, 2006; Wenger, Davies, Shahtahmasebi, & Scott, 1996). Regarding cross-national differences, findings indicated that the relatively high levels of loneliness in Spain were partially attributable to the relatively large group who no longer had living parents and the relatively large group providing personal care to a household member. The relatively high loneliness level in the Czech Republic was partially attributable to the relatively high proportion of older adults dependent on informal help from family members.

Whereas we were able to account for the relatively high rate of older adult loneliness in Greece, Spain, the Czech Republic, and Poland, we were unable to find an explanation for the relatively high prevalence of loneliness among French and Italian older adults. As regards France, the frequent reports of loneliness among their older residents might be a methodological artifact. Inspection of the French questionnaire revealed that respondents were asked whether they had felt alone (*senti(e) seul(e))* much of the time during the past week, rather than whether they had felt lonely. We suggest that respondents are less hesitant to report having felt "alone" than to having felt "lonely." As regards Italy, part of the explanation lies in economic deprivation and poor health in the older adult population. Demographic characteristics and social network characteristics failed to further contribute to the explanation. On the basis of our results, it is unclear why Italian older adults frequently report feeling lonely. Several possible interpretations warrant further investigation. It might be that Italian older adults have exceptionally high expectations of relationships that hardly can be fulfilled. They might be particularly vulnerable when they experience relationship losses. Italian society might attach great stigma to those who for whatever reason find themselves living alone. Unfortunately, our data set did not allow us to examine country variations in the loneliness effect of these issues. In future work, it will be important to consider people's normative orientations and vulnerabilities in the cultural context of the country in which they live.

Our study reveals that different types of factors play a role in explaining the observed country differences in Europe. High levels of loneliness in Spain, Italy, the Czech Republic, and Poland are largely associated with financial and health problems among their older adult population. This is not a self-evident finding, given that loneliness is usually conceptualized as a problem of relationships: having fewer close ties than desired, and not achieving the desired level of intimacy in relationships. Our results underscore that wealth and health are conditions for engaging in satisfying personal relationships and thus for the prevention and alleviation of loneliness (Hawkley et al., 2008; Victor, Scrambler, Bowling, & Bond, 2005). In southern and eastern European countries, improving the socioeconomic position of older adults and their health status is likely to result in a drop in loneliness.

Dykstra (2009) identified three sets of factors as explanations of cross-national differences in loneliness: differences in population composition, country-level characteristics, and interactions between individual characteristics and country. The current study focused on differences in population composition only yet considered a wide range of characteristics of the older adult population: demographic make-up, socioeconomic circumstances, health differentials, and social embeddedness. It remains an open question whether country indicators of wealth such as GDP help to explain cross-national differences in loneliness over and above individual income levels. Likewise, it remains an open question whether a factor such as having a network with limited support potential contributes more strongly to loneliness in certain countries rather than others. Previous work on cross-national differences in perceived family obligations suggests this might be the case. Norms of filial obligation tend to be strongly endorsed in the southeast of the European continent than in the northwest (Daatland, Herlofson, & Lima, 2011). It is conceivable that older adults are more prone to loneliness when support from adult children is not forthcoming in countries in southern and eastern Europe than in northern and western Europe. This issue merits further research.

Our study relied on a single item to measure loneliness. Over the years, the concept of loneliness has been measured in different ways, including direct single questions about feelings of loneliness (e.g., "I often felt lonely"), self-rating ("Do you categorize yourself in the group of 'not lonely', 'moderate lonely', 'lonely' or 'severely lonely'?"), and multiple-item measures such as the UCLA loneliness scale and De Jong Gierveld loneliness scale (De Jong Gierveld & Kamphuis, 1985; Russell, Peplau, & Cutrona, 1980). There is a general preference for loneliness scales—which, unfortunately, were not available in the SHARE survey—as they do not use the words "lonely" or "loneliness" and cover different aspects of loneliness. Moreover, direct, single-item measures of loneliness seem to address the emotional dimension of loneliness ("loss") more than social isolation (Dugan & Kivett, 1994). However, studies have shown that a single loneliness item is strongly related to the overall score obtained from a multi-item loneliness scale (De Jong Gierveld & Van Tilburg, 1999; DiTommasso & Spinner, 1993; Russell, Peplau, & Ferguson, 1978). We cannot rule out the possibility that the single direct question on loneliness influenced our findings. It is likely that nationals differ in the extent to which they feel they can openly express negative subjective experiences and personal concerns, with country differences in admitting loneliness as a result. There might also be country differences in the extent to which feelings of social isolation are conceived in terms of loneliness and relationship inadequacies rather than in terms of stress or general turmoil (Rokach, Orzeck, Cripps, Lackovic-Grgin, & Penezic, 2001). Clearly, additional comparative research on perceptions of the causes and manifestations of loneliness is needed.

There is an ongoing debate on whether loneliness is a single universal construct—an identical experience across countries—or an umbrella term that covers a variety of distinct distresses with some common features. Our findings do not help resolve this controversy. Although our findings point to correlates of the North/West–South/Central gradient in loneliness, the underlying mechanisms are not yet well identified. One example will serve to illustrate this point. To explain the contribution of the relatively large group of low socioeconomic-status individuals in the southern and central European countries to the high prevalence of adult loneliness in these countries, one may refer to the universal association between financial strain and psychological distress: regardless of the country in which they are living, older adults who lack economic resources are less able to participate in social activities, are less optimistic, and feel unable to control unwanted things that happen in their lives (Krause, Newsom, & Rook, 2008). Yet another mechanism might be relevant, one that goes beyond the individual's struggle to cope with everyday life and refers to the shared cultural experiences of economic and social changes. This is especially likely to apply to older residents in the central European countries (Petrov, 2007). During socialism, it was customary that elderly parents used their savings to help improve the life chances of their adult children. After the transitions of 1989–1990, pension schemes became more modest, and many of the older adults now have to rely on the financial help of children, who themselves are confronted with very high levels of unemployment, decreasing income levels, and increasing housing expenditures. These shared modes of stress, identified by Ries (1997) as "litanies of suffering," might result in a general reduction of trust and a widespread feeling of relative deprivation, leading to negative psychological outcomes (O'Rand, 2001), including loneliness.

Further cross-country comparative research is needed to disentangle the mechanisms underlying late-life loneliness across different environmental conditions and constraints. It is furthermore highly recommended to extend the number of central and eastern European countries under study. Apart from between-country comparisons, there is an urgent need for more loneliness research among different ethnic groups sharing the same environment. Most loneliness research has been conducted in the Western Hemisphere. The psychology of the individualistic cultures of the West, however, is likely to differ from the psychology of the collectivist cultures in other parts of the world (Triandis, 1996). Hence, there might be larger cross-ethnic differences than cross-country differences in loneliness. Due to the increasing number of older migrants from nonwestern countries in Europe, it would be particularly interesting to compare their loneliness experiences with those of their native peers.

REFERENCES

Adams, G., Anderson, S. L., & Adonu, J. K. (2004). The cultural grounding of closeness and intimacy. In D. J. Mashek & A. Aron (Eds.), *Handbook of closeness and intimacy* (pp. 321–339). Mahwah, NJ: Lawrence Erlbaum.

Ajrouch, K., Akiyama, H., & Antonucci, T. C. (2007). Cohort differences in social relations among the elderly. In H.-W. Wahl, C. Tesch-Römer, & A. Hoff (Eds.), *New dynamics in old age: Individual, environmental and societal perspectives* (pp. 43–63). New York: Baywood, Amityville.

Attias-Donfut, D., Ogg, J., & Wolff, F. (2005). European patterns of intergenerational financial and time transfers. *European Journal of Ageing*, *2*, 161–173.

Börsch-Supan, A., Brugiavini, A., Jürges, H., Kapteyn, A., Mackenbach, J., Siegrist, J., & Weber, G. (Eds.) (2008). *Health, ageing and retirement in Europe: Starting the longitudinal dimension (2004–2007)*. Mannheim, Germany: MEA.

Börsch-Supan, A., & Jürges, H. (Eds.). (2005). *The survey of health, ageing and retirement in Europe: Methodology*. Mannheim, Germany: MEA.

Cacioppo, J. T., Hawkley, L. C., Crawford, E. L., Ernst, J. M., Burleson, M. H., Kowalewski, R. B., ... Berntson, G. G. (2002). Loneliness and health: Potential mechanisms. *Psychosomatic Medicine*, *64*, 407–417.

Cornwell, E. Y., & Waite, L. J. (2009). Measuring social isolation among older adults using multiple indicators from the NSHAP study. *Journal of Gerontology: Social Sciences*, *64B*(suppl. 1), i38–i46.

Daatland, S. O., Herlofson, K., & Lima, I. A. (2011). Balancing generations: On the strength and character of family norms in the west and east of Europe. *Ageing & Society*, *31*, 1159–1179.

De Jong Gierveld, J., Broese van Groenou, M., Hoogendoorn, A. W., & Smit, J. H. (2009). Quality of marriages in later life and emotional and social loneliness. *Journals of Gerontology, Series B: Psychological Sciences and Social Sciences*, *64B*, 497–506.

De Jong Gierveld, J., & Dykstra, P. A. (2008). Virtue is its own reward? Support giving in the family and loneliness in middle and old age. *Ageing & Society*, *28*, 271–287.

De Jong Gierveld, J., & Kamphuis, F. H. (1985). The development of a Rasch-type loneliness-scale. *Applied Psychological Measurement*, *9*, 289–299.

De Jong Gierveld, J., & Van Tilburg, T. G. (1999). *Manual of the Loneliness Scale*. VU University Amsterdam, Department of Social Research Methodology. Available at http://home.fsw.vu.nl/TG.van.Tilburg/manual_loneliness_scale_1999.html

De Jong Gierveld, J., Van Tilburg, T., & Dykstra, P. A. (2006). Loneliness and social isolation. In A. Vangelisti & D. Perlman (Eds.), *Cambridge handbook of personal relationships* (pp. 485–500). Cambridge: Cambridge University Press.

DiTommaso, E., & Spinner, B. (1993). The development and initial validation of the Social and Emotional Loneliness Scale for Adults (SELSA). *Personality and Individual Differences*, *14*, 127–134.

Dugan, E., & Kivett, V. R. (1994). The importance of emotional and social isolation to loneliness among very old rural adults. *Gerontologist*, *34*, 340–346.

Dykstra, P. A. (2009). Older adult loneliness: Myths and realities. *European Journal of Ageing*, *6*, 91–100.

Dykstra, P. A., & De Jong Gierveld, J. (2004). Gender and marital-history differences in emotional and social loneliness among Dutch older adults. *Canadian Journal of Aging/La Revue Canadienne du Vieillissement*, *23*, 141–155.

Dykstra, P. A., & Fokkema, T. (2007). Social and emotional loneliness among divorced and married men and women: Comparing the deficit and cognitive perspectives. *Basic and Applied Social Psychology*, *29*, 1–12.

Dykstra, P. A., & Fokkema, T. (2011). Relationships between parents and their adult children: A West European typology of late-life families. *Ageing & Society*, *31*, 545–569.

Förster, M., & Mira d'Ercole, M. (2005). Income distribution and poverty in OECD countries second half of the 1990s. Working Paper OECD, nr. 22. Paris: OECD.

Generations and Gender Surveys, Contextual Database. Available at www.ggp-i.org/data.

Glaser, K., Tomassini, C., & Grundy, E. (2004). Revisiting convergence and divergence: Support for older people in Europe. *European Journal of Ageing, 1*, 64–72.

Guiaux, M., Van Tilburg, T., & Broese van Groenou, M. B. (2007). Changes in contact and social support exchange in personal networks after widowhood. *Personal Relationships, 14*, 457–473.

Halleröd, B. (2009). Ill, worried or worried sick? Inter-relationships among indicators of wellbeing among older people in Sweden. *Ageing & Society, 29*, 563–584.

Hank, K. (2007). Proximity and contact between older parents and their children: A European comparison. *Journal of Marriage and Family, 69*, 159–173.

Havens, B., & Hall, M. (2001). Social isolation, loneliness, and the health of older adults. *Indian Journal of Gerontology, 14*, 144–153.

Hawkley, L. C., Hughes, M. E., Waite, L. J., Masi, C. M., Thisted, R. A., & Cacioppo, J. T. (2008). From social structural factors to perceptions of relationship quality and loneliness: The Chicago health, aging, and social relations study. *Journal of Gerontology, Social Sciences, 63B*, S375–S384.

Höllinger, F., & Haller, M. (1990). Kinship and social networks in modern societies: A cross-cultural comparison among seven nations. *European Sociological Review, 6*, 103–124.

Johnson, D. P., & Mullins, L. C. (1987). Growing old and lonely in different societies: Toward a comparative perspective. *Journal of Cross-Cultural Gerontology, 2*, 257–275.

Jylhä, M. (2004). Old age and loneliness: Cross-sectional and longitudinal analyses in the Tampere longitudinal study on aging. *Canadian Journal on Aging/La Revue Canadienne du Vieillissement, 23*, 157–168.

Jylhä, M., & Jokela, J. (1990). Individual experiences as cultural: A cross-cultural study on loneliness among the elderly. *Ageing & Society, 10*, 295–315.

Kaufman, G., & Uhlenberg, P. (1998). Effects of life course transitions on the quality of relationships between adult children and their parents. *Journal of Marriage and the Family, 60*, 924–938.

Kitson, G. C., & Morgan, L. A. (1990). The multiple consequences of divorce: A decade review. *Journal of Marriage and the Family, 52*, 913–924.

Korporaal, M., Broese van Groenou, M., & Van Tilburg, T. G. (2008). Effects of own and spousal disability on loneliness among older adults. *Journal of Aging and Health, 20*, 306–325.

Kramer, S. E., Kapteyn, T. S., Kuik, D. J., & Deeg, D. J. H. (2002). The association of hearing impairment and chronic diseases with psychosocial health status in older age. *Journal of Aging and Health, 14*, 122–137.

Krause, N., Newsom, J. T., & Rook, K. S. (2008). Financial strain, negative social interaction, and self-rated health: Evidence from two United States nationwide longitudinal surveys. *Ageing & Society, 28*, 1001–1023.

Lehtinen, V., Sohlman, B., & Kovess-Masfety, V. (2005). Level of positive mental health in the European Union: Results from the Eurobarometer 2002 survey. *Clinical Practice and Epidemiology in Mental Health, 1*, 9.

Liefbroer, A. C. (1999). From youth to adulthood: Understanding changing patterns of family formation from a life course perspective. In L. J. G. van Wissen & P. A. Dykstra (Eds.), *Population issues: An interdisciplinary focus* (pp. 53–85). New York/Dordrecht: Kluwer Academic/Plenum Publishers.

Mackenbach, J. P., Stirbu, I., Roskam, A.-J. R., Schaap, M. M., Menvielle, G., Leinsalu, M., & Kunst, A. E. (2008). Socioeconomic inequalities in health in 22 European countries. *New England Journal of Medicine*, *358*, 2468–2481.

Manzi, C., Vignoles, V. L., Regalia, C., & Scabini, E. (2006). Cohesion and enmeshment revisited: Differentiation, identity and well-being in two European cultures. *Journal of Marriage and Family*, *68*, 673–689.

Mullins, L. C., Elston, C. H., & Gutkowski, S. M. (1996). Social determinants of loneliness among older Americans. *Genetic, Social and General Psychology Monographs*, *122*, 453–473.

Ó Luanaigh, C., & Lawlor, B. A. (2008). Loneliness and the health of older people. *International Journal of Geriatric Psychiatry*, *23*, 1213–1221.

O'Rand, A. M. (2001). Stratification and the life course: The forms of life-course capital and their interrelationships. In R. H. Binstock & L. K. George (Eds.), *Handbook of aging and the social sciences* (5th ed.; pp. 197–213). New York: Academic Press.

Penninx, B. W. J. H., Van Tilburg, T., Kriegsman, D. M. W., Boeke, A. J. P., Deeg, D. J. H., & Van Eijk, J. T. M. (1999). Social network, social support, and loneliness in older persons with different chronic diseases. *Journal of Aging and Health*, *11*, 151–168.

Peplau, L. A., & Perlman, D. (1982). Perspectives on loneliness. In L. A. Peplau & D. Perlman (Eds.), *Loneliness: A sourcebook of current theory, research and therapy* (pp. 1–18). New York: John Wiley.

Pérodeau, G.-M., & du Fort, G.-G. (2000). Psychotropic drug use and the relation between social support, life events, and mental health in the elderly. *Journal of Applied Gerontology*, *19*, 23–41.

Petrov, I. C. (2007). The elderly in a period of transition: Health, personality and social aspects of adaptation. *Annals of the New York Academy of Sciences*, *1114*, 300–309.

Pilusuk, M., & Minkler, M. (1980). Supportive networks: Life ties for the elderly. *Journal of Social Issues*, *36*, 95–116.

Pinquart, M. (2003). Loneliness in married, widowed, divorced, and never-married older adults. *Journal of Social and Personal Relationships*, *20*, 31–53.

Pinquart, M., & Sörensen, S. (2001). Influences on loneliness in older adults: A meta-analysis. *Basic and Applied Social Psychology*, *23*, 245–266.

Reher, D. S. (1998). Family ties in Western Europe: Persistent contrasts. *Population and Development Review*, *24*, 203–234.

Ries, N. (1997). *Russian talk: Culture and conversation during Perestroika*. Ithaca, NY: Cornell University Press.

Rokach, A. (2007). The effect of age and culture on the causes of loneliness. *Social Behavior and Personality*, *35*, 169–186.

Rokach, A. (2008). Coping with loneliness in North America and Spain. *Psychology Journal*, *5*, 51–68.

Rokach, A., & Brock, H. (1997). Loneliness: A multidimensional experience. *Psychology: A Journal of Human Behavior*, *34*, 1–9.

Rokach, A., & Neto, F. (2005). Age, culture, and the antecedents of loneliness. *Social Behavior and Personality*, *33*, 477–494.

Rokach, A., Orzeck, T., Cripps, J., Lackovic-Grgin, K., & Penezic, Z. (2001). The effects of culture on the meaning of loneliness. *Social Indicators Research*, *53*, 17–31.

Rokach, A., Orzeck, T., & Neto, F. (2004). Coping with loneliness in old age: A cross-cultural comparison. *Current Psychology*, *23*, 124–137.

Rosenmayr, L., & Köckeis, E. (1963). Propositions for a sociological theory of ageing and the family. *International Social Science Journal*, *XV*, 410–426.

Russell, D. W., Peplau, D. A., & Cutrona, C. E. (1980). The revised UCLA loneliness scale. *Journal of Personality & Social Psychology*, *39*, 471–480.

Russell, D., Peplau, L. A., & Ferguson, M. L. (1978). Developing a measure of loneliness. *Journal of Personality Assessment, 42*, 290–294.

Savikko, N., Routasalo, P. E., Tilvis, R. S., Strandberg, T. E., & Pitkala, K. H. (2005). Predictors and subjective causes of loneliness in an aged population. *Archives of Gerontology and Geriatrics, 41*, 223–233.

Scharf, T., & Smith, A. E. (2004). Older people in urban neighborhoods: Addressing the risk of social exclusion in later life. In C. Phillipson, G. Allan, & D. Morgan (Eds.), *Social networks and social exclusion: Sociological and political issues* (pp. 162–179). London: Ashgate.

Stack, S. (1998). Marriage, family, and loneliness: A cross-national study. *Sociological Perspectives, 41*, 415–432.

Stevens, N., & Westerhof, G. J. (2006). Marriage, social integration and loneliness in the second half of life: A comparison of Dutch and German men and women. *Research on Aging, 28*, 713–729.

Steverink, N., Westerhof, G. J., Bode, C., & Dittmann-Kohli, F. (2001). The personal experience of aging, individual resources, and subjective well-being. *Journal of Gerontology: Psychological Sciences, 65B*, 364–373.

Sundström, G., Fransson, E., Malmberg, B., & Davey, A. (2009). Loneliness among older Europeans. *European Journal of Ageing, 6*, 267–275.

Tesch-Römer, C., & Von Kondratowitz, H.-J. (2006). Unique as well as universal: Complexities of comparative ageing research. *European Journal of Ageing, 4*, 103–106.

Triandis, H. C. (1996). The psychological measurement of cultural syndromes. *American Psychologist, 51*, 407–415.

United Nations. (2010). *World population ageing 2009*. New York: Department of Economic and Social Affairs.

Väänänen, A., Buunk, B. P., Kivimäki, M., Pentti, J., & Vahtera, J. (2005). When it is better to give than to receive: Long-term health effects of perceived reciprocity in support exchange. *Journal of Personality and Social Psychology, 89*, 176–193.

Van de Kaa, D. J. (1987). Europe's second demographic transition. *Population Bulletin, 42*, 1–47.

Van Tilburg, T., De Jong Gierveld, J., Lecchini, L., & Marsiglia, D. (1998). Social integration and loneliness: A comparative study among older adults in the Netherlands and Tuscany, Italy. *Journal of Social and Personal Relationships, 15*, 740–754.

Van Tilburg, T., & Dykstra, P. A. (2008). Differences in older adults' loneliness and depression across Europe. In P. A. Dykstra (Ed.), *Ageing, intergenerational solidarity and age-specific vulnerabilities* (pp. 141–157). NIDI Report No. 77. The Hague, The Netherlands: KNAW Press.

Victor, C., Scambler, S., Bond, J., & Bowling, A. (2000). Being alone in later life: Loneliness, social isolation and living alone. *Reviews in Clinical Gerontology, 10*, 407–417.

Victor, C. R., Scrambler, S. J., Bowling, A., & Bond, J. (2005). The prevalence of, and risk factors for loneliness in later life: A survey of older people in Great Britain. *Ageing & Society, 25*, 357–375.

Wagner, M., Schütze, Y., & Lang, F. R. (1999). Social relationships in old age. In P. B. Baltes & K. U. Mayer (Eds.), *The Berlin Aging Study: Aging from 70 to 100* (pp. 282–301). New York: Cambridge University Press.

Waite, L. J., & Lehrer, E. L. (2003). The benefits from marriage and religion in the United States: A comparative analysis. *Population and Development Review, 29*, 255–275.

Walker, A. (1993). *Age and attitudes. Main results from a Eurobarometer survey*. Brussels, Belgium: Commission of the European Communities.

Wenger, G. C., Davies, R., Shahtahmasebi, S., & Scott, A. (1996). Social isolation and loneliness in old age: Review and model refinement. *Ageing & Society, 16*, 333–358.

Wilson, R. S., Krueger, K. R., Arnold, S. E., Schneider, J. A., Kelly, J. F., Barnes, L. L., ... Bennett, D. A. (2007). Loneliness and risk of Alzheimer Disease. *Archives of General Psychiatry*, *64*, 234–240.

PART III: LONELINESS AND OTHER CONDITIONS AND MALADAPTIVE BEHAVIORS

Loneliness in Patients with Rheumatic Diseases: The Significance of Invalidation and Lack of Social Support

MARIANNE B. KOOL
RINIE GEENEN
Utrecht University, University Medical Center Utrecht

ABSTRACT. Rheumatic diseases affect about 20% of the population, leading to common symptoms such as joint problems, pain, fatigue, and stiffness. Loneliness is prevalent in individuals with rheumatic diseases. This could be due to not receiving social support and being stigmatized and invalidated, which might be most common in fibromyalgia, a rheumatic disease that lacks medical evidence. The aim of this study was to compare loneliness in distinct rheumatic diseases and to examine the association of loneliness with social support and invalidation. Participants were 927 patients with ankylosing spondylitis ($n = 152$), fibromyalgia ($n = 341$), osteoarthritis ($n = 150$), rheumatoid arthritis ($n = 171$), or systemic diseases ($n = 113$). They completed online questionnaires including an 11-point Likert scale assessing loneliness, the Illness Invalidation Inventory (3*I; Kool et al., 2010), and the Social Support Survey (SSS; De Boer, Wijker, Speelman, & De Haes, 1996; Sherbourne & Stewart, 1991). Patients with fibromyalgia experienced significantly more loneliness than patients with ankylosing spondylitis and patients with rheumatoid arthritis. Besides being younger, having lower education, and not working, in multiple regression analyses both lack of social support and invalidation were independently correlated with loneliness. This suggests that to decrease loneliness, therapeutic attention should be given to both increasing social support as well as decreasing invalidation in patients with rheumatic diseases, especially in patients with fibromyalgia.

LONELINESS is prevalent in individuals with rheumatic diseases as compared to the general population (Laidmäe, Leppik, Tulva, & Hääl, 2009; Rokach, Lechcier-Kimel, & Safarov, 2006) and as compared to other chronic diseases (Penninx et al.,

This study was supported by a grant from the Dutch Arthritis Association. We are very grateful to the participants, to the collaborating colleagues of our research group, and to the patient representatives Paulien Vermaas and Miranda de Jong for their contributions to this project.

1999). Loneliness is perceived social isolation; it is the distressing feeling that accompanies the perception that one's social needs are not being met by the quantity or especially the quality of one's social relationships (Heinrich & Gullone, 2006). Loneliness has adverse effects on patients' well-being, functioning, and health (Hawkley & Cacioppo, 2010; Heinrich & Gullone, 2006), and it predicts increased mortality after account of age, sex, chronic diseases, alcohol use, and smoking (Penninx et al., 1997). Considering the high prevalence of rheumatic diseases (Klippel, Stone, Crofford, & White, 2008), the high occurrence of loneliness in rheumatic diseases, and the adverse effects of loneliness, it is important to get insight into risk factors of loneliness in this patient group to try to decrease loneliness.

There are more than 100 types of rheumatic diseases. The prevalence of self-reported doctor-diagnosed rheumatic diseases among adults is about 20% of the population with a female preponderance, a percentage that may increase up to 25% of the population in 2030 due to the aging and the increase of obesity (Klippel et al., 2008). Rheumatic diseases are characterized by musculoskeletal symptoms such as pain, stiffness, and swelling of joints, which can be due to inflammation and damage of musculoskeletal structures. Common rheumatic diseases are osteoarthritis, rheumatoid arthritis, ankylosing spondylitis, fibromyalgia, and systemic rheumatic diseases.

Osteoarthritis is the most common joint disease in humans, with an estimated prevalence of 6–10% of the population when it concerns hip and knee osteoarthritis (Felson & Zhang, 1998). It is strongly age-related. Symptoms are pain, short-lasting stiffness, cracking of joints, joint swelling, fatigue, and functional limitation (Klippel et al., 2008). Rheumatoid arthritis is a chronic systemic autoimmune inflammatory disease that is characterized by joint pain and swelling involving small distal joints, morning stiffness, and insidious fatigue. The prevalence of rheumatoid arthritis is about 1–2% of the population. In contrast to most other rheumatic diseases, ankylosing spondylitis is more common in men than in women (ratio = ~ 2:1). This disease involves chronic inflammation of the sacroiliac joints and spine as well as extraspinal lesions involving the eye, bowel, and heart. The estimated prevalence is 0.1–6.0% across different populations (Klippel et al., 2008). Systemic lupus erythematosus (SLE), Sjögren's syndrome, systemic sclerosis, inflammatory muscle diseases, and overlap syndromes are grouped as systemic rheumatic diseases or connective-tissue disorders, with the overlapping features of sustained inflammation, autoimmune processes with the development of specific autoantibodies, and the systemic clinical phenotype involving several organs. The estimated prevalence of this disease group is 0.5–3.0% of a given population (Gaubitz, 2006). Whereas most rheumatic disease can be diagnosed through objective physical or laboratory features or well-characterized pathologic findings, the rheumatic condition fibromyalgia is diagnosed using only the symptoms chronic widespread pain for at least three month and fatigue, unrefreshed sleep, and cognitive symptoms (Wolfe et al., 2010). The estimated population prevalence of fibromyalgia is 2% (Wolfe, Ross, Anderson, Russell, & Hebert, 1995).

Due to the burden of pain, fatigue, disabilities, and additional changes in a persons' life, patients can become more depressed (Axford et al., 2010; Isik, Koca, Ozturk, & Mermi, 2007; Kozora, Ellison, & West, 2006; Madenci, Herken, Keven, Yagiz, & Guersoy, 2007). Depression may partly explain loneliness (Cacioppo, Hughes, Waite, Hawkley, & Thisted, 2006). However, loneliness predicts increased depression, but depression does not predict increased loneliness (Cacioppo, Hawkley, & Thisted, 2010). Thus, other reasons than depression may also explain loneliness in rheumatic diseases. There are evolutionary reasons to expect that loneliness is common in chronic diseases. Ill people may be more often stigmatized and socially excluded, because isolation of ill people once prevented other people from becoming infected (Dijker & Koomen, 2006; Kurzban & Leary, 2001).

Also social exchange models, like the social contract theory (Cosmides, 1989), can explain the negative social attitude towards ill people. Reciprocal altruism requires that the individual is willing and able to reciprocate support (Kurzban & Leary, 2001). Reduced well-being and functioning of patients may hamper giving support in return for support. Moreover, core symptoms of rheumatic diseases—pain, stiffness, and fatigue—are mostly invisible. As a consequence, patients may be considered individuals who are receiving a benefit without paying a cost, resulting in exclusion of social exchanges. This may hold most for fibromyalgia, because this chronic pain condition lacks medical evidence. Indeed, patients with fibromyalgia report being considered to be cheaters or whiners who do not deserve benefits because they are not paying costs (Arnold et al., 2008; Kool, van Middendorp, Boeije, & Geenen, 2009), and in comparison with patients with rheumatoid arthritis, patients with fibromyalgia reported experiencing more invalidation, which refers to cognitive, affective, and behavioral responses of others who are perceived as denying, lecturing, overprotecting, not supporting, and not acknowledging with respect to the condition of the patient (Kool et al., 2009). Due to invalidation, patients with fibromyalgia may feel more often lonely than patients with other rheumatic diseases.

More loneliness has been related to less received social support (Beal & Stuifbergen, 2007; Kara & Mirici, 2004; Winningham & Pike, 2007), more negative social interactions (Cacioppo & Hawkley, 2009), and more stigmatization (Singer et al., 2007). Experimental and functional magnetic resonance imaging (fMRI) studies suggest that lonely people view their world as more threatening and punishing and that the brain of lonely people are on high alerts for social threats (Cacioppo & Hawkley, 2009). Thus, previous studies indicate that lack of social support and invalidation experiences of patients with rheumatic diseases could be related to more severe loneliness.

At this point, only one study has examined loneliness in the context of social interactions of patients with rheumatic diseases. In rheumatoid arthritis, associations were observed between less social support and loneliness in Dutch patients and between problematic support and loneliness in Egyptian patients (El-Mansoury et al., 2008). Our study will examine social support as well as invalidation in relation to loneliness. Our aim is to compare loneliness between distinct rheumatic diseases as well as to examine in patients with rheumatic diseases the association of loneliness with social support and invalidation. We expect that less social support and more invalidation are both associated with loneliness and that loneliness will be especially common among patients with fibromyalgia.

Method

Participants

Participants were 927 patients with a single rheumatic disease, either ankylosing spondylitis ($n = 152$), fibromyalgia ($n = 341$), osteoarthritis ($n = 150$), rheumatoid arthritis ($n = 171$), or a systemic disease such as Sjögren's syndrome, systemic lupus erythematosus, scleroderma, or mixed connective tissue disease ($n = 113$). We combined the systemic diseases in a single category because of the small sample size and because of overlapping features such as sustained inflammation, the development of specific autoantibodies, and the systemic clinical phenotype involving several organs (Gaubitz, 2006). Included were respondents with an age > 18 years who reported to be diagnosed by a specialist, general practitioner, or nurse practitioner. In all patient groups, most of the participants were female (69–96%), had a relationship (72–83%), had Dutch (85%) or Belgium (12%) nationality, and worked full-time or part-time (41–54%). Patients with osteoarthritis were significantly older (56.3 years) than all other patients groups ($p < .001$), and patients with rheumatoid arthritis were significant older (47.1 years) than the remaining patient groups ($p < .04$). On average, it was 5.1–10.6 years since participants had their diagnosis and 11.5–17.4 years since they experienced symptoms (Table 1).

Procedure

A hyperlink to an online questionnaire study was put on 14 websites of Dutch and Belgian patient associations of rheumatic diseases. In an accompanying text the aim and content of the study, sample criteria, and duration of participation were explained. Participants could always stop participating in the study if they wanted. Incomplete questionnaires were excluded from analyses.

Instruments

The online questionnaire included questions about demographic characteristics, such as age, gender, disease diagnosis, and work status, a single-item scale measuring loneliness, and two questionnaires.

TABLE 1. Demographic Characteristics of Patients with the Rheumatic Diseases Ankylosing Spondylitis, Fibromyalgia, Osteoarthritis, Rheumatoid Arthritis, or a Systemic Disease

Variable	Ankylosing spondylitis ($n = 152$)	Fibromyalgia ($n = 341$)	Osteoarthritis ($n = 150$)	Rheumatoid arthritis ($n = 171$)	Systemic diseases ($n = 113$)
Gender; female, *n*(%)	105 (69)	328 (96)	122 (81)	145 (85)	104 (92)
Age (years), *M* (*SD*)	42.1 (12.3)	40.5 (11.6)	56.3 (8.6)	47.1 (11.8)	43.1 (11.7)
Marital status, *n* (%)					
Single	23 (15)	53 (16)	*16 (11)*	23 (14)	24 (21)
Married/partnered	120 (79)	259 (76)	109 (73)	141 (83)	81 (72)
Divorced	5 (3)	16 (5)	14 (9)	1 (1)	4 (4)
Widowed	1 (1)	1 (0)	8 (5)	3 (2)	1 (1)
Years of education, *M* (*SD*)	15.3 (3.3)	14.2 (4)	13.8 (3.2)	15.4 (3.7)	14.9 (4.4)
Years with symptoms, *M* (*SD*)	17.4 (13.0)	12.9 (9.1)	12.1 (8.5)	11.5 (10.3)	12.2 (9.8)
Years since diagnosis, *M* (*SD*)	10.6 (11.4)	5.1 (4.7)	7.2 (6.7)	9.2 (9.3)	6.7 (6.9)
Work status, *n* (%)					
Employed full time	47 (31)	57 (17)	33 (22)	36 (21)	23 (20)
Employed part time	36 (24)	82 (24)	28 (19)	49 (29)	30 (27)
Unemployed	6 (4)	22 (7)	6 (4)	9 (5)	6 (6)
Retired	6 (4)	2 (1)	23 (5)	8 (5)	4 (4)
Receiving benefit or Workmen's Compensation Act	29 (19)	77 (23)	29 (19)	44 (26)	32 (28)
Housewife/student	12 (8)	45 (13)	19 (13)	11 (6)	10 (9)

Loneliness was measured with the question "How lonely did you feel last week?" Participants indicated their answer on an 11-point Likert scale (0 = *not at all lonely*, and 10 = *very lonely*). The one-item Likert-type scale has been shown to be an adequate way to measure a construct and useful when time or questionnaire space is limited (Davey, Barratt, Butow, & Deeks, 2007; Temel, Pirl, Recklitis, Cashavelly, & Lynch, 2006).

The Illness Invalidation Inventory (3*I) (Kool et al., 2010) measured the severity of invalidation experiences by each of five sources (spouse, family, medical professionals, work environment, and social services). It consists of two dimensions: lack of understanding (3 items) and discounting (5 items). The eight items were identical for each source, thus the 3*I includes 5 × 8 items (40 items). An example of an item is "*my family* makes me feel like I am an exaggerator." Participants indicated on a 5-point scale (1 = *never*, 2 = *seldom*, 3 = *sometimes*, 4 = *often*, 5 = *very often*) how often during the past year people within each category reacted to them in the described way. The 3*I showed good construct validity and reliability (Kool et al., 2010). The Cronbach's alphas in the current study were higher than .86 for discounting and higher than .83 for lack of understanding.

To measure social support, the MOS Social Support Survey-Dutch version was used (De Boer, Wijker, Speelman, & De Haes, 1996; Sherbourne & Stewart, 1991). Four dimensions of social support were assessed with 20 items: affectionate support (3 items), emotional/informational support (8 items), positive social interaction (3 items), and tangible support (4 items). Participants could indicate how often they perceived the specific support on a 5-point scale (1 = *none of the time*, 2 = *a little of the time*, 3 = *some of the time*, 4 = *most of the time*, 5 = *all of the time*). The psychometric properties of this widely used questionnaire are good (De Boer et al., 1996; Sherbourne & Stewart, 1991). In the current study, the Cronbach's alphas of the subscales were higher than .84. The mutual correlations between the dimensions were high ($r > .68$). A total social support score was calculated by adding the scores of the four subscales and dividing the sum by 4.

Statistical Analyses

All analyses were done with SPSS 16.0. Significance level was set at $p < 0.05$. Score distributions of all variables were normal.

Mean scores of loneliness for the five patient groups were compared using analysis of covariance with gender and age as covariates. The size of differences between the five patient groups was expressed by the effect size parameter partial eta-squared (partial η^2), with values of 0.01, 0.06, and 0.14 being considered small, moderate, and large, respectively. To illustrate the distribution of the loneliness scores in the groups, the percentages of participants were expressed for patients having "low" (0–1), "moderate" (2–4), and "high" (5–10) scores. These categories, which were chosen on the basis of consensus between the authors, were most close to a partitioning of scores in tertiles. Pearson correlation coefficients were calculated to examine the association of loneliness with demographic variables, social support, and invalidation. Variables that correlated significantly with loneliness were included in a hierarchical regression analyses to measure to what extent loneliness was predicted by the combination of variables. In regression analyses, the first step included the demographic variables age, gender, education, having a partner, and having work. Step 2 included having fibromyalgia (no/yes), because the severity of loneliness in fibromyalgia differed from the severity in the other rheumatic conditions. Step 3 included social support and invalidation (discounting or lack of understanding). Five hierarchical regression analyses were performed for the five different—though mutually correlated (Kool et al., 2010)—sources of invalidation (spouse, family, medical professionals, work, and social services). Each analysis included one of the sources of invalidation next to the demographic variables, fibromyalgia, and social support.

Results

Comparison of Loneliness Scores

In Table 2, the loneliness scores for the five patient groups are shown. In significance testing, the scores were adjusted for age and gender differences between groups. Patients with fibromyalgia experienced significantly more loneliness than patients with ankylosing spondylitis ($p = .02$, partial $\eta^2 = .02$) and patients with

TABLE 2. *M* and *SD* of Loneliness Scores for Patients with Ankylosing Spondylitis, Fibromyalgia, Osteoarthritis, Rheumatoid Arthritis, or Systemic Diseases (Sjögren's Syndrome, Systemic Lupus Erythematosus, Scleroderma, or Mixed Connective Tissue Disease)

	Loneliness	
Rheumatic disease	*M*	*SD*
Ankylosing spondylitis	3.1	3.1
Fibromyalgia	4.0	3.1
Osteoarthritis	3.2	3.2
Rheumatoid arthritis	3.1	3.0
Systemic diseases	3.1	3.0

The *M* score on loneliness of patients with fibromyalgia is significantly higher than the loneliness scores of patients with ankylosing spondylitis and patients with rheumatoid arthritis.

TABLE 3. Percentages of Patients with Ankylosing Spondylitis, Fibromyalgia, Osteoarthritis, Rheumatoid Arthritis, or Systemic Diseases Who Score Low (Score 0–1), Moderate (Score 2–4), or High (Score 5–10) on Loneliness

	Loneliness		
Rheumatic disease	Low (score 0–1)	Moderate (score 2–4)	High (score 5–10)
Ankylosing spondylitis	41%	27%	32%
Fibromyalgia	30%	21%	49%
Osteoarthritis	41%	29%	30%
Rheumatoid arthritis	42%	26%	32%
Systemic diseases	37%	29%	34%

rheumatoid arthritis ($p = .01$, partial $\eta^2 = .02$), but did not experience more loneliness than patients with osteoarthritis ($p = .17$) and patients with systemic diseases ($p = .053$). About half of the patients with fibromyalgia scored high on loneliness in comparison to about one third of the patients with other rheumatic diseases. Table 3

Associations with Loneliness

Table 4 shows the results of hierarchical multiple regression analyses predicting loneliness from three classes of independent variables. In most analyses, in Step 1 the demographic variables were significantly associated with loneliness: being younger ($-.19 < ß < -.13$), having a lower education ($-.19 < ß < -.12$), not having a relationship ($-.10 < ß < -.09$), and not working ($-.14 < ß < -.08$). After inclusion of fibromyalgia in the model (Step 2), the variables of Step 1 generally remained significant, and also having fibromyalgia was a significant determinant ($.11 < ß < .14$) of loneliness. In Step 3, social support and discounting (the five different sources separately) were included. For most social sources, being younger ($-.18 < ß < -.11$), having a lower education ($-.15 < ß < -.08$), and not working ($-.10 < ß < -.06$) remained significantly associated with loneliness. Furthermore, lack of social support ($-.41 < ß < -.33$) and discounting ($.16 < ß < .24$) were found to be independently associated with loneliness for all but one social source. About the same results were found for lack of understanding (not shown in the table); the ß- and p-values were, respectively: spouse $ß = .10$, $p = .01$; family $ß = .16$, $p < .001$; medical professionals $ß = .05$, $p = .17$; work $ß = .18$, $p < .001$; social services $ß = .11$, $p = .02$.

TABLE 4. Hierarchical Multiple Regression Analyses Predicting Loneliness From (1) the Demographic Variables Age, Gender, Education, Having a Spouse (Relationship), and Having Work, (2) Having Fibromyalgia, and (3) Social Support and Discounting by, Respectively, the Spouse, the Family, Medical Professionals, Colleagues at Work, and Employees at Social Services

		Loneliness									
		Spouse ($n = 699$)		Family ($n = 884$)		Medical professionals ($n = 884$)		Work environment ($n = 597$)		Social services ($n = 434$)	
Step	Variable	ß	Adj. R^2	ß	Adj. ΔR^2	ß	Adj. ΔR^2	ß	Adj. ΔR^2	ß	Adj. ΔR^2
1	Age	–.19**	.08	–.17**	.07	–.17**	.07	–.13**	.06	–.14**	.07
	Gender	–.07		–.06		–.06		–.06		–.05	
	Education	–.12**		–.11		–.11		–.12**		–.19**	
	Relationship	–.05		–.10**		–.10**		–.09*		–.08	
	Work	–.14**		–.12**		–.12**		–.08*		–.11*	
2	Age	–.17**	.08	–.14**	.08	–.14**	.08	–.10*	.08	–.11*	.09
	Gender	–.05		–.04		–.04		–.03		–.03	
	Education	–.10**		–.10**		–.10**		–.11*		–.17**	
	Relationship	–.05		–.10**		–.10**		–.09*		–.08	
	Work	–.13**		–.11**		–.11**		–.08		–.10*	
	Fibromyalgia	.10*		.13**		.13**		.14**		.16	
3	Age	–.17**	.26	–.15**	.24	–.18**	.27	–.11**	.28	–.12**	.24
	Gender	–.02		–.01		–.01		–.00		–.01	
	Education	–.09**		–.08*		–.08**		–.07		–.15**	
	Relationship	–.02		–.01		.02		.02		.04	
	Work	–.10**		–.06*		–.08*		–.04		–.04	
	Fibromyalgia	.06		.05		.07*		.07		.06	
	Social sup.	–.33**		–.35**		–.41**		–.36**		–.37**	
	Discounting										
	Spouse	.16**									
	Family			.2[illegible]**							
	Med prof.					.05					
	Work							.24**			
	Soc serv.									.16**	

Note. Sample sizes vary between social sources, because not all sources applied to each participant. Gender is encoded by 0 = female, and 1 = male.
$^*p < .05$. $^{**}p < .01$. Adj = adjusted; social sup. = social support; prof. = professionals; serv. = services.

Discussion

The aim of this study was to compare loneliness between rheumatic diseases and to examine in patients with rheumatic diseases the association of loneliness with social support and invalidation. The study showed that patients with fibromyalgia experience more loneliness than patients with ankylosing spondylitis and patients with rheumatoid arthritis. Within the total group of patients with rheumatic diseases, more severe loneliness was also found in younger patients and in patients with lower education and without work. After control for age, education, work, and fibromyalgia, both lack of social support and invalidation were found to be independently correlated with more severe loneliness in patients with rheumatic diseases.

A considerable number of patients with rheumatic diseases was indicated to experience loneliness. In support of the social exchange theory (Kurzban & Leary, 2001), loneliness scores were highest in patients with fibromyalgia. This suggests that a considerable number of patients with fibromyalgia feel lonely, and that feeling might have adverse effects on their well-being, functioning, and health on top of the burden of the illness itself. The lack of objective pathologic evidence in fibromyalgia leads to a disturbance in the social contact with others when patients are seen as cheaters or whiners who do not deserve benefits because they are not paying costs. Although these results are consistent with the social contract theory (Cosmides, 1989), our study does not yield definite proof for this theory. However, it is a significant observation that loneliness occurs most in the rheumatic condition that lacks medical evidence.

In line with other studies (Asnani, Fraser, Lewis, & Reid, 2010; Creed & Reynolds, 2001; Distel et al., 2010; El-Mansoury et al., 2008; Heinrich & Gullone, 2006), in the current study among patients with rheumatic diseases, younger age, lower education, and not working were associated with more loneliness. In the general population, the prevalence of loneliness peaks during adolescence and drops between young adulthood and middle age, with perhaps a slight increase in the elderly (Heinrich & Gullone, 2006), though higher loneliness in older patients was not observed in our study. The association between being single and loneliness disappeared fully when social support and invalidation were included in the regression model, suggesting that especially the quality of one's social relationships—more than being single or not—is important to prevent loneliness (Hawkley et al., 2008). Overall, next to patients who have negative social interactions, younger, low-educated, and not-working patients are most at risk of feeling lonely.

In agreement with a previous study (Demir & Tarhan, 2001; El-Mansoury et al., 2008), our study yields the suggestion that perceived invalidation and lack of social support may contribute to loneliness feelings in patients with rheumatic diseases. Although, social support is more clearly related to loneliness than invalidation, both are independent predictors that reflect that loneliness is highest when support is absent and invalidating responses are present such as lecturing, denying, and not acknowledging the symptoms. Also the opposite observation has face validity: Lonely individuals may see the social world as more threatening, and they may expect and remember more negative social interactions, as posited by the loneliness model (Hawkley & Cacioppo, 2010). These processes can lead to a downward spiral that may reduce the quality of lives of patients. To stop this, both loneliness and invalidation could be therapeutic targets.

A strength of this study is that it examines the potential significance of lack of social support and invalidation for loneliness in a large sample of patients with distinct rheumatic diseases. Limitations of the study are the use of a single item to assess loneliness, the absence of a control group for the general population, the cross-sectional design, and the self-selection that could have lead to a sample bias representing a relatively young—internet using—patient group. Moreover, the study does not take account of possible mediators between social variables and loneliness such as depression. The results of our study underscore the importance of longitudinal and clinical experimental studies examining lack of social support and invalidation as determinants of loneliness.

Social cognitive behavioral interventions that target maladaptive social cognitions have been suggested to be especially effective in decreasing loneliness, as a meta-analysis showed that this type of intervention is more effective than interventions enhancing social skills, providing social support, or increasing opportunities for social interaction (Hawkley & Cacioppo, 2010). Our study showed that lack of social support and invalidation are independently associated with loneliness in patients with rheumatic diseases and suggests that is could be fruitful to give therapeutic attention to both increasing social support and decreasing invalidation in patients with rheumatic diseases, especially in patients with fibromyalgia. This suggestion needs substantiation in longitudinal and clinical experimental research.

REFERENCES

Arnold, L. M., Crofford, L. J., Mease, P. J., Burgess, S. M., Palmer, S. C., Abetz, L., et al. (2008). Patient perspectives on the impact of fibromyalgia. *Patient Education and Counseling*, *73*, 114–120.

Asnani, M. R., Fraser, R., Lewis, N. A., & Reid, M. E. (2010). Depression and loneliness in Jamaicans with sickle cell disease. *BMC Psychiatry*, *10*, 40.

Axford, J., Butt, A., Heron, C., Hammond, J., Morgan, J., Alavi, A., et al. (2010). Prevalence of anxiety and depression in osteoarthritis: Use of the Hospital Anxiety and Depression Scale as a screening tool. *Clinical Rheumatology*, *29*, 1277–1283.

Beal, C. C., & Stuifbergen, A. (2007). Loneliness in women with multiple sclerosis. *Rehabilitation Nursing*, *32*, 165–171.

Cacioppo, J. T., & Hawkley, L. C. (2009). Perceived social isolation and cognition. *Trends in Cognitive Sciences*, *13*, 447–454.

Cacioppo, J. T., Hawkley, L. C., & Thisted, R. A. (2010). Perceived social isolation makes me sad: 5–year cross–lagged analyses of loneliness and depressive symptomatology in the Chicago Health, Aging, and Social Relations Study. *Psychology and Aging*, *25*, 453–463.

Cacioppo, J. T., Hughes, M. E., Waite, L. J., Hawkley, L. C., & Thisted, R. A. (2006). Loneliness as a specific risk factor for depressive symptoms: Cross-sectional and longitudinal analyses. *Psychology and Aging*, *21*, 140–151.

Cosmides, L. (1989). The logic of social-exchange: Has natural-selection shaped how humans reason: Studies with the Wason Selection Task. *Cognition*, *31*, 187–276.

Creed, P. A., & Reynolds, J. (2001). Economic deprivation, experiential deprivation and social loneliness in unemployed and employed youth. *Journal of Community & Applied Social Psychology*, *11*, 167–178.

Davey, H. M., Barratt, A. L., Butow, P. N., & Deeks, J. J. (2007). A one–item question with a Likert or visual analog scale adequately measured current anxiety. *Journal of Clinical Epidemiology*, *60*, 356–360.

De Boer, A. G. E. M., Wijker, W., Speelman, J. D., & De Haes, J. C. J. M. (1996). Quality of life in patients with Parkinson's disease: Development of a questionnaire. *Journal of Neurology Neurosurgery and Psychiatry*, *61*, 70–74.

Demir, A., & Tarhan, N. (2001). Loneliness and social dissatisfaction in Turkish adolescents. *Journal of Psychology*, *135*, 113–123.

Dijker, A. J., & Koomen, W. (2006). A psychological model of social control and stigmatization: Evolutionary background and practical implications. *Psychology, Health & Medicine*, *11*, 296–306.

Distel, M. A., Rebollo-Mesa, I., Abdellaoui, A., Derom, C. A., Willemsen, G., Cacioppo, J. T., et al. (2010). Familial resemblance for loneliness. *Behavior Genetics*, *40*, 480–494.

El-Mansoury, T. M., Taal, E., Abdel-Nasser, A. M., Riemsma, R. P., Mahfouz, R., Mahmoud, J. A., et al. (2008). Loneliness among women with rheumatoid arthritis: A cross-cultural study in the Netherlands and Egypt. *Clinical Rheumatology*, *27*, 1109–1118.

Felson, D. T., & Zhang, Y. Q. (1998). An update on the epidemiology of knee and hip osteoarthritis with a view to prevention. *Arthritis and Rheumatism*, *41*, 1343–1355.

Gaubitz, M. (2006). Epidemiology of connective tissue disorders. *Rheumatology*, *45*, 3–4.

Hawkley, L. C., & Cacioppo, J. T. (2010). Loneliness matters: A theoretical and empirical review of consequences and mechanisms. *Annals of Behavioral Medicine*, *40*, 218–227.

Hawkley, L. C., Hughes, M. E., Waite, L. J., Masi, C. M., Thisted, R. A., & Cacioppo, J. T. (2008). From social structural factors to perceptions of relationship quality and loneliness: The Chicago Health, Aging, and Social Relations Study. *Journals of Gerontology: Series B. Psychological Sciences and Social Sciences*, *63*, S375–S384.

Heinrich, L. A., & Gullone, E. (2006). The clinical significance of loneliness: A literature review. *Clinical Psychology Review*, *26*, 695–718.

Isik, A., Koca, S. S., Ozturk, A., & Mermi, O. (2007). Anxiety and depression in patients with rheumatoid arthritis. *Clinical Rheumatology*, *26*, 872–878.

Kara, M., & Mirici, A. (2004). Loneliness, depression, and social support of Turkish patients with chronic obstructive pulmonary disease and their spouses. *Journal of Nursing Scholarship*, *36*, 331–336.

Klippel, J. H., Stone, J. H., Crofford, L. J., & White, P. H. (Eds.). (2008). *Primer on the rheumatic diseases*. New York: Springer Science+Business Media.

Kool, M. B., van Middendorp, H., Boeije, H., & Geenen, R. (2009). Understanding the lack of understanding: Invalidation from the perspective of the patient with fibromyalgia. *Arthritis & Rheumatism-Arthritis Care & Research*, *61*, 1650–56.

Kool, M. B., van Middendorp, H., Lumley, M. A., Schenk, Y., Jacobs, J. W. G., Bijlsma, J. W. J., et al. (2010). Lack of understanding in fibromyalgia and rheumatoid arthritis: The Illness Invalidation Inventory (3*I). *Annals of the Rheumatic Diseases*, *69*, 1990–1995.

Kozora, E., Ellison, M. C., & West, S. (2006). Depression, fatigue, and pain in systemic lupus erythematosus (SLE): Relationship to the American College of Rheumatology SLE neuropsychological battery. *Arthritis & Rheumatism-Arthritis Care & Research*, *55*, 628–635.

Kurzban, R., & Leary, M. R. (2001). Evolutionary origins of stigmatization: The functions of social exclusion. *Psychological Bulletin*, *127*, 187–208.

Laidmäe, V., Leppik, L., Tulva, T., & Hääl, M. (2009). Disease-related social and family life: People coping with rheumatoid arthritis in Estonia. *Critical Public Health*, *19*, 87–105.

Madenci, E., Herken, H., Keven, S., Yagiz, E., & Guersoy, S. (2007). Alexithymia in patients with fibromyalgia syndrome [Fibromiyalji Sendromlu Hastalarda Aleksitimi]. *Turkiye Klinikleri Tip Bilimleri Dergisi*, *27*, 32–35.

Penninx, B. W. J. H., van Tilburg, T., Kriegsman, D. M. W., Boeke, A. J. P., Deeg, D. J. H., & van Eijk, J. T. M. (1999). Social network, social support, and loneliness in older persons with different chronic diseases. *Journal of Aging and Health*, *11*, 151–168.

Penninx, B. W. J. H., van Tilburg, T., Kriegsman, D. M. W., Deeg, D. J. H., Boeke, A. J. P., & van Eijk, J. T. M. (1997). Effects of social support and personal coping resources on mortality in older age: The Longitudinal Aging Study Amsterdam. *American Journal of Epidemiology*, *146*, 510–519.

Rokach, A., Lechcier-Kimel, R., & Safarov, A. (2006). Loneliness of people with physical disabilities. *Social Behavior and Personality*, *34*, 681–699.

Sherbourne, C. D., & Stewart, A. L. (1991). The Mos Social Support Survey. *Social Science & Medicine*, *32*, 705–714.

Singer, S., Danker, H., Bloching, M., Kluge, A., Schwenke, J., Oeken, J., et al. (2007). Perceived stigmatisation following laryngectomy. *Psychotherapie Psychosomatik Medizinische Psychologie*, *57*, 328–333.

Temel, J. S., Pirl, W. F., Recklitis, C. J., Cashavelly, B., & Lynch, T. J. (2006). Feasibility and validity of a one-item fatigue screen in a thoracic oncology clinic. *Journal of Thoracic Oncology*, *1*, 454–459.

Winningham, R. G., & Pike, N. L. (2007). A cognitive intervention to enhance institutionalized older adults' social support networks and decrease loneliness. *Aging & Mental Health*, *11*, 716–721.

Wolfe, F., Clauw, D. J., Fitzcharles, M., Goldenberg, D. L., Katz, R. S., Mease, P., et al. (2010). The American College of Rheumatology preliminary diagnostic criteria for fibromyalgia and measurement of symptom severity. *Arthritis Care & Research*, *62*, 600–610.

Wolfe, F., Ross, K., Anderson, J., Russell, I. J., & Hebert, L. (1995). The prevalence and characteristics of fibromyalgia in the general population. *Arthritis & Rheumatism*, *38*, 19–28.

Loneliness and Eating Disorders

MARTHA PEASLEE LEVINE
Penn State College of Medicine
Penn State Milton S. Hershey Medical Center

ABSTRACT. This article examines the link between loneliness and eating disorders. This concept is evaluated through a systematic review of the literature that links loneliness and eating disorders and through a survey of themes connecting the 2 conditions. Eating disorders—including anorexia nervosa, bulimia nervosa, and eating disorders that are not otherwise specified, which include binge eating disorder—are challenging health issues. Each of these diagnoses specifically relates to loneliness. This negative emotion contributes to and fuels eating disorder symptoms. Negative interpersonal relationships, both real experiences and individuals' skewed perceptions, exacerbate eating disorders and feelings of loneliness. Characteristics that have been associated with loneliness clearly relate to eating disorders. Understanding this relationship is vital, so that we can appreciate our patients' struggles and work to target these intense emotions within the treatment setting. We need to be aware of the power of loneliness as it applies to individuals in general and specifically to those struggling with disordered eating.

IN HIS SEMINAL TEXT, *Loneliness,* Moustakas (1961) said, "Loneliness anxiety results from a fundamental breach between what one is and what one pretends to be, a basic alienation between man and man and between man and his nature" (p. 24). The manifestation of loneliness in eating disorders embodies this quote. Not only are sufferers alienated from others through their symptom use, their low-self worth, and their negative perception of the world, but also they are alienated from their own inner drives of hunger. Food takes on an emotional quality and is used to numb feelings, including that of loneliness. The relationship between loneliness and eating disorders extends through the entire weight spectrum from anorexia nervosa to binge eating and obesity. This article will provide a systematic literature review of loneliness and eating disorders, examining not only this emotion's relationship to the various types of disordered eating, but also the associated intra- and interpersonal conflicts.

Types of Eating Disorders

Anorexia Nervosa

Anorexia nervosa (AN) is defined by severely low weight, intense fear of gaining weight, disturbed perception of body shape and weight, and amenorrhea (American Psychiatric Association [APA], 2000). It is a serious psychiatric condition with dangerous medical consequences. Sullivan (1995) found an elevated rate of mortality such that individuals with AN had an annual death rate due to all causes for females 15–24 years of age that was 12 times higher and a suicide rate that was more than 200 times greater. The serious nature of this illness makes it vital that we understand all associated risks and complications, including the impact of loneliness.

Eating disorders, such as anorexia nervosa, offer many functions for the individual. Arkell and Robinson's (2008) article about AN helps us understand the role of loneliness. The illness is viewed as a friend who is always there. One individual said, "It's a marriage or relationship I thought would come so easily with humans. It is always there for me stopping me feeling alone" (Arkell & Robinson, 2008, p. 653). Yet AN leads to social isolation by making it often impossible for individuals to participate in events that focus around food.

An eating disorder allows individuals to avoid feelings, to numb themselves. For AN, one individual describes, "I couldn't cope without it. Life would be harder and I would be more depressed and my feelings would be strange and not blocked by tiredness or lack of food" (Arkell & Robinson, 2008, p. 653). We hear in these descriptions Moustakas' (1961) perception of loneliness in both the interpersonal and intrapsychic realms. For many individuals, AN is used to cope with loneliness when relationships fail. They use it to numb their emotions, so that they can distance themselves from nature—their natural feelings.

From early on in the study of eating disorders, psychologists and psychiatrists have recognized feelings of powerlessness and loneliness as one factor in the development of anorexia nervosa (Whyte & Kaczkowski, 1983). Troop and Bifulco (2002) found that women with AN of the binge/purge subtype reported much higher levels of loneliness, shyness, and feelings of inferiority than non–eating disordered women. As one patient described it, loneliness is the real killer from anorexia: "The longer you're ill, the worse it is" (Treasure, Crane, McKnight, Buchanan, & Wolfe, 2011, Enabling, p. 299).

Bulimia Nervosa

Bulimia nervosa (BN) is characterized by recurrent episodes of binge eating occurring on a regular basis with compensatory behavior to prevent weight gain (APA, 2000). Individuals with bulimia experience a state that is "incommunicable," a nonspecific "extreme state of tension" (Esplen, Garfinkel, & Gallop, 2000 pp. 96–97). Difficulty in dealing with painful emotions, especially the sense of aloneness, may predispose individuals for an eating disorder or play a role in the perpetuation of bulimia nervosa (Esplen, Garfinkel, & Gallop). This is evident in the study of Pavlova, Uher, and Papezova (2008). They evaluated Czech au pairs. Loneliness, boredom, stress, and humiliation with the host families contributed to overeating and vomiting. In this study, the au pairs indicated that bingeing and purging helped them deal with unpleasant emotions, with the hurt of being laughed at because of language issues, and with their overall sense of loneliness, boredom, and undervaluation. Meyer and Waller (1999) demonstrated that women with bulimia struggled with overeating particularly related to abandonment (loneliness) cues.

Dolan, Lieberman, Evans, and Lacey (1990) suggested that women struggling with bulimia had poorer relationships with their parents and had observed their parents having poor marital relationships as compared with control persons. In this study, the bulimic women indicated that their parents did not spend much time with them and did not know them well. This was a compared with the control group who felt that their parents were interested in what they did. Loneliness is affected not only by the number of interpersonal relationships, but also by the quality of these relationships. This is an important aspect to keep in mind.

In women with bulimia as compared with women with depression, the BN group had a higher incidence of childhood sexual abuse and felt lonely despite family and friends (M. Nickel et al., 2006). Sexual abuse is significantly related to loneliness and inversely related to connectedness (Rew, 2002). This was studied in a homeless population, but it is a clearly understandable phenomenon. Abuse results in both physical and psychological long-term consequences with women being twice as likely to develop posttraumatic stress disorder (PTSD) that is secondary to exposure to violence as compared to men (Smith, 2009). Within a population of female victims of childhood abuse who were seeking treatment for substance abuse, relapse triggers included sadness or depression, anger, and loneliness (Smith). When individuals use food and their eating disorder to deal with the past abuse, loneliness becomes a trigger for a relapse in eating disorder symptom use.

Emotional abuse, which is at times insidious and ill-defined, can still be an important childhood experience when one examines trauma and its relationship to the development of eating disorders (Kent, Waller, & Dagnan, 1999). This experience can damage individuals' self-esteem and leave them feeling vulnerable and unable to approach others for help. A sense of loneliness despite family and friends occurs at a significantly higher level in BN individuals who are also at risk for suicide (C. Nickel et al., 2006). Interpersonal conflict leads to higher ratings of insecurity for individuals with BN, and this contributes to bulimic symptoms (Tuschen-Caffier & Vögele, 1999). In interactions, women struggling with bulimia have been found to focus increased attention on attractive female faces with the suggestion that they are hypervigilant towards this group because these attractive women are seen as a competitive threat (Maner et al., 2006). This demonstrates further the impaired interpersonal relationships associated with eating disorders and how they can impact individuals' emotions, particularly loneliness.

Guided imagery tasks that facilitate self-awareness about internal sensations increase the desire to binge (Tuschen-Caffier & Vögele, 1999). Both external and internal cues can trigger bulimic symptoms in individuals struggling with BN. Once bulimia has become established, the cycle is maintained by carbohydrate craving (96% individuals) and emotional distress with food being used for its sedative qualities to dampen negative emotional states, such as anger, frustration, loneliness, and boredom (78% individuals) (Lacey, Phil, Coker, & Birtchnell, 1986). Corstorphine, Waller, Ohanian, and Baker (2006) found that levels of anger/frustration and loneliness were high at the beginning of a binge-purge cycle and did not change throughout the cycle. So while individuals might feel that symptom use helps with these negative emotions, it is not apparent that loneliness actually changes during the cycle. What perpetuates the binge-purge cycle is that bingeing is reinforced by the effect of reducing hunger, but this then leads to increased guilt/shame and anxiety. The vomiting phase is then reinforced by lowering these negative emotions and increasing levels of happiness and relief (Corstorphine, Waller, Ohanian, & Baker, 2006).

Binge Eating Disorder (BED) and Obesity

Eating Disorders Not Otherwise Specified (EDNOS) is the category for disorders that do not meet the criteria for any other specific eating disorder (APA, 2000). Some patients may have symptoms similar to AN or BN, but do not meet all the criteria. Other specific conditions fall within EDNOS. One is binge-eating disorder (BED), characterized by binges without the compensatory behaviors seen in BN (APA, 2000). Obesity, while a health risk, has not been specifically designated as an "eating disorder," but it does have a relationship to loneliness and could be considered a disordered relationship with food. Not all individuals who are obese have binge eating disorder; however, most individuals with BED are overweight to obese because of the bingeing portion of the behavior without the compensatory activities to rid themselves of the excess calories.

One way to understand these illnesses (such as BED) is to realize that the lining of the digestive system has the same developmental roots as the skin, so eating acts as a kind of internal massage such that all food is to some extent comfort food (Cacioppo & Patrick, 2009). "Eating is a way of self-soothing that carries costs when we take it to excess, but that does not make it any less soothing in the moment" (Cacioppo & Patrick, 2009, p. 142).

The highest desire to eat when experiencing negative emotions is seen in BED (Zeeck, Stelzer, Linster, Joos, & Hartmann, 2011). Emotions, such as feeling depressed, being bored or lonely, often stand out as predominant binge eating triggers (Bruce & Agras, 1992). One study of binge eating disorder (BED) describes that over-eating in response to sadness, loneliness, tiredness, and anger occurs in between one-half and one-fourth of the binges, and emotional overeating relates to more frequent binge episodes and more severe eating disorder symptoms (Masheb

& Grilo, 2006). Masheb and Grilo (2006) reported that women were more likely to report overeating in response to loneliness than men.

Negative-interactional emotions are related to binges, and this relation demonstrates the importance of interpersonal issues in this population (Zeeck, Stelzer, Linster, Joos, & Hartmann, 2011). Striegel-Moore, Dohm, Pike, Wilfey, and Fairburn (2002) found that in women, physical abuse, sexual abuse, and bullying by peers were associated with increased risk for BED (binge eating disorder). Zeeck, Stelzer, Linster, Joos, and Hartmann (2011) found that "an urge to eat under feelings of loneliness, disgust or exhaustion appears to be more difficult to regulate" (Conclusion, para. 10). Healthy subjects had higher levels of hunger during joy and anger as compared with hunger in the BED group, which was associated with fear and sadness (Zeeck, Stelzer, Linster, Joos, & Hartmann, 2011).

For mild to severely obese individuals, emotional eating appears prominent in 60–90% of those studied (Ganley, 1989). Emotional overeating, eating triggered by emotions and often occurring in the absence of hunger, is most often precipitated by negative emotions such as anger, depression, boredom, anxiety, and loneliness (Ganley). Eating in these circumstances appears to be used to reduce affect and is often done secretively (Ganley). Emotional hunger correlates with "a longing for belonging and social relationships" (Grant, 2008, p. 127). When related to loneliness, eating provides a sense of comfort that takes the place of human connections, which the individuals long for but do not have (Grant). For some, food creates a connection that has never been there for these individuals; for others, it recreates a sense of contentment, which they experienced in the past (Grant). Food is used to self-medicate feelings of pain and conflict; eating becomes a way to fill emotional and social needs (Grant).

One participant indicated, "I found comfort in food. It was my best friend and I slowly gained weight. I didn't have anybody in my life, but I had food" (Grant, 2008, p. 128). One variation of EDNOS is night-eating syndrome (NES), which is characterized by excessive eating in the evening and nighttime awakening to eat. Morse and Katon (2006) studied a group with diabetes and found NES in 9.7% of patients. When compared with the other patients, the subgroup with NES was less likely to comply with diet, exercise, or glucose monitoring and were more likely to be obese and more likely to have two or more diabetes complications (Morse & Katon). These patients were more likely to be depressed, to have childhood abuse histories, to have nonsecure attachment styles, and to report eating in response to anger, sadness, loneliness, and worry (Morse & Katon).

Depressed obese men are substantially heavier than their nondepressed counterparts and are more passive, sedentary, and socially ineffective (Musante, Costanzo, & Friedman, 1998). Men typically demonstrate eating dysregulation in response to positive emotions (happiness, celebrating, socializing); women, though, are significantly more likely to experience eating dysregulation related to negative affects (anger, sadness, ineffectiveness, loneliness, and exhaustion) (Musante, Costanzo, & Friedman).

Overweight children often struggle with loneliness and spend too much time on their own, involved in sedentary activities with access to junk food (Mériaux, Berg, & Hellström, 2010). In addition, peer-victimization has been positively associated with loneliness and negatively associated with physical activity in overweight or at-risk-for-overweight youth; youth may end up avoiding activities, including opportunities for physical activities because of the risk of victimization (Storch et al., 2007). Also peer-victimization can lower rates for physical activity because of decreased motivation related to lowered mood, loneliness, and poor social connectedness (Storch et al.). Repeated peer victimization contributes to on-going social anxiety and loneliness (Devine et al., 2008). Libbey, Story, Neumark-Sztainer, and Boutelle (2008) found that frequent teasing by both family and/or peers is associated with greater disordered eating thoughts and behaviors, depression, anxiety, anger, and decreased self-esteem. In their study group 48% of the children experienced teasing by both peers and their family. One can understand how this teasing influences not only eating disorder thoughts and behaviors but also a sense of loneliness within these negative social interactions.

Isolation from others and from cliques is associated with depressive symptoms because children internalize the negative social experience and develop feelings of loneliness (Witvliet, Brendgen, van Lier, Koot, & Vitaro, 2010). Obesity and self-esteem have a significant relationship especially during early adolescence with obese white and Hispanic girls demonstrating significantly lower self-esteem by 13–14 years as compared with their nonobese counterparts (Strauss, 2000). In addition, obese children with decreased levels of self-esteem demonstrate significantly elevated levels of loneliness (Strauss).

Loneliness serves as an inhibitor of food consumption in nondieters and disinhibits food consumption for dieters (Rotenberg & Flood, 1999). It appears that when dieters experience loneliness, they perceive their diet as not working to improve social connections, and so when they are exposed to the opportunity to eat desirable foods, they abandon their diet and indulge (Rotenberg & Flood). In studies where participants are left feeling either socially disconnected or socially included, those who are socially disconnected consume about twice as much as those who feel that others want to work with them (Cacioppo & Patrick, 2009).

Eating Disorders, Loneliness, and Social Relationships

Perceptions of relationships are critical to the concept of loneliness. As described by Hawkley, Hughes, Waite, Thisted, and Cacioppo (2008), "People can live rather solitary lives and not feel lonely, or they can have many social relationships and nevertheless feel lonely" (p. S375). This can impact individuals struggling with eating disorders in many ways. As described, teasing can clearly impact eating disorders, but it can also affect individuals' feelings of connection. Fleming and Jacobsen (2009) showed that students who reported being bullied were more likely than nonbullied students to experience feelings of sadness, hopelessness, and loneliness. Within social relationships, if teasing or other critical or traumatizing events occur, individuals feel less of a positive connection and feel lonelier. In addition, at times individuals with eating disorders can misinterpret situations, and this can impact their social interactions and can fuel their eating disorders.

Purpose of Loneliness

To understand the extent of the potential impact of loneliness, it is vital to understand the functional role of loneliness. In this way, we can understand how something with evolutionary benefits ended up linked with behaviors that are potentially fatal to the individual. Cacioppo and Patrick (2009, p. 7) described that physical pain protects us from physical dangers and social pain, or loneliness, helps protect us from the danger of being isolated. Our distant ancestors needed social bonds for safety and for the successful passing on of their genes to offspring who then lived long enough to reproduce. Feelings of loneliness let individuals know when their protective bonds were in danger. While physical dangers are not lurking behind every bush and threatening us on a daily basis, the quality of loneliness continues to be passed on. Humans do not fare well if they live solitary lives or simply perceive themselves to be living in isolation (Cacioppo, Fowler, & Christakis, 2009). This experiential aspect is a key issue because individuals are at different levels of risk for experiencing loneliness.

Experience of Connections

Distel et al. (2010) demonstrated that loneliness is moderately heritable with a nonadditive genetic influence, such that individuals have different experiences of loneliness. Cacioppo and Patrick (2009, p. 4) indicated that individuals can have a predisposition or high sensitivity to feeling the absence of connection. This can be an issue if an individual with this high connection need is in an environment that fails to fulfill that need. This discrepancy between experiential needs and the environment is one that is seen in individuals struggling with eating disorders.

In her book, *Eating in the Light of the Moon,* Johnston (2000, p. 17) describes how individuals who later develop eating disorders are often exceedingly aware of undercurrents within the family and interpersonal relationships. However, this sensitivity to issues within the family is dangerous and can often bring about ridicule, rejection, abuse, or even disintegration of the family. Consider then these individuals who are acutely intuitive but must bury their perceptions and accept others' perceptions and expectations. This can lead to an existential loneliness. These individuals are no longer in touch with their inner selves.

Many of Johnston's descriptions of individuals with eating disorders parallel Moustakas' descriptions of loneliness. This provides the bedrock for understanding how deeply loneliness and eating disorders are interconnected. For example, Moustakas describes: "He learns to respond with surface or approved thoughts. He learns to use devious and indirect ways, and to base his behavior on the standards and expectations of others" (Moustakas, 1961, p. 31). "In attempting to overcome loneliness anxiety, the individual sometimes gives up his individuality and submerges himself in dependency relations" (Moustakas, 1961, p. 30). The lonely person learns to base behaviors on others' expectations. And what happens to those with eating disorders? Such an individual is often "accepting others' perceptions of reality and rejecting her own" (Johnston, 2000, p. 17). What does this rejection of self stem from and lead to? The answer is "Loneliness."

> This rejection of a large part of her being, however, eventually takes its toll. As the years go by, she is plagued with a vague, uneasy sense of emptiness. So she tries to fill herself up. Since she is no longer clear about what she longs for she assumes her hunger is a physical one. And so she either eats compulsively or becomes horrified at her seemingly insatiable appetite and proceeds to starve herself. (Johnston, 2000, p. 18)

In this extreme fear of loneliness, the person tries to stop feeling altogether and tries to live solely by rational means and cognitive control (Moustakas, 1961, p. 34). This attempt at control and operating only by rational means rather than on the emotional level is a fundamental part of an eating disorder. "All addictive processes represent an effort to keep feelings under control. Even more than that, they represent an effort to keep the flow of *life itself* under control" (Johnston, 2000, p. 32). Loneliness and eating disorders are linked through their inherent experience and attempted controls to avoid experience.

Separation Anxiety and Attachment Styles

Another challenge for individuals with eating disorders is the impairment in their interpersonal attachments. Armstrong and Roth (1989) demonstrated that both anorexic and bulimic individuals have elevations in separation anxiety. In their study, both the eating-disordered and the control group struggled with major separations, but there was a significant difference in mildly stressful separations for the eating-disordered population. For any situation, this group often draws on underlying beliefs to understand why they have been left by a "parental figure" (Armstrong & Roth, 1989). Even small ripples of rejection can trigger deep waves of loneliness in individuals struggling with eating disorders. Not dissimilarly, lonely individuals are more likely to perceive daily events as stressful (Hawkley & Cacioppo, 2003).

This separation anxiety affects how individuals evaluate current relationships and base them on past relationships. If they had not felt stable and interested attachments in their youth, this situation can impact their perceptions and expectations of relationships in the future. In addition, the "risk of disappointment, pain, and rejection may prevent one from reaching out, thus perpetuating feelings of loneliness" (Karnick, 2005, p. 7).

In preadolescent and adolescent girls, attachment styles influence weight concerns and can place individuals at risk for eating disorders (Sharpe et al., 1998). Insecurely attached girls appear more likely to internalize and idealize society's appearance-related messages; they, therefore, strive for a "perfect" body in order to gain acceptance from others (Sharpe et al., 1998). These girls feel at the edge of the social fabric and work to wrap themselves tighter into the weave of connections. In these attempts, they become even more disconnected from their inner selves and their bodies, often forcing their bodies to say what they themselves cannot say.

Negative Self-Esteem

In addition, these individuals (eating disordered and/or lonely) have an impaired sense of self-worth and perceived competence. When they feel so negatively about themselves, they often do not believe others want to have relationships with them. A common theme is the individuals' willingness to sacrifice their own desires in order to please others. They feel that they have to bury their own needs in order to maintain the relationship. Individuals can feel lonely even within relationships—not believing that others know their true selves or that they would maintain the relationship if they did know. This leads to an inner loneliness—the need to hide their true selves in order to please everyone around them. "Feeling lonely" reflects the distance one feels between one's self and others (Karnick, 2005). Individuals with eating disorders and individuals who are lonely constantly grapple with the distance that they feel from their inner self and the distance that they feel from others. Individuals with eating disorders struggle with and do not believe in the viability of healthy, stable, intimate relationships (Armstrong & Roth, 1989).

Hypervigilance

Perceived social isolation is equal to feeling unsafe and sets off hypervigilance for social threats in the environment (Hawkley & Cacioppo, 2010). Through this surveillance, lonely people see the world as a more threatening place, expect more negative social interactions, and remember more negative social information, which then confirm the lonely persons' expectations (Hawkley & Cacioppo, 2010). Even the brains of lonely individuals are on higher alert for social threats contributing to their tendency to view their social world as threatening and punitive as compared with nonlonely individuals (Cacioppo & Hawkley, 2009). McFillin et al. (in press) found that when individuals with eating disorders are presented with ambiguous social situations, they tend to view the situation as more hostile than do control persons and frequently will not challenge their misperceptions, but instead will use eating disorder symptoms to sooth the negative feelings that have been triggered.

Lonely individuals appear to have increased social memory and heightened ability to decode social cues in faces and voices, but are not able to make social connections, despite a desire for increased involvement. This appears related to social anxiety, which impairs social interactions or causes individuals to avoid them altogether (Gardner, Pickett, Jefferies, & Knowles, 2005). Lonely people (and individuals with eating disorders) are on one level quite intuitive to social cues, but their anxiety often impairs interactions. In addition, negative interactions are more easily remembered for individuals. If they detect even slight rejection, that escalates their perception of danger (Armstrong & Roth, 1989) and can cause them to avoid future social interactions. Although women with eating disorders tend to make adequate first impressions, the issue arises in how they thought they were being perceived (Rofey, Kisler-van Reede, Landsbaugh, & Corcoran, 2007). Negative self-biases cause them to assume the worst about their impression, and this can then limit their ability to participate in future interactions (Rofey, Kisler-van Reede, Landsbaugh, & Corcoran, 2007).

As Moustakas (1961) noted, "The person suffering from loneliness anxiety is deeply suspicious. Even the slightest criticism hurts him. He often perceives nonexistent deprecation in surface or tangential remarks" (p. 30). This is born out by the studies that demonstrate individuals with eating disorders as being more sensitive to rejection, carrying negative meta-perceptions about themselves, and can even be seen with individuals who in recovery find criticism in comments that they are looking *healthier*. In their mindset, this means that they are *fat*. This demonstrates the often suspicious and perceived "nonexistent deprecation" that individuals with eating disorders bring to social interactions.

This misinterpretation of social cues can affect the expression of romantic interest. Similarly to individuals with eating disorders who thought they were coming across more negatively than they actually were, individuals with high or moderate attachment anxiety often perceive that more romantic interest was communicated in their overtures (Vorauer, Cameron, Holmes, & Pearce, 2003). In a series of studies, Vorauer, Cameron, Holmes, and Pearce (2003) demonstrated that individuals experiencing fears of rejection exhibited a "signal amplification bias" such that they believed their social overtures demonstrated more romantic interest to potential partners than they actually did. The skewed views of their roles in social interactions make it challenging for lonely individuals and individuals with eating disorders to improve their social connections. They have difficulty in even understanding how they are actually being perceived. "Many individuals long fervently to be with others and to find love, but they are held back by their own restraining fears" (Moustakas, 1961, p. 28).

Trust

Low trust beliefs are a probable cause of loneliness (Rotenberg et al., 2010). Individuals who hold low rather than high trust beliefs see others as unreliable, emotionally untrustworthy and dishonest; subsequently, they develop a lack of connectedness and experience an elevated state of loneliness (Rotenberg et al.). With their fear of negative evaluation, lonely individuals engage in overly cautious social behaviors that can continue their social isolation. Lonely individuals tend to be more prevention focused, working to achieve security and avoid negative outcomes as opposed to being promotion focused, working towards positive outcomes and trying to avoid missed opportunities (Lucas, Knowles, Gardner, Molden, & Jefferis, 2010).

This limited trust is exacerbated by the fact that individuals with eating disorders have an increased incidence of sexual abuse (Wonderlich et al., 2001), which confirms the danger of the environment and relationships. It hinders their ability to form trusting relationships. When women are sexually abused, they experience shame as a recurrent theme. They often express feelings of loneliness and being estranged from others (Rahm, Renck, & Ringsberg, 2006). These feelings negatively affect not only the individuals' mental health but also their relationships to others.

Cycle of Loneliness

Once individuals are lonely and disconnected, they are at greater risk for becoming even more disconnected. Cacioppo, Fowler, and Christakis (2009) demonstrated that "loneliness is both a cause and a consequence of becoming disconnected" (p. 983). Cacioppo, Fowler, and Christakis described the reinforcing nature of loneliness such that "people with few friends are more likely to become lonelier over time, which then makes it less likely that they will attract or try to form new social ties" (p. 984). It is also of note that women report higher levels of loneliness than men (Cacioppo, Fowler, & Christakis). Even as lonely members of a group may try to reconnect, humans work to drive away lonely members of their species; in this way those who have felt socially isolated, now become objectively isolated (Cacioppo, Fowler, & Christakis). Loneliness threatens the cohesiveness of a network and this is the reason that humans push the lonely clusters to the periphery of the social networks (Cacioppo, Fowler, & Christakis). Loneliness spreads more quickly among friends than family such that lonely individuals are more forcibly rejected by networks that they select rather than those who they inherit (Cacioppo, Fowler, & Christakis). You can choose your friends but you cannot chose your family.

This disconnection can prove to be a risk for individuals for eating disorders because, at times, their identity and ability to develop a social network relate only to their eating disorders. A major negative consequence of an eating disorder is isolation and loneliness (Treasure, Crane, McKnight, Buchanan, & Wolfe, 2011). These authors point out that "services can set up a vicious circle whereby the clinician or inpatient service provides the main social network" (Treasure, Crane, McKnight, Buchanan, & Wolfe, 2011, Enabling, p. 299).

Conclusion

Social exclusion causes a global reduction in the perception of life as meaningful with a reduction in one's sense of purpose, one's sense of control, one's sense of social value, and one's sense of self-worth (Stillman et al., 2009). As Stillman et al. indicate, "even a small dose of such an experience can be sufficient to begin to erode one's ordinary sense of life as meaningful" (Discussion, para. 6).

The sense of loneliness can have far-reaching ramifications. The clear association with loneliness and eating disorders supports the need to assess this issue, explore attachments and perceptions that individuals bring to relationships, and work to help individuals with eating disorders improve healthy social connections within their lives. "The escape from loneliness is actually an escape from facing the fear of loneliness" (Moustakas, 1961, p. 32). The real escape is by recognizing the depth of the loneliness for our patients and helping them to face the fear and the unknown.

REFERENCES

American Psychiatric Association. (2000). *Diagnostic and statistical manual of mental disorders* (4th ed., text rev.). Washington, DC: Author.

Arkell, J. R., & Robinson, P. (2008). A pilot case series using qualitative and quantitative methods: Biological, psychological and social outcome in severe and enduring eating disorder (anorexia nervosa). *International Journal of Eating Disorders, 41*(7), 650–656.

Armstrong, J. G., & Roth, D. M. (1989). Attachment and separation difficulties in eating disorders: A preliminary investigation. *International Journal of Eating Disorders, 8*(2), 141–155.

Bruce, B., & Agras, W. S. (1992). Binge eating in females: A population-based investigation. *International Journal of Eating Disorders, 12*(4), 365–373.

Cacioppo, J. T., Fowler, J. H., & Christakis, N. A. (2009). Alone in the crowd: The structure and spread of loneliness in a large social network. *Journal of Personality and Social Psychology, 97*(6), 977–991.

Cacioppo, J. T., & Hawkley, L.C. (2009). Perceived social isolation and cognition. *Trends in Cognitive Sciences, 13*(10), 447–454.

Cacioppo, J. T., & Patrick, W. (2009). *Loneliness: Human nature and the need for social connection.* New York: W. W. Norton & Company.

Corstorphine, E., Waller, G., Ohanian, V., & Baker, M. (2006). Changes in internal states across the binge-vomit cycle in bulimia nervosa. *Journal of Nervous and Mental Disease, 194*(6), 446–449. doi: 10.1097/01.nmd.0000221303.64098.23

Devine, K. A., Storch, E. A., Gefken, G. R., Freddo, M., Humphrey, J. L., & Silverstein, J. H. (2008). Prospective studies of peer victimization and social-psychological adjustment in children with endocrine disorders. *Journal of Child Health Care, 12*(1), 76–86.

Distel, M. A., Rebollo-Mesa, I., Abdellaoui, A., Derom, C. A., Willemsen, G., Cacioppo, J. T., & Boomsma, D. I. (2010). Familial resemblance for loneliness. *Behavioral Genetics, 40*, 480–494.

Dolan, B. M., Lieberman, S., Evans, C., & Lacey, J. H. (1990). Family features associated with normal body weight bulimia. *International Journal of Eating Disorders, 9*(6), 639–647.

Esplen, M. J., Garfinkel, P., & Gallop, R. (2000). Relationship between self-soothing, aloneness, and evocative memory in bulimia nervosa. *International Journal of Eating Disorders, 27*, 96–100.

Fleming, L. C., & Jacobsen, K. H. (2009). Bullying among middle-school students is low and middle income countries. *Health Promotion International, 25*(1), 73–84.

Ganley, R. M. (1989). Emotion and eating in obesity: A review of the literature. *International Journal of Eating Disorders, 8*(3), 343–361.

Gardner, W. L., Pickett, C. L., Jefferies, V., & Knowles, M. (2005). On the outside looking in: Loneliness and social monitoring. *Personality and Social Psychology Bulletin, 31*(11), 1549–1560.

Grant, P. G. (2008). Food for the soul: Social and emotional origins of comfort eating in the morbidly obese. In J. Buckroyd & S. Rother (Eds.), *Psychological responses to eating disorders and obesity: Recent and innovative work* (pp. 121–137). West Sussex, England: John Wiley & Sons.

Hawkley, L. C., & Cacioppo, J. T. (2003). Loneliness and pathways to disease. *Brain, Behavior, and Immunity, 17*, S98–S105.

Hawkley, L., & Cacioppo, J. T. (2010). Loneliness Matters: A theoretical and empirical review of consequences and mechanisms. *Annuals of Behavioral Medicine, 40*, 218–227.

Hawkley, L. C., Hughes, M. E., Waite, L. J., Masi, C. M., Thisted, R. A., & Cacioppo, J. T. (2008). From social structural factors to perceptions of relationship quality and loneliness: The Chicago health, aging, and social relations study. *Journal Gerontology "B Series," Psychological Sciences, Social Sciences, 63*(6), S375–S384.

Johnston, A. (2000). *Eating in the light of the moon*. Carlsbad, CA: Gurze Books.

Karnick, P. M. (2005). Feeling lonely: Theoretical perspectives. *Nursing Science Quarterly, 18*(1), 7–12.

Kent, A., Waller, G., & Dagnan, D. (1999). A greater role of emotional than physical or sexual abuse in predicting disordered eating attitudes: The role of mediating variables. *International Journal of Eating Disorders, 25*, 159–167.

Lacey, J. H., Phil, M., Coker, S., & Birtchnell, S. A. (1986). Bulimia: Factors associated with its etiology and maintenance. *International Journal of Eating Disorders, 5*(3), 475–487.

Libbey, H. P., Story, M. T., Neumark-Sztainer, D. R., & Boutelle, K. N. (2008). Teasing, disordered eating behaviors, and psychological morbidities among overweight adolescents. *Obesity, 16*(2), S24–S29.

Lucas, G. M., Knowles, M. L., Gardner, W. L., Molden, D. C., & Jefferis, V. E. (2010). Increasing social engagement among lonely individuals: The role of acceptance cues and promotion motivations. *Personality and Social Psychology Bulletin, 36*(10), 1346–1359. doi: 10.1177/0146167210382662

Maner, J. K., Holm-Denoma, J. M., Van Orden, K. A., Gailliot, M. T., Gordon, K. H., & Joiner, Jr., T. E. (2006). Evidence for attentional bias in women exhibiting bulimotypic symptoms. *International Journal of Eating Disorders, 39*, 55–61.

Masheb, R. M., & Grilo, C. M. (2006). Emotional overeating and its associations with eating disorder psychopathology among overweight patients with binge eating disorder. *International Journal of Eating Disorders, 39*, 141–146.

McFillin, R. K., Cahn, S. C., Burks, V. S., Levine, M. P., Loney, S. L., & Levine, R. L. (in press.). Social information-processing and coping in adolescent females diagnosed with an eating disorder: Toward a greater understanding of control. *Eating Disorders: Journal of Treatment and Prevention.*

Mériaux, B. G., Berg, M., & Hellström, A. L. (2010). Everyday experiences of life, body and well-being in children with overweight. *Scandinavian Journal of Caring Sciences, 24*(1), 14–23.

Meyer, C., & Waller, G. (1999). The impact of emotion upon eating behavior: The role of subliminal visual processing of threat cues. *International Journal of Eating Disorders, 25*, 319–326.

Morse, S. A., & Katon, W. J. (2006). Isn't this just bedtime snacking? The potential adverse effects of night-eating symptoms on treatment adherence and outcomes in patients with diabetes. *Diabetes Care, 29*, 1800–1804.

Moustakas, C. E. (1961). *Loneliness*. Englewood Cliffs, NJ: Prentice-Hall.

Musante, G. J., Costanzo, P. R., & Friedman, K. E. (1998). The comorbidity of depression and eating dysregulation processes in a diet-seeking obese population: A matter of gender specificity. *International Journal of Eating Disorders, 23*, 65–75.

Nickel, C., Simek, M., Moleda, A., Muehlbacher, M., Buschmann, W., Fartacek, R., ... Nickel, M. K. (2006). Suicide attempts versus suicidal ideation in bulimic female adolescents. *Pediatrics International, 48*, 374–381.

Nickel, M. K., Simek, M., Lojewski, N., Muehlbacher, M., Fartacek, R., Kettler, ... Nickel, C. (2006). Familial and sociopsychopathological risk factors for suicide attempt in bulimic and in depressed women: Prospective Study. *International Journal of Eating Disorders, 39*, 410–417.

Pavlova, B., Uher, R., & Papezova, H. (2008). It would not have happened to me at home: Qualitative exploration of sojourns abroad and eating disorders in young Czech women. *European Eating Disorders Review, 16*, 207–214.

Rahm, G. B., Renck, B., & Ringsberg, K. C. (2006). "Disgust, disgust beyond description": Shame cues to detect shame in disguise, in interviews with women who were sexually abused during childhood. *Journal of Psychiatric and Mental Health Nursing, 13*, 100–109.

Rew, L. (2002). Relationships of sexual abuse, connectedness, and loneliness to perceived well-being in homeless youth. *Journal for Specialists in Pediatric Nursing, 7*(2), 51–63.

Rofey, D., Kisler-van Reede, V., Landsbaugh, J., & Corcoran, K. J. (2007). Perceptions and metaperceptions of same-sex social interactions in college women with disordered eating patterns. *Body Image, 4*, 61–68.

Rotenberg, K. J., Addis, N., Betts, L. R., Corrigan, A., Fox, C., Hobson, Z., ... Boulton, M. J. (2010). The relation between trust beliefs and loneliness during early childhood, middle childhood, and adulthood. *Personality and Social Psychology Bulletin, 36*(8), 1086–1100.

Rotenberg, K. J., & Flood, D. (1999). Loneliness, dysphoria, dietary restraint, and eating behavior. *International Journal of Eating Disorders, 25*, 55–64.

Sharpe, T. M., Killen, J. D., Bryson, S. W., Shisslak, C. M., Estes, L. S., Gray, N., ... Taylor, C. B. (1998). Attachment style and weight concerns in preadolescent and adolescent girls. *International Journal of Eating Disorders, 23*, 39–44.

Smith, C. S. (2009). Substance abuse, chronic sorrow, and mothering loss: Relapse triggers among female victims of child abuse. *Journal of Pediatric Nursing, 24*(5), 401–412.

Stillman, T. F., Baumeister, R. F., Lambert, N. M., Crescioni, A. W., DeWall, C. N., & Fincham, F. D. (2009). Alone and without purpose: Life loses meaning following social exclusion. *Journal of Experimental Social Psychology, 45*(4), 686–694.

Storch, E. A., Milsom, V. A., DeBraganza, N., Lewin, A. B., Geffken, G. R., & Silverstein, J. H. (2007). Peer victimization, psychosocial adjustment, and physical activity in overweight and at-risk-for-overweight youth. *Journal of Pediatric Psychology, 32*(1), 80–89.

Strauss, R. S. (2000, January). Childhood obesity and self-esteem. *Pediatrics, 105*(1). http://www.pediatrics.org/cgi/content/full/105/1/e15

Striegel-Moore, R. H., Dohm, F., Pike, K. M., Wilfley, D. E., & Fairburn, C. G. (2002). Abuse, bullying, and discrimination as risk factors for binge eating disorder. *American Journal of Psychiatry, 159*, 1902–1907.

Sullivan, P. F. (1995). Mortality in anorexia nervosa. *American Journal of Psychiatry, 152*(7), 1073–1074.

Treasure, J., Crane, A., McKnight, R., Buchanan, E., & Wolfe, M. (2011). First do no harm: Iatrogenic maintaining factors in anorexia nervosa. *European Eating Disorders Review, 19*(4), 296–302. doi: 10.1002/erv.1056.

Troop, N. A., & Bifulco, A. (2002). Childhood social arena and cognitive sets in eating disorders. *British Journal of Clinical Psychology, 41*, 205–211.

Tuschen-Caffier, B., & Vögele, C. (1999). Psychological and physiological reactivity to stress: An experimental study on bulimic patients, restrained eaters and controls. *Psychotherapy and Psychosomatics, 68*(6), 333–340.

Vorauer, J. D., Cameron, J. J., Holmes, J. G., & Pearce, D. G. (2003). Invisible overtures: Fears of rejection and the signal amplification bias. *Journal of Personality and Social Psychology, 84*(4), 793–812.

Whyte, B. L., & Kaczkowski, H. (1983). Anorexia nervosa: A study of psychiatrists' and psychologists' opinions and practices. *International Journal of Eating Disorders, 2*(3), 87–92.

Witvliet, M., Brendgen, M., van Lier, P. A., Koot, H. M., & Vitaro, F. (2010). Early adolescent depressive symptoms: Prediction from clique isolation, loneliness, and perceived social acceptance. *Journal of Abnormal Child Psychology, 38*, 1045–1056.

Wonderlich, S. A., Crosby, R. D., Mitchell, J. E., Thompson, K. M., Redlin, J., Demuth, G., ... Hasletine, B. (2001). Eating disturbance and sexual trauma in childhood and adulthood. *International Journal of Eating Disorders, 30*(4), 401–412.

Zeeck, A., Stelzer, N., Linster, H. W., Joos, A., & Hartmann, A. (2011). Emotion and eating in binge eating disorder. *European Eating Disorders Review, 19*(5), 426–431. doi: 10.1002/erv.1066.

Loneliness and Depressive Symptoms: The Mediating and Moderating Role of Uncontrollable Ruminative Thoughts

JANNE VANHALST
KOEN LUYCKX
FILIP RAES
LUC GOOSSENS
Catholic University of Leuven

ABSTRACT. Although feelings of loneliness often are accompanied by depressive symptoms, little is known about underlying mechanisms in this association. The present study sampled 370 college freshmen and investigated whether rumination (and its components of Uncontrollability, Causal Analysis, and Understanding) functioned as a mediator or moderator in the relationship between 2 types of loneliness (as experienced in the relationship with parents and with peers, respectively) and depressive symptoms. Results indicated that rumination partially mediated the relationship between peer-related loneliness and depressive symptoms and moderated the relationship between parent-related loneliness and depressive symptoms. In addition, the uncontrollable nature, rather than the content, of these ruminative thoughts about parent- and peer-related loneliness was particularly harmful in the development of depressive symptoms. Implications and suggestions for future research are discussed.

EXPERIENCING LONELINESS (i.e., the negative emotional response to a discrepancy between the desired quality and the achieved quality of one's social network; Peplau & Perlman, 1982) is strongly associated with depressive symptoms (i.e., cognitive, somatic, and psychological markers of depression; Radloff, 1977) in adolescence (for a review, see Mahon, Yarcheski, Yarcheski, Cannella, & Hanks, 2006). However, only few studies have focused on explaining this relationship. An exception is the study by Vanhalst, Luyckx, and Goossens (2009),

Funding was provided by Grant OT/08/013 of the Research Council, Catholic University of Leuven.

which demonstrated that loneliness predicted depressive symptoms over time and that this relationship was mediated by maladaptive emotion regulation strategies. Emerging adults experiencing loneliness seemed to rely on maladaptive ways to cope with these feelings (e.g., by blaming themselves), which, in turn, made them more vulnerable to depressive symptoms.

The present study tried to expand on this finding in three important ways. First, the present study focused on a more specific aspect of maladaptive cognitive coping (i.e., rumination and its subcomponents) crucial for the development of depressive symptoms (Aldao, Nolen-Hoeksema, & Schweizer, 2009). Second, we examined not only mediation in the relationship between loneliness and depressive symptoms, but also moderation. More specifically, mediation implies that loneliness gives rise to depressive symptoms *because* the former is generally associated with rumination, whereas moderation implies that loneliness gives rise to depressive symptoms *only or especially when* it is accompanied by rumination. Third, we investigated whether these underlying processes occurred for different aspects of loneliness, because loneliness may have a different meaning in different relationships. So far, most studies used general measures of loneliness (which have been shown to capture peer-related loneliness; Goossens et al., 2009) or specific measures of peer-related loneliness when linking loneliness to depressive symptoms. In the present study, both peer-related and parent-related loneliness are considered.

It is particularly relevant to investigate the interplay between loneliness, rumination, and depressive symptoms during the transition to college because this is a turbulent period in terms of maintaining the quality of social relationships and subsequent social and emotional adjustment (Montgomery & Côté, 2003; Shaver, Furman, & Buhrmester, 1985). Freshmen not only have to adapt to a new academic environment, but most of them also have to adapt to a new living situation. Most freshmen can no longer rely on their social network of friends and family and have to deal with many life changes and choices, which may cause feelings of loneliness and depression (Kenny & Sirin, 2006; Oswald & Clark, 2003; Stroebe, van Vliet, Hewstone, & Willis, 2002). Furthermore, the transition to college might also be a risk period for increased ruminative thoughts. Specifically, substantial changes in the lives of adolescents (such as transitioning to college) are often accompanied by a struggle of finding a balance between striving for autonomy and safeguarding feelings of connectedness to peers and parents, which induces rumination (Peled & Moretti, 2007).

Peer- and Parent-Related Loneliness

Loneliness has a different meaning in parent versus peer relationships (Goossens et al., 2009), suggesting that there are different consequences of both types of loneliness for well-being. We hypothesized that, in college students, peer-related loneliness would be more strongly associated with depressive symptoms than parent-related loneliness, mainly for two reasons. First, emerging adults devote more time outside and less time inside the family and increasingly turn to peers (Nelis & Rae, 2009). In that way, peer-related loneliness may be more stressful than parent-related loneliness, and, thus, may be more strongly related to the development of depressive feelings. Second, the close relationship theory (Laursen & Bukowski, 1997) states that parent relationships are permanent, whereas peer relationships are potentially impermanent. In permanent relationships, the ties that bind individuals together are largely unrelated to interaction outcomes. In impermanent relationships, partners tend to participate as long as interactions remain mutually advantageous, and thus, the threat of relationship dissolution is omnipresent. Hence, loneliness may be more threatening in a possibly impermanent peer relationship than in a permanent parent relationship.

Rumination and its Subcomponents

A growing literature shows the existence of both adaptive and maladaptive forms of self-focused attention in general (e.g., Trapnell & Campbell, 1999) and of rumination as a specific type of self-focused attention, in particular (e.g., Treynor, Gonzalez, & Nolen-Hoeksema, 2003). *Rumination* is defined here as repetitively and passively focusing on symptoms of distress (such as feelings of loneliness) and on the possible causes and consequences of these symptoms (Nolen-Hoeksema, 1991). Recently, researchers have started to emphasize the importance of distinguishing different forms or subcomponents of rumination. For example, Treynor et al. (2003) distinguished a brooding and a reflective form of rumination. Several studies have shown that the brooding facet of rumination, compared to the reflection subcomponent, represents the more maladaptive form of rumination (e.g., Raes & Hermans, 2008; Treynor et al., 2003). This maladaptive form is a passive comparison of one's actual situation to one's ideal situation and is motivated by perceived threats, losses, or injustices. Specifically, several studies showed that brooding is a stronger within-time and over-time predictor of depressive symptoms than reflection is (Armey et al., 2009; Grassia & Gibb, 2008).

More recently, Raes, Hermans, Williams, Bijttebier, and Eelen (2008) distinguished three components of rumination, including not only different aspects of rumination itself, but also different beliefs or appraisals about the process of rumination. First, Causal Analysis refers to the process of figuring out what may be the causes of one's distress, and is viewed as the component most closely related to reflection. The second component, Uncontrollability, concerns the experience (i.e., its repetitive nature) rather than the content of rumination and refers to the experience that ruminative thinking processes are difficult to stop. This component appears to be the most maladaptive form of rumination, as demonstrated by its high association with depressive symptoms and with the cognitive risk factor of thought suppression (Raes et al., 2008). Third, Understanding refers to the process of trying to understand oneself and the meaning of one's distress and lies somewhat in between the other two rumination components. Hence, in the present study, we hypothesized that the subcomponent Uncontrollability is a particularly important mechanism in the link between loneliness and depressive symptoms, more so than Causal Analysis or Understanding are.

Loneliness and Depressive Symptoms: Rumination as Modulating Variable

Forming and maintaining social relationships are important sources of life satisfaction, and numerous studies have indicated that loneliness is related to symptoms of poor mental health such as depression (Heinrich & Gullone, 2006). Specifically, the relation between loneliness and depressive symptoms is in the range of a large effect size ($r = .61 - .62$), as revealed by a meta-analysis conducted on 33 adolescent samples (Mahon et al., 2006). Loneliness was found to predict depressive symptoms both within time (e.g., Hagerty & Williams, 1999) and across time (e.g., Heikkinen & Kauppinen, 2004). In addition, the importance of feelings of loneliness as a key role in the etiology of depressive symptoms has frequently been acknowledged by leading theories. For instance, attachment theory states that insecurely attached individuals are more susceptible to depression because of their negative views of relationships with others (Bowlby, 1973). Cognitive theories put forth that some individuals define their self-worth by means of their relationships, which makes them more vulnerable to depression in response to interpersonal difficulties (Blatt, 1990). Behavioral theories posit that certain individuals are vulnerable to depression because they have poor social skills, making it difficult for them to elicit positive reinforcement from others and deal with relationship stressors (Lewinsohn, 1974). These theoretical assumptions are confirmed by empirical research showing an association between loneliness and depressive symptoms, both within (Mahon et al., 2006) and across time (Joiner, 1997).

We consider rumination as a prime candidate to mediate or moderate this strong relationship between loneliness and depressive symptoms, because rumination causes people to remain fixated on their negative experiences (such as loneliness) and impairs problem solving (Nolen-Hoeksema, Wisco, & Lyubomirsky, 2008). We anticipate that rumination is likely to occur when feeling lonely, because loneliness has been found to affect cognitive thinking (Heinrich & Gullone, 2006). Lonely people tend to have maladaptive attributional styles (Anderson, 1999) and inflexible friendship beliefs (Lavallee & Parker, 2009), both of which are related to rumination. Also, ruminative thinking is a discrepancy-based processing style, as people often start ruminating when they are confronted with a painful discrepancy between a current situation and a desired situation (e.g., Martin & Tesser, 1996; Schoofs, Hermans, & Raes, 2010). Recall that loneliness can be seen as the result of such an instance of a painful discrepancy, namely between the current and desired qualities of one's social network (Peplau & Perlman, 1982). Furthermore, previous research suggests that rumination plays a key role in maintaining negative mood following interpersonal harm (Wade, Vogel, Liao, & Goldman, 2008). Particularly in the first weeks of college, freshmen might be increasingly aware and concerned about being accepted and their self-presentation. Therefore, feeling lonely is likely to evoke ruminative thinking in these individuals. For example, research about homesickness among freshman college students suggested that students who missed their friends and family were found to ruminate about loneliness, which was associated with depressive symptoms (Stroebe et al., 2002).

Whereas the link between loneliness and ruminative thoughts is rather unexplored, a vast amount of research demonstrated the association between rumination and depressive symptoms (for reviews, see Nolen-Hoeksema et al., 2008; Smith & Alloy, 2009). Specifically, prospective longitudinal studies showed that adolescents engaging in rumination when distressed were more likely to develop depressive disorders (e.g., Nolen-Hoeksema, Stice, Wade, & Bohon, 2007) and that rumination played an important role in the maintenance of depression (e.g., Grassia & Gibb, 2008).

In sum, the present study examined whether rumination—and, more specifically, its subcomponents Causal Analysis, Understanding, and Uncontrollability—mediate or moderate the relationship between (peer- and parent-related) loneliness and depressive symptoms. We tentatively hypothesized that mediation would mainly occur in the relationship between peer-related loneliness and depressive symptoms and that moderation would mainly occur in the relationship between parent-related loneliness and depressive symptoms, based on the titration hypothesis in the vulnerability-stress model discussed in hopelessness theory (Abramson, Alloy, & Hogan, 1997). This hypothesis states that the less negative a person's cognitive style (or, applied to our study, the less one ruminates), the more negative an event must be to generate ruminative thoughts and give rise to depressive symptoms. Recall that loneliness is expected to be more stressful in the relationship with peers than in the relationship with parents (Laursen & Bukowski, 1997; Nelis & Rae, 2009). Altogether, at lower levels of stress (i.e., parent-related loneliness), only cognitively vulnerable individuals may ruminate and experience depressive symptoms, whereas at high levels of stress (i.e., peer-related loneliness), both cognitively vulnerable and nonvulnerable individuals may start ruminating and experience depressive symptoms. Furthermore, we expected the rumination subcomponent Uncontrollability to be a stronger mediator or moderator in the association between loneliness and depressive symptoms, more so than Causal Analysis or Understanding.

Method

Participants and Procedure

Participants were psychology students from a large university in Belgium, attending college for just 1 month. This university mainly attracts Caucasian students from middle-class backgrounds. A total of 370 students (M_{age} = 18.22 years, SD = 1.21 years) participated (83.5% were female). Of these, 26% lived with their parents, and 74% lived mainly on their own (typically in a student facility). Students participated during group sessions and received course credit for their participation. All participants signed an informed consent form.

Measures

Depressive symptoms. Depressive symptoms were measured using the well-known Center for Epidemiologic Studies Depression Scale (CES-D; Radloff, 1977), which was translated into Dutch by Hooge, Decaluwé, and Goossens (2000). To avoid item overlap with the loneliness measures, the item "During the last week, I felt lonely" was dropped, and we proceeded with a 19-item version. Each item asks participants to indicate how often they experienced symptoms of depression during the week prior to assessment, by using a 4-point Likert-type rating scale ranging from 0 (*seldom*) to 3 (*most of the time or always*). Cronbach's alpha for the 19-item version was .88.

Loneliness. Two subscales—parent-related loneliness and peer-related loneliness—of the Loneliness and Aloneness Scale for Children and Adolescents (LACA; Marcoen, Goossens, & Caes, 1987) were used to capture loneliness. Both subscales contain 12 items answered on a 4-point Likert-type scale ranging from 1 (*never*) to 4 (*often*). Because the questionnaire was developed for school-aged children and adolescents, some of the items were adapted to make them more appropriate for a college population (e.g., "I feel left out by my classmates" was changed to "I feel left out by my fellow students"). Sample items are "I have the feeling that I belong to my parents" (parent-related loneliness, reverse coded), and "I think I have fewer friends than others have" (peer-related loneliness). Cronbach's alphas were .92 and .88, respectively. Confirmatory factor analysis (CFA) indicated that a two-factor model fit the data adequately: SBS-$\chi^2(251) = 617.211$, $p < .001$, CFI = .96, RMSEA = .06. Standardized pattern coefficients ranged from .53 to .82 ($ps < .001$).

Rumination. Rumination was measured using the Leuven Adaptation of the Rumination on Sadness Scale (LARSS; Raes et al., 2008), capturing three rumination components: Causal Analysis (5 items), Understanding (6 items), and Uncontrollability (6 items). These three subscales can be summed to yield a composite measure of rumination. In the original version of the LARSS, participants are asked to indicate what they think when feeling sad (i.e., rumination on sadness). We adapted this instruction to what they think when feeling "left outside, lonely, or not supported by peers, fellow students, or family" (i.e., rumination on loneliness), using a 5-point Likert-type scale ranging from 1 (*almost never*) to 5 (*almost always*). Sample items read "I keep asking myself what could have contributed to this feeling" (Causal Analysis), "I repeatedly think about what might be the meaning of my feelings" (Understanding), and "I have difficulty getting myself to stop thinking about how lonely I am" (Uncontrollability). Cronbach's alphas were .95 for the total measure, and .88, .88, and .93 for Causal Analysis, Understanding, and Uncontrollability, respectively. CFA confirmed the three-dimensional structure: SBS-$\chi^2(116) = 439.084$ ($p < .001$), CFI = .97, RMSEA = .09. Standardized pattern coefficients ranged from .54 to .89 ($ps < .001$).

To further strengthen the validity of the LARSS, we correlated the LARSS with the well-validated Rumination and Reflection Questionnaire (RRQ;

Trapnell & Campbell, 1999), tapping into an adaptive and maladaptive form of self-attentiveness, that is, rumination and reflection. Sample items are "I always seem to be rehashing in my mind recent things I've said or done" and "I love exploring my inner self," respectively. Both subscales contain 8 items answered on a 5-point Likert-type scale ranging from 1 (*strongly disagree*) to 5 (*strongly agree*). Cronbach's alpha in our sample was .87 for the subscale rumination and .85 for reflection. The subscales rumination and reflection of the RRQ correlated .65 and .44, respectively, with our total LARSS-score, and their difference was significant (t (367) = 11.07; $p < .001$). Partial correlations of both RRQ scales with the LARSS scale (i.e., correlations with reflection controlled for rumination, and vice versa) yielded similar results, that is, $r = .65$ for rumination and $r = .43$ for reflection. Hence, the total LARSS scale is more indicative of maladaptive rumination than it is of adaptive reflection. With respect to partial correlations of both RRQ subscales with the three LARSS subscales, Uncontrollability is more strongly correlated with rumination ($r = .71$; $p < .001$) than with reflection ($r = .13$; $p < .05$; t (367) = 12.13; $p < .001$). The same result, although to a lesser extent, holds for Causal Analysis ($r = .51$; $p < .001$; and $r = .41$; $p < .001$; t (367) = 7.54; $p < .001$). The subscale Understanding, on the contrary, has more in common with reflection ($r = .54$; $p < .001$) than with rumination ($r = .44$; $p < .001$; t (367) = 6.51; $p < .001$), although the difference is rather small. Because the RRQ was merely used to validate the LARSS, this measure was dropped from all subsequent analyses.

Results

Preliminary Analyses

To investigate multivariate effects of participants' age, gender, and living arrangement, a MANCOVA was performed, with age as covariate, gender and living arrangement as fixed factors, and all study variables as dependent variables. This yielded a significant multivariate effect of gender (Wilks' $\lambda = .92$; F (7,342) = 3.99, $p < .001$), but no overall age effects (Wilks' $\lambda = .98$; F (7,342) = .89, *ns*) or effects of living arrangement (Wilks' $\lambda = .99$; F (7,342) = .34, *ns*). Follow-up analyses indicated that women scored higher than men on depressive symptoms and all rumination measures (except for the subscale Understanding) (see Table 1).

Table 2 presents correlations among loneliness, depressive symptoms, and rumination components. As expected, we found a high correlation between peer-related loneliness and depressive symptoms ($r = .58$, $p < .001$) and a lower—$t(367) = 8.53$, $p < .001$—but still significant correlation between parent-related loneliness and depressive symptoms ($r = .23$, $p < .001$). In addition, peer-related loneliness had a significant positive correlation with all rumination subscales, whereas parent-related loneliness was unrelated to these rumination subscales. Furthermore, the three rumination subscales were highly associated

TABLE 1. Mean Differences as a Function of Gender

	M (SD)			
Scale	Full sample	Men	Women	F(1, 353)
Parent-related loneliness	1.55 (0.51)	1.65 (0.49)	1.53 (0.51)	3.20
Peer-related loneliness	1.71 (0.49)	1.63 (0.51)	1.73 (0.49)	1.87
Depressive symptoms	0.60 (0.42)	0.45 (0.34)	0.63 (0.43)	9.43**
Rumination (Total)	2.70 (0.87)	2.42 (0.64)	2.76 (0.89)	7.39**
Causal analysis	2.99 (0.90)	2.72 (0.69)	3.04 (0.93)	6.17*
Understanding	2.45 (0.92)	2.42 (0.70)	2.46 (0.96)	0.07
Uncontrollability	2.72 (1.06)	2.16 (0.81)	2.82 (1.07)	19.15***

$^{*}p < .05$. $^{**}p < .01$. $^{***}p < .001$.

with each other and with the total rumination score. Lastly, peer-related loneliness and depressive symptoms were more strongly associated with Uncontrollability than with Causal Analysis—for peer-related loneliness, $t(367) = 9.77$, $p < .001$; for depressive symptoms, $t(367) = 6.99$; $p < .001$—and with Understanding—for peer-related loneliness, $t(367) = 5.92$, $p < .001$; for depressive symptoms, $t(367) = 3.28$; $p < .001$.

Mediation Analyses

The intervening role of rumination in the relationship between loneliness and depressive feelings was examined by means of path analysis using LISREL 8.54 (Jöreskog & Sörbom, 1993). Gender was controlled for by allowing

TABLE 2. Intercorrelations Among Loneliness, Depressive Symptoms, and Rumination

Variable	2	3	4	5	6	7
1. Parent-related loneliness	.13*	.23***	.06	.02	.09	.05
2. Peer-related loneliness		.58***	.26***	.19***	.17**	.32***
3. Depressive symptoms			.37***	.26***	.24***	.47***
4. Rumination (Total)				.93***	.89***	.89***
5. Rumination (Causal Analysis)					.80***	.74***
6. Rumination (Understanding)						.62***
7. Rumination (Uncontrollability)						

$^{*}p < .05$. $^{**}p < .01$. $^{***}p < .001$.

paths from gender to all other variables in the model. Three models were estimated and compared: (a) a direct effects model including the direct effects of loneliness on depressive symptoms; (b) a full mediation model in which loneliness is only indirectly related to depressive symptoms through the hypothesized mediator (i.e., rumination); and (c) a partial mediation model including direct paths from loneliness to depressive symptoms and indirect paths through rumination.

First, (a) the direct effects model was saturated (i.e., it had zero degrees of freedom), and, by definition, provided a perfect fit to the data. In this model, peer-related loneliness ($\beta = .54$; $p < .001$) was a stronger predictor of depressive symptoms than parent-related loneliness ($\beta = .16$; $p < .01$). Next, we tested (b) the full mediation model by including paths from parent- and peer-related loneliness to rumination and from rumination to depressive feelings. This model showed an insufficient fit to the data: SBS-$\chi^2(2) = 37.90$, $p < .001$; CFI = .42; RMSEA = .23. Subsequently, (c) the partial mediation model was tested, by adding paths from parent- and peer-related loneliness to depressive feelings. Allowing these direct paths resulted again in a saturated model with perfect fit. However, the path from parent-related loneliness to rumination did not reach significance, and, subsequently, was trimmed from the model. This final model, represented in Figure 1a, had a near-perfect fit to the data: SBS-$\chi^2(1) = 0.38$, *ns;* CFI = 1.00; RMSEA < .01. To assess the significance of the indirect effect of peer-related loneliness over rumination on depressive feelings, we performed the Sobel (1982) test, which resulted in a significant value, $z = 3.30$, $p < .001$. In sum, the strong association between peer-related loneliness (but not parent-related loneliness) and depressive symptoms was partially explained by rumination.

To investigate which rumination subscale (i.e., Causal Analysis, Understanding, or Uncontrollability) acted as the strongest mediator in the relationship between loneliness and depressive feelings, we repeated the mediation analysis with the separate rumination subscales as mediators. The full mediation model showed a less than optimal fit to the data—SBS-$\chi^2(2) = 40.14$, $p < .001$; CFI = .87; RMSEA = .23—and the partial mediation model resulted in a saturated model. Inspection of the individual paths in the partial mediation model showed that only peer-related loneliness (and not parent-related loneliness) predicted all three rumination components significantly. However, only the subscale Uncontrollability showed a significant path towards depressive symptoms. The nonsignificant paths were trimmed from the model, resulting in the more parsimonious model as shown in Figure 1b: SBS-$\chi^2(5) = 8.16$, *ns*; CFI = 1.00; RMSEA = .04. The Sobel (1982) test indicated that the indirect effect of peer-related loneliness over Uncontrollability on depressive feelings was significant, $z = 3.93$, $p < .001$. In sum, the rumination subscale Uncontrollability (and not Causal Analysis or Understanding) was found to be a partial mediator in the relationship between loneliness and depressive symptoms.

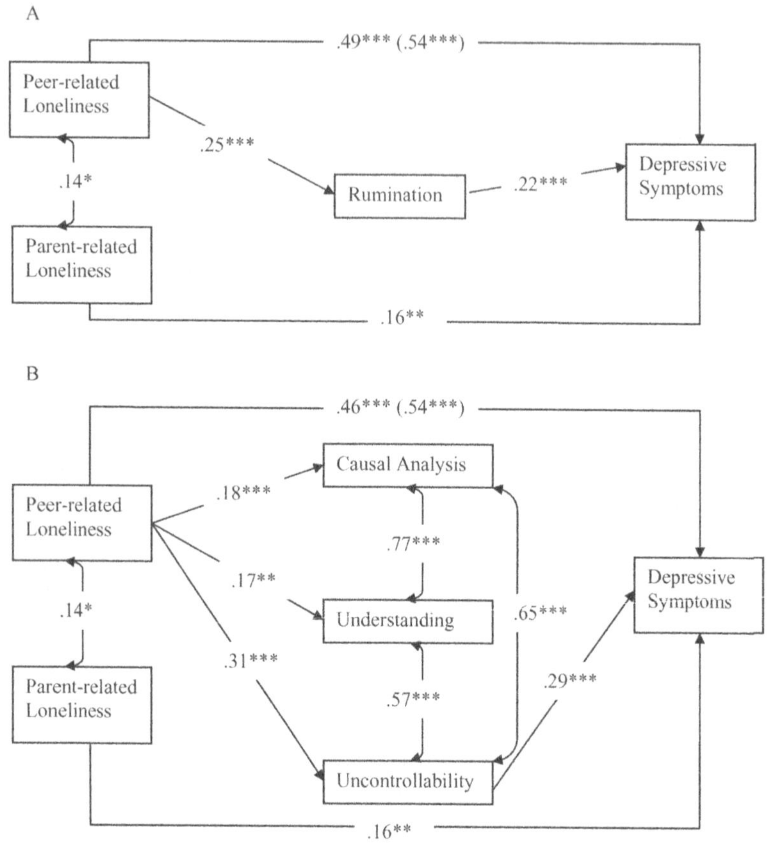

FIGURE 1. Trimmed partial mediation model with total rumination scale (Panel A) and three rumination subscales (Panel B) as mediator. $^{*}p < .05$. $^{**}p < .01$. $^{***}p < .001$.

Because directionality cannot be empirically tested in a cross-sectional design, we tested an alternative model in which ruminative thoughts predicted depressive symptoms, which, in turn, predicted parent- and peer-related loneliness. This alternative model was compared to our final model, using the Akaike information criterion (AIC; Keith, 2006), where a smaller AIC value indicates a better fit. Based on Raftery's (1995) criterion, suggesting that an AIC difference of 10 points or more is strong, we rejected the alternative model in favor of our final model (ΔAIC = 24.58).

Moderation Analyses

We conducted hierarchical regression analyses with two-way interaction terms to investigate whether rumination could act as a moderator between feelings of loneliness and depressive symptoms. Loneliness and rumination scores were centered, and interaction terms were computed by multiplying the centered means (Aiken, West, & Reno, 1991).

In a first step, gender was entered as a control variable, which resulted in a significant prediction of depressive symptoms, $\beta = .16, p < .01$. In a second step, main effects of parent- and peer-related loneliness on depressive symptoms were examined. Both main effects explained an additional significant portion of the variance in depressive symptoms, with peer-related loneliness, $\beta = .54, p < .001$, acting as a stronger predictor than parent-related loneliness, $\beta = .17, p < .001$. In a third step, the moderator variable (i.e., rumination) was included, which also added significantly to the prediction of depressive symptoms, $\beta = .22, p < .001$. In a last step, both interaction terms (that involved rumination and parent- and peer-related loneliness, respectively) were entered. Only the interaction term with parent-related loneliness, $\beta = .09, p < .05$, reached significance. Thus, rumination interacted with parent-related loneliness, but not with peer-related loneliness, in the prediction of depressive symptoms.

To interpret this interaction, simple slopes of parent-related loneliness predicting depressive symptoms were examined at low (1 *SD* below *M*) and high (1 *SD* above *M*) levels of the moderator (i.e., rumination). Whereas parent-related loneliness did not significantly predict depressive symptoms at low levels of rumination (simple slope = 0.08; $t = 1.30$; *ns*), parent-related loneliness did significantly predict depressive symptoms at high levels of rumination (simple slope = .24; $t = 4.00$; $p < .001$). In other words, loneliness in the relationship with parents is associated with depressive feelings only when accompanied by a high amount of ruminative thinking about these feelings of loneliness. Figure 2 gives a graphical representation of these simple slopes.

In an ancillary set of analyses, we explored which of the three rumination subscales (i.e., Causal Analysis, Understanding, and Uncontrollability) acted specifically as a moderator in the relationship between parent-related loneliness and depressive feelings. Therefore, we performed a set of three moderator analyses (i.e., one for each rumination subscale), following the same four steps as described above. Including the three subscales as a moderator in Step 3 added significantly to the prediction of depressive symptoms in each analysis, with, as expected, Uncontrollability ($\beta = .44$; $p < .001$) being a stronger predictor than Causal Analysis ($\beta = .23$; $p < .001$) and Understanding ($\beta = .22$; $p < .001$). Interaction terms of parent-related loneliness with each rumination subscale were entered at Step 4. The interaction terms with Causal Analysis ($\beta = .11$; $p < .05$) and Uncontrollability ($\beta = .13$; $p < .01$) reached significance, whereas the interaction term with Understanding ($\beta = .07$; *ns*) did not. Simple slopes analyses showed that parent-related loneliness only predicted depressive symptoms at high levels of Causal

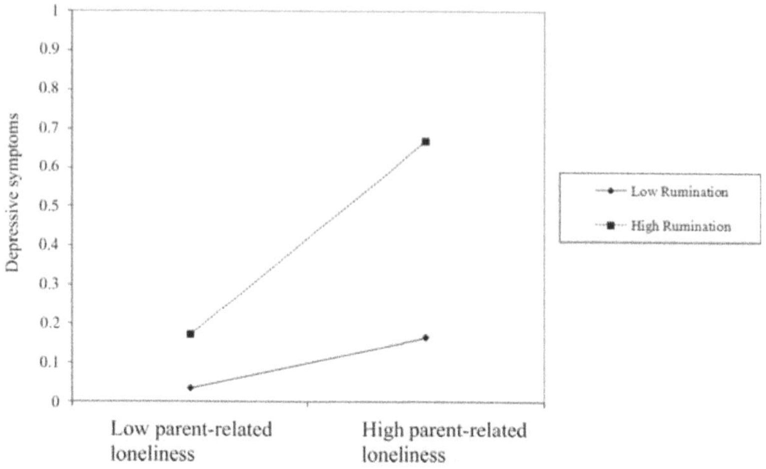

FIGURE 2. Simple slopes of parent-related loneliness predicting depressive symptoms at low (1 *SD* below *M*) and high (1 *SD* above *M*) levels of ruminative thinking.

Analysis (simple slope = 0.27; $t = 4.43$; $p < .001$) and Uncontrollability (simple slope = 0.26; $t = 5.60$; $p < .001$), and not at low levels of Causal Analysis (simple slope = 0.08; $t = 1.29$; $p < .001$) or Uncontrollability (simple slope = .05; $t = .10$; *ns*). Therefore, we conclude that two out of the three subscales moderated the relationship between parent-related loneliness and depressive symptoms.

Discussion

This study was the first to explore whether rumination acted as a mediator or moderator in the relationship between loneliness and depressive symptoms, measuring both loneliness and rumination in multidimensional fashion. More specifically, we examined loneliness in the relationship with both peers and parents (Goossens et al., 2009) and investigated the separate role of three components of rumination: Causal Analysis, Understanding, and Uncontrollability (Raes et al., 2008). Our results indicated that rumination partially mediated the relationship between peer-related loneliness and depressive symptoms and moderated the relationship between parent-related loneliness and depressive feelings. In addition, our results revealed that the most harmful component of rumination was Uncontrollability, suggesting that the process of rumination itself is more important than the actual content of one's ruminative thoughts. As expected, we found that both types of loneliness were experienced differently, with peer-related loneliness having a greater negative impact on students' well-being than parent-related loneliness.

Rumination as a Mediator and a Moderator Between Loneliness and Depressive Symptoms

Our mediation analyses indicated that when college students felt lonely in their relationship with peers, they tended to ruminate about it, which was, in turn, associated with depressive symptoms. In addition, this was especially the case when these ruminative thoughts were perceived as uncontrollable. Our moderation analyses showed that when college students felt lonely in the relationship with their parents and when, on top of that, they could not help but ruminating about the causes of these feelings, they were more vulnerable to depressive symptoms. Taken together, our results suggest that ruminative thoughts about loneliness may be an important element in understanding what makes lonely adolescents vulnerable for depressive symptoms.

The differences we found between the three components of rumination demonstrated the need to consider rumination as a multifaceted construct. The fact that we found the uncontrollability—rather than the content—of ruminative thoughts about parent- and peer loneliness to be particularly harmful is in line with previous research (e.g., Raes et al., 2008) and supports the idea that this component is most closely related to the maladaptive aspects of rumination. This finding is also in line with the notion that beliefs that ruminators hold about their own thinking style (i.e., meta-rumination) can play an important role in determining the outcomes of rumination (Papageorgiou & Wells, 2003). More specifically, individuals can initially engage in rumination because they believe in the benefits of rumination (e.g., to find the causes of one's loneliness). However, this engagement can result in harmful consequences of ruminating and the experience that this ruminative thinking is beyond their own control. The meta-rumination theory states that especially these negative beliefs about rumination will in turn increase depressive feelings (Papageorgiou & Wells, 2003). Trying to understand oneself and one's loneliness, on the contrary, was more related to adaptive reflection than to maladaptive rumination, which could explain why Understanding did not function as a mediator or moderator between loneliness and depression in the present study. Indeed, previous research investigating rumination and reflection as a mediator between childhood emotional abuse and depressed mood showed that only rumination, and not reflection, functioned as a mediator (Raes & Hermans, 2008). Further research is needed to replicate these findings.

Differences Between Parent- and Peer-Related Loneliness

Our results clearly indicated that parent-related and peer-related loneliness need to be distinguished in emerging adulthood. As expected, depressive symptoms were more strongly associated with peer-related loneliness than with parent-related loneliness. In addition, all rumination subcomponents were significantly associated with peer-related loneliness, whereas there were no associations with parent-related loneliness. This finding is in line with the assumption that peer-related loneliness is a more stressful problem than parent-related loneliness because of the typical relationship shifts in this age period (Oswald & Clark, 2003; Stroebe et al., 2002). This result is also consistent with the close relationship theory (Laursen & Bukowski, 1997), which argues that loneliness may be more threatening in a possibly impermanent peer relationship than in a permanent parent relationship.

The fact that mediation (and not moderation) occurred in the relation between peer-related loneliness and depression and moderation (and not mediation) in the relation between parent-related loneliness and depression can be explained both theoretically and statistically. Theoretically, our results are in line with the titration hypothesis forwarded in the vulnerability-stress model (Abramson et al., 1997), as discussed in the introduction. Statistically, and closely related to the previous explanation, mediation is most suitable in the case of a strong relationship, whereas moderation is most suitable in the case of a weak relation between the predictor and criterion variable (Baron & Kenny, 1986). Indeed, in our study, we found rumination to mediate the strong direct relationship between peer-related loneliness and depression, and we found rumination to moderate the weaker relationship between parent-related loneliness and depressive symptoms.

Clinical Implications

Provided that the present findings are replicated in independent samples, the present study can have implications for clinical prevention and intervention programs. Our results stressed the importance of ruminative thoughts about one's loneliness for the development of depressive symptoms, especially when these ruminative thoughts are perceived as beyond one's control. More specifically, uncontrollable ruminative thoughts can partly explain why peer-related loneliness gives rise to more depressive symptoms, and they are a condition under which parent-related loneliness brings about depressive symptoms. Therefore, reducing uncontrollable ruminative thoughts about loneliness or changing people's perceptions about the control over their ruminative thoughts should be an important goal in intervention programs of loneliness or in prevention programs of depression. Reducing uncontrollable ruminative thoughts about loneliness (or sadness) might end the vicious circle that results in continued feelings of loneliness or sadness. Given the fact that the transition to college life is a risk period in terms of experiencing loneliness and depressive symptoms (Kenny & Sirin, 2006; Stroebe et al., 2002), more attention should be given to students' emotional support and counseling.

Limitations and Suggestions for Future Research

Although the present article revealed several interesting findings, some limitations need to be mentioned. First, participants were mainly Caucasian female college students. A more balanced sample in terms of gender, educational level, and ethnic background would be more appropriate to generalize our findings to the broader population of emerging adulthood. Also, our research questions would be interesting to investigate in a clinical population. Second, our study relied exclusively on self-report measures. Such an approach can cause shared method variance, which, in turn, might partially account for the effects obtained. However, the variables of interest in this article are internal and subjective processes, which are most appropriate to be investigated by use of self-report measures. Third, other mediators or moderators that modulate the relationship between loneliness and depressive symptoms should be investigated, given the fact that rumination only explains a small part of the association between loneliness and depressive symptoms. Fourth, the instructions of our rumination on loneliness measure could be further improved in future research, as they may emphasize the role of peers in one's sense of loneliness, relative to family members. Lastly, a cross-sectional design was used, making it impossible to make statements about the direction of effects. In this study, loneliness is assumed to be an antecedent of depressive symptoms, in accordance with the dominant path described in the literature that goes from social vulnerability and loneliness to depressive symptoms. Nevertheless, other theories recognize the importance of the opposite path, which states that depressive episodes produce an array of interpersonal problems and cause damage in close relationships, which might give rise to loneliness (Joiner, 2000). Empirical evidence on the dynamics between loneliness and depressive symptoms is scarce and shows mixed results (e.g., Cacioppo, Hawkley, & Thisted, 2010; Cacioppo, Hughes, Waite, Hawkley, & Thisted, 2006; Lasgaard, Goossens, & Elklit, 2011; Weeks, Michela, Peplau, & Bragg, 1980). Hence, longitudinal research on this topic is needed.

Despite these limitations, the present study indicated that rumination acted as an underlying mechanism in the association between loneliness and depressive symptoms in 1st-year college students. Specifically, rumination partially mediated the relationship between peer-related loneliness and depressive symptoms and moderated the relationship between parent-related loneliness and depressive symptoms. Uncontrollability was found to be the most harmful subcomponent of rumination, suggesting that lonely adolescents are particularly vulnerable to depressive symptoms when they experience their ruminative thoughts about loneliness as beyond their control.

REFERENCES

Abramson, L. Y., Alloy, L. B., & Hogan, M. E. (1997). Cognitive/personality subtypes of depression: Theories in search of disorders. *Cognitive Therapy and Research, 21*, 247–265.

Aiken, L. S., West, S. G., & Reno, R. R. (1991). *Multiple regression: Testing and interpreting interactions*. Newbury Park, CA: Sage.

Aldao, A., Nolen-Hoeksema, S., & Schweizer, S. (2009). Emotion-regulation strategies across psychopathology: A meta-analytic review. *Clinical Psychology Review, 30*, 217–237.

Anderson, C. A. (1999). Attributional style, depression, and loneliness: A cross-cultural comparison of American and Chinese students. *Personality and Social Psychology Bulletin, 25*, 482–499.

Armey, M. F., Fresco, D. M., Moore, M. T., Mennin, D. S., Turk, C. L., Heimberg, R. G., et al. (2009). Brooding and pondering: Isolating the active ingredients of depressive rumination with exploratory factor analysis and structural equation modeling. *Assessment, 16*, 315–327.

Baron, R. M., & Kenny, D. A. (1986). The moderator mediator variable distinction in social psychological research: Conceptual, strategic, and statistical considerations. *Journal of Personality and Social Psychology, 51*, 1173–1182.

Blatt, S. J. (1990). Interpersonal relatedness and self-definition: Two personality configurations and their implications for psychopathology and psychotherapy. In J. Singer (Ed.), *Repression: Defense mechanisms and personality* (pp. 299–335). Chicago: University of Chicago Press.

Bowlby, J. (1973). *Attachment and loss: Vol. 2. Separation: Anxiety and anger*. New York: Basic Books.

Cacioppo, J. T., Hawkley, L. C., & Thisted, R. A. (2010). Perceived social isolation makes me sad: 5-year cross-lagged analyses of loneliness and depressive symptomatology in the Chicago health, aging, and social relations study. *Psychology and Aging, 25*, 453–463.

Cacioppo, J. T., Hughes, M. E., Waite, L. J., Hawkley, L. C., & Thisted, R. A. (2006). Loneliness as a specific risk factor for depressive symptoms: Cross-sectional and longitudinal analyses. *Psychology and Aging, 21*, 140–151.

Goossens, L., Lasgaard, M., Luyckx, K., Vanhalst, J., Mathias, S., & Masy, E. (2009). Loneliness and solitude in adolescence: A confirmatory factor analysis of alternative models. *Personality and Individual Differences, 47*, 890–894.

Grassia, M., & Gibb, B. E. (2008). Rumination and prospective changes in depressive symptoms. *Journal of Social and Clinical Psychology, 27*, 931–948.

Hagerty, B. M., & Williams, R. A. (1999). The effects of sense of belonging, social support, conflict, and loneliness on depression. *Nursing Research, 48*, 215–219.

Heikkinen, R. L., & Kauppinen, M. (2004). Depressive symptoms in late life: A 10-year follow-up. *Archives of Gerontology and Geriatrics, 38*, 239–250.

Heinrich, L. A., & Gullone, E. (2006). The clinical significance of loneliness: A literature review. *Clinical Psychology Review, 26*, 695–718.

Hooge, J., Decaluwé, L., & Goossens, L. (2000). Identiteit en psychisch welbevinden [Identity and well-being]. In H. De Witte, J. Hooge, & L. Walgrave (Eds.), *Jongeren in Vlaanderen: Gemeten en geteld. 12- tot 18-jarigen over hun leefwereld en toekomst* [Youth in Flanders: 12 to 18-year-olds about their lifeworld and future] (pp. 35–58). Leuven, Belgium: Universitaire Pers Leuven.

Joiner, T. E. (1997). Shyness and low social support as interactive diatheses, with loneliness as mediator: Testing an interpersonal-personality view of vulnerability to depressive symptoms. *Journal of Abnormal Psychology*, *106*, 386–394.

Joiner, T. E. (2000). Depression's vicious scree: Self-propagating and erosive processes in depression chronicity. *Clinical Psychology: Science and Practice*, *7*, 203–218.

Jöreskog, K. G., & Sörbom, D. (1993). *LISREL 8 users' reference guide* [software manual]. Mooresville, IN: Scientific Software.

Keith, T. Z. (2006). *Multiple regression and beyond*. Boston: Allyn and Bacon.

Kenny, M. E., & Sirin, S. R. (2006). Parental attachment, self-worth, and depressive symptoms among emerging adults. *Journal of Counseling and Development*, *84*, 61–71.

Lasgaard, M., Goossens, L., & Elklit, A. (2011). Loneliness, depressive symptomatology, and suicide ideation in adolescence: Cross-sectional and longitudinal analyses. *Journal of Abnormal Child Psychology*, *39*, 137–150.

Laursen, B., & Bukowski, W. M. (1997). A developmental guide to the organisation of close relationships. *International Journal of Behavioral Development*, *21*, 747–770.

Lavallee, K. L., & Parker, J. G. (2009). The role of inflexible friendship beliefs, rumination, and low self-worth in early adolescents' friendship jealousy and adjustment. *Journal of Abnormal Child Psychology*, *37*, 873–885.

Lewinsohn, P. M. (1974). A behavioral approach to depression. In R. J. Friendman & M. Katz (Eds.), *The psychology of depression: Contemporary theory and research* (pp. 157–178). Washington, DC: Winston-Wiley.

Mahon, N. E., Yarcheski, A., Yarcheski, T. J., Cannella, B. L., & Hanks, M. M. (2006). A meta-analytic study of predictors for loneliness during adolescence. *Nursing Research*, *55*, 308–315.

Marcoen, A., Goossens, L., & Caes, P. (1987). Loneliness in pre- through late adolescence: Exploring the contributions of a multidimensional approach. *Journal of Youth and Adolescence*, *16*, 561–577.

Martin, L. L., & Tesser, A. (1996). Some ruminative thoughts. In R. S. Wyer (Ed.), *Ruminative thoughts: Advances in social cognition* (Vol. 9, pp. 1–47). Hillsdale, NJ: Erlbaum.

Montgomery, M. J., & Côté, J. E. (2003). College as a transition to adulthood. In G. R. Adams & M. D. Berzonsky (Eds.), *Blackwell handbook of adolescence* (pp. 149–172). Malden, MA: Blackwell.

Nelis, S. M., & Rae, G. (2009). Brief report: Peer attachment in adolescents. *Journal of Adolescence*, *32*, 443–447.

Nolen-Hoeksema, S. (1991). Responses to depression and their effects on the duration of depressive episodes. *Journal of Abnormal Psychology*, *100*, 569–582.

Nolen-Hoeksema, S., Stice, E., Wade, E., & Bohon, C. (2007). Reciprocal relations between rumination and bulimic, substance abuse, and depressive symptoms in female adolescents. *Journal of Abnormal Psychology*, *116*, 198–207.

Nolen-Hoeksema, S., Wisco, B. E., & Lyubomirsky, S. (2008). Rethinking rumination. *Perspectives on Psychological Science*, *3*, 400–424.

Oswald, D. L., & Clark, E. M. (2003). Best friends forever? High school best friendships and the transition to college. *Personal Relationships*, *10*, 187–196.

Papageorgiou, C., & Wells, A. (2003). An empirical test of a clinical metacognitive model of rumination and depression. *Cognitive Therapy and Research*, *27*, 261–273.

Peled, M., & Moretti, M. M. (2007). Rumination on anger and sadness in adolescence: Fueling of fury and deepening of despair. *Journal of Clinical Child and Adolescent Psychology*, *36*, 66–75.

Peplau, L. A., & Perlman, D. (1982). Perspectives on loneliness. In L. A. Peplau & D. Perlman (Eds.), *Loneliness: A sourcebook of current theory, research, and therapy* (pp. 1–20). New York: Wiley.

Radloff, L. S. (1977). The Center for Epidemiologic Studies Depression Scale: A self-report depression scale for research in the general population. *Journal of Applied Psychological Measurement, 1*, 185–401.

Raes, F., & Hermans, D. (2008). On the mediating role of subtypes of rumination in the relationship between childhood emotional abuse and depressed mood: Brooding versus reflection. *Depression and Anxiety, 25*, 1067–1070.

Raes, F., Hermans, D., Williams, J. M. G., Bijttebier, P., & Eelen, P. (2008). A "Triple W" model of rumination on sadness: Why am I feeling sad, what's the meaning of my sadness, and wish I could stop thinking about my sadness (but I can't!). *Cognitive Therapy and Research, 32*, 526–541.

Raftery, A. E. (1995). Bayesian model selection in social research (with discussion). *Sociological Methodology, 25*, 111–195.

Schoofs, H., Hermans, D., & Raes, F. (2010). *Self-discrepancy leads to reduced memory specificity in students and depressed patients*. Manuscript submitted for publication.

Shaver, P. R., Furman, W. C., & Buhrmester, D. (1985). Transition to college: Network changes, social skills, and loneliness. In S. Duck & D. Perlman (Eds.), *Understanding personal relationships: An interdisciplinary approach* (pp. 193–219). London: Sage.

Smith, J. M., & Alloy, L. B. (2009). A roadmap to rumination: A review of the definition, assessment, and conceptualization of this multifaceted construct. *Clinical Psychology Review, 29*, 116–128.

Sobel, M. E. (1982). Asymptotic intervals for indirect effects in structural equations models. In S. Leinhart (Ed.), *Sociological methodology* (pp. 290–312). San Francisco: Jossey-Bass.

Stroebe, M., van Vliet, T., Hewstone, M., & Willis, H. (2002). Homesickness among students in two cultures: Antecedents and consequences. *British Journal of Psychology, 93*, 147–168.

Trapnell, P. D., & Campbell, J. D. (1999). Private self-consciousness and the five-factor model of personality: Distinguishing rumination from reflection. *Journal of Personality and Social Psychology, 76*, 284–304.

Treynor, W., Gonzalez, R., & Nolen-Hoeksema, S. (2003). Rumination reconsidered: A psychometric analysis. *Cognitive Therapy and Research, 27*, 247–259.

Vanhalst, J., Luyckx, K., & Goossens, L. (2009, August). *Loneliness, coping, and depressive symptoms: Moderating and mediating mechanisms in late adolescence*. Poster presentation at the 14th European Conference on Developmental Psychology (ESDP), Vilnius, Lithuania.

Wade, N. G., Vogel, D. L., Liao, K. Y. H., & Goldman, D. B. (2008). Measuring state-specific rumination: Development of the rumination about an interpersonal offense scale. *Journal of Counseling Psychology, 55*, 419–426.

Weeks, D. G., Michela, J. L., Peplau, L. A., & Bragg, M. E. (1980). Relation between loneliness and depression: A structural equation analysis. *Journal of Personality and Social Psychology, 39*, 1238–1244.

Medicine, Radiology, Hospitalization, and Loneliness

BEN ROKACH
Memorial University of Newfoundland, Canada

AMI ROKACH
York University, Toronto Canada, Centre for Academic Studies, Or Yehuda, Israel, Walden University, USA.

ABSTRACT. In this chapter we survey the effects of illness, diagnostic procedures, hospitalization, and impending death on the patient and the loneliness he thus experiences. While hospitals, medical procedures, and treatment are all geared to help the patient survive illness, it is the anxiety, powerlessness, alienation, disconnection, and loneliness that the patient needs to deal with, and which medicine is not well equipped to address. This chapter, rather than being an experiment, is written in order to summarize and highlight the emotional, psychological, and social needs of the patient. Indications of what can be changed in medical settings and approach are intertwined throughout the discussion.

> "For the past 200 years medicine has pursued the positivist goal of erasing the subject [of death] from medical perception. A fully objective view of disease was made possible when the autopsy was integrated into clinical medicine through clinico-pathological correlation...The observed body became the project of modern medicine" (Sullivan, 2003; p. 1596)

I (BEN) AM A RESIDENT in a major medical center in Canada. I specialize in Radiology. The idea to write this article came from observing how the medical "machinery" works, and how loneliness is often present in the hospital together with illness, pain, treatment, and hope. I would suggest that radiology, as a field, is particularly prone to induce hope or despair, but many times loneliness and alienation as well.

Modern medical science has been focused, and at times obsessed, with death. It attempts to help conquer the death-causing diseases. Physicians were, and often still are, seen as possessing supernatural abilities in their fight with serious diseases and death (Sullivan, 2003). In that context, radiology provides physicians with the ability to see what no other human, with a naked eye, can see – the inside of the human body, and thus the ability to diagnose, and then decide how to treat one's ailment (see also Brant & Helms, 2007).

Radiology, or diagnostic imaging, encompasses the various technologies used in medicine to see inside the body in order to help provide information about the patient's anatomy or as a means of reaching a diagnosis. The radiological technologies include those that involve radiation, such as computed tomography (CT) or conventional x-rays, and those that do not, such as ultrasound or magnetic resonance imaging (MRI). Interventional radiology is a specialized field within diagnostic imaging (Brant & Helms, 2007). This subfield provides various diagnostic or therapeutic procedures, or interventions, which are performed with the help of imaging, which serves to guide the physician performing the medical intervention. Often times these procedures are less time consuming and less invasive than their traditional counterparts, such as surgery (Flory & Lang, 2011).

Loneliness Associated with Medical Diagnosis

Many patients are familiar with the feelings of anxiety and loneliness following the diagnosis of a disease or illness. However, equally as distressing is the experience associated with awaiting a diagnosis or procedure (see, for example, Chappy, 2004). While there is a paucity of studies that examine how patients feel while undergoing radiological procedures, or when they are awaiting a diagnosis, research has demonstrated that patients during those times are prone to feelings of uncertainty and anxiety (Liao, Chen, Chen, & Chen, 2008). Mishel (1988) proposed the Uncertainty-in -Illness theory to illuminate the process that patients who are at that stage undergo. Accordingly, he maintained that uncertainty is a cognitive state which is experienced when one does not have sufficient information to categorize an event, or in this case an illness. This can result in anxiety, when being uncertain of what is to come and feeling powerless to determine it. That, à la Mishel (1988), is perceived as a state of danger.

One of the common procedures performed by radiology is women's mammograms. Breast cancer is one of the most common and deadly cancers amongst women. Several studies have, thus, examined women's experience with abnormal mammograms and the reactions of women who were suspected of having breast cancer. Women reported that they experience anxiety once a breast lump is discovered, or an abnormal mammogram report is received. Their anxiety reaches its peak when they prepare for a breast biopsy (Chappy, 2004). Interviewing women awaiting a diagnosis after an abnormal mammogram was detected, Thorne, Harris, Hislop, and Vestrup (1999) found that the women described the time period when they were undergoing radiological studies, and until a diagnosis was reached, as a time of being "in limbo." Many women experienced serious disruptions to their daily existence, they complained of insomnia, panic attacks, inability to concentrate at work, and anxiety. They considered themselves suspended from their participation of normal living. In addition, some women kept their abnormal mammogram results a secret from loved ones. Consequently, such disconnection from normal daily routines, and from loved ones, commonly results in feelings of isolation and loneliness. People who have been afflicted with cancer reported that as the diagnosis is completed, the treatments commence, and their ability to cope with the disease decreases, the quality of their social interactions deteriorates (Bloom & Spiegel, 1984; De Haes & Van Knipperberg, 1985).

Compared with other types of medical procedures and surgeries, image-guided diagnostic procedures (such as CT Scans and MRI) are "cutting edge" and less invasive. Awaiting these procedures, patients report experiencing anxiety, fear of the unknown, worrying about the possibility of further needed interventions, disruption of life plans, a pervasive loss of control they experience, and their dread of disability (see Johnston, 1980; Viegas, Turrini, & da Silva Bastos Cerullo, 2010). While medical professionals often assume that such minimally invasive diagnostic tests create less distress than more risky invasive approaches, such procedures do indeed create uncertainty and stress (Mishel, 1984). Flory and Lang (2011) conducted a study in which they compared distress levels in several groups of ill women: those awaiting large core breast biopsy, women undergoing invasive, and potentially risky, treatment of diagnosed malignancies of the liver, and those undergoing invasive, potentially risky, treatment of diagnosed benign uterine tumors. All three groups of women experienced abnormally high levels of perceived stress and depressed mood, but it was the women awaiting breast biopsy (the least invasive of the three diagnostic procedures) who experienced the highest anxiety levels. Flory and Lang (2011) concluded that the invasiveness of the procedure has less influence on patients' distress and the concomitant feelings of alienation than does the uncertainty of treatment outcome.

Patients report considerable anxiety while waiting for those interventional procedures, despite the fact that their physicians may consider them easy to perform and undergo (Mueller, Biswal, Halpern, Kaufman, & Lee, 2000). Such procedures, which may, potentially, be followed by a diagnosis of an illness or even a serious or life-threatening malady, no doubt cause the patients to feel alone in their waiting for answers to their queries; answers that may determine how their future will unfold, and become central in their desire to remain alive and healthy.

To conclude, the experience of awaiting a diagnosis or a radiological procedure often takes an emotional toll on the patient. In fact, most of the resources in the hospital are focused on helping patients deal with their diagnoses once they were shared with them. To our knowledge, there are but minimal support infrastructures designed to help patients cope with their anxiety and loneliness while *awaiting* their diagnoses. Feelings of hopelessness, uncertainty, helplessness, disconnection from daily activities, difficulty maintaining social activities, and fear of death are present in the minds of patients fearing a possible diagnosis of major illness. The lack of social and emotional support that they desperately need and which may not be available may, naturally, lead to loneliness (Cohen, 1985; Friedman, Florian, & Zernitsky-Shurka, 1989).

How does Loneliness Affect Patients?

Social relationships play a large role in achieving and maintaining healthy emotional and cognitive functions as well as appropriate behavioural adjustment (Hawkley & Cacioppo, 2003). The number of social relationships decrease and the social events associated with loneliness increase as we age. When these psychosocial challenges are combined with physical aging and feelings of loneliness, prolonged stress responses and illness are more likely (Hawkley & Cacioppo, 2003). Uchino, Cacioppo, and Kiecolt-Glaser (1996) revealed that lower blood pressure, better immune response, and lower levels of stress hormones are associated with perceived social connectedness or support. Other research has highlighted the effects of social support on illness.

Hawkley and Cacioppo (2003) outlined several different mechanisms through which loneliness may lead to ill health, or exacerbate it. Lonely individuals are thought to engage in fewer health-promoting behaviors and more health-compromising behaviors (see also Seeman, 2000). Lonely individuals, suggested Hawkley and Cacioppo (2003), are more likely to perceive daily events as stressful when compared with non-lonely individuals. In addition, lonely individuals demonstrated different patterns of cardiovascular function both in the short and long term when faced with psychological stressors. The authors suspected that the pattern of cardiovascular function demonstrated by the lonely would contribute to impaired cardiovascular functioning in the long term. In addition, increased levels of catecholamines (the body's fight or flight hormones) and cortisol were found in the blood samples of lonely individuals in their study.

Social relationships have also shown to have an impact on physiological repair and maintenance processes. For example, natural killer (NK) cells are involved in the immune system's response to cancer and are shown to be at lower levels in lonely individuals (Kiecolt-Glaser et al., 1984a, 1984b). In those afflicted with Epstein-Barr virus, lonely individuals had higher antibody levels of the virus indicating the inadequacy of their immune system (Kiecolt-Glaser, Speicher, Holliday, & Glaser 1984c). Sleep, which has been shown to have restorative and recuperative functions, is altered in lonely individuals. Sleep efficiency is lower and wake time after sleep onset has been shown to be higher in lonely individuals (Cacioppo et al., 2003). All in all, when individuals undergo diagnosis or medical treatment, while at home or even more importantly in the hospital, it is quite clear that as they need the medical establishment to help them in arresting or curing their ailment, they must have a solid support system to aid them emotionally, which eventually can help them heal physically as well.

Loneliness and Chronic Disease

Chronic illness is one of the most common health problems in the United States (and North America in general) with increasing incidence (Centers for Disease Control and Prevention, 2012). Chronic illness is by definition long lasting, often permanent, and at risk of worsening and deterioration. The experience of illness has been described as a "life disturbance" and creating a feeling of disorder (Ohman, Soderberg, & Lundman, 2003). When dealing with illness, either as an in- or outpatient, individuals describe feelings of vulnerability, reduced capacity, and being acutely aware of their limitations (Toombs, 1992). According to Strauss et al. (1984), chronic illness is associated with reduced social contacts, social isolation and loneliness, depression, and the feeling of being a burden (see also Charmaz, 1983).

Persons suffering from chronic illness frequently view themselves as different, feeling separate from healthy individuals. This, in turn, may lead to social withdrawal (Miller, 1985). Aggravating the situation, individuals close to those with chronic illness often withdraw from the ill person (Miller, 1983). As a result, people suffering from chronic illness lack support networks with whom to share their concerns and experience. The inability of the ill to fulfill formal or occupational roles further enhances their feelings of isolation and loneliness (Black, 1973).

Ohman, Soderberg, and Lundman (2003) interviewed individuals with chronic illnesses in an attempt to understand the experience of illness and presented similar findings. One of the major themes they discovered was what they titled "Being Alone in Illness." Individuals described feeling different and therefore isolated, as others stopped visiting them and they avoided meeting friends and others in their social network. They also explained that individuals in their social network displayed a lack of understanding and insight into their illness which further intensified their feelings of loneliness.

It appears that in addition to chronic illness being associated with loneliness, the type of illness that one suffers can have additional impact on the social network and support patterns of the chronically ill (Penninx, van Tilburg, Kriegsman, Boeke, Deeg, & van Eijk, 1999). Researchers have suggested that disease characteristics such as progression and visibility of symptoms, as well as functional disability that the sick suffer from, have a significant effect on support patterns that are offered to the ill (Fitzpatrick, Newman, Archer, & Shipley 1991; Lyons, 1991). Diseases that are associated with functional limitations such as arthritis or those who are paraplegic are less able to perform certain roles and tasks and require more instrumental support with a limited ability to reciprocate. This, consequently, creates an imbalance in their social relationships which can limit their social support (Depner & Ingersoll-Dayton, 1988; Dowd, 1984).

Similarly, the course and prognosis of a disease can be equally as influential on one's loneliness. For example, individuals suffering stroke or diabetes, illnesses with relatively stable courses with occasional changes, report that they are satisfied with the support they receive (Irwin & Kramer, 1988; Kutner, 1987; Neuling & Winefield, 1988; Wilson et al., 1986). In contrast, diseases with episodic courses, such as chronic lung disease, are associated with a social network that is not continually aware of the consequences or symptoms of the disease (Williams, 1989). We would like to emphasize that treating people with chronic illnesses should address more than just the physical dimension. It needs to care also for the patient's social and emotional ones, as they are major contributors in healing and recuperation.

Hospitalization

The modern hospital environment is supposed to provide a safe and healing environment for people inflicted with a variety of illnesses, be it for short term visits and minor health problems, or as a result of more serious conditions requiring long term treatment and care. In the Western hemisphere, patients receive the most contemporary care available, benefiting from modern technology and the expertise of professional staff. And although the hospital might be geared to be a "safe house" for the sick patients, the experience of illness and hospitalization is one of the most distressful events people might actually experience in their lifetime (Hughes, 2001). Brannon and Feist (2004) observed that the admitted patient becomes part of an institution and assumes a role within that entity. "That role includes some difficult aspects: being treated as a 'nonperson', tolerating lack of information, and losing control of daily activities" (p. 64). For hospitalized patients, all but their illness becomes invisible, and to wit, one may hear a physician telling the nurse to "attend to the multiple fractures in room...." It was also observed that, under some circumstances, patients' comments and questions, and their emotional needs, may be ignored by the hospital staff (Yarnold, Michelson, Thompson, & Adams, 1998). Patients having to eat the hospital food, or having to sleep on different beds, may bring about emotional discomfort, as they no longer "feel at home," and as such have minimal personal control over their choices and for as long as they need to stay in hospital (Williams & Irurita, 2005; Williams, Dawson, & Kristjanson 2008). Feelings of alienation and loneliness are, thus, not far behind (Incalzi, Gemma, Capparella, & Muzzolon, 1991; Pressman, Meyer, Peterson, Greenspon, & Figueroa, 1997).

Let's accompany Helen, an imaginary patient, as she enters the hospital. Upon admission to the hospital, Helen will experience a disruption in her daily routines, a profound change of her living environment, and for the duration of her stay the hospital environment will become her new "home." Despite her feisty nature and active lifestyle, Helen will be expected to resign herself to the care of physicians and nurses, get used to the, often unpleasant, experiences associated with the course of diagnosis and treatment, and to being told what to do and when; as Brannon and Feist (2004) maintained that "For efficiency of the organization, uniform treatment and conformity to hospital routine are desirable, even though they deprive patients of information and control" (p. 65). Research indicated that Helen will, most probably, live now in a state of constant worry as she will be expected to instil her complete faith in the medical professionals (Paul & Rattray, 2008; Hallström & Elander, 2007). All in all, it is quite apparent that the patient as well as her family and caregivers are not only subject to the debilitating aspects of the physical illness, but also to the added stressors inherent in the experience of being hospitalized (Williams & Irurita, 2005; Rokach, Matalon, Safarov, & Bercovitch, 2007).

Sellick and Edwardson (2007) observed that illness is a major stressor on one's life. Various symptoms that the patient may have contribute to a state of continuous stress which may include pain, fatigue, and in more severe cases, immobility and even loss of bodily functions (Rowe, 1996). In general, it is not only the physical suffering and distress that the patient has to endure, but also factors that negatively affect his or her psychological state (Rattray, Johnston, & Wildsmith, 2005). These include perceived threat to one's life, the uncontrollable and unpredictable nature of one's condition, and the state of apprehension and hopelessness, which can have a considerable effect on the thoughts, emotions, and behaviors of the patient (Raps, Peterson, Jonas, & Seligman 1982; Seeman & Seeman, 1983; Mishel, 1997). Other factors related to such inconveniences as double occupancy rooms, which might impede patients' privacy and quality of rest, or lack of fresh air, possibly influence the individuals' experience of physical and emotional comfort (Rollins, 2004; Williams, Dawson, & Kristjanson, 2008).

In circumstances of life threatening illnesses which may include severe symptoms, and which require intensive, isolated care and nursing, the combination of these factors is enhanced and might even alter their previously held perception of themselves and their sense of how they are perceived by others. Consequently, they might feel disorganized, and disengaged (Parkinson, 2006). Indeed, the lingering, long term psychological effects of severe illnesses have been observed to induce anxiety, depression, and loneliness (Mayou & Smith, 1997; Scragg, Jones, & Fauvel, 2001; Tattersall, Bennett, & Pugh, 1999).

In addition to the technical aspects of care in the hospital facilities, the attitude and behavior of the medical staff towards the patients appears to be a key factor in perceived quality of care, and whether patients' coping with the stress of their illness is helpful (Attree, 2001; Thomas & Bond, 1996). With the exception of the (limited) visiting time of their family and friends, hospitalized patients' social contact is limited to interaction with the medical staff. Albeit, this being an imbalanced interaction, on one side are the patients, who feel and are quite powerless and dependent, and on the other side are the doctors, nurses, and supporting staff, who are in complete charge of almost every aspect of the patients' care with all the knowledge, authority, and power (Hughes, 2001). The result of this imbalanced and unnatural situation (natural for the hospital, but not for our way of life) is that patients may be feeling even more hopeless and emotionally distressed, particularly in settings where the doctors and nurses treat the patients in a mechanical, insensitive, or distant manner (Attree, 2001). An indicator of such a power differential is the frequent use of complex medical jargon by the medical staff (Phillips, 1996). Patients may, consequently, experience heightened levels of anxiety since they might feel deprived of the much-needed feelings of control and knowledge about their health and recovery (Raps, Peterson, Jonas, & Seligman, 1982; Williams & Irurita, 2005). More specifically, these patients may feel "dehumanized," and while the health professionals treat their bodies, the staff may not be fully aware and attentive to their human spirit and the wholeness of their existence (see Eddleston, White, & Guthrie, 2000; Hughes, 2001). That may lead to considerable distress and feelings of helplessness and loneliness in patients (Polimeni & Moore, 2002).

The Dying

As we mentioned in the beginning of this article, medicine sees death as "the enemy" that needs to be conquered, or at least postponed indefinitely.

As Rando (1984) so poignantly indicated, death "is not romantic. It is not graceful. It is not beautiful. In fact, death stinks – literally and figuratively! It is clammy too. It can sound bad, and it often is ugly" (p. 272). Consequently, people with terminal illnesses may be spending the more advanced stages of their illness in a hospice, with the goal of achieving the best possible quality of life for themselves and for their families, and in order to lower their distress for their final days (Tang, McCorkle & Bradley, 2004). Palliative care provides physical, emotional, spiritual, and informational support geared to enhance the quality of life of the dying while recognizing the patient and family as the principal decision makers (Van Bommel, 1992). It centers on offering a support system that encourages patients to live as actively as possible until death, and helps the family (during the patient's illness) cope with the bereavement, anticipatory, and post-mortem grief (Faull & Woof, 2002).

The dying may pose particular demands for their carers. They may, actually, be difficult to care for because of their pathology, which may affect behavior and/or personality. Conditions that may result in such difficulties are brain tumors, cerebrovascular disease, or concurrent illnesses, e.g., hypothyroidism. Additionally, psychological factors and psychiatric disorders may include anger, mistrust, fear, or shame, which are directed toward the carers, or depression and paranoia, and may result in a patient who is very demanding and difficult to handle (Twycross, 2003). Loneliness has been documented to be an integral part of ill health, for both the patient and his or her caregivers. One of the most excruciating elements of death is the leaving behind of all that the patient owned, had, and knew. Separating from friends and family is not only one of the most heart-wrenching aspects of dying—,but also a precursor of loneliness and aloneness (see Doka, 1997; Rokach, Matalon, Safarov & Bercovitch, 2007).

Death is not only distressing and overwhelming, but it is frequently accompanied by loneliness—both, for the dying and for their caregivers (Chentsova-Dutton et al., 2000). In our own research, we compared the loneliness of people on their deathbed in a hospice with the one experienced by their caregivers (see Rokach, Matalon, Safarov, & Bercovitch, 2007; Rokach & Rokach, 2005). What we focused on was not the quantity or intensity of loneliness, but rather its qualitative aspects.

We utilized the loneliness model developed by the second author and which included five factors, or dimensions. The most salient factor was Emotional distress. This included items that captured the intense pain, inner turmoil, hopelessness, and feelings of emptiness associated with loneliness. The second factor, Social inadequacy and alienation, addressed the perception and concomitant self-generated social detachment that were reported as part of the loneliness experience. The third factor, Growth and discovery, captured the positive, growth-enhancing, and enriching aspects of loneliness and the increased feelings of inner strength and self-reliance that follow. Interpersonal isolation was the fourth factor. It depicted feelings of alienation, abandonment, and rejection, which were reported as related to a general lack of close relationships and/or absence of a primary romantic relationship. The fifth factor, Self-alienation, described a detachment from one's self that is characterized by numbness, immobilization, and denial.

Results indicated that loneliness is experienced differently in or out of the hospice. While our loneliness model includes five dimensions, that difference was confined to the Growth and discovery and the Self-alienation dimensions of our loneliness model. These addressed, on the one hand, the growth and personal development that may accompany loneliness in some individuals, and on the other hand the need to escape the unbearable pain of alienation which results in one disconnecting from one's self and one's feelings and experiences. The general population scored significantly lower than the other two subgroups, on both those elements. It is intuitively apparent, and easier to explain, the higher mean subscale scores of the patients and their caregivers. The pain, emotional turmoil, and the sense of terror that both death and loneliness many evoke could mobilize a reaction akin to fainting, which is a physical response to acute pain. Self-alienation may be present as a reaction to loneliness and to their impending death. Connor (1998) observed that people respond differently to their impending death. Most often their behavior is characterized by ambivalence—"fearful avoidance and the desire for release" (p. 46). Results of our investigations, thus, indicated that in the midst of that ambivalence—which is so often experienced by the patient and the caregiver—Self-alienation may be the dimension of loneliness that they most acutely experience. And indeed, a form of distancing and numbing may be needed in facing the end of life and the impending separation from loved ones. The Growth and discovery higher scores of the dying and their caregivers were not intuitively expected. In light of the "moments of truth," the shirking of social "niceties" and expectations, and the order that the dying are putting in their affairs, both the patient and the caregiver may find the strength, inner resources, and personal capabilities to deal with loneliness and with the impending separation and loss (see Rokach, 2005).

To summarize, psychological variables, including loneliness, have been shown to be associated with changes in immune functioning and may, thus, adversely affect the body's capacity to fight disease (Kennedy, Kiecolt-Glaser, & Glaser, 1988). Kiecolt-Glaser, McGuire, Robles, and Glaser (2002) pointed out that more and more research now indicates that psychological factors are clinically significant and are correlated with immune-related health outcomes, including infectious disease, cancer, autoimmune disease, and HIV. These factors include, as we pointed out, the anxiety, uncertainty, diminished social support, feelings of alienation, and the loneliness that often accompany medical procedures, diagnostic radiological protocols, hospitalization, and ultimately, dying. In these pages we have highlighted the emotional consequences, the loneliness, and disconnection that hospitalized patients frequently report, and that the dying face. While it is clear that the main function of the medical establishment is to care for people's illnesses and injuries, it must be remembered that the patient is more than just a sick body. He is a whole human being whose feelings may help or hinder his recovery, adjustment, and coping with the disease.

REFERENCES

Attree, M. (2001). Patients' and relatives' experiences and perspectives of "Good"and "Not so Good" quality care. *Journal of Advanced Nursing*, *33*(4), 456–466.

Black, K. (1973). Social isolation and the nursing process. *Nursing Clinics of North America*, *8*(4), 575–585.

Bloom, J. R., & Spiegel, D. (1984). The relationship of two dimensions of social support to the psychological well being and social functioning of women with advanced breast cancer. *Social Science and Medicine*, *19,* 831–837.

Brannon, L., & Feist, J. (2004). *Health psychology: An introduction to behaviour and health.* Toronto, Canada: Thomson Wadsworth.

Brant, W., & Helms, C. (2007). *Fundamentals of Diagnostic Radiology* (3rd Ed.). Philadelphia: Lippincott Williams & Wilkins.

Chappy, S. (2004). Women's experience with breast biopsy. *AORN Journal*, *80*(5), 885–901.

Charmaz, K. (1983). Loss of self: A fundamental form of suffering in the chronically ill. *Sociology of Health and Illness*, *5*, 168–195.

Chentsova-Dutton, Y., Schucter, S., & Hutchin, S. et al. (2002). Depression and grief reactions in hospice caregivers: From death to one year afterwards. *Journal of Affective Disorders*, *69*, 53–60.

Cohen, I. S. (1985). Psychosomatic death: Voodoo death in modern perspective. *Integrative Psychiatry*, *16,* 46–51.

Cohen, S., & Syme, S. L. (1985). Issues in the study and application of social support. In S. Cohen & S. L. Syme (Eds.), *Social Support and Health*. New York: Academic Press.

Connor, S. R. (1998). *Hospice: Practice, pitfalls, and promise*. Washington, DC: Taylor & Francis.

Dale, W., Bilir, P., Han., M, & Meltzer, D. (2005). The role of anxiety in prostate carcinoma. *Cancer, 104*(3), 467–478.

De Haes, J. C. J. M., & Van Knipperberg, F. C. E. (1985). The quality of life of cancer patients: A review of the literature. *Social Science and Medicine, 20*, 809–817.

Depner, C. E., & Ingersoll-Dayton, B. (1988). Supportive relationships in later life. *Psychology and Aging, 3*, 348–357.

Doka, K. J. (1997). When illness is prolonged: implications for grief. In K. J Doka (Ed.), *Living with Grief When Illness is Prolonged* (pp. 5–16). Washington, DC: Hospice Foundation of America.

Dowd, J. J., (1984). Beneficence and the aged. *Journal of Gerontology, 39*, S102–S108.

Eddleston, J. M., White, P., &, Guthrie, E. (2000). Survival, morbidity, and quality of life after discharge from intensive care. *Critical Care Medicine, 28*(7), 2293–2299.

Fitzpatrick, R., Newman, S., Archer, R., & Shipley, M. (1991). Social support, disability and depression: A longitudinal study of Rheumatoid arthritis. *Social Science and Medicine, 33*, 605–611.

Flory, N., & Lang, E. (2011). Distress in the radiology waiting room. *Radiology, 260*, 166–173.

Friedman, G., Florian, V., & Zernitsky-Shurka, E. (1989). The experience of loneliness among young adult cancer patients. *Journal of Psychosocial Oncology, 7*, 1–15.

Hallström, I., & Elander, G. (2007). Families' needs when a child is long-term ill: A literature review with reference to nursing research. *International Journal of Nursing Practice, 13*, 193–200.

Hawkley, L. C., & Cacioppo, J. P. (2003). Loneliness and pathways to disease. *Brain, Behavior, and Immunity, 17*, S98–S105.

Hughes, B. (2001). Psychology, hospitalization, and some thoughts on medical training. *European Journal of Psychotherapy and Counselling, 4*(1), 7–26.

Incalzi, R. A., Gema, A., Capparella, O., & Muzzolon, R. (1991). Effects of hospitalization on affective status of elderly patients. *International Psychogeriatrics, 3*(1), 67–74.

Irwin, P.H., & Kramer, S. (1988). Social support and cancer: Sustained emotional support and successful adaptation. *Journal of Psychosocial Oncology, 6*, 53–73.

Johnston, M. (1980). Anxiety in surgical patients. *Psychological Medicine, 10*(1), 145–152.

Kennedy, S., Keicolt-Glaser, J. K., & Glaser, R. (1988). Immunological consequences of acute and chronic stressors: Mediating role of interpersonal relationships. *British Journal of Medical Psychology, 61*, 77–85.

Kiecolt-Glaser, J. K., Garner, W., Speicher, C. E., Penn, G. M., Holliday, J., & Glaser, R. (1984a). Psychosocial modifiers of immunocompetence in medical students. *Psychosomatic Medicine, 46*, 7–14.

Kiecolt-Glaser, J. K., Icker, D., George, J., Messick, G., Speicher, C.E., Garner, W., et al. (1984b). Urinary cortisol levels, cellular immunocompetency, and loneliness in psychiatric inpatients. *Psychosomatic Medicine, 46*, 15–23.

Kiecolt-Glaser, J. K., Speicher, C. E., Holliday, J. E., & Glaser, R. (1984c). Stress and transformation of lymphocytes by Epstein-Barr virus. *Journal of Behavioral Medicine, 7*, 1–12.

Kutner, N. G. (1987). Social ties, social support, and perceived health status among chronically disabled people. *Social Science and Medicine, 25*, 29–34.

Liao, M., Chen, M., Chen, S., & Chen, P. (2008). Uncertainty and anxiety during the diagnostic period for women with suspected breast cancer. *Cancer Nursing, 31*(4), 274–283.

Lyons, R. F. (1991). The effects of acquired illness and disability on friendship. In D. Perlman & W.H. Jones (Eds.), *Advances in Personal Relationships 3* (pp. 233–276). London: Jessica Kingsley.

Mayou, R. A., & Smith, K. A. (1997). Post traumatic symptoms following medical illness and treatment. *Journal of Psychosomatic Research, 43*, 121–123.

Miller, J. F. (1983). Coping with chronic illness: Overcoming powerlessness. Philadelphia, PA: F. A. Dais.

Miller, J. F. (1985). Assessment of loneliness and spiritual well-being in chronically ill and healthy adults. *Journal of Professional Nursing, 1*(2), 79–85.

Mishel, M. (1984). Perceived uncertainty and stress in Illness. *Reseach in Nursing & Health, 7*(3), 163–171.

Mishel, M. (1988). Uncertainty in illness. *Journal of Nursing Scholarship, 20* (4), 225–232.

Mishel, M. H. (1997). Uncertainty in acute illness. *Annual Review of Nursing Research, 15*, 57–80.

Mueller, P., Biswal, S., Halpern, E., Kaufman, J., & Lee, M. (2000). Interventional radiologic procedures: Patient anxiety, perception of pain, understanding of procedure, and satisfaction with medication – a prospective study. *Radiology, 215*, 684–688.

Neuling, J. S., & Winefield, H. R. (1988). Social support and recovery after surgery for breast cancer: Frequency and correlates of supportive behaviours by family, friends and surgeon. *Social Science and Medicine, 27*, 385–392.

Ohman, M., Soderberg, S., & Lundman, B. (2003). Hovering between suffering and enduring: The meaning of living with serious chronic illness. *Qualitative Health Research, 13*(4), 528–542.

Parkinson, J. (2006). Experiences of selves in isolation: A psychodynamic approach to the care of patients being treated in a specialized medical hospital unit. *Psychodynamic Practice, 12*(2), 149–163.

Paul, F. & Rattray, J. (2008). Short- and long-term impact of critical illness relatives: literature review. *Journal of Advanced Nursing, 62*(3), 276–292.

Phillips, D. (1996). Medical professional dominance and client dissatisfaction: study of doctor–patient interaction and reported dissatisfaction with medical care among female patients at four hospitals in Trinidad and Tobago. *Social Science & Medicine, 42*, 1419–1425.

Polimeni, A. & Moore, S. (2002). Insight into women's experiences of hospital stays: perceived control, powerlessness and satisfaction. *Behaviour Change, 19*(1), 52–64.

Pressman, M. R., Meyer, T. J., Peterson, D. D., Greenspon, L. W., & Figueroa, W. G. (1997). *Effects of Hospitalization, Surgery, and Anesthesia on Sleep and Biological Rhythms*. Washington, DC: American Psychological Association.

Rando, T. (1984). *Grief, Dying and Death*. Champaign, Ill: Research Press.

Raps, C. S., Peterson, C., Jonas, M., & Seligman, M. E. P. (1982). Patient behavior in hospitals: Helplessness, reactance, or both? *Journal of Personality and Social Psychology, 42*, 1036–1041.

Rattray, M., Johnston, J. A., & Wildsmith, W. (2005). Predictors of emotional outcomes of intensive care. *Anesthesia, 60,* 1085–1092.

Rokach, A. (2005). Caring for those who care for the dying: Coping with the demands on palliative care workers. *Palliative and Supportive Care, 3*, 325–332.

Rokach, A., & Rokach, B. (2005). *The dying and the living: Caring for the patient and for the professional who treats him/her.* A keynote address delivered at the eighth annual Conference of Palliative Medicine, Tzfat, Israel, May 19.

Rokach, A., Matalon, R., Safarov, A., & Bercovitch, M. (2007). The loneliness experience of the dying and of those who care for them. *Palliative and Supportive Care, 5*, 153–159.

Rollins, J. A. (2004). Evidence-based hospital design improves health care outcomes for patients, families and staff. *Pediatric Nursing, 30*(4), 338–339.

Rowe, M. A. (1996). The impact of internal and external resources on functional outcome in chronic illness. *Research and Nursing in Health, 19*(6), 485–497.

Scragg, P., Jones, A., & Fauvel, N. (2001). Psychological problems following ICU treatment. *Anaesthesia, 56* (1), 9–14.

Seeman, M., & Seeman, T. E. (1983). Health behavior and personal autonomy: a longitudinal study of the sense of control in illness. *Journal of Health and Social Behavior, 24*(2), 144–160.

Seeman, T. E. (2000). Health promoting effects of friends and family on health outcomes in older adults. *American Journal of Health Promotion, 14*, 362–370.

Sellick, S. M., & Edwardson, A. D. (2007). Screening new cancer patients for psychological distress using the hospital anxiety and depression scale. *Psycho-Oncology, 16* (6), 534–542.

Strauss, A. L., Corbin, J., Fagerhaugh, S., Glaser, B. G., Maines, D., Suczek, B. et al. (1984). *Chronic Illness and the Quality of Life* (2nd Ed.). St. Louis, MO: C.V. Mosby.

Sullivan, M. (2003). The new subjective medicine: Taking the patient's point of view on health care and health. *Social Science & Medicine, 56*, 1595–1604.

Tattersall, A. J., Bennett, P., & Pugh, S. (1999). Stress and coping in hospitals. *Stress Medicine, 15*, 109–113.

Tang, S. L., McCorkle, R., & Bradley, E. H. (2004). Determinants of death in an inpatient hospice for terminally ill cancer patients. *Palliative and Supportive Care, 2*, 361–370.

Thomas, L. H., & Bond, S. (1996). Measuring patients' satisfaction with nursing: 1990–1994. *Journal of Advanced Nursing, 23*, 747–756.

Thorne, S., Harris, S., Hislop, G., & Vestrup, J. (1999). The experience of waiting for diagnosis after an abnormal mammogram. *The Breast Journal, 5*(1), 42–51.

Toombs, S. K. (1992). *The Meaning of Illness: A phenomenological account of the different perspectives of physician and patient.* Dordrecht, The Netherlands: Kluwer Academic.

Twycross, R. (2003). *Introducing palliative care* (4th Ed.). Oxford, UK: Radcliffe Medical Press.

Uchino, B. N., Cacioppo, J. T., & Kiecolt-Glaser, J. K. (1996). The relationship between social support and physiological processes: A review with emphasis on underlying mechanisms and implications for health. *Psychological Bulletin, 119*, 488–531.

Van Bommel, H. (1992). *Dying for Care: Hospice care or euthanasia*. Toronto: NC Press.

Viegas, L., Turrini, R., & da Silva Bastos Cerullo, J. (2010). An analysis of nursing diagnoses for patients undergoing procedures in a Brazilian interventional radiology suite. *AORN Journal*, *91*(5), 544–547.

William, A. M., Dawson, S., & Kristjanson, L. J. (2008). Exploring the relationship between personal control and the hospital environment. *Journal of Clinical Nursing, 17*(12), 1601–1609.

Williams, A. M., & Irurita, V. F. (2005). Enhancing the therapeutic potential of hospital environment by increasing the personal control and emotional comfort of hospitalized patients. *Applied Nursing Research*, *18*, 22–28.

Williams, S. J. (1989). Chronic respiratory illness and disability: A critical review of the psychological literature. *Social Science and Medicine*, *28*, 791–803.

Wilson, W., Ary, D. V., Biglan, A., Glasgow, R. E., Toobert, D. J., & Campbell, D. R. (1986).

Psychosocial predictors of self-care behaviours (compliance) and glycemic control in non-insulin-dependent diabetes mellitus. *Diabetes Care*, *9*, 614–622.

Yarnold, P. R., Michelson, E. A., Thompson, D. A., & Adams, S. L. (1998). Predicting patient satisfaction: A study of two emergency departments. *Journal of Behavioral Medicine, 21*, 545–563.

Index

Made in United States
North Haven, CT
10 November 2026

22095621R00174